P9-CRR-817

The influence of John Locke's thought on American politics has been tremendous. It provided the basic ideas put forward in justification of the American Revolution, supplied a formula by which written constitutions could be worked out, and has continued to be the centerpiece of liberal democratic theory in the modern era. This volume is the most comprehensive collection of Locke's writings to date, and it contains both of Locke's most famous works of political philosophy: *The Second Treatise of Government* and *A Letter Concerning Toleration*. It also provides complete texts of all the key works that are central to the long-running debates over how to interpret Locke—never before collected into one volume. In addition, David Wootton's masterful introduction offers a new account of the development of Locke's ideas and original interpretations of the texts.

DAVID WOOTTON has previously edited *Divine Right and Democracy*. He is the author of *Paolo Sarpi: Between Renaissance and Enlightenment* and the co-editor, with Michael Hunter, of *Atheism from the Reformation to the Enlightenment*. He holds the Lansdowne Chair in Humanities at the University of Victoria, Canada.

JOHN LOCKE

Political Writings

Edited and with an Introduction by
DAVID WOOTTON

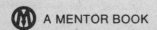 A MENTOR BOOK

MENTOR
Published by the Penguin Group
Penguin Books USA Inc., 375 Hudson Street,
New York, New York 10014, U.S.A.
Penguin Books Ltd, 27 Wrights Lane, London W8 5TZ, England
Penguin Books Australia Ltd, Ringwood, Victoria, Australia
Penguin Books Canada Ltd, 10 Alcorn Avenue,
Toronto, Ontario, Canada M4V 3B2
Penguin Books (N.Z.) Ltd, 182-190 Wairau Road,
Auckland 10, New Zealand

Penguin Books Ltd, Registered Offices:
Harmondsworth, Middlesex, England

Published by Mentor,
an imprint of New American Library,
a division of Penguin Books USA Inc.
Published by arrangement with Penguin Books Ltd.

First Mentor Printing, August, 1993
10 9 8 7 6 5 4 3 2 1

(M) REGISTERED TRADEMARK—MARCA REGISTRADA

LIBRARY OF CONGRESS CATALOGING CARD NUMBER: 93-77945

Printed in the United States of America

Contents

Acknowledgements viii

Preface 1

Introduction 7

Locke's liberalism (p. 7); Locke's life (p. 16); Locke before Shaftesbury (p. 26); Locke and Shaftesbury (p. 36); Locke and Tyrrell (p. 49); *The First Treatise of Government* (p. 64); *The Second Treatise of Government* (p. 77); Interlude: Seeds and trees, locks and ciphers (p. 89); *A Letter Concerning Toleration* (p. 94); Some more equal than others? (p. 110); Notes (p. 119).

Suggestions for Further Reading 123

A Note on the Texts 131

1. Letter to S.H. [Henry Stubbe] (mid-September? 1659; published 1967) 137

2. Letter to Tom (20 October 1659; published 1976) 139

3. From: 'Question: Whether the civil magistrate may lawfully impose and determine the use of indifferent things in reference to religious worship. Answer: Yes' (*First Tract on Government*, 1660; published 1961) 141

4. 'Preface to the Reader' from the *First Tract on Government* (1661; published 1961) 146

5. 'Question: Can the civil magistrate specify indifferent things to be included within the order of divine worship, and impose them upon the people? Answer: Yes' (*Second Tract on Government*, c. 1662; published 1961). Translated from the Latin 152

6. 'Question: Is each man's private interest the foundation of the law of nature? Answer: No' (*Essays on the Law of Nature*, No. VIII, 1664; published 1954). Translated from the Latin 177

7. Letter to the Hon. Robert Boyle (12/22 December 1665; published 1744) 184

8. *An Essay Concerning Toleration* (1667; published 1876) 186

9. *The Fundamental Constitutions of Carolina* (1669; published c. 1670) 210

94640

10. 'Philanthropy, or The Christian Philosophers' (1675; published 1972)   232

11. 'Obligation of Penal Laws' (Journal, 25 February 1676; published 1829)   234

12. 'Law' (Journal, 21 April 1678; published 1829)   236

13. 'Credit, Disgrace' (Journal, 12 December 1678; published 1829)   236

14. 'The Idea We Have of God' (Journal, 1 August 1680; published 1829)   237

15. 'Inspiration' (Journal, 3 April 1681; published 1829)   238

16. 'Virtus' (1681; from the 1661 Commonplace Book; published 1829)   240

17. From *The First Treatise of Government* (*c*. 1681, published 1689)   242

    CHAPTER FIVE: Of Adam's Title to Sovereignty by the Subjection of Eve   242

    CHAPTER NINE: Of Monarchy by Inheritance from Adam   249

18. 'Two Sorts of Knowledge' (Journal, 26 June 1681; published 1829)   259

19. *The Second Treatise of Government* (*c*. 1681, published 1689)   261

    CHAPTER ONE: 261

    CHAPTER TWO: Of the State of Nature   262

    CHAPTER THREE: Of the State of War   269

    CHAPTER FOUR: Of Slavery   272

    CHAPTER FIVE: Of Property   273

    CHAPTER SIX: Of Paternal Power   286

    CHAPTER SEVEN: Of Political or Civil Society   300

    CHAPTER EIGHT: Of the Beginning of Political Societies   309

    CHAPTER NINE: Of the Ends of Political Society and Government   324

    CHAPTER TEN: Of the Forms of a Commonwealth   327

    CHAPTER ELEVEN: Of the Extent of the Legislative Power   328

    CHAPTER TWELVE: Of the Legislative, Executive, and Federative Power of the Commonwealth   335

    CHAPTER THIRTEEN: Of the Subordination of the Powers of the Commonwealth   337

CHAPTER FOURTEEN: Of Prerogative 344

CHAPTER FIFTEEN: Of Paternal, Political, and Despotical Power Considered Together 349

CHAPTER SIXTEEN: Of Conquest 352

CHAPTER SEVENTEEN: Of Usurpation 362

CHAPTER EIGHTEEN: Of Tyranny 363

CHAPTER NINETEEN: Of the Dissolution of Government 369

20. Letter to Edward Clarke (27 January/6 February 1685; published 1927) 387

21. *A Letter Concerning Toleration*, trans. William Popple (1685; published 1689) 390

22. Letter to Edward Clarke (29 January/8 February 1689; published 1927) 436

23. Preface to *Two Treatises of Government* (written and published 1689) 438

24. 'Labour' (1693; from the 1661 Commonplace Book; published 1991) 440

25. 'Venditio' (1695; from the 1661 Commonplace Book; published 1968) 442

26. *Draft of a Representation Containing a Scheme of Methods for the Employment of the Poor. Proposed by Mr Locke, the 26th October 1697* (published 1789) 446

Bibliography 462

Index 471

Acknowledgements

The cover illustration is reproduced by permission of the Bodleian Library. The text of the *Two Treatises* is reproduced by permission of the Master and Fellows of Christ's College, Cambridge. The texts of 'Virtus', 'Labour', and 'Venditio' are reproduced with the permission of the private collector who owns the 1661 Commonplace Book.

I would like to thank those scholars who were kind enough to show me pre-publication copies of their work while I was working on this book: John Dunn, Mark Goldie, Ian Harris, Alan Houston, John Marshall, Jonathan Scott, James Tully.

I am grateful to Constantin Fasolt and Julius Kirshner for inviting me to talk to their history seminar at the University of Chicago; Stephen Holmes and Nathan Tarcov for inviting me to talk to their political science seminar there; Blair Worden for inviting me to talk to his history seminar in Oxford; and John Robertson for inviting me to give a public lecture in Oxford. Students and colleagues, first in London, Ontario, and then in Victoria, British Columbia, have listened to me on the subject of Locke over and over again.

I am immensely grateful to Richard Ashcraft, John Dunn, Jeffrey Friedman, Mark Goldie, Alan Houston and Paul Wood for patiently reading the Introduction in draft. I have not adopted all their suggestions, and so the faults that remain are mine alone. I believe I am prepared, as Locke claimed to be, 'to resign any opinion I have, or to recede from anything I have writ, upon the first evidence of any error in it', but there is scope for some difference of opinion as to how this principle should be implemented in practice.

Finally I want to thank two Locke scholars, John Dunn and Ed Hundert, who have made me feel at home on both sides of the Atlantic, and who supported me long before I began work on this book.

Preface

Two events mark the beginning of modern Locke scholarship: Eric Stokes's discovery, in 1944 or 1945, in the library of Christ's College, Cambridge, of a revised text of the *Two Treatises of Government*, prepared by Locke for the printer (Laslett in Locke 1967b, xiv); and the purchase of the Earl of Lovelace's collection of Locke manuscripts by the Bodleian Library in 1947 (Long 1959). The first event gave rise to Peter Laslett's brilliant edition of the *Two Treatises* (1960), and to the work of a long series of Locke scholars trained in Cambridge, including John Dunn, Patrick Kelly, Philip Abrams, Richard Tuck, and James Tully. The second led to the Clarendon Edition of Locke's works, which is still in progress, and to the work of scholars such as Peter Nidditch, E. S. De Beer, W. von Leyden, and G. A. J. Rogers. Meanwhile a series of North American scholars – John Yolton, Leo Strauss, C. B. Macpherson, Richard Ashcraft, and others – have provided sharply contrasting accounts of Locke's intellectual commitments.

It is this distinguished body of modern scholarship that makes a selection of Locke's political writings timely, for students and a wider public need to have easy access to the texts that scholars have long been debating. Where this is the first wide-ranging selection from Locke's political works, there are by now numerous competing introductions to Locke's political thought: my Introduction is not intended to replace them, but to help those reading Locke for the first time to find their way among them and, at the same time, to provide a new account of the place of religion in Locke's political thought (an account that places particular stress on Socinianism), and a new account of the development of Locke's political ideas (an account that emphasizes the importance of James Tyrrell's *Patriarcha non Monarcha*).

My main principle of selection has been a straightforward one. I simply excluded those works by Locke that were primarily polemical, and concentrated instead on those in which he was mainly concerned to express his own views. This meant excluding the greater part of the *First Tract on Government* (1660) and the three *Letters Concerning Toleration* he wrote after the first (1685). It also meant excluding the bulk of the *First Treatise*. Laslett, who insisted that the *Two Treatises* were a single work directed against Filmer, acknowledged that Locke probably approved the separate publication of the *Second Treatise* in French translation, and he himself found remarkably little to say about the argument of the *First Treatise*. In my Introduction I defend the view that the two works were originally intended to serve quite different purposes, while suggesting that one section of the *First Treatise* may be read as an immediate prelude to the *Second*, and trying to explain why Locke thought the whole of the surviving fragment of the *First Treatise* worth publishing.

The texts presented here are all based on the original manuscripts, except in the case of the *Second Tract* and the eighth of the *Essays on the Law of Nature*, where I have made my own translations of the Latin originals; the letter to Robert Boyle, where there is no surviving manuscript; the *Constitutions of Carolina*, where I have followed the first edition; the *Two Treatises*, where I have followed the Christ's College copy, corrected by Locke for the press; and the *Letter Concerning Toleration*, where I have followed the second, corrected edition of Popple's translation. In every case I have modernized the spelling and, to the extent that it seemed necessary to make the text easier to read, punctuation: I apologize to scholars, but in almost every case there is a scholarly edition to which they can turn, and their loss is outweighed by the gain of those readers who are less accustomed to seventeenth-century spelling and punctuation, and who may be saved, for example, from the error of thinking that 'propriety' in Locke means something other than 'property'.

As I have worked on Locke, I have been acutely conscious of my debt to my predecessors and contemporaries. The progress of Locke scholarship since the war has been a collective accomplishment, the result of both cooperation and conflict among scholars. If there is little agreement over the interpretation of Locke, there is no doubt that the range and subtlety of arguments, and the quality and quantity of information, have advanced immeasurably. Many before me have set out on that arduous intellectual journey that begins in the Duke Humphrey reading room of the Bodleian Library, where scholars now read Locke's papers, sitting at desks on which Locke himself must once have worked, surrounded by copies of the books that Locke and his contemporaries read and over which they argued. Sitting in Duke Humphrey, you are close to where the Oxford Parliament met in March of 1681 in the final trial of strength between Charles II and the supporters of Exclusion; only a few steps from where Stephen College was executed in August for saying things Locke thought; a few yards from where a selection of dangerous books was burnt by order of the University authorities in 1683, while Locke's *Two Treatises*, which summarized many of their arguments, lay safely in hiding, and Locke himself began to make preparations to flee into exile. Though he returned to England in 1689, Locke never returned to Oxford, which continued to be dominated by his opponents and enemies. The University authorities went so far as to ban the reading of his masterpiece, *An Essay Concerning Human Understanding*, in 1703. Nevertheless, it was by bequeathing copies of the *Two Treatises* and the *Letter Concerning Toleration* to the Bodleian that Locke confirmed he was their author, and it is appropriate that our voyage of discovery (a voyage we can now plan with the help of excellent maps and guides, so that it is now much less arduous than once it was) begins in a room that has changed little since his day, and that so many of the key events with which we shall be concerned took place close by.

Locke left no autobiography, no account of his own intellectual career. We do not know if he watched College hang, or saw the flames flicker among the volumes of Milton, Hunton and Hobbes. We do not know whether his immediate reaction to these events was one of anger or of fear. We do know that the author of the *Two Treatises* had good reason to fear both the censor and the executioner. History is the art of making sense of the evidence that survives, and the historian's task is hardest when the evidence has been pre-selected. Locke was a cautious philosopher, anxious in those dangerous months and years to avoid self-incrimination. He took care to leave no record of much of what he thought and did, and went to elaborate lengths to conceal his authorship of both the *Two Treatises* and the *Letter Concerning Toleration* during his lifetime. In this volume you will find both the key political works that Locke published, and the most important surviving evidence from among his papers relating to his political philosophy.

This evidence leaves many questions unanswered and poses many puzzles: the introduction represents my attempt to find a key to Locke.

Locke himself wrote a short essay on the difficulties of interpreting a classic text: it appears as the Preface to his most important posthumous work, *A Paraphrase and Notes on the Epistles of St Paul*. There, among the many difficulties and dangers he discusses, two are especially apposite: the difficulty of re-establishing the context that can alone make clear what an author was discussing, and what he or she was trying to accomplish (to whom was St Paul writing, and what knowledge did he and his first readers share and take for granted?), and the danger of trying to make an author speak in terms that are familiar to us, and reach conclusions with which we agree. Locke's view was that the 'touchstone' for the interpretation of St Paul was to read him, not as a theologian, but as a Church leader pursuing practical objectives, as someone who 'knew how to prosecute his purpose with strength of argument and close reasoning, without incoherent sallies, or the intermixing of things foreign to his business' (Locke 1987, 109, 111). Locke had started off feeling he understood Paul's 'practical directions', but not his doctrine (103); he ended up reinterpreting his doctrine in the light of those directions.

Locke had time to prepare for death. He died expecting his *Paraphrases* to be published, and having made arrangements for the long-kept secret of his authorship of the works that have made his reputation as a political philosopher, the *Two Treatises* and the *Letter Concerning Toleration*, to be finally made public. He would not have thought it inappropriate to apply to his own works the principles of interpretation he had applied to St Paul. But he could not foresee the day when he himself would become the subject of seemingly endless commentary when he wrote these words in defence of the enterprise upon which he had embarked: 'To go about to explain any of St Paul's Epistles, after so great a train of expositors and commentators, might seem an attempt of vanity, censurable for its needlessness, did not the daily and approved examples of pious and learned men justify it. This may be some excuse for me to the public, if ever these following papers should chance to come abroad: but to myself, for whose use this work was undertaken, I need make no apology' (103).

Introduction

Locke chose the following epigraph for the posthumous edition of the *Two Treatises*:

Quod si nihil cum potentiore juris humani relinquitur inopi, at ego ad Deos vindices humanae superbiae confugiam: et precabor ut iras suas vertant in eos, quibus non suae res, non alienae satis sint quorum saevitiam non mors noxiorum exatiet: placari nequeant, nisi hauriendum sanguinem laniandaque viscera nostra praebuerimus.

Livy, bk 9, ch. 1

[But if the weak are left no civil rights to protect them from the mighty, nevertheless I will seek protection from the Gods, who punish human pride. And I will pray that they will grow angry with those who are never content, not with their own possessions, nor with those they take from others. Their blood lust is not satiated by the execution of the guilty. They will not be satisfied unless we offer them our blood to drink, and our entrails to tear out.]

Locke's liberalism

There are at most two or three English authors of the seventeenth century about whom we know more than we know about John Locke. We have thousands of letters to and from Locke, volumes of his journals, drafts of many of his works, his commonplace books, the catalogue of his library. Locke's surviving papers provide a vast mass of information on almost every aspect of his life, and would attract historians even if he was a figure of the second rank, a minor Oxford academic. Anyone who turned to Locke's papers for an insight into his life and times, in the way that we turn to Samuel Pepys, John Evelyn, or Anthony Wood, would, however, be sadly disappointed. They wrote to expose themselves and their contemporaries to their own gaze or to that of posterity. Locke has no interest in his own peculiarities, or those of his friends. He was fascinated by the inner workings of the mind, but had no desire to expose his own to the public's eye. We know so much about him because he was orderly, thoughtful, and systematic, but what we know often leaves us in the dark regarding his hopes and fears, motives and aspirations. Building a picture of the man and his life out of the papers he left behind is far from straightforward. If Locke scholars persist it is only partly because there is so much to learn; above all it is because they are so eager to know.

Most of the scholars who work on Locke, and most of the students who read him, are not historians. Some are philosophers, but the greatest number are studying political theory. They come to Locke because they want to know more about the intellectual origins of liberalism.[1] In the past Locke's political theory has had a particular resonance for Americans, even though (paradoxically) the term 'liberal' has come to be a term of abuse in American political life. Nathan Tarcov has written of the

very real sense in which Americans can say that Locke is *our* political

7

philosopher. The document by virtue of which we Americans are an independent people, occupying our special station among the powers of the earth, derives its principles and even some of its language from the political philosophy of John Locke. Practically speaking, we can recognize in his work something like our separation of powers, our belief in representative government, our hostility to all forms of tyranny, our insistence on the rule of law, our faith in toleration, our demand for limited government, and our confidence that the common good is ultimately served by the regulated private acquisition and control of property as well as by the free development and application of science. As for fundamental political principles, it can be safely assumed that every one of us, before we ever heard of Locke, had heard that all men are created equal, that they are endowed with certain inalienable rights, that among them are life, liberty, and the pursuit of happiness, that to secure these rights governments are instituted among men, deriving their just powers from the consent of the governed, and that, whenever any form of government becomes destructive of these ends, it is the right of the people to alter or abolish it. (Tarcov 1984, 1)

It is less than a decade since Tarcov wrote these words, but they no longer read like a list of peculiarly 'American' principles. It is important, however, to remember that only recently they still did. If the American constitution was founded on Lockean principles, the English constitution, notoriously, was founded on their opposite, the principles of Burke. The sovereignty of Parliament (which included the monarch and a chamber dominated by a hereditary peerage), the powers of a government that was unlimited in law (and so could not be held accountable in the courts for its actions), and the privileges of a state Church were justified by an ultimate appeal not to rights or principles, but to the sanction of tradition and custom. At the same time, over much of the world, communist governments recognized no limits on their power, and denied that their citizens could lay claim to any inalienable rights.

A few years ago it was a remarkable fact that there was hardly a country in the world that did not claim to be a democracy or to be on the road to democracy (Dunn 1979). The exceptions (e.g. Kuwait, South Africa) were obvious anomalies. At the same time, though, the differences between the so-called people's democracies and their opponents, the bourgeois democracies, were so great that nobody could imagine there was one common set of political principles recognized throughout the world. It was merely that one word passed as common currency in several different languages. Now the situation is totally different. As communism in eastern Europe has collapsed, it has suddenly begun to look as though liberal democracy, founded on the separation of powers, representative government, freedom of speech and conscience, and the right to pursue wealth, will become the norm throughout the world. Even in England calls for constitutional reform are increasingly heard, and it is now possible to appeal against the decrees of a semi-sovereign Parliament to a court of rights in Strasbourg. We are all, it would seem, liberals now. Almost all of us can now say that Locke is *our* political philosopher.

Liberalism, of course, comes in many different forms. For some it means the principles of the free market, of *laissez-faire*. 'Conservative liberals' are hostile to the state, and look to the family and the market as the key institutions that provide the cement of society. Others think that the rights to life and to the pursuit of happiness imply a right to divorce and abortion, and a right, not only to universal education, but also to universal health insurance and to generous welfare provision. But these are disputes within an overall consensus, quarrels over the social and political implications of liberal principles. Locke does not speak straightforwardly for either side in these disputes: one can portray him as being both for and against the free market, for and against the welfare state, for and against divorce. Those on both sides of these disputes use arguments whose force he would have recognized.

Is Locke then to be revered as the founder of liberalism, the philosopher of the day? Two decades ago John Dunn, in an immensely influential book on Locke's political philosophy, insisted that Locke's arguments were now irrelevant (Dunn 1969a). In Dunn's view, our reasoning was now so fundamentally different from Locke's that it was different in kind. None of us would argue in terms of a social contract reached in a state of nature; few of us would wish to ground our political philosophy in a divinely ordained law of nature. Even if we were liberals, what we could mainly learn from Locke was that the intellectual difficulties, the paradoxes and tensions, with which we had to struggle were ones that had dogged liberalism from its inception. Best though to forget about 'Locke and Liberalism', and concentrate simply on Locke. Dunn offered us history, not contemporary political theory.

Dunn is an Englishman; an American would have expressed himself more cautiously. Within a few years, in any case, academic fashions had changed. With the arguments of Rawls and Nozick the social contract tradition, which the English had long seen as a historical curiosity, the tradition of Hobbes, Locke, and Rousseau, rendered irrelevant by Hume, Mill, and Marx, was reborn. The new technology of the computer even came to the support of the Lockeans, for it was easy to programme computers to play out games between rational actors making and breaking contracts. Meanwhile American scholars working in the tradition of Leo Strauss continued to insist that Locke's thinking was fundamentally secular, not religious, and primarily about practical interests, not abstract rights, and that it was therefore quintessentially 'modern'.

Even if Locke's arguments now seem more relevant than they did twenty years ago, there has been a continuing obstacle to his intellectual rehabilitation. In an influential article, Dunn went so far as to claim that Locke was not only a historical anachronism, but that he had had little impact on history (Dunn 1969b). This argument was much reinforced by J. G. A. Pocock's *The Machiavellian Moment* (1975), which argued that the major intellectual tradition which prepared the ground for the American revolution was not that of Lockean liberalism, but rather that of Machiavellian republicanism. As Machiavelli's star rose, Locke's went into decline. Only recently has there been a sustained attack on the view that the Whig tradition which inspired the American revolution owed little to Locke (e.g. Dworetz 1990, Hamowy 1990, Houston 1991). Even Dunn recently gracefully admitted that something is still alive in the political philosophy of John Locke (Dunn 1990).

Locke is a seventeenth-century, not a twentieth-century, political philosopher. If any political theorist has continuing relevance, then it is he. The newest constitutions embody his principles. The most fashionable political philosophers argue from premises recognizably related to his. But it is not my purpose here to stress the respects in which Locke is 'our' political philosopher. I want to tackle the basic historical questions which have to be asked if we are to understand why Locke wrote what were to become the classic texts of liberal political theory. Such questions as: When did Locke write the *Two Treatises*? What was his political purpose in doing so? What intellectual resources did he draw upon? When and how did he come to hold the views he expressed there? Did he continue to find them convincing? It should quickly become apparent that it is always dangerous to say that John Locke thought this or that. In the first place, his views changed radically over time. What Locke thought in 1661 is quite different from what he thought in 1681. And in the second place, scholars disagree sharply about how to interpret his key texts. Where one sees a defence of democracy, another sees an unthinking acceptance of oligarchy; where one discovers ill-concealed contempt for Christianity, another finds an authentic piety; where one argues that he wrote as a detached philosopher, another claims that he was a party propagandist. These disagreements about what Locke was actually saying can be resolved only by clarifying the context in which he was saying it, by finding out what Locke took for granted and did not think it necessary to explain, by reading Locke as he himself sought to read St Paul. Only when we have a proper grasp of Locke's meaning can we go on to debate how far his arguments are still relevant in our very different circumstances.

Dunn was right to stress that Locke could not see us coming. The word 'liberalism' did not exist in his vocabulary. Nor did he have the comfort our liberals have, of holding views that are widely approved. The principles he espoused in the *Second Treatise* were far from fashionable. The only major revolution of which Locke had knowledge, the English Civil War, had ended in abject failure with the restoration of the monarchy in 1660. If Locke's party, the Whigs, triumphed in the years after the milk and water revolution of 1688, it was only because they supported war against the Catholic absolutism of Louis XIV in Europe; not because the King or the nation had been converted to their political principles. In any case, the principles of the *Second Treatise* were far from being those of the Whig movement as a whole. Locke's political ideas had few supporters in his own day (Thompson 1976, Nelson 1978, Thompson 1979, Ashcraft and Goldsmith 1983); they gained at best a precarious respectability when Locke owned them at his death, by which date his reputation as a philosopher of knowledge was secure. Because the *Two Treatises* and the *Letter Concerning Toleration* were included in the editions of his *Works*, they were widely available when, at last, there were people eager to put them to use. But for this circumstance they would have faded into obscurity.

People sometimes write as if Locke spoke for his age: nothing could be further from the truth. More sophisticated scholars have a tendency to want to make Locke the spokesman for a particular movement in the intellectual or political life of his day – Baconianism (Wood 1983, Wood 1984), radical Whiggism (Ashcraft 1986) – but even these categories fail to do justice to the eccentric individuality of his thought. If we want to understand Locke's political philosophy we have to put to one side our approval of those principles that we hold in common with him, to put aside even our desire to situate him within the major intellectual movements of the time, and concentrate instead on the substantial gap between his views and those of most of his contemporaries. Locke himself warns us of the danger of explaining authors' meanings 'by what they never thought of whilst they were writing, which is not,' he said, 'the way to find their sense in what they delivered, but our own, and to take up from their writings not what they left there for us, but what we bring along with us in our selves' (1987, 114). Locke may be, of necessity, our philosopher: the *our* no longer needs to be underlined. But this brings us no nearer to understanding his political philosophy as he himself conceived it; no nearer either to understanding the place of the *Second Treatise* and the *Letter Concerning Toleration* in Locke's life.

We shall not make much progress towards this end if we think of Locke as inventing liberal political principles from scratch. Every single one of the principles enumerated by Tarcov as being those of the American Declaration of Independence can be traced back before Locke to the Levellers, and almost all of them can be traced back even further, to the winter of 1642/3, the first winter of the English Civil War (Wootton 1990). If we want to locate the intellectual origins of liberalism we can follow this path backwards until we reach that moment in time when liberal doctrines spring seemingly from nowhere, like a stream bubbling up from underground.

The obscure men who first gave voice to them were however following the logic of arguments that had long been around: arguments that founded government in an original act of consent, and made rulers ultimately answerable to their subjects. It was desperation, the desperation of military defeat, that drove them to follow those arguments through to the unpalatable conclusion that legitimate government might be at an end, the state of nature might be restored, and that men, gathered together as equals, might have to build a new political order from scratch. Thus they made the momentous transition from claiming that rulers must ultimately be answerable to their subjects to maintaining that subjects could not be bound by the decisions of their ancestors.

Already one author, whose works were completely unknown at the time, had swiftly sketched out the liberal position simply and solely in order to attack it. Sir Robert Filmer's *Patriarcha* was written, almost certainly, by 1631 (Filmer 1991, viii, xxxii–iv); but it was not published until 1680, when it was immediately seized on by the supporters of royal absolutism as a brilliant presentation of their views. Filmer's claim was that Adam was owner of the world and monarch of all his descendants; that the powers of kings and fathers were identical and unlimited; and that monarchs should be regarded as substitutes for Adam and as the fathers of their peoples. There were obvious problems with his argument, for it was hard to see how Charles II could have inherited Adam's rights, or could have come by those of a father over his family by virtue of being King of England. But one reason for Filmer's popularity was that the straw men that Filmer had constructed in the 1630s in order to hack at them with his sickle had become men of flesh and blood in the meantime, men armed with guns: it was hard not to read him as someone commenting upon, rather than foreseeing, the arguments of the Civil War (Wallace 1980; Ashcraft 1986, 250n–251n).

In 1680 it was widely feared that the issues and conflicts of the Civil War were once more coming to the fore. The Whigs, under the leadership of Shaftesbury, claimed that there was a Catholic plot to assassinate the King and establish his Catholic brother and heir, James, Duke of York, on the throne. Arguing that any Catholic ruler would be bound to undermine the Church of England and would seek to establish an absolute government, they sought to persuade Parliament – that is, the House of Commons, the House of Lords, and the King, who each had a veto on new legislation – to exclude James from the throne. Between 1679 and 1681 they twice won majorities in the House of Commons in national elections; each time they failed to persuade the King to abandon the hereditary principle and name a Protestant successor. Filmer was long dead, but his claim that the principle of hereditary succession had been established by divine law seemed directly relevant to the conflicts of the day.

In 1680 and the years immediately following it, in the midst of the Exclusion Crisis and the Tory reaction that succeeded it, three men sat down to write replies to Filmer. James Tyrrell, a close friend of Locke's, published *Patriarcha non Monarcha* in the first half of 1681. He was to go on to become the leading proponent of a respectable Whig philosophy in the years after the revolution of 1688, when James (who had succeeded to the throne on Charles's death in 1685) was finally overthrown. Algernon Sidney, long a republican, was to die on the scaffold in 1683, suspected of having participated in the Rye House Plot, convicted of having written a series of *Discourses* in reply to Filmer. These discourses were to be published by Toland in 1698 and, supported by Sidney's posthumous reputation as a Whig martyr, were to make Sidney a more influential political theorist than Locke through most of the eighteenth century. It seems that Sidney did not begin work on his *Discourses* until August 1681 at the earliest (Worden 1985, 15). The third, and for long the least important of the three as a political philosopher, was Locke.

There are numerous points at which the arguments of Tyrrell, Sidney, and Locke overlap. Many of the similarities between their works are due simply to the fact that they had in Filmer a common opponent, but others suggest, as I will argue below, that Locke had been influenced by Tyrrell. On the basis of this and other evidence I shall argue that Locke's *Second Treatise* was written in the second half of 1681.

Between them Tyrrell, Sidney, and Locke covered the range of argument that had been propounded by the opponents of the monarchy during the decade of the Civil War. Tyrrell's sympathies were with Philip Hunton, who had recognized that subjects might have to rebel, but only, he believed, to defend the principles of the established constitution. Sidney's sympathies were with the republicans, who had looked to Italy – to the austerity of ancient Rome, to the realism of Machiavelli, and to the constitution of Venice – in order to learn how to construct a new political order based on liberty, virtue, and martial valour.

As for Locke, he was the only one of the three who fully accepted the challenge presented by Filmer. He did not only attack the positions Filmer had defended; he systematically defended the views Filmer had attacked. Filmer, not Locke, invented liberalism. He defined the position he was attacking as the belief that 'Mankind is naturally endowed and born with freedom from all subjection, and at liberty to choose what form of government it please, and that the power which any one man hath over others was at first by human right bestowed according to the discretion of the multitude.' From the 'supposed natural freedom and equality of mankind, and liberty to choose what form of government it please', there followed, he believed, 'as a necessary consequence' the view that rulers are 'subject to the censures and deprivations of their subjects'. It was also a consequence of this view, he held, that there must be freedom of inquiry and of speech: those who affirmed the natural liberty of mankind were obliged not to 'deny by retail that liberty they affirm by wholesale' (Filmer 1991, 2–4). Filmer knew that most people did not accept that these conclusions followed from the premise of original liberty. They thought that liberty once given up could never be reclaimed; that rebellion could only be justified to restore, but never to transform, the constitution; and that freedom of speech must be curtailed in order to protect religion and the law. Despite his pretence that he was writing against real opponents, it was he who had imagined 'the whole fabric of this vast engine of popular sedition' (Filmer 1991, 3; Tarcov 1984, 22–34).

We do not know whether Locke had read any of the Civil War radicals, whether he was familiar with Lilburne or Overton. Because he set out to defend the view that Filmer had attacked, his arguments were bound to parallel theirs, and he was surely aware that there were Civil War precedents for what he wanted to say, should he choose to look for them. But Locke's defence of the principles of the natural freedom and equality of mankind, of inalienable rights, and of the ultimate right to revolution (principles that we may reasonably label 'liberal') was immeasurably more sophisticated and uncompromising than anything that had gone before. There is no mystery about where the fundamental principles of the *Second Treatise* came from: they came from Filmer. What is puzzling is Locke's willingness to adopt these principles, his willingness to allow Filmer to dictate the terms of the debate.

Locke's life

John Locke was born in Somerset in 1632.[2] His paternal grandfather was a wealthy clothier. His father, a lawyer and small landowner who served in the Parliamentary army during the Civil War, lost rather than made money. John Locke senior was lawyer to Alexander Popham, an MP for a West Country constituency. It was Popham who arranged for young John to attend Westminster School in London in 1647.

If Locke's background was Puritan and Parliamentary, his school was royalist and High Church. From Westminster he went to Christ Church, Oxford, in 1652. The University had recently been purged of royalists, and Christ Church was under secure, but relatively tolerant, Parliamentary control. The Dean of Christ Church and Vice Chancellor of the University, John Owen, was a prominent advocate of religious toleration. The educational curriculum was, however, unreformed: Locke was trained as a conventional scholastic (that is, Aristotelian) philosopher, although he soon developed an extra-curricular interest in the study of medicine, an interest that brought him into contact with the small group of empirical natural philosophers and physicians at Oxford whose regular meetings were later to be a model for the Royal Society.

In 1658 Locke obtained his MA and an untenured fellowship at Christ Church. That same year Oliver Cromwell died, and the prolonged crisis that was to lead to the Restoration of the King in 1660 began. Locke himself welcomed the Restoration: 'All the freedom I can wish my country or myself is to enjoy the protection of those laws which the prudence and providence of our ancestors established and the happy return of his Majesty has restored' (below, pp. 149–50). The year before he had been in favour of religious toleration. Between late 1660 and the end of 1662 he wrote two tracts insisting that rulers were under no obligation to allow diversity in forms of religious worship. The first was directed against a colleague, Edward Bagshaw, who had defended toleration at the moment when the exact nature of the Restoration settlement was yet to be established. Locke's tracts (in which he argued that subjects never had the right to resist their rulers) remained unpublished, but he had firmly attached himself to the winning side: Bagshaw lost his job and was soon in prison.

A year later Locke wrote a series of *Essays on the Law of Nature* (that is, not on science, but on the moral law that should govern the behaviour of all rational beings): these are remarkable for their insistence that there can be no innate knowledge. Everything we know, including our knowledge of right and wrong, is an inference that we have drawn on the basis of our experience. Locke was to remain an empiricist to the end of his life, and his essays of 1663 contain the germ of the theory of knowledge of the *Essay Concerning Human Understanding*. Nevertheless Locke insisted that we could have an adequate knowledge of right and wrong, and that we could be confident that those who sought to ground morality in mere self-interest (the modern reader thinks at once of Hobbes, and so, in all probability, did Locke) were mistaken.[3]

The empiricism of the *Essays on the Law of Nature* constitutes Locke's first independent intellectual commitment. In the same year he made a decision that he knew was likely to govern the future course of his life: he decided not to take religious orders, despite the fact that of the fifty-five tenured jobs at Christ Church, only five could be held by laymen. Locke was jeopardizing his future, for reasons about which we can only speculate. Perhaps he was doubtful as to whether he should stay in academic life. Fellows of colleges were forbidden to marry, and Locke was clearly interested in courtship and romance. In 1665 he explored the possibility of starting a new career, going as secretary on a diplomatic mission to Brandenburg, where he saw Protestants and Catholics living amicably together. Locke was offered the opportunity to continue in diplomacy; he may well have had the chance to marry a young lady to whom he wrote under the pseudonym of 'Scribelia'. Instead he seems to have decided to be a bachelor, a don, and a layman, and to devote himself to the study of medicine. His failure to become ordained at this juncture, when his career was potentially at stake, suggests that he was far from comfortable with the doctrines of the Anglican Church, but we cannot prove what we may reasonably suspect.

In 1666 Locke was asked to give medical advice to Lord Ashley, the future Earl of Shaftesbury and the leading advocate of religious toleration in the far-from-tolerant Restoration Parliament. Evidently the two quickly formed an alliance. Ashley sought to secure Locke's position at the University, despite his failure to take orders, seeking to obtain for him a dispensation so that he could proceed directly to a doctorate in medicine, brushing aside the fact that he had not taken his bachelor's or master's degrees in that field: this would have opened the way for Locke to obtain one of the few fellowships reserved for laymen. Ashley was unsuccessful in furthering Locke's medical career, but he did secure his position at the University, obtaining a letter from the King dispensing Locke from the obligation to be ordained if he wanted to retain his fellowship.

Next year Locke went to live in Ashley's household in London. He was in charge of Ashley's medical care (carrying out an operation on Ashley's liver in 1668). In 1667 he wrote an *Essay Concerning Toleration*, which was apparently intended to be shown to the King by Ashley, who had recently become a minister of the Crown. Next year he become a Fellow of the Royal Society. He wrote an essay for Ashley arguing against legislation to control interest rates. He became secretary to the Lords Proprietors of Carolina, a colony effectively governed by Ashley, and drafted a remarkable constitution for the new settlement. He took charge of the education, and the marriage, of Ashley's son, and played a role, in due course, in the education of his famous grandson, the third Earl of Shaftesbury.

In 1671 Locke and five or six friends formed a little group that met periodically to discuss 'the principles of morality and revealed religion'. In the course of these meetings Locke declared that they could not proceed without a better grasp of the nature of knowledge in general: two early drafts of the *Essay Concerning Human Understanding* were completed in the course of this year.

In 1672 Ashley became the Earl of Shaftesbury and, by the end of the year, Lord Chancellor; he masterminded a trade war between England and Holland; and he oversaw the royal Declaration of Indulgence, which suspended all legal penalties against Puritan Nonconformists (or Dissenters) and against Catholics. Locke, as Shaftesbury's associate, was rewarded with a government sinecure, Secretary of Presentations, worth £300 a year, rather more than he earned from the estates in Somerset which he had inherited on his father's death.

But Shaftesbury soon began to suspect that there was more to the King's policies than there seemed. Two years before, Charles had signed a treaty with Louis XIV. In secret clauses attached to it he promised to convert to Catholicism, in return for which he was assured of a French subsidy and the support of French troops. As suspicions regarding the terms of this treaty spread, Shaftesbury expressed increasing hostility to France and to Catholicism, and towards the end of 1673 he was dismissed from office. By then Locke had obtained the important post of Secretary to the Council of Trade and Plantations, a position he was to hold for a year and a half. By 1675 Shaftesbury was the leader of opposition to the King, and in particular to royal attempts to impose on the clergy, office holders, and members of Parliament an oath declaring illegal any armed resistance to the King and any attempt to change the constitution of the Church.

The views of the opposition were forcibly expressed in *A Letter from a Person of Quality to His Friend in the Country*, a pamphlet that was written by Shaftesbury or someone close to him, perhaps even Locke himself. Shortly after the pamphlet was condemned to be burnt by the hangman, Locke left on a lengthy journey to France. Ostensibly he went because he was in ill-health. He may have feared being identified as the author of *A Letter*. He may have been needed in France because of secret negotiations that were taking place between the opposition to Charles and the French court, for both shared a temporary common interest in undermining the King's chief minister, Danby, who was building up the strength of the Church party. We cannot be sure whether Locke during these years is best described as a convalescent philosopher, a political exile, or a secret agent.

By the time Locke returned to London, in the spring of 1679, the crisis of the Popish Plot had engulfed English political life. Titus Oates claimed to have evidence of a plot to kill the King; Shaftesbury (who was now in the government as a result of Danby's fall, despite the fact that he had only recently emerged from a year's imprisonment in the Tower that had been his penalty for opposition to the King) gave his support to Oates; and numerous people, many of them Catholic, were condemned to death on the basis of false testimony. We do not know whether Shaftesbury and Locke believed Oates's lies. What is clear is that Shaftesbury and his supporters were determined to exploit Oates's testimony in order to exclude James from succession to the throne. Locke's close relationship to Shaftesbury placed him at the centre of the plotting, the political campaigning, and the propaganda wars of the Exclusion Crisis.

In March 1681, in Oxford, Charles opened what was to be the last of the three Exclusion Parliaments. After eight days, with no prospect of a compromise, he dissolved it. He was determined, we now know, to govern in future without Parliament. In July Shaftesbury was charged with high treason. The same month, a London jury rejected charges of treason brought against Stephen College, a supporter of Shaftesbury who had distributed around Oxford at the time of the Parliament a cartoon and a doggerel poem calling on the House of Commons to seize control and make the King obey them. The prosecution moved the case to Oxford, where College was condemned and executed. Shaftesbury, who had reason to fear that his own case would follow College's to trial in front of a royalist Oxford jury, paid for College's lawyer; Locke arranged for his accommodation. Spies reported to the government on Locke's movements and conversations. But they did not know that Locke was writing the *Second Treatise*: in doing so he was running the risk of sharing College's fate.

At the end of the year Shaftesbury was released from the Tower by a London jury. There was no longer any prospect of legal opposition, for there was no hope of Parliament being called, or of the King agreeing to Exclusion. The radical policy for which College had died – calling on the Commons to seize power from the King – could no longer be pursued. The choice seemed to be between an armed *coup d'état* and acquiescence in the ultimate victory of Catholicism and absolutism. There were soon plans afoot to seize the King and his brother – plans, presumably, to assassinate them. From December 1681 until the discovery of the Rye House Plot in July of 1683 the conspiracy was hatched, uninterrupted even by Shaftesbury's death in exile in Holland. The discovery of the plot meant the final victory of reaction. Algernon Sidney and Lords Essex and Russell were arrested: Sidney and Russell were soon to be executed, Essex to die mysteriously in prison. In Oxford books justifying resistance were burnt by order of the University, and Tory mobs jeered known Whigs in the street. In August, in great secrecy and in such haste that he could neither order his financial affairs nor pack his clothes, Locke fled for Holland. There was, and is, no incontrovertible evidence of his involvement in the Rye House Plot, but everything points to it.

During his five years of exile in Holland, Locke was occupied with redrafting the *Essay Concerning Human Understanding* and writing the *Letter Concerning Toleration*. We know that he was also acquiring and reading works of Socinian (i.e. Unitarian) theology. More urgently, the government suspected him of involvement in treasonous plotting. In November 1684 the King demanded that he be expelled from his position at Christ Church, although Locke, writing from Holland, defended himself as a dutiful subject and denied consorting with the King's enemies. He was in Holland, he claimed, not because it was the centre of conspiracy against the King, but because he liked the beer! Perhaps he was involved in helping to organize Monmouth's invasion, which took place after the death of Charles and the accession of James to the throne in the summer of 1685. The rebellion was an ignominious failure: even Locke's closest friends in England avoided being implicated in it. In Holland, Locke went into hiding: the English government had named him among the conspirators it wanted extradited to stand trial. He was in danger of being kidnapped or assassinated by English agents.

In England Tory principles were not long in the ascendant. James was determined to introduce toleration for Catholics, despite the fierce opposition of Tories and High Churchmen. He turned for support to many of his former opponents, offering toleration to the Dissenters. Among those willing to cooperate with James were close associates of Locke, who urged him to seek a pardon and come home. Locke, however, shows no sign of having wavered in his opposition to James, whose position rapidly became precarious as Tories and intransigent Whigs united against him. The Queen's pregnancy, and the eventual birth of a son, opened up the prospect of a Catholic dynasty. In Holland, William of Orange, James's son-in-law, saw his overthrow as the only way to bring England into the Continental struggle against the power of Louis XIV's France. In November 1688, William, encouraged by a majority of Whigs and Tories alike, invaded England. James's army melted away and he fled abroad. The Convention Parliament offered William and Mary, his wife, the throne.

By the time Locke returned, in February 1689, the revolution was over. He was offered the position of ambassador to Branden-burg, and refused. He quickly published the *Essay Concerning Human Understanding* (an abridgement of which had been published in French in 1687) and, anonymously, *Two Treatises of Government*. The *Letter Concerning Toleration* also appeared anonymously the same year, first in Latin, published at Gouda, and then in an English translation by a Socinian, William Popple. At the age of fifty-seven, Locke had at last become an author to be reckoned with. He divided his time between London and a country house at Oates, in Essex, where he lived with Lady Masham, daughter of the Cambridge philosopher Ralph Cudworth and a formidable intel-lect in her own right, and her husband. The marriage had taken place while Locke was in exile. In 1682, Damaris Cudworth (as she then was) and Locke had been in love. Perhaps rumours to this effect reached Locke's enemies, one of whom referred to 'the seraglio at Oates'.

In 1692 Locke published *Some Considerations of the Consequences of the Lowering of Interest*, a work based on his memorandum to Shaftesbury of 1668. In 1693 there followed *Some Thoughts Concern-ing Education*, a re-working of some letters he had written from exile in Holland to a close friend, Edward Clarke, on how best to educate his son. The *Letter Concerning Toleration* embroiled Locke in a prolonged controversy with Jonas Proast. The *Essay Concerning Human Understanding* had provoked a number of criticisms, to some of which Locke tried to respond in the second edition of 1692. But it was the publication in 1695 of *The Reasonableness of Christianity* that provoked the wrath of the orthodox. Locke's version of Christianity appeared to leave no place for the doctrines of original sin or the Trinity. Its stress upon reason seemed to make revealed truth subject to human judgement. John Edwards quickly launched a formidable attack upon it, accusing Locke of Socinianism. Others, suspecting Locke's authorship of the *Reasonableness*, re-read the *Essay* in the light of it and found Socinian arguments there: Locke was to be enmeshed in the resulting controversies until his death.

At the same time Locke was embarking on his last major period of political activity. In 1695 he published *Further Considerations Concerning the Raising the Value of Money*, advocating re-coinage (a policy the government adopted, with disastrous results). The next year he was appointed a Commissioner of a newly established Board of Trade: he was, despite recurrent ill-health, to be the dominant member of the Board until he finally retired in 1700. For the last years of his life (he died in 1704) Locke's health was poor, but he was still active. He was at work on the *Paraphrase and Notes on the Epistles of St Paul*. And he was still making new friends: it was in 1703 that he formed a close friendship with a young freethinker, Anthony Collins. Increasingly his arguments were being taken up by deists and sceptics such as Toland, Tindal, and Collins: his future importance for Enlightenment philosophy was prefigured in their approval of his works.

Locke died a wealthy man: since the beginning of his association with Shaftesbury he had invested wisely, not in land, but in shares, bonds, and private loans. He also died famous: his *Essay Concerning Human Understanding* was widely regarded as one of the most important works of philosophy since Descartes. That he was the author of *A Letter Concerning Toleration* was widely believed; that he was the author of *Two Treatises of Government* was suspected by those few who concerned themselves with such matters. That these last two were works whose reputation would grow from century to century no one imagined.

I have sketched in the outline of Locke's life, but it is of limited help in making sense of his political philosophy. We cannot learn from it whether Locke agreed in 1682 with those Whig plotters who wanted to preserve the ancient constitution, or with those who wanted to transform it. We cannot tell from it whether the respectable civil servant of the late 1690s regretted or approved his earlier support for revolutionary principles. Only the details of the story can answer questions like these.

Forget for a moment the basic facts we now know. Come with me into the bookshop of Awnsham and John Churchill, at the sign of the Black Swan in Paternoster Row, near St Paul's Cathedral. The year is 1695. Churchill is one of the leading publishers, booksellers, and stationers of his day. Here you can buy books imported from the Continent, books bought in from other London printers and from Cambridge and Oxford, almanacs and newssheets, not to mention reams of paper and several qualities of ink.

But what a confusing place it is! For there are, to a twentieth-century eye, scarcely any books to be seen. The few bound volumes are reserved, waiting to be picked up by those who have ordered them, or are samples to attract your attention. Churchill's stock, stored at the back, consists of reams of printed paper, each page as big as a newspaper. There are a few booklets, ephemera like almanacs that are sold like magazines, stitched together, but the opportunities for browsing are limited: you have to order from the catalogue and rely on the Churchills' own description of their wares. You have come to buy what will, when bound, become a small volume, *Further Considerations Concerning Raising the Value of Money*, by John Locke.

Locke's book is an attack on a proposal to devalue the coinage. The silver coins with which you pay for it are evidently damaged: illegally clipped, they weigh only about two-thirds their official weight. The purloined silver has been melted down and, by now, either exported or taken to the mint to be turned into money. England is at war with France, her trade disrupted, taxes high, the government's finances stretched to the limit. And her currency is beginning to collapse: full-weight coins now command a premium because the silver of which they are made is worth more than their face value. They are hoarded, and scarcely to be found. Nobody has confidence in the light-weight coins that you are pleased to pass on to Churchill – one day soon they may be rejected as illegal tender.

This, you know, is Locke's proposal and the proposal of the government. The old coinage is to be called in. The key question is: Will you be allowed to exchange a light-weight coin for a full-weight one; or will the old coins be valued by their weight, not their denomination? Locke's view, Awnsham Churchill tells you, is that the coins should be valued at their weight. Everybody would lose something in the process, but speculators and hoarders would lose the most; the poor, with little money in hand, would lose the least. The government, on the other hand, proposes to compensate those who promptly hand in old coins by giving them the same number of new ones. Churchill tells you that Locke fears that this policy, designed to prevent the devaluation of the pound in your pocket, will prove a disaster: the existing coinage will rapidly disappear from circulation, but will only slowly be replaced. As a result, trade will come to a standstill, creditors will be unable to collect their debts. Speculators will buy up the newly illegal light-weight coins at a discount from those unable to get to the mint, or required to pay their taxes promptly; they will then cash them in at the mint for their full value, pocketing huge profits at the expense of the disadvantaged.

Shortly, these dire predictions will come to pass. But why, before the test of experience, should Churchill take Locke's opinion seriously? Locke, he tells you, is just establishing his reputation as a great philosopher. His *Essay Concerning Human Understanding* is a best-seller; he has only a few copies left of the third edition. If you prefer your philosophy in Latin he can sell you the *Logica* of Jean le Clerc: written by a friend of Locke's, it employs similar principles. If you have children, you might like to read Locke's essay on how they should be educated. Locke, too, is a man with a long-standing interest in financial affairs: Churchill has two other pamphlets by him on money that he can sell you. Locke, he tells you, is to be a member of the new Board of Trade. If only the government were planning to follow his advice!

The conversation I am describing, of course, is imaginary. We do not know what Awnsham Churchill told his customers about John Locke, or whether Churchill foresaw the disastrous outcome of the great re-coinage, for which Locke has long, unjustly, been held responsible (Locke 1991, 12–39). We do know, though, what he did not tell them. As he sold John Locke's *Essay* and his *Further Considerations*, he had, listed in his catalogue, stacked in his warehouse, a number of other books by the same John Locke: the *Reasonableness of Christianity*, the *Letter Concerning Toleration*, *Two Treatises of Government*.[4] The first two of these had provoked considerable controversy. Locke had written replies to his attackers, and Churchill had forwarded to him letters sent by well-wishers of the anonymous author, whose identity was widely suspected, but never confirmed until Locke's death in 1704. The third had attracted much less attention. It was in its second edition, and would go into a third before Locke's death, but no one was very interested in its authorship, no one had bothered to devote an essay to attacking it. It is barely possible that even Churchill was not certain who had written it.[5]

If we are going to understand Locke's political philosophy we are going to have to dig beneath the surface of his life. Neither the young Oxford don, nor the associate of Shaftesbury, nor the member of the Board of Trade professed in public the principles for which Locke is now famous. To understand Locke's liberalism we have to see him as even his friends could not; we have to enter into the private recesses of his thoughts. We have to start with a most revealing document, his letter to a friend called Tom.

Locke before Shaftesbury

''Tis fancy that rules us all under the title of reason . . . Men live upon trust, and their knowledge is nothing but opinion moulded up between custom and interest, the two great luminaries of the world, the only lights they walk by' (below, p. 140). Locke's letter to Tom, written in 1659 when the Restoration crisis was at its height, is a straightforward declaration of scepticism, and sceptical themes run through his early writings. In 1660: 'Our deformity is others' beauty, our rudeness others' civility, and there is nothing so uncouth and unhandsome to us which doth not somewhere or other find applause and approbation' (Locke 1967a, 146). In 1661: 'the generality of men, conducted either by chance or advantage, take to themselves their opinions as they do their wives, which when they have once espoused they think themselves concerned to maintain, though for no other reason but because they are theirs' (below, p. 146). In 1663 he outlines the diversity of human moral behaviour, and concludes: 'It may be justly doubted whether the law of nature is binding on all mankind, unsettled and uncertain as men are, accustomed to the most diverse institutions, and driven by impulses in quite opposite directions; for that the decrees of nature are so obscure that they are hidden from whole nations is hard to believe' (Locke 1954, 191).

Like all sceptics, Locke is faced with an obvious problem: What to do, if one does not know what one ought to do? The conventional sceptical answer, propounded for example by Descartes in the *Discourse on Method* (1637), was that one should follow custom. In 1659 this was a less than helpful recommendation, for in a time of upheaval there were few established customs on which one could rely. Locke at first proposes not only following custom but also interest. Even this is hardly specific enough. So he resolves to pursue virtue and honour. 'Let us make it our interest to honour our maker, and be useful to our fellows, and content with ourselves . . . let us content ourselves with the most beautiful and useful opinions' (below, p. 140).

It is easy to disregard the letter to Tom, for it seems to have no obvious bearing on Locke's early writings, the *Two Tracts on Government* and the *Essays on the Law of Nature*. Scholars reading these works have placed them in traditions that have little to do with scepticism. The *Second Tract*, we are told, follows so closely the Anglican and royalist theologian Robert Sanderson that it comes close to plagiarism, while the *Essays on the Law of Nature* are firmly in the tradition of the neo-Platonist natural law theorist Nathaniel Culverwell, who was Locke's precursor in insisting that knowledge of the natural law was not innate, nor could it be discovered through tradition or universal consent: it could only be established by reason working upon the lessons of experience (Abrams in Locke 1967a, 71–2; von Leyden in Locke 1954, 39–43). In both works Locke relies upon the claim that we can have adequate knowledge of the moral law, and in both works he seems to be writing in the tradition of scholastic philosophy.

At the same time, in all his early works Locke gives forceful expression to traditional sceptical arguments. At the heart of Locke's *Essays on the Law of Nature*, when he is arguing that we do not have knowledge of the law of nature from the general consent of mankind, we find a paraphrase of a passage from the most famous sceptic of the century, Pierre Charron:

There is almost no vice, no infringement of natural law, no moral wrong, which anyone who consults the history of the world and observes the affairs of men will not readily perceive to have been not only privately committed somewhere on earth, but also approved by public authority and custom. Nor has there been anything so shameful in its nature that it has not been either sanctified somewhere by religion, or put in the place of virtue and abundantly rewarded with praise. Hence it is easy to see what has been the opinion of men in this matter, since they believed that by such deeds they either reverently honoured the Gods or were themselves made godlike. I shall say nothing here of the various religions of the nations, some of which are ridiculous in their ceremonies, others irreverent in their rites and impious in respect of the cult itself, so that the other nations shudder at the very name of them ... (Locke 1954, 167)[6]

Charron's *Of Wisdom* stressed, like many of Locke's works, the limits of reason, the power of custom, the prevalence of self-interest. Like Locke's *Two Tracts* it laid great emphasis on the need for an absolute state authority to impose religious orthodoxy and political unity, so much so that Charron has been seen as a precursor of Hobbes, and did indeed almost certainly influence him (Tuck 1988, Grendler 1963). If Charron's political philosophy is similar to that of the young Locke, echoes of Charron's other arguments continue to reverberate through his work long after his political opinions had been radicalized, for the attack on the claim that there were some truths that commanded universal consent or were inscribed in the hearts of all mankind, which Locke may well have first learnt from Charron, lay at the heart of the *Essay Concerning Human Understanding*, where Locke also echoed Charron's complaints about the power of custom in shaping opinion (Wootton 1992b).

Having discussed custom, Locke turned, in the *Essays on the Law of Nature* as in the letter to Tom, to interest: Is self-interest the only proper guide to action? The answer he gives is once again 'no' (below, p. 177). The question, as he formulated it, makes us immediately think of Hobbes, but, in the form in which he posed it, it derived from the founder of the modern natural-law tradition, Hugo Grotius, who, like Locke, had invoked a philosopher of ancient Greece, Carneades, as a spokesman for scepticism (Tuck 1983, Tuck 1987). Locke insists that neither custom nor self-interest are true guides to action, but that reason, which we all share, can identify our moral obligations. In these early *Essays* he is determined to oppose scepticism, but at the same time he accepts fully the sceptical account of what the world is actually like. He is engaged in an intimate dialogue with sceptical themes, sceptical arguments, and, we must presume, sceptical authors.

It was a convention among the sceptics to insist that they were prepared to abandon their scepticism as soon as it became dangerous. Did scepticism appear to undermine religious faith? Not at all, they insisted, for by stressing the limits of reason it destroyed the weapons that could be used against belief. In any case, sceptics, they claimed, would be the first to defer to religion because it played such an important role in preserving a social order that was constantly under threat from the unruly passions of mankind, embodied in the dangerous multitude. It was characteristic of the sceptics to argue, as Locke did in the *First Tract*, that religion, which ought to teach obedience, was widely exploited by those seeking to overthrow the existing political order and seize power. Scepticism, because it was hostile to doctrinaire faith, was, they insisted, a bulwark of orthodoxy and guarantor of stability. Sceptics would obediently accept the religion of the authorities, and support neither innovation in religion nor sedition in politics.

Reading sceptics like Charron one often comes away with the impression that it is their political philosophy and their view of human nature that cause them to approve of religion; that they do not accept religion for its own sake, on its own terms, but only for its secular consequences. So too Locke says in his letter to Tom that he will make it his interest to honour his maker: a strange phrase that suggests that he, not his maker, has the final say. Many years later he says that we should regulate our politics, morality, and religion by the public interest, as if we should construct a religion to suit our purposes (Locke 1989, 180).

I do not want to claim that Locke was, at the beginning of his career, a thorough-going sceptic: his objective was to refute scepticism, not to uphold it. What I want to stress is that, for all the rationalist statements in the *Essays on the Law of Nature*, there are important respects in which his thinking in these early years parallels that of sceptics like Charron, and that scepticism went hand in hand with political conservatism of the sort Locke espoused in the *Two Tracts*. The letter to Tom describes what is for Locke a genuine intellectual temptation, and opens the way to a lifelong dialogue with sceptical arguments. Moreover it offers a clear challenge: What is the nature of reason, and what are its limits? Because we know that Locke began the *Essay Concerning Human Understanding* in 1671, it is tempting to try to ground his interest in epistemology in the events of that period, when Locke was reading Samuel Parker's arguments against toleration: to see the *Essay* as a consequence of Locke's political commitments in the 1670s and 1680s, as a work of Whig philosophy. This approach, which Richard Ashcraft has developed, has some merit: the debate on toleration did raise fundamental problems of epistemology (Ashcraft 1986, 39–74). But the *Essay* has intellectual origins which predate the controversy provoked by Parker. Locke sought to respond to Parker by writing a book on epistemology, not merely because this was an astute move in a particular polemical context, but also because the problem of knowledge was of long-standing personal importance for the author of the letter to Tom.

Other scholars have argued that Locke's later work grew naturally out of the *Two Tracts*. There he had appealed to the law of nature; in the *Essays on the Law of Nature* he tried to clarify what that law was; to succeed, he eventually realized, he had to give a fuller account of knowledge in general (Abrams in Locke 1967a, 84–107, von Leyden in Locke 1954, 60–82). But it is surely a mistake to see Locke as moving from unexamined assumptions to ever more profound inquiries: the letter to Tom shows that from the beginning Locke knew that conventional arguments would not sustain the weight one needed to place on them, and that all assumptions had to be examined.

Scholars have failed to stress the impact of scepticism on Locke's thought because they have failed to notice the presence of Charron in the *Essays*, and because one hardly associates scepticism with the claims Locke makes there for man's ability to discover moral truth (although Charron too, it should be stressed, thought that there was one form of wisdom common to all men: Gregory 1992). What some have suspected is that the early works are influenced by Hobbes, and they have gone so far as to maintain that the young Locke deliberately gives religious scepticism and self-interest the stronger arguments, that he does not believe in the Christian religion and the moral law that he claims to recognize. Does he in fact intend to undermine the position he pretends to defend? In my view a persuasive argument of this sort can be made for authors such as Charron and Hobbes when they write about religion (Wootton 1992b). But the argument for interpreting Locke in this way has been carelessly formulated: Kraynak, for example, misdates a key text, tears quotations out of context, and sees Hobbes's influence where that of other, less suspect, authors is equally possible (Kraynak 1980).[7] Just because Locke could not satisfactorily answer the sceptical challenge, we need not conclude that he was not making his best effort to overcome it. Evidently he wanted at all costs to escape from the uncertainties that plagued him (and the nation) in 1659.

One route of escape was to turn to authority. In the early 1660s Locke was convinced that the greatest threat to society came from the unruly mob; in the 1680s, by contrast, he would come to think the mob more trustworthy than the government. To control the mob he insisted on the necessity for an absolute ruler: resistance to the magistrate – i.e. the head of state – could never be legitimate. The magistrate must have unlimited authority, for 'a man cannot part with his liberty and have it too' (below, p. 141). The powers of government cannot be limited or they will be destroyed. Locke believed that this conclusion obtained no matter how one thought government originated. One could hold that the ruler's authority came directly from God, or that it was established by a compact of the people. One could (as Locke seems to have wanted to do) hold that the people originally chose their rulers, but God gave them authority, for rulers have a right to kill that individuals do not have, and that must come from God, not man. In any case one must recognize the need for an unchecked authority, be it a single individual or an assembly.

31

Locke's claim, in the early 1660s, was that there could be no limitation on the powers of governments: rulers must answer to God alone. But he also maintained this was true only of legitimate governments: we are, after all, entitled to resist pirates and highwaymen. We do not have to take orders from just anyone. It is essential, then, that we can identify our legitimate rulers. What, though, is the legitimate government of England? Locke heralds the Restoration as 'the happy return of our ancient freedom and felicity' (Locke 1967a, 119, 125), but he does not tell us whether he thinks it is the King who has been restored, or the King-in-Parliament. The implication of his argument, however, would seem to be that if one can have no limited government, then one can have no mixed constitution. There must be a single ultimate authority, for if there is a system of checks and balances, in times of crisis people will not know whom to obey. Mixed constitutions involve limitations on power and are merely attempts to ensure that people can both give away their liberty and keep it still, which is precisely what Locke thought impossible. In England, the powers of the Crown must be unchecked. The legislative power must lie in the hands of the King alone. Locke deliberately avoids spelling out this conclusion, but it is, I think, one he hopes to persuade us to adopt.

Philip Abrams has maintained that it is wrong to read the argument of the *Two Tracts* as authoritarian. To do so is to miss Locke's 'sense of balance, tension, and ambiguity'. In the preface to the reader that Locke wrote when he planned to publish the *First Tract* he stressed both his submission to authority and his love of liberty. Moreover, in Abrams's view, the scope of Locke's argument is much more limited than it might seem: 'He asserts the need for authority specifically and exclusively in respect of issues which the champions of liberty themselves "confess to be little and at most are but indifferent",' issues such as whether the priest should wear a surplice, whether one should kneel at the sign of the cross (Abrams in Locke 1967a, 9).

In order to assess whether Abrams is right or not, it is essential to grasp this key concept of 'indifferency' that runs right through Locke's *Two Tracts*. It derived from a theological distinction between those beliefs that were necessary for salvation (belief in the Trinity, the resurrection of the dead, the remission of sins, etc.)

and those beliefs and practices that were not essential, but could be altered to suit times and circumstances: the design of churches, the order of service, the clothes of worshippers. There was a good deal of dispute about how extensive this category of optional beliefs and practices was (Was belief in predestination necessary or optional? Must all true Churches have bishops, or might they be dispensed with?), but almost everyone was agreed that some religious beliefs and practices were necessary and others optional, or, as they termed them, 'indifferent'. The same distinction also applied in secular affairs. Murder is wrong, whether the magistrate has legislated against it or not, because it is contrary to God's law. But if the magistrate decreed that all houses must be built of stone in order to prevent fires, he or she would be legislating on an indifferent question, and wooden houses, once legal, would become overnight illegal.

To the modern reader it seems obvious that the government may reasonably require that churches be safely constructed, but that it may not require people to kneel when they pray. But most seventeenth-century intellectuals thought it was entirely appropriate for governments to impose religious uniformity. In the Old Testament, God required that all members of the state of Israel should share a common faith, and he seemed to impose upon rulers an obligation to enforce the Ten Commandments, which implied that all should be required to worship the true God. Where differences of practice and belief were tolerated, disagreements over fundamental questions of faith must soon follow. And such disagreements must quickly give rise to political conflict. The seventeenth century was a century of religious warfare, and there was plenty of experience to suggest that religious differences led rapidly to civil war. There were few who were prepared to defend toleration as correct in principle, or viable in practice.

Locke's *Two Tracts* dealt with issues raised by Edward Bagshaw, who had argued for a limited toleration. He maintained that where indifferent matters were concerned the state should allow each individual to go his or her own way, imposing uniformity only in those matters that were necessary for salvation. Locke's response was that if the matters were indeed indifferent, nobody could claim a conscientious right to freedom with respect to them. The state, if it ordered clergymen to wear surplices, was no more exceeding its rights than if it ordered ships to carry lights at night, or regulated any other indifferent question for the public good. Indeed, Locke insisted that one could not draw a water-tight distinction between religious and secular questions. Bagshaw recognized that the state could impose a building code. But what if the subject claimed his religion required him to worship in a wooden building? Bagshaw's argument depended on the claim that one could reliably separate religious and secular issues, and on the claim that individuals had freedom of choice regarding indifferent religious (but not secular) practices. Locke insisted that all indifferent practices were comparable, and that all fell under the magistrate's jurisdiction.

Locke thus concentrates on the question of indifferent practices because both he and Bagshaw agree that the magistrate can exercise compulsion against those who act contrary to what the magistrate defines as essential requirements of the faith: they both take an underlying intolerance for granted. The magistrate, of course, may be mistaken about what is essential and what is not, in which case the conscientious Christian will refuse to obey and patiently take the consequences.[8] The magistrate certainly will be wrong if he tries to legislate regarding, not just the public behaviour of his subjects, but also their intimate convictions (below, p. 175). Bagshaw and Locke can agree that the Anabaptist who claims that it is contrary to his religion to pay tithes, or the Quaker who has a religious objection to doffing his hat to his social superior or taking an oath of loyalty to his ruler, must be compelled to conform. Locke sees no need to assert the need for authority in such cases because it is not in dispute.

The truth of the matter is that for all its apparent moderation and balance, Locke's argument comes down firmly on the side of authority, and offers no protection at all for liberty. The balanced statements that impress Abrams are no more than rhetorical window dressing. When he says, for example, 'I have not therefore the same apprehensions of liberty that I find some have' he is not saying that he dreads liberty less than some do; rather the contrary. He is saying that he has a different conception of liberty from the one that many people have, for he knows that 'a general freedom is but a general bondage' (below, pp. 148-9)

And yet, only a year before, Locke had been in favour of religious toleration. There has been some disagreement about the significance of Locke's letter of 1659 to Hobbes's associate, Henry Stubbe (below, pp. 137–9). Abrams argues that in it Locke does not in fact endorse toleration. In support of this view he offers two arguments. First, he quotes a passage in which Locke writes of the dangers of toleration, expressing doubt as to whether liberty 'can consist with the security of the nation' (in Locke 1967a, 8–9). He fails to note that Locke here is writing about liberty for Catholics. Throughout his life Locke argued that the Catholic obligation to obey the pope was at odds with a recognition of the legitimate authority of secular rulers: Catholics, in effect, were subjects of the pope, and so could not be citizens of any country other than the papal states. If Locke's comments on Catholicism in 1659 are to be taken as evidence that he was opposed to religious toleration, similar comments in the *Letter Concerning Toleration* could be used to show that he remained intolerant to the end. Second, Abrams claims that Locke is being transparently ironical when he says that the testimony of daily experience shows that men can live in peace together despite differences in religion, citing the examples of Holland, France, and Poland (243). There is no doubt that the testimony of experience in England, France, or Poland was somewhat mixed, but Locke would certainly not have cited the example of Holland had he intended to be obviously ironical, for there, it was generally agreed, toleration had been an extraordinary practical success. There men had indeed been allowed to 'take different ways towards heaven' (below, p. 138). In Locke's letter to Stubbe the question of whether toleration is practical is open, not closed.

Despite Abrams (and Ashcraft 1986, 90), then, we can reasonably view Locke in 1659, as in 1665 (when he wrote the letter to Boyle: below, pp. 184–5), as sympathetic to toleration. Even in 1660 he wished that men would be tolerant. The problem was that in practice, in England, they were not. One had to disappoint either those who wanted religious freedom and diversity, or those who wanted (and believed that God demanded) religious uniformity. Either choice involved dismissing the arguments of conscientious objectors. Either choice involved an element of compulsion. The only question for Locke was which was most likely to work in practice. In the end, this was a question not for the private individual but for the magistrate. And the crisis that shook Christ Church during 1660 as contending factions disputed how services should be conducted in the college chapel had persuaded Locke that a sensible magistrate would opt for uniformity.

It would be easy to draw a simple portrait of Locke in 1660 as a loyal member of the Church of England, a scholastic philosopher, an authoritarian, and an absolutist. By and large this portrait would be correct, but it would miss the most important aspect of Locke's early works: the dialogue that Locke encourages among contrasting positions. Although he does not endorse scepticism, he states sceptical arguments in their strongest form. He endorses neither divine right monarchy nor contractarianism, but gives both their say. He advocates religious uniformity, but writes, as Roger Williams and the most radical advocates of toleration had, of an ideal world in which religion is merely a matter of individual belief and does not prevent men from recognizing their common interest in peace and mutual security, a world in which Church and State are separate (below, p. 145). Locke's sympathy with the arguments of his opponents marks him out as no straightforward Anglican or scholastic. The one issue, though, on which he shows no hesitation is that of political authority. Even the prospect that the magistrate may prove an Egyptian taskmaster does not make him flinch (Exodus 1; below, p. 142). Men may fly from oppression, but they must never resist it. 'As for myself,' writes Locke in 1661, 'there is no one can have a greater respect and veneration for authority than I' (below, p. 148). If someone in the early 1660s had predicted that Locke would in time become a philosopher of inalienable rights and an advocate of revolution, we can be sure that no one would have been more incredulous than Locke himself.

Locke and Shaftesbury

Locke's *Essay Concerning Toleration* of 1667 appears to belong to a different world from that inhabited by the author of the *Two Tracts*. That there had been a profound transformation in Locke's thought, and that this transformation coincided approximately with the beginning of his close association with Shaftesbury is evident. What we are most in danger of doing, in fact, is underestimating the radicalism of the *Essay* in the context of the day.

Soon after the Restoration, Charles II and the Restoration Parliament had opted for a policy of intolerance towards Nonconformists or Dissenters, a policy embodied in the Clarendon Code. Despite severe civil disabilities imposed on those who failed to worship in the Church of England (penalties that could be escaped by what was termed 'occasional conformity') and even stiffer penalties imposed on those who worshipped in other churches, a large section of the English population had, for the first time in history, refused to join an established national religion that had the full support of the law. In 1661 Locke may have thought that it would not be difficult to impose uniformity. By the time of the *Essay Concerning Toleration*, he may well have concluded that it would be virtually impossible. Most Church leaders, however, continued to believe that a vigorous policy of enforcing uniformity must eventually succeed.

Since Locke's primary argument for intolerance had been that it was most likely to ensure peace and order, it would not be at all surprising to find him in 1667 advocating tolerance as more expedient than intolerance. Moreover the failure of persecution to bring rapid results presented a puzzle: why, if the dispute between conformists and Nonconformists was not over the fundamentals of the faith but over secondary issues, were the Nonconformists so reluctant to conform? In response to this puzzle, Locke's *Essay* rejects the view of religious worship that he had defended in the *Two Tracts* (below, pp. 154–8, 189). There he had maintained that worship was primarily an inward relationship between the individual and his God; the outward acts by which it was accompanied were indifferent, and could be regulated by the magistrate. Now he recognized that the outward acts of worship were directed to an audience, and that audience was not the magistrate, but God. Far from being secondary, or irrelevant, they were a means for the worshipper to communicate with God, and the worshipper was bound therefore to prefer those modes of behaviour that he thought God would approve over those selected by the magistrate.

But this new view of worship had far-reaching implications.

Locke used it to argue that worship, because it was a form of communication between an individual and his God, was not properly speaking a public act at all, despite the fact that it was a collective activity. Locke's new argument hinged upon his distinction between the public and the private, a distinction that has become characteristic of liberalism, and that makes the *Essay Concerning Toleration* a founding text in the liberal tradition. The state, he maintained, was concerned only with public order, and with creating the conditions where individuals could successfully pursue their private goods. Its concerns lay entirely in this world, and extended only to those aspects of behaviour that needed to be regulated for the protection of the public. It was not concerned with the welfare of the individual's soul. It was not concerned with virtue and vice as such, but only with outward behaviour that affected the interests of others. And consequently it was not concerned either with religious worship or with what Locke terms 'speculative opinions' – a term covering not only theology, but also science. Locke in the *Essay* stands at the beginning of a line of argument that will lead to the watchman state of Adam Smith.

Locke's argument is not without its internal tensions, some of which imply a deliberate strategy of literary subterfuge. In the first place, he has to insist that the magistrate must regulate marriage, for example, passing laws dealing with monogamy, polygamy, adultery, divorce, not on the basis of what he thinks is virtuous or moral, but simply on the basis of what he thinks is likely to be publicly beneficial. The magistrate is thus required to treat these matters as indifferent even if he believes that, morally speaking, they are not. He is not allowed to legislate against something simply because it is wrong; he can only legislate against things that are harmful to society. At the same time the subject must not lay claim to a right of conscientious disobedience in such matters. Freedom of worship is not to be extended into a wider liberty of conscience. Locke's argument thus depends on his being able to draw the distinction between what is religious and what is not that he had insisted was invalid when made by Bagshaw. The magistrate is not to act as a Christian magistrate, or strive in his official capacity to create a Christian society. He is not to enforce the Ten Commandments, neither the commandments of the first table (those that relate to belief in the true God), nor those of the second (that relate to moral behaviour). The state is to be a secular institution with secular ends.

We are so used to secular states that we are liable to forget that the primary objection to them is theological, and may therefore not notice that Locke's argument involves a series of theological choices. First of all, he sees religion as voluntary. But within conventional Christianity the child is welcomed into the Church at baptism, and is then educated, instructed, and (in the seventeenth century) disciplined to ensure he or she becomes a true believer. To stress the voluntary nature of religion is to take a crucial step towards the theology of the Anabaptists and the Socinians, who argued that infant baptism went hand in hand with compulsory religion and persecution, and rejected it for that reason. Second, there is no continuity between the tolerant state and the state of the Old Testament, which had enforced conformity and required faith. And this implies a view of the New Testament as having replaced, rather than fulfilled, the Old. The unity of religious community and political society established by Moses is, on this view, as incompatible with Christianity as ceremonial circumcision and animal sacrifices. The magistrate's commands are not to be seen as an expansion of the principles of the Ten Commandments, but as different in kind and intent.

Locke suggests in the *Essay Concerning Toleration* that intolerance is the mark only of Catholicism, and that Protestants can unite around the principles he is advocating. Tolerant principles, indeed, will make it easier to draw people into an amorphous national religion. But he knows perfectly well that Anglicans, Lutherans, and the varieties of Calvinists (Presbyterians, Huguenots) had all traditionally insisted on the need for religious uniformity, a godly society, and a Christian magistrate. To accept the argument of the *Essay* one must be prepared to break, not only with Catholicism, but with the mainstream of Protestantism. If we want to find a parallel for Locke's arguments in the *Essay* it is to the Baptist Roger Williams or to the Levellers that we must turn (Wootton 1991, 438–42). It is important, therefore, to recognize that when Locke argues that intolerant religions are the product of 'ambitious human nature' he is sidestepping a theological debate.

But Locke's radicalism does not end with his rejection of established religion. He insists that England has a limited, and therefore not a divine-right, monarchy. As a consequence he appears to opt for a contractarian political theory. It seems somewhat inconsistent of him, therefore, to insist that the subject may never actively resist the magistrate, but may only passively suffer when conscience forbids active obedience. But how sincere is Locke in this limitation on the subject's rights? In the first place he maintains that people will in practice resist persecution: 'For let divines preach duty as long as they will, 'twas never known that men lay down quietly under the oppression, and submitted their backs to the blows of others when they thought they had strength enough to defend themselves' (below, p. 205). 'I say not this to justify such proceedings,' he adds, but how can he appeal to Magna Carta, as he does at the beginning, without implicitly justifying the revolt that forced the King to sign it? The answer, perhaps, is that Locke had come to accept the theory of resistance that was orthodox among those who maintained the possibility of a limited monarchy and a mixed constitution: that individuals had no right to resist, but that they might have to choose between competing authorities when King fell out with Parliament or Commons with Lords. When rulers resist rulers and magistrates resist magistrates, subjects are under no obligation to stand idly by.

At the same time, though, Locke recognizes in the magistrate an absolute right to make war upon his subjects if they appear to constitute a political threat. It is wrong to persecute men for their faith; but perfectly justified to persecute them if they are a danger to civil order. Locke recognizes no limits on the powers of the state once it has identified an enemy within: in particular he seems to want to justify the horrific persecution of Quakers that was taking place at the time. And Locke insists that there is one speculative opinion that cannot be tolerated: atheism. Despite his secular conception of the state, and despite his recognition that in Japan those who denied the existence of a life after death (a view whose practical consequences were, to Locke's way of thinking, indistinguishable from atheism) were tolerated, Locke is not prepared to follow the Levellers in insisting that thought should be free, and only actions should be punished.

The *Essay* is thus a deeply ambiguous text: both Christian and secular, both authoritarian and libertarian, both in favour of passive obedience and sympathetic to resistance. But these ambiguities are the result of Locke's attempts to limit the consequences of his fundamental premise: if people have a right not to be interfered with in their private lives, and if the state is only an umpire intended to moderate conflicts between individuals, it is not hard to conclude that subjects have inalienable rights and that rulers should be answerable to the ruled. The *Letter Concerning Toleration* and the *Two Treatises* are in a sense natural developments of the *Essay*. We should be wary though of the deceptive word 'natural'. Philosophers' lives do not have the elegance of geometrical proofs. Locke in 1667 was not trying to formulate a liberal political philosophy. He had changed his mind on royal absolutism and on toleration. But he was still deeply fearful of disorder, and his argument for toleration was first and foremost a prudential one. What he was recommending was a strange combination of secular state and ancient constitution.

If we want to get a clear understanding of Locke's political ideals in the late 1660s and early 1670s, what we must read is the *Constitutions of Carolina* (below, pp. 210–32). Shaftesbury and a few of his associates were the proprietors of Carolina, Locke their secretary. They were free to draw up for the colony any constitution on which they could agree among themselves and for which they could obtain royal consent. In 1669, the year in which the *Constitutions* were written, there was no doubt at all that Shaftesbury was the dominant figure among the proprietors: the final text was bound to reflect his views. It seems clear that the final text was also very much Locke's work. Certainly this was what contemporaries assumed: one wrote to him referring to 'that excellent form of government in the composure of which you had so great a hand'. A draft exists in Locke's handwriting that differs in only one significant respect from the final text. The final text provided for the establishment of the Church of England as the state Church: those who knew Locke well later claimed that he insisted that this clause was inserted contrary to his wishes, and the draft in his own hand provides for a true separation of Church and State. This was contrary to the colony's charter, which required the establishment of the Church of England, so that it is not surprising that the final text provided for the eventual establishment of a state Church, supported by taxation, alongside voluntary Churches. It seems reasonable to conclude that the rest of the text met with Locke's approval (Haley 1968, 238–45).

What, then, was the form of government that Locke and Shaftesbury saw as a workable ideal in 1669? Obviously not a democratic one. Only the well-to-do were to have the vote; only the wealthy the right to be elected to parliament. Though there were to be biennial parliaments, the agenda of parliament was to be entirely controlled by the proprietors' council; the speaker of parliament was to be a proprietor; and debates were to take place in the presence of the proprietors and the aristocracy, who would vote with the commons and have almost half the votes. In passing we may note too the provision for compulsory military service: it had been a principle of the Levellers, whose democratic theories were here being rejected, that there should be no conscription. If this was to be a constitutional monarchy in which the proprietors collectively were to fulfil the role of monarch, then the powers of the monarch were to be extensive indeed. Above all, the executive was to remain entirely in their hands.

Second, the constitution is a peculiar adaptation of Harringtonianism. James Harrington (1611–77) had insisted that the secret ballot was the best way to conduct elections, and the constitution provides for balloting. More importantly, Harrington had argued that power necessarily follows wealth, and that if one could stabilize the distribution of landed wealth in a society one could also stabilize the distribution of power. It was just such a 'balance' that the constitution, using Harrington's term, sought to establish. The ratio of land held by the proprietors and the two orders of nobles was to remain constant. Indeed each noble estate was to be preserved intact, inherited or sold only as a whole. This was the opposite of the division of estates encouraged by Harrington in order to spread power through society. On the other hand the constitution prevented the accumulation of noble estates in a few hands: the number and wealth of the nobility was to remain fixed. The goal seems to have been to create a balance of power between proprietors, nobles, and free men, while ensuring that the proprietors' wishes would normally predominate.

Third, as is often remarked, the constitution provided for an extraordinary measure of religious toleration. All that was required of anybody was that he or she should belong to a religious association. As long as that association recognized a God and provided for some form of solemn oath-taking (a stipulation that would have excluded the Quakers), its members were free to believe what they liked and practise as they chose. This freedom extended even to slaves, who, despite the fact that they had rational souls, were to be entirely, in every other respect, at the disposal of their masters.

But the most significant aspect of the constitution is its most peculiar: the provision for a class of 'leet-men'. This has been described as 'curious', but the full extent of the curiosity is missed if one then proceeds to remark that 'the attempt to transplant manors and courts leet across the Atlantic was not so anachronistically medieval as it sounds' (Haley 1968, 244, 247). For the proposed 'leet-men' of Carolina bear no resemblance to those recognized as 'leet-men' in seventeenth-century England, who were, in essence, individuals entitled to poor relief. In the first place, the leet-men of Carolina, unlike any English man or woman, have no right of appeal beyond their lord's court. In the second, they have no freedom of movement: they are obliged to remain on their lord's land, and are to be bought and sold with the land. Above all, it may have been envisaged that the first leet-men would be volunteers, but the status was to be hereditary: 'All the children of leet-men shall be leet-men, and so to all generations' (§23). There is no question as to what this institution is: it is serfdom by another name.[9]

By 1669 serfdom had completely disappeared in England. As far as I am aware there was no attempt to establish hereditary serfdom anywhere in North America outside Carolina. It is quite inconceivable that the proprietors were under royal pressure to embody any such peculiar institution in the constitution. Nor was it imposed upon a reluctant Shaftesbury and Locke by their associates, for in 1674 the two of them were urging the impoverished settlers of Carolina, who had fallen deep into debt to the proprietors, to register as leet-men. A year later the two of them were to insist that a new colony they sought to establish should be independent of the old, 'For it is as bad as a state of war for men that are in want to have the making of laws over men that have estates' (Wootton 1992a, 85). Their intention was to ensure the reverse: that men with estates would make the laws for those in want.

I say 'the two of them', but I must confess to the suspicion that the sentence I have just quoted was written by Locke. Few of Shaftesbury's letters survive, so we have little with which to compare the letters that went out over Shaftesbury's name between 1668 and 1675 while Locke was secretary to the proprietors. Haley says of them: 'They are always written directly to the point, crystal-clear in meaning and with scarcely a word wasted . . . without ambiguity, doubt, or hesitation' (Haley 1968, 253). We may well wonder whether this is not a better description of Locke's prose style than Shaftesbury's. At any rate, our uncertainty on this question was also that of the contemporary in the best position to know. The secretary who copied Shaftesbury's official correspondence with Carolina into a letterbook signed one letter, in a thoughtless moment, not 'Shaftesbury' but 'Locke'.[10] It seems likely that he was copying a text handed to him by Locke, and in Locke's handwriting. But he may also have known he was copying a text written by Locke, not dictated to him by Shaftesbury.

In their emphasis on religious freedom, and in smaller details (such as the oath of allegiance required as a prerequisite for the inheritance of land), the *Constitutions of Carolina* foreshadow the works Locke published in 1689. But it is clear that in 1669 (and still in 1675, when they continued to try to recruit 'leet-men') neither Locke nor Shaftesbury believed in any inalienable right other than the right to freedom of religion; the only political rights they recognized were the rights of men with estates. It is this that we need to bear in mind when we turn to consider *A Letter from a Person of Quality to his Friend in the Country* (1675), which has been described as 'the decisive step to the mature theory of justified armed resistance in the *Two Treatises*' (Tully in Locke 1983, 9; also Viano 1960, 198–201).

By the time *A Letter* was written Shaftesbury was the leader of the opposition to a monarchy that was suspected of seeking to establish absolutism and Catholicism. *A Letter* is the first in the series of anti-government pamphlets that was to culminate in Tyrrell's *Patriarcha non Monarcha*, Locke's *Two Treatises*, and Sidney's

Discourses. It may have been written by Locke (Ashcraft 1986, 120–23). I have not included it here because we have no manuscript in Locke's hand, nor any acknowledgement of authorship by Locke. In 1684 Locke was to insist 'in the presence of God that I am not the author, not only of any libel, but not of any pamphlet or treatise whatever in part good, bad, or indifferent'. Locke was trying to clear himself of government suspicions and retain his Christ Church fellowship. He may have been lying, though I rather doubt that he would have invoked the name of God in a downright lie. He was certainly equivocating, for he had written, if not published, the *Two Treatises.* According to Des Maizeaux, who published *A Letter* as Locke's after Locke's death, Locke wrote *A Letter*, but he did so 'under his lordship's inspection, and only committed to writing what my Lord Shaftesbury did in a manner dictate to him'. In other words, the two collaborated, but the major role was Shaftesbury's. *A Letter* is an important guide to Locke's thinking in 1675, but only because it is reasonable to assume that, after almost a decade of close association, he and Shaftesbury thought alike.

In 1675 Shaftesbury was opposing a king who had abandoned toleration for a policy of alliance with the Church party. A new oath was to be required of all officers of Church and State and all members of both houses of Parliament: 'I do declare that it is not lawful, upon any pretence whatsoever, to take up arms against the King; and that I do abhor that traiterous position of taking arms by his authority, against his person, or against those that are commissioned by him in pursuance of such commission. And I do swear that I will not at any time endeavour the alteration of the government, either in Church or State.' Thus the doctrine of passive obedience was to be enshrined in law, and alongside it the rights and privileges of the Anglican clergy. The monarchy was to be, in effect, declared absolute. For the government that was to be protected from alteration was not to be the old limited monarchy of King-in-Parliament, but a new, divine-right monarchy. It is not surprising to find the author of *A Letter* echoing the point with which Locke had begun his essay of 1667: divine-right monarchy is incompatible with Magna Carta, which made of England a limited, not an absolute, monarchy. But now it is necessary to spell out the conclusion, denied in 1667, that in any limited monarchy there must be an ultimate right of rebellion against tyranny.

Resistance theories, however, are not interchangeable. The consistent claim of the opposition in the late 1670s was that the constitution established the rights of both prince and people, and that it was only by preserving the ancient constitution that either would have any secure claim. In October 1675 Shaftesbury said: 'My principle is that the King is king by law, and by the same law that the poor man enjoys his cottage' (*State Tracts* 1689, 60). The same year Locke too found it natural to associate the rights of kings and beggars as having the same foundation: ''Tis the greatest charity to preserve the laws and rights of the nation whereof we are. A good man, and a charitable man, is to give to every man his due. From the king upon the throne to the beggar in the street' (below, p. 234). In a notebook entry of 1676 Locke treated authority, rank, and property in land as comparable in kind, all being consequent to, and dependent upon, the same human laws (below, p. 234). 'We have the same right,' wrote Marvell in *An Account of the Growth of Popery and Arbitrary Government* (1677), '. . . in our property that the prince hath in his regality' (*State Tracts* 1689, 70).

Thus all rights were of the same sort, and none of them were natural. The King's authority must be under the law if it was to be compatible with the rights of others; to place it under the law was to make it one of a hierarchy of rights stretching from king to beggar. A crucial place in that hierarchy was held by the House of Lords. 'My principle is also,' Shaftesbury continued, 'that the Lords' House, and the judicature and rights belonging to it, are an essential part of the government, and established by the same law.' The Lords were essential because they had a crucial role to play in counter-balancing one of the two forces, the clergy and the army, that stood to gain from absolutism. The clergy must be counter-balanced by tolerating dissenters. The army must be counter-balanced by the wealth and military might of the peerage. As *A Letter* put it, in neo-Harringtonian terms, 'the power of Peerage and a standing-army are like two buckets, the proportion that one goes down, the other exactly goes up' (*State Tracts* 1689, 55).

The resistance theory of *A Letter* was thus poles apart from a resistance theory grounded in a claim to equal, individual, inalienable, natural rights. *A Letter* insisted that the rights of each were inseparable from the rights of all; that rights were naturally collective and unequal; and that far from being truly natural they were historical and constitutional. Men could, if they were careless, sell themselves into slavery. It was not at all clear that, if men agreed to the new oath, they could not be properly said to have given up any claim to liberty (e.g. *The Character of a Popish Successor* (1681), in *State Tracts* 1689, 162): there were, after all, legitimate arbitrary governments to be found elsewhere in the world.

In 1675 Locke wrote in his notebook that the clergy invite us to worship, under the guise of truth, merely their own interests. *A Letter* ends by forecasting the dreadful day when 'Priest and Prince may, like Castor and Pollux, be worshipped together as divine, in the same temple, by us poor lay-subjects; and that sense and reason, law, properties, rights, and liberties shall be understood as the oracles of those deities shall interpret or give signification to them, and ne'r be made use of in the world to oppose the absolute and free will of either of them' (*State Tracts* 1689, 56). The political solution to the threat from Priest and Prince lay in the Peerage and Toleration. But how was a philosopher to behave in a world where ideas were so nakedly shaped by interests, or, even less intelligibly, 'by example and fashion', by 'credit and disgrace', by our old acquaintance, custom?

Locke's response, he tells us in a journal note of 1675, had been to form a small society of those concerned to reinforce each other's commitment to the pursuit of truth. If men were inevitably governed by interest, one must find a way of turning truth into a group interest; and if converts to truth were to be won, one must evidently appeal to men's interests and fashions. One scholar has complained that Locke never stopped to discuss 'the life and self-understanding of the philosopher' (Pangle 1988, 266), but this is clearly what he does do in 'Philanthropy, or The Christian Philosophers'. And in doing so he stresses the politics of truth – the need to defeat enemies, win support, appeal to allies. He does not, though, suggest that in the end the philosopher must compromise the truth or conceal it. On the contrary, truth is, in the end, in everyone's best interests. Far from being subversive of the existing order it is its best support, for philosophy teaches us not to appeal to divine right, or abstract knowledge, but to recognize our obligation to give every man his due, be he king or beggar.

'Philanthropy' entitles us to suspect that it was to this society of fellow truth-seekers that Locke read the first draft of the *Essay Concerning Human Understanding* in 1671. It clarifies the sense in which Locke saw philosophical inquiry as a form of political action. But it also shows that the framework within which Locke originally conceived his philosophical activity was not, as has been suggested, that of a Baconianism directed at establishing a new agrarian capitalism (Wood 1984). He did not even embark upon philosophical inquiry because he was seeking the intellectual foundations on which one could build a defence of toleration. Nor was he, as others have claimed, someone who thought philosophers must conceal the truth lest they suffer the fate of Socrates (e.g. Strauss 1953, 207–9). He became a philosopher because he thought that the interests of the clergy, the universities, and the Crown were at odds with the constitutional status quo. He saw the task of the philosopher as being to preserve the existing order against the subversive threat of change. Where custom was no longer reliable, truth must come to its support. Unless Locke had, by 1675, come to misremember the motives that had shaped his philosophical thinking a few years before, those motives were primarily political: he was seeking to defend conservatism in the state, and his motive in pressing for toleration was his fear of the alliance between Crown and clergy.

Nevertheless, such conservatism was deeply subversive. In 1660 Locke had repeatedly stressed that we are under a conscientious obligation to obey our superiors. By 1676 he thought we had no obligation to obey them in indifferent things (below, p. 235). Our obligation was merely not to resist them in so far as they served to preserve peace and safety. This was to admit, tacitly, that there might be circumstances where we were entitled to disobey actively as well as passively to order to preserve peace and safety. It was also to make the biblical injunction to obey your superiors irrelevant: 'The Gospel alters not in the least civil affairs, but leaves husband and wife, master and servant, magistrate and subject, every one of them, with the very same power and privileges that it found them [with], neither more nor less.' Locke thus left open the possibility that political authorities might have fewer rightful privileges than was generally assumed. Political systems were not divinely ordained. They were human contrivances. And their purpose was not simply to protect order against the threat of anarchy, against the threatening sea of popular discontent he had so feared in 1661. These were contrivances designed to establish powers and privileges, not just for rulers, but also for their subjects. Entry into civil society was a way of creating, not giving up, rights.

Locke had come a vast distance from the authoritarianism of the *Two Tracts*. Where once he had looked to authority to preserve order, he now suspected it of seeking to establish tyranny. He was now prepared to countenance disobedience and even resistance. But the only equal, natural right he recognized was the right to religious freedom, for this was a right that nobody could give up. (Locke was consequently prepared to defend the 1672 Declaration of Indulgence, which had used prerogative power to suspend parliamentary legislation, but had done so in order to bring a halt to religious persecution.) All other rights were alienable. All types of government, even that over slave and serf, were potentially legitimate. The Locke who returned from exile in 1679 was still no liberal. If his political theory between 1667 and 1679 is quite different in character from that of the *Two Tracts*, it also bears little resemblance to that of the *Second Treatise*. To see it as a step in that direction is to argue from hindsight. Locke could not foresee the direction in which his thought would develop.

Locke and Tyrrell

We come now to the heart of any study of Locke's political thought, the *Two Treatises of Government*. Unfortunately, we also come to a vexed problem in Lockean scholarship, that of dating the composition of this work. Unless we know when it was written, we can have no hope of understanding the purposes it was originally intended to serve. The obvious place to start is the Preface, with its references to the events of 1688. For generations of scholars there was no cause to look further. The obvious context in which to read the *Two Treatises* was Locke's claim that his objective was to justify the revolution of 1688 and William III's title to the throne. Access to Locke's papers, however, made it clear that the *Two Treatises* were not written by Locke in the months after the revolution. When then were they written?

In 1960 Laslett argued that the bulk of the *Second Treatise* was written in the winter of 1679–80. Early in 1680, after publication of Filmer's *Patriarcha* in January 1680, the *First Treatise* was added. In the summer of 1681 Locke revised the *Second Treatise*: it was then that he bought Hooker (on 13 June), and added the quotations from and references to him that run through the *Second Treatise*. Further revisions took place in 1682 and 1683, and in 1689, when chapters 1, 9, and 15 may have been added (Locke 1967b, 45–66; Locke 1988, 123–6).

Laslett's dating depends upon two key pieces of information. At the only point in the *Second Treatise* at which Locke refers to a specific page in Filmer he was, as can easily be shown, using the 1679 edition of Filmer's political tracts, an edition that did not include *Patriarcha*, which was published for the first time only in 1680. Alongside this fact Laslett placed what he took to be evidence that Locke had read the 1679 edition of Filmer in the year of its publication, for in a note-pad, on a page that Locke had begun using in 1679, he found a note taken from the 1679 edition of Filmer. Throughout the *First Treatise*, however, Locke aims his attacks at *Patriarcha*, and uses the 1680 edition of Filmer's works, which includes *Patriarcha*. On this basis Laslett concluded that the first draft of the *Second Treatise* predated the *First Treatise*, which was an addition written in response to the publication of *Patriarcha*.

There are problems with this thesis. In the first place, it is almost impossible to make sense of the *Second Treatise* as a work written in 1679–80. The *Second Treatise* is obviously a work written in defence of revolution, and yet supporters of Shaftesbury in 1679–80 were not thinking in terms of revolution: their concern was to demonstrate the urgent need for Exclusion, and the legal right of King-in-Parliament to determine the succession. At their most extreme, the Whigs were looking for ways in which Parliament might force the King's hand: by the swearing of a Bond of Association (similar to that which had been sworn when Mary Queen of Scots had been plotting against Elizabeth), for example. The most radical Whig view during the Exclusion crisis is represented by Stephen College's cartoon, distributed during the meeting of the Oxford Parliament and reproduced in part on the cover of this book, which shows the House of Commons (which the King is portrayed as thinking he could control like a puppet show) rebelling and seizing control of King and Lords. College was not claiming that individuals had a right to resist the King, but only that the constitutional representatives of the people had a right to act. This was a theory of magisterial, not popular, resistance, and of resistance aimed at protecting, not transforming, the constitution.

The question then is: How sound is the tie between the *Second Treatise* and 1679? Ashcraft has argued that the fact that Locke began his page of notes in his note-pad in 1679 does not mean that the note he made on Filmer was written in that year. He argues that the note-pad was something Locke carried around with him when he was away from home, in the way that one might carry an address book. Just as the entries on the page of an address book may be separated by some years, so entries on particular pages of this note-pad were made at widely differing dates. In addition, Ashcraft musters crucial evidence to cast doubt on a 1679–80 date for the *Second Treatise* by a detailed analysis of Locke's book purchases. It is not just Hooker whom Locke acquires in the summer of 1681. All the evidence suggests that Locke began reading around the themes of the *Two Treatises* in 1680, not 1679. It was in June 1680, for example, that he bought Barclay, whom he quotes at length at the end of the *Second Treatise* (Ashcraft 1987, 286–97).

Ashcraft therefore proposed a straightforward alternative. The *First Treatise*, he argued, was written in 1680–81 in defence of Exclusion. It was finished or abandoned when, in March 1681, Charles II dissolved the third Exclusion Parliament in Oxford. That moment marked the end of Exclusion as a coherent policy, for Exclusion depended upon Charles being willing to approve parliamentary legislation altering the succession. By the end of March it was apparent that Charles was determined to resist such legislation, and likely that he would try in the future to avoid summoning a Parliament that would propose it. The only option left open to the Whigs was rebellion, for only by force of arms could they now hope to impose their will upon the King. In June, as Laslett had recognized, Locke was at work on the *Second Treatise*, and at the same time writing notes in his journal on Hooker: but what he was at work on was not a second but a first draft. Work may have continued until Locke went into exile in 1683, and coincided with the Whig plotting that culminated in the Rye House Plot. The volume published in 1689 thus combined a *First Treatise* which was an Exclusion tract and a *Second Treatise* which was a Rye House tract. The *First Treatise* is about how power needs to be exercised within a constitutional framework; the *Second* is about how tyrannical power can rightly be resisted by each and every individual. Ashcraft's thesis provides a better account of the external evidence (the testimony of Locke's notebooks) than does Laslett's. It also makes possible a more straightforward reading of the texts themselves, for it gives each of them a distinct political purpose.

It has however a number of flaws. First, Locke refers in §124 of the *First Treatise* to James Tyrrell's *Patriarcha non Monarcha*, a work that he purchased on 2 June 1681. In §87 of the *First Treatise* he clearly refers to a passage in the *Second Treatise*. Are these just isolated sentences tacked in at a later date, or were substantial sections of the *First Treatise* written after the collapse of the Oxford Parliament? (I will suggest an answer to this question in the next section.)

Second, the lengthy quotations from Hooker that Locke copied into his journal on 22 June 1681 come just before and just after the passage quoted in §5 of the *Second Treatise*. Locke's journal notes from Hooker, which are scattered through late June, in fact never include the passages referred to in the *Second Treatise*. If Locke was copying the passages he needed for the *Second Treatise* into another notebook, or copying them directly into the manuscript as he composed it, he had a clear conception of the argument of the *Second Treatise*, and of what he would need to develop it, by the second half of June 1681. Had revolutionary resistance been adopted as a political strategy by the end of June 1681?

Ashcraft's answer is that it had (Ashcraft 1986, 290–91, 314–37). Later testimony, he points out, was that there was no thought of resistance before the dissolution of the Oxford Parliament, but there was talk of it soon after (cf. de Krey 1990, 147). The crucial evidence he seeks to adduce is a paper found in Shaftesbury's possession when he was arrested on 2 July 1681 that called for an Association to resist the establishment of Catholicism in England and to prevent the Duke of York taking the throne. This paper, he maintains, reflects a decisive shift in Whig strategy which took place after the defeat of the Exclusion Bill in the House of Lords in November 1680. From this point the Whigs recognized that it might be necessary to use force to prevent James from succeeding to the throne.

There is no question that the Association, like College's cartoon, represented a threat that force would be used. But between the threat of force and practical plans for rebellion there is a significant gap. Almost all the hard evidence for revolutionary plotting seems to date from after July 1682, when the Whigs lost control of the City of London, and with it control over the selection of juries (de Krey 1990, 147–8; Scott 1991a, 272). In the summer of 1681 there were still hopes that there might be future parliamentary opportunities to press for Exclusion (*State Tracts* 1689, 187): these dissipated only as the extent of the royalist reaction became apparent with the trials of Fitzharris (condemned to death for treason 9 June, executed 1 July) and College (condemned to death for treason 18 August – largely on the evidence of the cartoon – and executed 31 August: Rahn 1972). From 2 July Shaftesbury himself was under threat of death, held in the Tower awaiting trial: he was released on 24 November by a carefully packed London jury that insisted there was no case for him to answer. In the second half of 1681 legal manoeuvring, not rebellion, was the first priority of the embattled Whigs.

Ashcraft's position is that the writing of the *Second Treatise* probably stretched over the period 1681–3, when resistance was envisaged, threatened, and planned. An alternative view is that it is a revolutionary text, and that revolutionary plotting is confined to 1682–3. Consequently it must have been written contemporaneously with Sidney's *Discourses*. Thus John Pocock has written: 'We are now sure that Locke wrote his *Second Treatise* somewhere between 1680 and 1683; the later the more plausible, since writing it needs to be situated in the process of the Whigs' turning to desperate courses in the experience of defeat' (Pocock 1988, 162). Only if the composition of the *Second Treatise* is moved back in time will it be possible to see it, as Ashcraft originally hoped to do, as 'an outgrowth' of a pre-existing 'revolutionary movement' (Ashcraft 1980, 486). As I write this introduction, this third view, supported in particular by John Marshall, seems on the point of becoming a new orthodoxy (Marshall 1990, ch. 8). It has, though, one obvious disadvantage. It involves putting aside, not only the evidence of the note-pad (discounted by Ashcraft), but also the evidence of the journal notes on Hooker (accepted by both Laslett and Ashcraft). The view I put forward here seeks to revise Ashcraft's argument in the other direction. Far from arguing that Locke wrote the *Second Treatise* in 1682–3, I am of the opinion that he composed it, more or less in its entirety, in 1681, when there was no practical prospect of revolution, but when discussion of theories of resistance was under way.

Suppose for a moment that Locke began writing the *Second Treatise* when he made his journal notes on Hooker. In that case Locke conceived the work shortly after Fitzharris had been condemned, despite all the efforts of the Whig peers, the House of Commons, and the sheriffs of the City of London to preserve his life. Fitzharris was condemned for having written a seditious treatise in February of 1681, a treatise calling for an uprising. At the time he may well have been acting as an *agent provocateur* (rebellion, after all, was not Whig policy), and it was the Whigs he was trying to entrap who made sure he was arrested; but after his arrest he tried to win a pardon by offering testimony relating to the Popish Plot. Thus he ensured that the King sought his condemnation while the Whigs sought to protect him, but he had unfortunately changed sides at the wrong moment. The Whigs could no longer control the courts (Haley 1968, 629–51).

It was not difficult to predict, during the second half of June, as Locke made notes on Hooker, that others would follow Fitzharris into the dock: it was for this very reason that the Whigs had fought desperately to protect him during the Oxford Parliament. Francis Smith, for example, had been arrested on 15 April and charged with treason for saying 'he would never leave printing and writing till this kingdom was brought to a free state' (Haley 1968, 640). But it would have been rather harder to predict that there would soon be serious Whig plans for an uprising. The *Second Treatise*, written in the summer of 1681, would not be a defence of an uprising that was currently being planned (in the way that Sidney's *Discourses*, written while the Rye House Plot was underway, are, and in the way that the *Second Treatise* itself is, if the arguments of Marshall are accepted). Locke, in writing a sustained defence of resistance when no rebellion was planned, was endangering himself for no immediate purpose.

If the *Second Treatise* was conceived before the beginning of serious plots for an uprising, it is difficult to understand why Locke wrote it. But before we abandon this line of speculation and turn to adopt the new orthodoxy, we need to consider the possibility that the context we are looking for, the context that would be adequate to 'explain' the writing of the *Second Treatise*, need not be that of revolutionary politics. Written in the second half of 1681, it comes too soon to be closely linked to Shaftesbury's revolutionary strategy. But it does not come too soon to fit neatly into the wider political debates of the hour. Consider the evidence of Dryden's masterful attack on the Whigs, *Absalom and Achitophel*, published in November 1681, which asked:

> What shall we think? Can people give away,
> Both for themselves and sons, their native sway?
> Then they are left defenceless to the sword
> Of each unbounded, arbitrary lord:
> And laws are vain, by which we right enjoy,
> If kings unquestion'd can those laws destroy.
> Yet if the crowd be judge of fit and just,
> And kings are only officers in trust,
> Then this resuming covenant was declared
> When kings were made, or is for ever barr'd.
> If those who gave the sceptre could not tie
> By their own deed their own posterity,

How then could Adam bind his future race?
How could his forfeit on mankind take place?
Or how could heavenly justice damn us all,
Who ne'er consented to our father's fall?
Then kings are slaves to those whom they command,
And tenants to their people's pleasure stand.
Add, that the power for property allow'd
Is mischievously seated in the crowd:
For who can be secure of private right,
If sovereign sway may be dissolved by might?
Nor is the people's judgement always true:
The most may err as grossly as the few,
And faultless kings run down by common cry,
For vice, oppression, and for tyranny . . .
If they may give and take whene'er they please,
Not kings alone, the Godhead's images,
But government itself at length must fall
To nature's state, where all have right to all.

In the second half of 1681 it was part of practical political debate to ask whether kings are officers in trust; whether the decisions of our ancestors are binding on us; whether property was best protected by giving power to king or people; and, indeed, what our rights are if government is dissolved and we find ourselves in a state of nature. All these are questions Locke set out to answer. He did so because the intellectual debate was running ahead of political events. And this was partly because everyone was conscious of the precedents of the English Civil War, where Henry Parker's defence of the rights of the House of Commons had been followed by the fall of monarchy and Leveller arguments for democracy. Indeed Charles II in his *Declaration* of 8 April had called on his subjects to consider 'the rise and progress of the late troubles' and to remember that 'religion, liberty, and property were all lost and gone when the monarchy was shaken off' (Haley 1968, 639).

Of course the evidence of Dryden's poem might be dismissed: it was in his interest to exaggerate the radical character of Whig speculation. But *Absalom and Achitophel* was probably in part a response to *A Just and Modest Vindication of the Proceedings of the Two Last Parliaments*. This work has rightly been described as marking the moment when Whig polemicists moved into radical territory (Worden 1985, 15). Its authors (for there seems to have been more than one) warned that if James came to the throne the nation would be forced to take up arms in its own defence.[11] But the immediate conflict in which they were engaged was an intellectual one: 'Let the people to whom the appeal is made [by the King and his ministers in their vindication of their actions] judge then between them and us; and let reason and the law be the rules, according unto which the controversy may be decided. But if by denying this, they shall like beasts recur to force, they will thereby acknowledge that they want the arms that belong to rational creatures' (*State Tracts* 1689, 186–7). Before there could be any thought of responding to force with force, 'the arms that belong to rational creatures' had to be prepared: the pamphlet went on to claim that its side had the 'greater intellectuals', and could be confident of winning any rational debate. Here the language of the *Second Treatise*, the language of appeal to the people and resistance against those who, like beasts, reject the rule of law, is already in use, but the context is primarily one of intellectual conflict, the chief demand that of free access to the press. 'We desire only . . . that the press may be open for our justification' (186). When James's opponents were making appeals such as this, what task could be more urgent than the construction of a political theory that could justify their claim to have reason on their side?

The language of the authors of *A Modest Vindication* and that of Dryden thus makes it, I think, perfectly plausible that Locke might have set himself the task of writing the *Second Treatise* as early as June 1681. But we can, I think, go much further to establish the immediate intellectual context in which it was written, for we know that on 2 June 1681 Locke purchased a copy of James Tyrrell's *Patriarcha non Monarcha*.[12] It has long been recognized that this work is crucial for an understanding of the *Second Treatise*. 'There are,' writes Ashcraft, 'too many parallels between James Tyrrell's *Patriarcha non Monarcha* and the *Second Treatise* – literally scores of them – to list here. Not only the notions of "the state of nature" or "that great Law of Nature, that every man ought to endeavour the common good of mankind", but also the dissolution of government, the state of war, "tacit consent", private property arising from the "labor and industry" of the individual, the example of the Indians living in America, and many more specific parts of Locke's argument first appear in Tyrrell's work' (Ashcraft 1980, 444).

This is, as we shall see, indeed an incomplete list, but it is sufficient to justify asking: If Locke started the *Second Treatise* shortly after acquiring Tyrrell, and if Locke's central themes are the same as Tyrrell's, is the work perhaps best read, not as a commentary on Whig plans for rebellion, but as a response to Tyrrell's version of resistance theory? Before we can press this question, however, we must consider the possibility that it was not Locke who was responding to Tyrrell but, on the contrary, Tyrrell who was responding to Locke.

Everybody who reads *Patriarcha non Monarcha* quickly realizes that something went wrong as the book went through the press. The page numbering runs from 1 to 136, then from 97 to 160, and then from 209 on. Seventeenth-century books, however, carry another set of identifying marks, more important even than page numbers. An octavo book like *Patriarcha non Monarcha* was produced by printing eight pages at a time on each side of a large sheet of paper the size of a newspaper. Folded up into a little booklet by the binder, these pages constituted a 'gathering'. Gatherings were sewn together to make a volume, the edges of which were then guillotined, and the whole was bound. To ensure that the binder made no mistake when folding and sewing together the sheets, the first page of each gathering was marked at the bottom with a letter of the alphabet: in the case of *Patriarcha non Monarcha* the gatherings run from A to S. Gathering A, on which the preface alone appears, and which may have been written last, consists of a half sheet of eight pages. So does gathering S, which must have been printed last (perhaps on the same sheet as A), for it carries an errata sheet that refers to all the other gatherings. Richard Tuck has perceptively noted that gathering P begins on page 209, and that this is the right page number for an octavo book in which page 1 is B1. The misnumbered pages, gatherings L to O, pp. 97–160, were, he argues, interpolated into what was once a complete series (Tuck 1979, 169–70). Clearly Tyrrell changed his mind about something.

Tuck points out that the most striking similarity between *Patriarcha non Monarcha* and the *Second Treatise* appears in these pages, in Tyrrell's account of property. Suppose Laslett was right about the dating of the *Second Treatise* and it was indeed written in 1679. Then, in Tuck's view, what has happened is obvious: Tyrrell has read Locke while his book is in the press; has realized his treatment of property is inadequate; and has added to the book a version of Locke's new theory. Indeed in 1681 Tyrrell and Locke were in close collaboration – Tyrrell served for a time as Locke's amanuensis in the writing of a long manuscript on toleration.[13] Given this, Tuck argues, the similarities between the *Second Treatise* and *Patriarcha non Monarcha* are evidence of Locke's influence on Tyrrell, not vice versa.

But there is a flaw in Tuck's argument. He has not noticed that gathering K, pages 128–36, is a half sheet. Clearly this gathering too was pulled from the press. The compositors reset the first eight pages on a half sheet while Tyrrell rewrote the beginning of chapter 4 (the new gathering L), and kept on rewriting for page after page, for otherwise there would have been no need to disturb gatherings M, N, and O. Yet for all this rewriting, the end result was a book eight pages shorter (barely, for small print had to be used to squeeze everything in at the end of gathering O), not, as Tuck assumes, longer than the original. Tyrrell was cutting, not adding. At the beginning of chapter 4, where the cuts began, Tyrrell tells the reader he is not going to discuss Filmer's pamphlet on Hobbes, nor his pamphlet on Milton. Hobbes was always dangerous, but Milton more so. 'And less shall I take upon me to vindicate Milton,' says Tyrrell, 'since that were at once to defend downright murder and rebellion.'

The obvious explanation of the botched text of *Patriarcha non Monarcha* is that Tyrrell was not at first quite so cautious. The book was probably going through the press when the Oxford Parliament was dissolved: it eventually appeared in May (Menake 1981, Menake 1982). Fitzharris had already been arrested and charged for writing a seditious pamphlet. Between March 1679 and June 1685 there was no Licensing Act in force, but the government had ample legal resources for the enforcement of post-publication censorship (Patterson 1990). Perhaps under pressure from his publisher, Tyrrell wrote a preface saying that he would discuss the legitimacy of tyrannicide not here but elsewhere. He cut his discussion of Milton, and all later references to it in the succeeding pages. If gathering P had already been set in print the result was bound to be a botched job, with pages missing, but it was made worse when a careless compositor numbered the first page of gathering L '97' instead of '137'. Tuck's thesis is that Tyrrell revised his discussion of Filmer on Grotius to take account of Locke on property. But why then did gatherings N and O, which are concerned with Hunton on limited and mixed monarchy, have to be reset? And why is the end result shorter, not longer, than the original? The only satisfactory answer to these questions is that the original text fell victim to self-censorship.

Tuck thought he had discovered evidence that tended to support Laslett's dating: he imagined Tyrrell reading a draft of the *Second Treatise*. Ashcraft, who thinks the *Second Treatise* had yet to be written as *Patriarcha non Monarcha* went through the press, is seduced into thinking that perhaps Tyrrell had seen some draft essay by Locke on property, a draft predating the *Second Treatise* itself (Ashcraft 1986, 251). But the logic of his argument should have brought him to a quite different conclusion. Far from Locke influencing Tyrrell, Tyrrell influenced Locke. Indeed Tyrrell's *Patriarcha non Monarcha* was the immediate cause of the *Second Treatise*.

This is an obvious hypothesis, but what makes it convincing is the fact that it is not mine, but Tyrrell's. In 1690 Tyrrell read the *Two Treatises*. He noted that they contained a reference to *Patriarcha non Monarcha*. He noted too the similarity between them and his own work: 'whoever writ it . . . agreed perfectly with my conceptions in *Patriarcha non Monarcha*' (Gough 1976, 597). Had he read Locke on property before writing *Patriarcha non Monarcha*, or while it was in press, he might not have been so sure that it was he and not Locke who had influenced the author of the *Two Treatises*. He might have said, writing to Locke, 'he agrees with us'; or (if Locke had from the first concealed his own authorship) 'he agrees with me and the author of that essay you showed me'. But he was in no doubt that the ideas in *Patriarcha non Monarcha* were his own, and in no doubt, therefore, about which way the causal chain ran.

Consequently, Tyrrell reached the conclusion (even though he did not know exactly when the *Two Treatises* had been written) that *Patriarcha non Monarcha* had inspired the *Two Treatises*. He was virtually certain that their author was Locke, and he was obliged to conclude that Locke's text was much more closely derived from his own than it acknowledged. In 1692 he sent Locke a copy of his soon-to-be-published epitome of Cumberland on the law of nature, expressing the hope that 'it may provoke you to publish something more perfect'. A few months later he wrote again, repeating his hope that his own 'small performances' might serve as 'a foil to set off' the work of Locke's 'greater hand'. If Locke would publish on the subject 'I shall no more resent it than the publishing of the 2 Treatises of Government after Patriarcha non Monarcha . . . since I have (I thank God) learnt so far that master principle in Dr Cumberland's book, as to prefer the common good of mankind before my own fame and all the small reputation of an author' (599–600). It is clear that Tyrrell's view was that the *Two Treatises* had been 'provoked' by *Patriarcha non Monarcha*. Tyrrell's problem, and ours, was simple: Why did the author of the *Two Treatises*, who had made a favourable reference to *Patriarcha non Monarcha* in the *First*, make no acknowledgement of his extensive debt to it in the *Second*?

Tyrrell's relationship with Locke, which had been so close in 1681, was under strain even before he charged Locke with having written the *Two Treatises*. But it is hard not to think, as one reads the tense correspondence between the two over the years, that Tyrrell did resent Locke's having stolen his best ideas. Tyrrell owed Locke money, but somehow could not bring himself to repay it. Tyrrell had charge of some of Locke's possessions that Locke had left with him when he went into exile, but acted as if he had no desire to return them. Evidently he had grown fond of Locke's barometer, his telescope, his rugs, which now furnished his study. Did he feel that since Locke had taken something of his, the exchange was fair? Certainly his next work, the

Bibliotheca Politica (1692–1702), opens with the claim that he has gone to great lengths to cite his sources so that he will not be suspected of plagiarism: one might almost think he was offering Locke (who is one of his sources, and to whom he sent a copy) an example of how to behave.

Nor was this complicated exchange one-sided. Locke would never, in his lifetime, admit to Tyrrell that he had written the *Two Treatises*. But, near the end of his life, he invited Tyrrell to act as his intermediary when the Bodleian Library asked him for copies of his works. He made Tyrrell make sure that his gift of the works that he acknowledged as his appeared in the book of benefactors (he had to increase the value of the gift to qualify), and that there was space for more additions. Tyrrell must therefore have been among the first to know the terms of Locke's will, in which he acknowledged authorship of the *Two Treatises* and the *Letter Concerning Toleration*, and he would assuredly have been told when the new titles were added to the inscription in the book of benefactors. This new information was at the centre of the biographical essay Tyrrell wrote for the *Great Historical Dictionary* next year. But it was the *Letter* and the economic writings, not the *Two Treatises*, for which Tyrrell expressed admiration: not just because he could not have admired the *Two Treatises* without admiring his own work, but also because he was far from agreeing with the radical political message of the *Second Treatise*. Working with materials derived from Tyrrell, Locke had reached quite different, and much more subversive, conclusions. Tyrrell may have been exploring arguments in favour of tyrannicide in the spring of 1681, but there is no evidence that he would ever have accepted Locke's conclusion that there was no need to be bound by past constitutional precedent, that tyrannicide could legitimately be the prelude to revolution. Their conceptions did not, in fact, 'agree perfectly'.

This is, perhaps, why Locke had not acknowledged his debt, for to do so would have been to offer a hostage to a conservative critic. It may also be that Locke thought there was no need for one anonymous author to acknowledge another. He may even have recognized that the Tyrrell/Locke theory of property provided for property in objects, but not ideas. In any case, though Locke never offered Tyrrell an apology, he does seem to have wanted to ensure that Tyrrell should be among the first to know for sure that John Locke, philosopher and economist, was the author of the *Two Treatises*. Locke's bequest to Tyrrell was, we might say, a silent acknowledgement of an unpaid debt.

So: the evidence suggests that the *First Treatise* was, as Laslett, Ashcraft, and Marshall agree, an Exclusion tract, and was largely written by March 1681, although perhaps Locke was still at work on it when he first read *Patriarcha non Monarcha*. But the *Second* came second, as Ashcraft and Marshall recognize. If Locke began work on it (as his journal notes suggest) in June of 1681, then he was not writing to justify a specific revolutionary conspiracy: the *Second Treatise* is not a Rye House tract. But we do not need to conclude, as Marshall does, that he began work on it later. If Locke's immediate inspiration was *Patriarcha non Monarcha*, there is no reason why the *Second Treatise* could not have been conceived within a few days of Locke acquiring his copies of Tyrrell and Hooker, and why almost the whole of it should not have been written in the summer of 1681. The issues of revolutionary resistance which Locke addressed in the *Second Treatise* may not yet have been practical politics, but Tyrrell and the Whig pamphleteers had placed them on the intellectual agenda, as Dryden was quick to recognize.

Writing to satisfy his own curiosity, hoping to resolve the leading intellectual problems of the hour, driven onwards by his need to make intellectual coherence out of the arguments that had brought Fitzharris and College to the scaffold, and perhaps with some rash plan of resorting to clandestine publication, Locke wrote a work that he immediately went to great lengths to conceal and preserve because it promptly became of growing practical political relevance, as the question of resistance became not a matter of abstract debate but of practical organization.

The cover name by which Locke referred to this dangerous text, a name that recurs among his papers from July of 1681 on, and that he used when asking friends whether they still had it safe in their possession, was *Tractatus de Morbo Gallico*, the medical term for syphilis (Locke 1967b, 62–4). Locke's book was an attack on absolutism, and absolutism was a French disease. But there was one moment when English absolutism appeared particularly in this guise: the King's *Declaration* of April was, according to *A Just and Modest Vindication*, so full of Gallicisms that it appeared to be a translation from the French; and indeed the French ambassador had a copy in his hands before the King's Council had seen it (*State Tracts* 1689, 166–7). Within three months Locke's treatise had acquired its code name. At least one person knew of its contents: among Shaftesbury's papers when he was arrested in July were his personal notes taken from a work entitled *Mors Gallicus*. Did Shaftesbury have in his possession a draft of the *Second Treatise* as well as the *First*? Were the authors of *A Just and Modest Vindication* already aware of the existence of a treatise on the people's right to judge when they so confidently claimed that their side could rely on 'some persons . . . of greater intellectuals' than the advisers to the King?[14] These are questions we cannot answer with certainty, but we shall soon see that there is further evidence in Locke's journals, apart from his notes on Hooker, for dating the *Second Treatise* to June 1681.

The First Treatise of Government

Locke tells us that the bulk of the original manuscript of the *First Treatise of Government* was lost or destroyed. What survives appears at first sight to be primarily a close analysis of Sir Robert Filmer's use of biblical quotations to support his patriarchal theory. Presumably the original text went on to discuss those sections of Filmer's works that relied less heavily on the Bible. Still, Locke thought it worth publishing this truncated and narrowly biblical version of his original argument, and there is no doubt that his first priority in the text we have is to establish that Filmer wilfully distorts Scripture. When the Ten Commandments say 'Honour thy Father and Mother', for example, Filmer drops the reference to mothers, and uses the text to justify a claim for paternal authority over mothers and for the eldest brother's authority over his siblings (1.§60). Thus the 'express text of Scripture' is distorted: 'but God must not be believed, though he speaks it himself, when he says he does anything which will not consist with Sir Robert's hypothesis' (1.§32). 'The prejudices of our own ill-grounded opinions, however by us called probable, cannot authorize us to understand Scripture contrary to the direct and plain meaning of the words' (1.§36). To undermine Filmer's claim to biblical sanction for his arguments was to destroy his authority.

What Locke is much slower to advertise is the fact that his own reading of Scripture is potentially subversive of orthodox religious belief. For example, the standard interpretation of Genesis 3.19 – 'In the sweat of thy face, shalt thou eat thy bread' – was that it was, as Locke says, 'not spoken personally to Adam, but in him, as their representative, to all mankind, this being a curse upon mankind, because of the Fall'. This in fact was the key biblical passage for the doctrine of original sin, the damnation of all men and women in punishment for the fall of Adam and Eve. Original sin was a doctrine with important implications for political theory: conventionally government was held to have been made necessary to restrain man's sinful nature; and, as we saw Dryden insist, the punishment of the descendants of Adam and Eve for their transgression was the paradigm case of the acts of individuals binding their descendants. To question the doctrine of original sin was thus a first step to questioning the foundations of conventional Christian political theory.

And indeed in the next paragraph Locke clearly, if indirectly, rejects the conventional interpretation of this passage (1.§46). Moreover, according to the conventional interpretation, the punishment of Adam and Eve had been unequal because Eve was more directly responsible for the Fall than Adam. Genesis 3 was thus a classic text for arguments designed to demonstrate the necessary inferiority of women to men. Locke, by contrast, goes on to hint that there is no necessary subjection of women to men: the circumstances of a woman's condition or her marriage contract may make her equal or superior to her husband. We learn from a journal note of 1681 that Locke thought that according to nature women were 'at their own disposal', as free as the men with whom they had relations (below, p. 241).

One of the confirmations that one would hope to offer in support of any dating of the *Two Treatises* would be links of this kind between the themes Locke discussed in his notebooks and journals and the argument of the *Two Treatises*. Since everyone accepts that the *First Treatise* was almost certainly written in 1680–81, it seems natural to turn to Locke's journals for that year to see if they cast any light on his attitude to the two vexed questions he touches on here: the supposed inferiority of women to men (which is discussed in his note on 'Virtus', to which I have just referred), and the related question of original sin. Strangely, the evidence of the journals has been largely overlooked.

It is apparent from Locke's journal entry for 1 August 1680 on 'The Idea We Have of God' that Locke (at the time when he was writing the *First Treatise*) cannot have believed in the doctrine of original sin, for belief in this doctrine required believing that God had ordained men to misery, and believing that he had punished them, not so that they would learn to behave better, or to benefit them, but in such a way that better behaviour and self-improvement became impossible for them. This, Locke assures us, is contrary to the idea we have of a good God (below, pp. 237–8).[15] The author of 'The Idea We Have of God' could not, therefore, have been an orthodox Christian. If one were to ask oneself what sort of Christian he was, one would be tempted to answer that he was probably a Socinian, for the followers of Socinus were not only Unitarians, but also the only Christians to be systematic in their rejection of the doctrine of original sin. We know that Locke was familiar with Socinian theology. In 1679 he was reading a substantial work in that tradition, George Enyedi's *Explicationes* (Marshall 1990, 494), and on 4 February 1680 he acquired a small collection of Socinian books, the titles of which he entered in his journal (Wootton 1989, 56). In later years, accused of Socinianism, he was to deny ever having read any Socinian books, despite the fact that during his years of exile in Holland he had built up a substantial collection of works by Socinian theologians. We should envisage Locke reading the pamphlets he bought in 1680, I suggest, at the same time as he first read *Patriarcha*. He was probably proud to have got hold of them, for most of them had been condemned to be burnt by the hangman for their heretical content, and they were rare indeed.

We have in our hands here, I think, a clue which helps resolve a number of delicate problems in Locke scholarship. A useful starting point is provided by an ambiguous passage in John Dunn's *Political Thought of John Locke* where he maintains that:

> the Lockean social and political theory is to be seen as the elaboration of Calvinist social values, in the absence of a terrestrial focus of theological authority and in response to a series of particular challenges. The explanation of why it was *Calvinist* social values which Locke continued to expound is that he was brought up in a Calvinist family. And the reason why he *continued* to expound them is that his own experience was too dominated by 'uneasiness', too anxious, to make a self-confident naturalism a tolerable interpretation of the world. A 'state of licence' did not seem an enhancement of liberty but simply a destruction of security. His own psychology and his own biography conspired to retain him within the inherited theological framework and in consequence the honesty and force of his thought were devoted to making such sense as could be made of this framework instead of replacing it. (Dunn 1969a, 259)

It is important to be clear about what Dunn is claiming here. He is certainly claiming that Locke's social values had their roots in 'the Protestant ethic' (213, 222–8, 250–54). He is also insisting that Locke's religion was profoundly individualistic: he did not recognize the authority of any ecclesiastical community, and did not seek to make his doctrinal beliefs correspond to any predetermined orthodoxy (249, 257). But it is easy to read him as maintaining that Locke continued throughout his life to accept an essentially Calvinist theological framework. Dunn was well aware, as is apparent from his discussion of Locke's *The Reasonableness of Christianity* (1695), that this was not in fact the case (e.g. 192–3, 195), and he is best understood as holding that Locke's outlook was religious, not secular, rather than that it was Calvinist as opposed, say, to latitudinarian.

Dunn's view is not, therefore, strictly incompatible with William Spellman's view that Locke was a latitudinarian rather than a Calvinist (Spellman 1988). Latitudinarians, like Locke, argued that theological details were of limited importance, that the essence of Christianity lay in its moral teaching, and that there should be both toleration for differing varieties of Christian faith and a national Church embracing as many Christians as possible.

Locke certainly had friends and associates among the latitudinarians and expresses his support for 'latitudinism' at the end of the *Essay Concerning Toleration*. But latitudinarians, despite the accusations that were often levelled against them, were careful to remain orthodox on key doctrines, particularly belief in the Trinity and original sin. It is precisely evidence of such orthodoxy that is missing from works such as *The Reasonableness of Christianity*, and Locke's private notebooks in later life suggest that he was a Unitarian, not a Trinitarian (Marshall, forthcoming). If we turn to Locke's *Some Thoughts Concerning Education*, too, we find an emphasis on the malleability of human nature and on man's potential goodness that is at odds with the Christian orthodoxy of the day, even as cautiously stated by latitudinarian thinkers.

Dunn's view is however incompatible with that of the followers of Leo Strauss. They regard Locke as an enemy of orthodox religion, as a secret deist, or atheist, and as a man who, in particular, did not believe in the immortality of the soul. Straussians have argued that Locke's *First Treatise* is a key text in which he insinuates his contempt for the Bible while pretending to follow it closely (Zuckert 1979). In fact, they claim, Locke is following Hobbes, and like him is seeking to combine a superficial acceptance of Christianity with a systematic attack upon religion.

The differing Straussian interpretations all share two over-simplifications. In the first place they over-simplify the place of Hobbes in late-seventeenth-century political philosophy. Hobbes, for example, argues in terms of a state of nature, and this seems to Strauss a fundamentally irreligious mode of argument: the Bible talks of man's state before and after the Fall, but neither corresponds to a state of nature in which men were dependent only upon their own instincts and reason (Strauss 1953, 215). Locke takes over Hobbes's concept of a state of nature, and in doing so, Straussians claim, accepts its irreligious implications. But this argument completely obscures the way in which the concept of a state of nature had been adopted within orthodox intellectual debate. Above all, Pufendorf, who was much admired by Tyrrell and Locke, had been influential both for his attacks on Hobbes and for his adoption of a whole series of concepts out of Hobbes, including the concept of a state of nature. If we are going to argue that Locke's state of nature is

Hobbesian in inspiration, we need to show it is not Pufendorfian; if we are going to claim it implies religious scepticism, we need to show that the same charge can successfully be levelled against Pufendorf (a rather unlikely eventuality), or that Locke's concept is different in kind from Pufendorf's. The Straussians have yet to undertake this sort of elementary comparative analysis of Locke in relationship to his sources.

The second simplification the Straussians make is to assume that where they find an argument that seems to them to be at odds with orthodox religion, they can reasonably conclude that its author is seeking to inculcate irreligion. They never pause to consider the possibility that the author is religious, but not orthodox. Thus the fact that Locke seems to undermine the biblical foundation for belief in original sin does not prove he is no Christian: it merely implies that he is not an orthodox Christian. Again, Locke appeals in the *Second Treatise* to Cain's statement that 'Every one that findeth me shall slay me' as evidence of a natural right to punish murderers with death, omitting to mention that God specifically forbids the killing of Cain himself (2.§11). To the Straussians this seems like a deliberate distortion of the biblical text at least as remarkable as any perpetrated by Filmer (Cox 1960, 54–6). They fail to note, though, that the same argument had been put forward by Grotius (1925, bk I, ch. 2, §4) and Tyrrell (1681, 12, 115–18). Grotius had explicitly raised the question of the contradiction between certain biblical injunctions (e.g. 'turn the other cheek') and the teaching of reason, and had insisted that the Bible must be interpreted in the light of reason (Grotius 1925, bk I, ch. 3, §3). Thus one need not always turn the other cheek, and, but for God's intervention, it would have been right to kill Cain. When he quoted Cain as providing evidence of a natural right to punish murderers, Locke was merely summarizing a view that others had insisted was compatible with orthodox Christianity. Again, a comparative analysis is necessary: either the charge of deliberate distortion of the Bible must be extended to Grotius, or Locke's argument must be shown to be different from his.

There is no doubt, as Locke's short essay 'Inspiration' of April 1681 makes abundantly clear, that Locke was committed to the view that the Bible must be interpreted in the light of reason, and that one must reject all claims made on behalf of religion that were incompatible with reason (below, p. 239). Locke's insistence that religion must be reasonable long predates his writing of *The Reasonableness of Christianity* in the 1690s. This emphasis on reason was potentially corrosive of faith, and was to be put to irreligious purposes in Toland's *Christianity not Mysterious* (1696), and in the *Discourse of Freethinking* (1713) of Locke's close friend, Anthony Collins. But there is no evidence that Locke ever concluded that reason and faith were incompatible. His argument in 'Inspiration' is of precisely the sort that was used in good faith by Protestants against the Catholic doctrine of Transubstantiation, and also, indeed, by Socinians against original sin and the Trinity, doctrines that they held to be contrary to reason.

When *The Reasonableness of Christianity* was published in 1695 many contemporaries noted its insistence that our knowledge of the immortality of the soul derives from the resurrection of Jesus, and its silence on the Trinity. Socinian theologians did not regard Christ's crucifixion as a sacrifice for our sins, and did not believe that Christ's death had freed men in general, or the elect in particular, from the guilt of original sin. The central emphasis of their theology lay therefore not on the crucifixion but the resurrection: by rising from the dead Christ had shown us that there was a life after death. Natural reason alone could not establish this fact, because it, by contrast, showed man to be naturally mortal. Immortality was a truth established only by revelation (Wootton 1989).

What sort of immortality could we expect? Orthodox theologians insisted that our bodies would rise again, miraculously reassembled at the Last Judgement. (Sceptics were puzzled: if Tom drowns and is eaten by an eel, and Joe then catches the eel and eats it, surely what was once Tom's body becomes Joe's body? How then are the two to be separated at the last trump (Locke 1823, vol. 9, 257–8)?) Socinians favoured the notion that there would be no literal resurrection of the old body: instead God would provide a new and immortal body.

Once the question of whether Locke was a Socinian is asked, a whole series of arguments in the *Essay Concerning Human Understanding* take on a new significance. There Locke had argued that there was no rational demonstration of the immortality of the soul, he had attacked the theory of substances that was traditionally used to explain the Trinity, and (in the second edition of 1694) he had argued that our personal identity has nothing to do with the physical continuity of our bodies. I would still be me if I woke up and found myself inhabiting your body, or (to take a modern example) if my brain was transplanted into your body. It was easy to conclude that the *Essay* was a sustained exercise in Socinian philosophy, and was to be rejected by orthodox Christians for that very reason (Yolton 1956, Jolley 1984).

When did Locke become a Socinian? The evidence for thinking that he was very close to Socinianism, even if he did not agree with every aspect of Socinian theology, is strong for the 1690s (Marshall, forthcoming). But it seems to me that we have enough evidence to argue backwards, as contemporaries did, from the *Reasonableness* to the *Essay*, and indeed from the *Essay* to the *First Treatise* and these journal notes of 1681. In support of this strategy we have the testimony of Damaris Cudworth, who probably knew Locke better than anyone else, and who reported that the main shift in his religious beliefs occurred some years before he went into exile (Fox Bourne 1876, vol. 2, 282). Ferguson (who was, alas, not always truthful) later claimed that Locke had converted Shaftesbury to Socinianism, and that Shaftesbury confessed as much on his deathbed in 1682. Ferguson was Shaftesbury's chaplain at the time, and so in a good position to know (Haley 1968, 732).

Straussians are right, then, to claim that something strange is going on when Locke appeals to the Bible, but wrong to conclude that Locke's intention is to undermine faith.[16] In fact, he is trying to insinuate a rationalist, Socinian reading of the Bible. This, I suspect, is one reason why he still wanted to publish the *First Treatise* in 1689, despite the fact, which he stressed in the Preface, that the arguments of Sir Robert Filmer were now irrelevant and scarcely worth rebutting. The whole question of how to interpret the Bible was still immediately relevant, and the *First Treatise* gave a clear indication of Locke's view on this question.

In §86 Locke makes clear that, for all his apparent willingness to enslave himself to the Bible text, he was in fact boldly asserting the claim of reason to govern the interpretation of the text. God spoke to man through his senses and reason, telling him that he might eat other creatures: 'And therefore I doubt not, but before these words were pronounced, I Gen. 28, 29 (if they must be understood literally to have been spoken) and without any such verbal donation, man had a right to a use of the creatures . . .' Yet in the previous paragraph Locke had said 'positive grants give no title further than the express words convey it'. Relying on this premise, he had argued against Filmer that God had not given Adam a property in all creatures, because God gave him permission to eat only vegetable and not animal life: consequently Adam was apparently confined to a vegetarian diet. Only after the Flood were Noah and his sons told to eat the animals (1. §§38–9). In this way Locke enjoyed using biblical literalism against Filmer, but §86 exposes this argument as insincere: the right to eat the animals derives not from God's explicit donation, or from the Bible, but from sense, instinct, and reason. The *First Treatise* thus contains the germs of the rationalist testing of the Bible text that 'Inspiration' demands.

One must wonder, though, whether Locke intended to contradict himself so transparently. Rather, the conflict between §85 and §86 may be evidence that Locke wrote these two paragraphs at different times. The section that runs from §86 to §100 is quite exceptional in the *First Treatise* for its virtual absence of references to Filmer. It also contains four references ahead: one of which is clearly an anticipation of the discussion of property in the *Second Treatise*. Finally it argues that children in the state of nature had a right to a stable family life and to the equal inheritance of their parents' property. This is at odds with an entry in Locke's commonplace book, 'Virtus', dated 1681 (below, pp. 240–42) that takes the conventional view that men and women in a state of nature were under no obligation to preserve stable family units: a view that fitted well with Whig strategy before the Oxford Parliament, for one of their options was to press for Charles to divorce his barren Queen and re-marry.

The conventional view of the state of nature is well summed up by the opening lines of *Absalom and Achitophel*, which were made more piquant by their satirical reference to Charles I's numerous bastards. According to this view, just as property was the creation of the political order, so too were monogamy and inheritance:

> In pious times ere priestcraft did begin,
> Before polygamy was made a sin;
> When man on many multiplied his kind,
> Ere one to one was cursedly confined;
> When nature prompted and no law denied
> Promiscuous use of concubine and bride;
> Then Israel's monarch after Heaven's own heart,
> His vigorous warmth did variously impart
> To wives and slaves; and wide as his command,
> Scatter'd his Maker's image through the land.

This is the state of nature discussed in 'Virtus', but it is quite different from the picture of men's and women's natural moral responsibilities that Locke draws in this section of the *First Treatise*.

Between writing 'Virtus' and writing §86 of the *First Treatise* Locke had, I believe, come up with a new theory of men's rights and properties in nature: a theory that was a response to his reading of Tyrrell in May or June of 1681. What he has to say in this section should be read alongside 'Two Sorts of Knowledge', which he wrote on 26 June 1681 (below, pp. 259–61). Where before he had accepted without complaint the bounds set by 'custom and reputation' in deciding what virtue is, now he appeals to abstract reasoning against 'the lazy traditional way of talking one after another'. Someone with a demonstrative knowledge of moral principles of the sort to which Locke laid claim in June of 1681 could use them, as Locke does in 1.§90, to pass judgement on the 'absurd' practices of existing societies and to justify a sharp attack on contemporary institutions.

Locke's discussion of a right to inherit would have been immediately relevant in the summer of 1681. Under English law men convicted of a felony forfeited their property to the state: the families of Fitzharris and College faced paupery as a result of their condemnations. Shaftesbury was to busy himself in 1682 with mortgaging his estates to ensure that there would be friends who would have a prior claim on them should he be found guilty of treason

(Haley 1968, 725–6). Locke's insistence that children have a right to inherit, and his attack on the laws of his own society, mark a significant step towards the radical position of the *Second Treatise*. It foreshadows the argument, not only of chapter 5 of the *Second Treatise*, but also of 2.§182, which insists on the right of children to inherit from their fathers even if their fathers have been justly condemned. This whole section was, I believe, added when Locke was first sketching out the arguments of the *Second Treatise*: his theory of inheritance is indeed, as we shall see, a crucial precondition for the role he gives to property in that work. When he came to write this section, Locke had not only forgotten what he had written in §38–9. He even failed to notice the contradiction between his new natural-law argument, founded on abstract reason, and his own insistence in §85 on the need to adhere closely to the Bible text.

On 18 September 1681 Locke recorded in his journal a view about inheritance that clearly bears on the argument of the *Two Treatises*, but that has been overlooked in all the debates about their date. Locke wrote (and signed with his initials, a practice he adopted when he felt he had made up his mind on a disputed question): 'In the inheritance of anything indivisible, the next of blood is the eldest son, for want of sons the eldest daughter, for want of issue the father, unless the inheritance came by the mother, and then she is next heir. This one rule (wherein is preferred the natural right of nearness of blood) being observed, there can be no dispute about the next heir' (Ms Locke f 5, 121–2). Locke does not seem to have any clear principle of this sort in mind when he wrote the final surviving chapter of the *First Treatise*, 'Who Heir?'. Later, as I take it, when he wrote about inheritance in §§86–97, he discussed the right of parents to inherit from their children, and stressed the view (which he takes for granted in September) that all children had normally an equal right to inherit. The journal note goes beyond the discussion in the *First Treatise* in dealing with the limit case of the inheritance of something indivisible, and in distinguishing between mothers and fathers. But it also goes beyond the discussion in the *Second*. If the *Second Treatise* had yet to be written in September 1681, why did Locke not introduce into it 'this one rule' that he had so carefully recorded in his journal? The sensible conclusion seems to be that the journal entry was written after this section of the *First Treatise* was composed, and after the sections of the *Second Treatise* to which it refers. That in turn suggests that by September 1681 Locke had finished or abandoned the *First Treatise* and had written all or most of the *Second*. This fragment of evidence provides additional support for the dating I have proposed.

How far had Locke got with the *First Treatise* when he conceived of the *Second*? On the one hand we have the claim in the Preface that there once existed a complete manuscript, of which only part survived. On the other hand we have the internal evidence of the last chapter, 'Who Heir?', as it stands: a rambling mess, it is hard to see it as anything more than a careless first draft, and difficult to believe that Locke could have advanced much further before he had paused to sort out its structure. Despite Locke's testimony to the fact that he had written more than survives, I am tempted to think that he broke off his work on a still incomplete *First Treatise* when he recognized the need for a *Second*.

In any case it is clear what his original plan was. His intention was to demonstrate how Filmer's account provided no coherent picture of the four ways of transmitting power that he recognized: inheritance, grant, usurpation, and election (1.§80). What survives is primarily a discussion of inheritance, of Filmer's argument that kings rule as Adam's heirs. Locke's intention is to show that Filmer's principles, whether taken separately or together, provide no guide to who has the right to rule: 'since men cannot obey anything that cannot command, and ideas of government in the fancy, though never so perfect, though never so right, cannot give laws, nor prescribe rules to the actions of men; it would be of no behoof for the settling of order, and establishment of government in its exercise and use amongst men, unless there were a way also taught how to know the person, to whom it belonged to have this power, and exercise this dominion over others. 'Tis in vain then to talk of subjection and obedience, without telling us whom we are to obey' (1.§81). 'The great question which in all ages has disturbed mankind, and brought on them the greatest part of those mischiefs which have ruined cities, depopulated countries, and disordered the peace of the world, has been, not whether there be power in the world, nor whence it came, but who should have it' (1.§106).

Locke's original intention, then, was to answer the question 'Whom should we obey?' His purpose was not just to argue that the laws of inheritance were artificial, not natural, and that James could therefore be put aside in favour of an alternative heir: this was merely the first step. He also had to undermine Filmer's claim that one should always obey the King. What the Whigs foresaw as they planned a Bond of Association, and expected as they waited for the Oxford Parliament to meet, was that individuals might one day have to choose, as they had had to in 1642, whether they would obey King or Commons. If Locke foresaw a *Second Treatise* as he began work on the *First*, it would presumably have been one that established the claims of the representatives of the people. To do this he would have had to analyse the role of consent in government and say something about the nature of man's natural freedom.

However, what is astonishing about the *First Treatise* is how far Locke avoids committing himself to any substantial theory of natural freedom and equality: in his only discussion of the question he does not go beyond endorsing the view of a divine-right theorist such as Barclay (1.§67). He seems to take for granted the condition of hereditary slavery, and to accept the conventional belief that men might legitimately be forced to consent to a complete subordination to their rulers (1.§§42–3, 130). There is no indication that he believes, as he did when he wrote the *Second Treatise*, that all men are born with an inalienable right to freedom, and that there are key freedoms (beyond the right to religious toleration) that no man can alienate. There is no evidence that the Locke who wrote the *First Treatise* had yet discovered what we regard as the founding principles of liberalism. The *First Treatise* is written by someone concerned to refute Filmer; the *Second* by someone prepared to adopt the position that Filmer is attacking, that men are born equal and free, and with an inalienable right to change their government. Yet again, our search for the origins of Locke's liberalism has drawn a blank: the Locke of the *First Treatise* is not yet a liberal.

The Second Treatise of Government

We have seen that, according to Laslett, the *Second Treatise* was largely written in the winter of 1679–80. Some fifty paragraphs were added in the summer of 1681 (the Hooker references, and chapters 16, 17, 18, and part of chapter 8). Parts of chapter 18 and the final chapter, he believes, date to the plots of 1682 and 1683; and further revisions were made in 1689. The view put forward here is that almost the entire treatise was written in the summer and autumn of 1681.[17] There is nothing in the sections that Laslett thinks were written in 1679–80 that conclusively dates them to that period; nor is there anything in the sections he dates to 1682–3 that could not have been written earlier. There are a few passages which do seem to date to 1689, and involve direct references to the government of James II, though not perhaps as many as Laslett thinks. Apart from these passages, the last date at which we can be confident Locke was still working on the *Two Treatises* is August 1681, when he purchased 'the late relation of Ceylon' that he refers to in 2.§92. Since the *Second Treatise* is a work in defence of revolution, it is tempting to date it, as Marshall does, to 1682–3, but there is no substantial evidence to support this dating. In favour of the idea that the *Second Treatise* was written rapidly in the summer of 1681 is the evidence of the references to Hooker and the discussion of 'Two Sorts of Knowledge' in the journal entries for June, the discussion of inheritance in September, and the fact that every single one of the central themes of the *Second Treatise* would arise naturally out of a consideration of Tyrrell's *Patriarcha non Monarcha*, which we know Locke had in his possession by June of 1681.

Once we recognize that the *Second Treatise* was almost certainly written after *Patriarcha non Monarcha*, and, moreover, that there is no evidence that Locke influenced the argument of *Patriarcha non Monarcha*, then the close dependence of Locke's work upon Tyrrell's becomes apparent.[18] In order to clarify this dependence we need to concentrate on those arguments that are common to *Patriarcha non Monarcha* and the *Second Treatise*. Large sections of *Patriarcha non Monarcha* are irrelevant to Locke's argument, and at certain key points, as we shall see, Locke disagreed with Tyrrell. But we can understand the intellectual enterprise on which he was engaged only if we see that the bulk of his 'Essay of Civil Government' was derived directly from Tyrrell. In writing the *Second Treatise* Locke was not thinking about political philosophy in the abstract, nor was he primarily interested in Filmer or Hobbes. He was interested in seeing what he could do with Tyrrell's arguments if he detached them from a number of conservative assumptions to be found in Tyrrell, sharpened them, and used them to address the problem that Tyrrell had side-stepped: the problem of resistance to tyranny.

The importance of Tyrrell's *Patriarcha non Monarcha* lies in five key principles on which his argument rests:

(i) All men (and, in principle, women) are born free and equal (Tyrrell 1681, 86–9).[19] Tyrrell was the first author to press this claim to its logical conclusion. For Hobbes men are born free and equal if they are born in a state of nature; but children born into society are born subjects, and the children of slaves are born in servitude. For Pufendorf too men are in theory born free and equal, but children born into society are obliged to accept the contracts entered into by their forebears. How, Pufendorf asked, if men are born free, could the child of a slave be born a slave (Pufendorf 1934, bk VI, ch. 3; 1991, 131)? Because, he answered, the child of a slave owed its nourishment and upbringing to its owner. This debt could never be repaid, and as a consequence the child, by the time it reached adulthood, had no claim to the freedom that was notionally its right at the moment of birth.

Tyrrell's response was uncompromising (Tyrrell 1681, 32, 75–6). The child of a slave had a right to freedom. Any debt to its owner could be paid off within a few years, after which point it would have earned freedom. To argue otherwise was to give someone who saved you from drowning the right to claim that you owed your life to him (or indeed her) and so must be his or her slave (an argument repeated by Locke). Similarly, the children of subjects were not themselves subjects (87). Rather they were in the same position as foreigners: obliged by a passive or tacit consent to abide by the laws of the country they were in as long as they remained there, but with a fundamental right to leave and join another community.

Only an act that committed one to citizenship – such as the taking of an oath of allegiance, or the inheritance of an estate to which was attached the condition that it could only be possessed by a citizen – obliged one to give up one's natural freedom.

Tyrrell was the first natural-law theorist to argue that all men are born with a title to freedom, become free when they reach maturity, and cannot lose their freedom except through an act of their own. This argument Locke takes over wholesale from Tyrrell. They differ only on minor details. Thus Locke claims that the laws of states recognize that men are not born subjects (2.§118); Tyrrell, more realistically, recognizes that the laws pretend that men are born subjects, but insists these laws are not binding on the conscience. We have a right to emigrate, even if the government tries to stop us (Tyrrell 1681, 87–8). Tyrrell, however, argues that people ought to join the society their ancestors have established, because political systems benefit mankind, and so we have a moral obligation to support them (76–7). Locke chooses not to stress this moral limitation placed on our natural liberty. Tyrrell talks as if possession of all goods in a society carried with it, under existing law, consent to membership (86–7). Locke recognizes that this is not necessarily true of all or even any goods (2.§§119–21). Both are writing in the context of a legal system that required an oath of allegiance from all freeholders, although neither of them makes clear this fundamental distinction between freeholders and others.

It is a consequence of the claim that all men are born with a title to freedom that no man can enter into an obligation that binds another without his consent, and that all legitimate authority (except in the limit case of authority over those who have deserved to be condemned to death) is founded in consent: this is a consequence that Tyrrell states, but, as we shall see, Locke is much more systematic than Tyrrell in applying this principle (Tyrrell 1681, 80). Both Locke and Tyrrell insist that there are historical examples of governments founded in consent, and both give the examples of Rome and Venice (Tyrrell 1681, 84; Locke 2.§102). Both agree that when men consent to form a political society they agree, of necessity, to be bound by the will of the majority (Tyrrell 1681, 84; Locke 2. §96). Both deny that a conqueror can establish himself as an absolute ruler, if only because conquest gives him no right of absolute rule

over those who have fought alongside him (Tyrrell 1681, 85; Locke
2.§177). Both men maintain that there are certain inalienable rights.
Locke appears to claim that every individual must preserve his own
life; Tyrrell claims that no man may give up his own life except for
a higher moral end, such as the defence of the nation (Tyrrell 1681,
116–17). No one, therefore, can enter into a contract that abrogates
the right of self-defence against arbitrary violence.

(ii) The powers of governments are based entirely on powers
transferred to them by individuals, and governments have no rights
that are peculiar to them (Tyrrell 1681, 115–18; Locke 2.§87–9).
Most importantly, the right to punish is one that individuals have
in a state of nature (Tyrrell 1681, 11). It is not (as was standardly
claimed in seventeenth-century political thought) a peculiar attribute of divinely ordained authority. Both Locke and Tyrrell
place restraints on this right to punish. You may not seek revenge
for its own sake, but may seek recompense for losses, and may
punish individuals to reform them, or to deter them or others who
may seek to imitate them (Tyrrell 1681, 25–9; Locke 2.§8). Thus
you may kill someone who uses force to steal from you, and Cain
was right to think that his murder of Abel gave every individual the
right to kill him. Tyrrell was developing here an argument made by
Grotius, but he was the first to grasp the possibility of treating
governments as having rights no different in kind from those of
individuals in a state of nature, while insisting those rights were not
(as Hobbes had claimed) unlimited.[20] Locke simply follows Tyrrell,
while clarifying his vocabulary. Thus Tyrrell had said that punishment implied a relationship between superior and inferior, classify-
ing as 'natural punishments' the penalties inflicted by equals upon
each other or by inferiors on superiors. Locke simply dropped this
confusing distinction, and argued not only for a natural right of
self-defence, but also for a natural right to punish.

It may be noted, however, that just as Locke's theory of a right
to inheritance was at odds with the English law governing felony,
and his theory of natural freedom was at odds with the English law
on citizenship, so his theory of a natural right of self-defence and
punishment was at odds with the English law of murder. Under
English law someone who killed in self-defence was in fact liable to
the forfeiture of his goods, although he could expect to be pardoned.

This is surprising to us, because we have come to accept a Lockean principle of self-defence; it was not surprising to contemporaries, who held that only a legitimate ruler had the right to kill (Hale 1736, 478–96).

(iii) Both Locke and Tyrrell agree that the state of nature is not necessarily a state of war of all against all. It has a law to govern it, the law of nature, and both agree that this law requires the pursuit of the common good. Before political society was established, men were therefore capable of living orderly and moral lives. Above all, they could establish and identify private property rights. For although the world was given to all men in common, men can by labour appropriate private property without having to obtain the consent of their fellow commoners. Private property thus precedes the establishment of government, and men in a state of nature can enter into contracts to transfer property from one to another. In a state of nature, men may lay claim only to property for which they have a use, and must leave enough over to satisfy the needs of others (Tyrrell 1681, 65, *108–14*[21]; Locke 2.§§33, 37). In a primitive society, where much of the land continues to be held in common, there will be few occasions for conflict, and no need for a state. America is for both of them an example of such a primitive world where most property is still held in common. Under such conditions, rulers are temporary military commanders whose rights should cease with the end of the military campaign. Such rulers are likely to be the heads of extended families, and so the state has its distant origins in patriarchal authority (Tyrrell 1681, 35–9; Locke 2.§§74, 76).

Locke is more systematic than Tyrrell in arguing that labour is the only claim to property. Tyrrell allows for a claim from occupation: if you walk into a lecture theatre in which the seats are unassigned, you have a claim on the seat you occupy, and no one has a right to throw you out of it. But you may occupy only what you can use: and in the case of land you may occupy only the area that you can transform through labour. In any case, Locke's insistence on labour as the basis of property right is somewhat misleading. Both give the example of a common dish placed on a table at a meal: the meat I serve myself belongs to me (Tyrrell 1681, *108–14*; Locke 2.§29). It is hardly my labour that makes it mine, for all the real labour took place before the food got to table. Serving myself is much more like occupying a seat in a lecture hall than like clearing a forest to sow grain.

(iv) For all their agreement with conventional seventeenth-century political theory over the historical importance of patriarchy, Locke and Tyrrell also agree in distinguishing sharply between five types of authority: the authority of a ruler over his or her subjects (political authority), of a father over his children, a husband over his wife, a master over his servants, and a slave-owner over his slaves. The authority of a father over his children is a function of his obligation to raise and educate the child, and extends no further than is necessary for this purpose. He has no right on the grounds that he has made the child, for it is God, not he, who has given the child being. Once the child is grown he or she owes a debt of gratitude to his or her parents, but is under no lasting obligation to obey them. A father or mother who fails to look after a child loses all right to obedience, while a loving foster-father acquires the same rights as a natural father (Tyrrell 1681, 13–20; Locke 2.§§52–76).

The authority of husbands over wives is based on the contract they enter into in marriage. Such a contract may give the wife a measure of independence, even equality, and a right to divorce. Because husband and wife constitute a committee of two, it is necessary that one of them should have a deciding vote, and natural that this should normally be held by the man. Both thus allow for the possibility of a society in which men and women will be treated equally (Tyrrell 1681, 14–15, 109–13; Locke 2.§§82–3).

(v) Finally both agree that tyrannical behaviour dissolves legitimate authority, and restores the natural freedom and equality that exists in a state of nature. Thus if a father tries to murder his child or his wife, Tyrrell insists they have a right to defend themselves (Tyrrell 1681, 23–4). A ruler who leaves no recourse open to the subject who is the victim of injustice obliges him to consider whether he will regard the government as having been dissolved and lay claim to his natural right to punish his oppressor. In short, he creates a state of war in which subject and ruler meet as juristic equals. This has the unfortunate consequence that it makes the individual a judge in his own cause, but this is inescapable; and there are certain types of injustice (e.g., in England, taxation without consent) that are so transparent that individuals need not hesitate to trust to their own judgement. In such circumstances each individual must (as Hunton had argued) decide in the light of his own conscience whether to support the government or join the rebellion (Tyrrell 1681, *132*, *153–4*, 218–19, 229, 231, 235). In Tyrrell's view one should only rebel if one is defending the public good, not in order to protect a merely private interest. In Locke's view men have an inalienable right to stand up for themselves; but rebellion will be futile if others do not recognize that the interests you are defending are theirs too (Locke 2.§§167, 208–9).

Both accept that it is a principle of the English constitution that the King cannot be held to have done wrong, and cannot be punished, although those acting under his orders can. There is thus no constitutional, but only a natural, right to hold a King of England to account, and this right can be exercised only when his actions have gone so far as to destroy his claim to authority (Tyrrell 1681, *159*, 231; Locke 2.§205).

In other words, almost all the principles that we think of as being distinctly Lockean are in fact borrowed by Locke from Tyrrell. Some of Tyrrell's arguments were far from original: he is deeply in debt to Pufendorf for his theory of natural freedom; part of his resistance theory comes from Hunton; and his theory of a natural right to punish comes from Grotius. Locke had certainly read Grotius for himself. He bought a key work of Pufendorf's in May 1681 (Locke 1967b, 143). He may never have read Hunton. In each case, though, Tyrrell had selected from his sources precisely those elements that Locke was to draw upon. We do not need to think of Locke writing with a large pile of volumes on his desk: all he needed was Tyrrell. And, with Tyrrell to hand, he must have been able to work quickly. All he had to do was isolate the arguments I have identified from Tyrrell's long-winded text, and decide in what order to present them. Nevertheless, there are fundamental differences between Locke's argument and Tyrrell's, and it is those differences that make the *Second Treatise*, not *Patriarcha non Monarcha*, the founding text of liberal political theory.

The key difference is simple. In Locke's view no contract entered into under duress is valid (Locke 2.§§23, 176). A Christian captured and sold as a slave in Algiers has the right to escape. In Tyrrell's view (and this seems to have been Locke's view in the *First Treatise*) there was no simple distinction to be made between choice and compulsion. A merchant who throws his cargo overboard during a storm so that the ship will float higher in the waves has acted under compulsion, but he has also acted voluntarily. A captive may reach agreement with his captor that he will not try to escape if the other will feed him and not work him to death (Tyrrell 1681, 103–9, *122*). Tyrrell calls such a contract a contract for slavery; Locke, who insists in the *Second Treatise* that compact and slavery are incompatible, would call it drudgery (Locke 2.§24). On Tyrrell's view slave-owners do not have the right to kill their slaves, once they are out of chains; on Locke's view they do. Tyrrell's broad definition of a voluntary action thus gives virtually everyone, including slaves, some rights. The position of a slave should be no worse than that of a serf, who could own no property, yet if he was killed his wife could have recourse to the courts.

Tyrrell's broad definition of a voluntary action, however, means that (despite his insistence that certain rights are inalienable) he thinks that there can be legitimate absolute governments, for one may alienate everything but one's right to life (and to freedom of worship) to the government. For Locke, by contrast, absolute governments cannot be legitimate because they provide for no impartial arbitrator in disputes between the subject and his ruler, and so leave subject and ruler in a state of nature with regard to each other (Locke 2.§13). In Locke's view, everyone who is not a slave has a right not only to life, but also to property. Locke's narrow definition of a voluntary action means that no one can be compelled to give up his or her right to property. Promises made to highwaymen are not binding, nor are contracts imposed on the conquered by their conquerors. Only a limited government that recognizes that all individuals (other than slaves) have a broad range of rights can be legitimate. Locke thus insists on a more extensive definition of inalienable rights as a consequence of his narrow definition of a voluntary action.

There is a second important difference between Tyrrell and Locke. Both insist that property exists in a state of nature; that political society is established to protect property; and that political society also regulates property, determining, for example, whether daughters can inherit as well as sons. (The protection of property is only a primary reason in Tyrrell's view, while it is the sole reason in Locke's, for establishing government. The difference between them on this point derives from the fact that Locke has a more extensive definition of property, including property in oneself and one's rights – although Tyrrell at one point implies that one's life is a property.) But in Locke's view the purpose of political society is to protect property rights established prior to its existence, and so, even in political society, there can be no taxation without consent. In Tyrrell's view the creation of political society voids all previous property rights, for it replaces a purely personal relationship between a particular individual and his property by a legal relationship that is no longer necessarily dependent on occupancy or labour. In a state of nature, because property rights are purely personal, there is no right to inherit. My labour can establish a right only for me: when I die the right dies with me (Tyrrell 1681, 49). If I leave the lecture theatre at the end of the lecture, I have no claim on the seat if I return later in the day. Locke on the other hand insists that there is a natural right of inheritance. As a consequence I can have a right to land I have never worked, to goods I have never purchased, and political society is obliged to protect my right to the product of the labour of others.

In Tyrrell's view what drives men into society is growing density of population (*108–14*). As all the land comes to be cultivated there is none left over for others, and conflicts become inevitable. Political society establishes a division of land that overrides the natural obligation to leave as good for others and to take only what you can use, leaving in their place only a limited duty of charity to the dispossessed. For some, political society is therefore disadvantageous (*107*). They are obliged either to emigrate to where there is still common land available, or to accept the status quo because it is in the interests of mankind as a whole, even if it is not in their own interests.

In Locke's view, even before population density has inevitably led to the disappearance of land as a common property, the invention of money as an agreed store of wealth makes possible accumulation beyond the immediate needs of the individual and his family, bringing with it the extension of land ownership and the growth of commercial society. Here too the old limitations on the accumulation of property disappear, but not out of necessity. Rather men have agreed to waive them. And such agreement is reasonable because everyone is a beneficiary. The growth of commerce and the improvement of land increase productivity, so that in commercial society everyone is better off than in a primitive society: there are no losers, even if some gain more than others (Locke 2.§§37, 40–50).

Locke's definition of property is thus more extensive than Tyrrell's in three respects: it includes our property in ourselves, our right to inherit wealth, and our entitlement to accumulate wealth. In his view, then, political society merely protects a broad range of natural property rights; while in Tyrrell's view political society replaces natural rights by governmentally determined ones. In Locke's view our natural right to property acts as a continuing check on the powers of government; while in Tyrrell's view we have few inalienable rights beyond a natural right to life.

Locke's narrow definition of a voluntary action and his broad definition of natural property rights thus make all the difference between his political theory and Tyrrell's. On his theory all absolute governments are illegitimate, as is all taxation without representation. On Tyrrell's view it is merely a historical fact that England is a limited not an absolute monarchy, and that Englishmen have the right not to be taxed without the consent of Parliament. Over time these rights may come to be extended, or they may be lost. Tyrrell approves of the rebels who imposed Magna Carta on the King; but it is difficult to see how he could justify their action if one could show they were seeking to establish new rights, not reaffirm old ones. Nor is it surprising that Tyrrell was to find it hard to justify the exclusion of James II's son from the throne (Carlyle 1885–1900). If James might be resisted because he sought to destroy the constitution, this did not mean that a Convention Parliament had the right substantially to alter it. To do this the agreement of the King would be necessary; even if James could be held to have abdicated, no one could disinherit his son. Tyrrell thus (like Hunton before him) has a clear concept of the natural and civil right to resist tyranny; but he is far from clear that we have any right to change the existing constitution by non-constitutional means.

There is a third important difference between Locke's political theory and Tyrrell's. Both were in principle committed to a systematic individualism by their view that all men are born free. But Tyrrell was happy to accept that, because patriarchal households were a natural development, it was appropriate for heads of households to act on behalf of their wives, children, and servants. The consent that was needed to establish a government was thus not the consent of all – Tyrrell dreaded democracy – but only the consent of independent adult males 'at their own dispose' (Tyrrell 1681, 73–4). Locke was much more consistent in applying the principle that nobody could act on another's behalf without their genuine consent. He never claims that heads of households can act for their servants, or employers for their employees, in political affairs. Implicit in Locke's argument was thus the possibility of a democratic conception of consent. Tyrrell, on the other hand, not only allowed servants to be bound by their masters, but also insisted that we should consider ourselves bound by the decisions of our ancestors. A people, he said when at his most Burkean, was like a river: individuals might be born and die, just as drops of rain entered the stream and eventually reached the ocean. But the nation, the constitution, the political community could survive substantially unchanged, just as the river did (77). Locke, by contrast, was keen to insist that the fact that things had been done in a certain way in the past did not imply that they ought to be done that way in the future. There was no need for the river to continue to run between its old banks.

Locke had constructed a systematic liberalism on the foundations provided by Tyrrell. But precisely because his argument was more systematic, it was harder to reconcile it with the real world. On Locke's view, as on Tyrrell's, nobody could be born a slave; but nobody could be born into servitude either. The clear implication of Locke's argument was that there could be no chattel slavery of any sort, while Tyrrell's argument implied that slaves had some rights, but not necessarily the right to freedom. Similarly Locke's argument, by refusing to treat servants as consenting to the actions of their employers, was fundamentally egalitarian; but this egalitarianism could be reconciled with the existing constitution of England only if one assumed that most people living in England had no right to representation because they were not properly citizens; in which case, of course, they were under no obligation to defend those who were. Locke's insistence on an obligation to preserve oneself makes it hard to see how anyone could be obliged to fight; even if citizens could impose such an obligation on each other, they certainly could not impose it on non-citizens. A conscript army, on Locke's principles, implies a democratic constitution.

Locke's adaptation of Tyrrell thus had dangerously radical implications for slavery and oligarchy. Whether he accepted these implications reluctantly or willingly, or whether he thought there was some way in which he could evade them, we do not know, any more than we know if he approved or disapproved when his close friend Molyneux took up the arguments of the *Second Treatise* in *The Case of Ireland* (1698), and used them to claim that the Protestant Irish had a right of self-government, a line of argument which provoked the obvious and dangerous riposte that if the Protestants could lay claim to such rights, so too could the Catholics (Hont 1990, 80–84; Dunn 1969b, 66). But these subversive implications were the necessary consequence of extending the natural rights of men and women to the point where it was clear that they had a right to rebel, not just when their religion was overthrown, but when there was the danger that it might be; not just when their property was taxed without their consent, but when their legislature was prevented from meeting; not just when all were in danger, but merely when the actions of the government against a few seemed to jeopardize the security of all.

In order to establish a right to resistance in the circumstances that obtained in the summer of 1681, Locke had to formulate a political theory more radical than any constructed since the Restoration. For us the obvious precursors are the Levellers, and perhaps Locke was influenced by them. His language, for example, is often reminiscent of Edward Sexby's classic defence of tyrannicide in *Killing No Murder* (Wootton 1986, 360–88). But whatever other works may have been to hand as he wrote the *Second Treatise*, his main purpose was to produce a radical reconstruction of the argument of *Patriarcha non Monarcha*. There is no evidence that Locke had adopted liberal political principles before the dissolution of the Oxford Parliament and the trial of Fitzharris. His liberalism does not date from his first meeting with Shaftesbury, or from the publication of *A Letter from a Person of Quality to his Friend in the*

Country, or from the beginning of the Exclusion Crisis. It was a hasty response to a combination of events. On the one hand there were the political events of the spring and summer of 1681: without these the *Second Treatise* is inconceivable. On the other, though, and equally important, there was a remarkable intellectual event: the publication of *Patriarcha non Monarcha*. Tyrrell's work was a compendium of radical arguments, some old but many new, and yet its author flinched before radical conclusions. Intellectually, he failed to take voluntary consent seriously enough. Personally, he compromised, bowdlerizing his book as it went through the press.

For such compromises Locke had no time. His argument made no concessions to constitutional propriety. He seemed to leave no space at all for juristic inequality. If he defended economic inequality, he also insisted that nobody should suffer as a result of it. In the circumstances of the time the *Second Treatise* was completely unpublishable, and likely to remain so. Its most probable consequence would be the arrest and execution of its author on charges similar to those faced by Fitzharris, College, and, eventually, Sidney. As early as July 1681 Locke was hiding copies out of harm's way (somewhat ironically, Tyrrell was the first to be entrusted with Locke's parcel of papers, though he was not told what they contained), for Locke was already fearful that his rooms would be searched.

Had the *Second Treatise* been intended as the manifesto of a political movement, we could understand why Locke might have taken such risks to write it. But, if I am right about its date, there was nothing timely in what he had to say when he first said it. The only thing to be said in favour of his argument was that it was self-evidently right. And, as far as we can tell, Locke never did persuade himself to think differently. When the argument was once more a political liability, when Locke had become a loyal supporter of an established government, he continued to work on revising the *Second Treatise*, and took steps to ensure its posthumous publication.

Interlude: Seeds and trees; locks and ciphers

From 1681 to 1688 Locke was a political activist suspected of operating outside the law, first in England and then in Holland. It is very hard for us now, at this distance in time, to establish exactly what he was doing, to learn how far (or indeed whether) he was involved in the Rye House Plot, the planning of Monmouth's invasion, and the preparations for William's invasion. Locke was an immensely cautious man; which was fortunate for him, for he was in a situation where caution was absolutely necessary, where a false step might lead to his death. In the winter of 1685, for example, when Locke happened to be writing the *Letter Concerning Toleration*, the English government was seeking to have him extradited from Holland. Extradition would have led to a trial, and a trial, in the circumstances of the time, to condemnation. Even if the government's attempts to extradite him should fail, there was a real risk of kidnapping or assassination by government agents. We should scarcely be surprised that Locke went into hiding under an assumed name. What we cannot tell is quite how far the suspicions of the government were justified.

This sceptical view was challenged by Richard Ashcraft in *Revolutionary Politics and Locke's 'Two Treatises of Government'* (1986), a work that opened a new chapter in the history of Locke scholarship. Ashcraft set out to make a case for Locke's active involvement in revolutionary activity between 1681 and 1688. The reading of Locke's political thought that I am presenting here does not depend on this particular part of Ashcraft's overall argument being either true or false. But since the argument is of considerable intrinsic interest, it is worth pausing for a moment to look at the evidence on which it is based. Moreover Ashcraft wishes to interpret Locke as the spokesman for a political movement. If he can show that Locke was deeply and continuously involved in political conspiracies, his reading of the *Second Treatise* is strengthened. If he cannot, it becomes easier to view the *Second Treatise* as a work which Locke valued for intellectual as much as for immediate political reasons.

Ashcraft successfully shows that conspirators in the 1680s adopted a series of catch phrases and coded terms with which to identify each other and to test out the allegiances of those outside their circle. Thus discussion of the duty of resistance to an invader could prepare the ground for insinuating that James II was no better than an invader.[22] But Ashcraft suspects the existence of more specific codes that he thinks he can identify in the letters to and from Locke: conspiratorial codes designed to convey secret information and instructions. Certainly Locke did employ codes for some of his communications: false names, or numbers in place of names, were designed to protect friends and associates should his correspondence fall into government hands. Was he, though, engaged in a common conspiracy with these friends and associates, and if so with which of them? Ashcraft's problem here is that, once one starts reading a text looking for hidden meanings, one is likely to find them where none exist. So, for example, Tyrrell wrote a chatty letter to Locke on 27 May 1683, in which he remarked 'A dog fell mad last week, and has bit divers children and amongst the rest Jo. Clark's little boy (a very pretty child) by the hand.' This was written around the time the Rye House Plot was discovered by the government, and probably received by Locke just before he went into hiding. Ashcraft concedes that Tyrrell is scarcely likely to have been one of the Rye House Plotters; he has no evidence that Tyrrell knew more than Locke about the discovery of the plot; or that Locke and Tyrrell had established a code with which to communicate. Nevertheless, on the basis primarily of the coincidence in timing, he concludes that 'the message could be a warning to Locke', and that it was as a result of receiving it that Locke went into hiding (Ashcraft 1986, 387–8).

Frankly, I find this implausible. Locke had spent a great deal of time at Tyrrell's house, and we need not be surprised to find Tyrrell entertaining him with gossip about friends and neighbours. To suggest that this sentence was anything more than gossip we would need to be confident that Locke could ascribe to it a determinate meaning. To do this he would have needed to know more than that references to 'mad dogs' were sometimes employed in discussions about the government. He would have had to know who was meant by 'Jo. Clark's little boy', for otherwise he would have had no way of knowing that the government's action was a threat to him in particular. This, though, implies that Locke and Tyrrell would have had occasion to establish a sophisticated code for communication: yet this is scarcely plausible if Tyrrell was not a co-conspirator, for if he was not, why would he and Locke have expected to have secret information to impart to each other? Ashcraft has not established the existence of a code, or successfully

deciphered a coded message. Nor has he shown that secret information has in fact been conveyed. In the circumstances, though the
coincidence in timing is suspicious, it seems wisest to conclude that
there was indeed a mad dog, and that Tyrrell's neighbour's child
really was pretty.

One of Ashcraft's most persuasive claims is that Locke was
engaged in a coded correspondence with his friend Edward Clarke,
in which references to plants stood for references to troops and
guns. Ashcraft claims to be able to decode these letters (although he makes no attempt to show that he has truly 'cracked' a
code, as opposed to merely guessing at hidden meanings). The
crucial piece of evidence that seems to justify his procedure is a
letter from Locke to Clarke that Clarke annotated: 'J.L. his letter
received the 2d February 1684 [i.e. 1685 new style]: with an account
of seeds etc. and some ciphers on it' (below, p. 389). Ashcraft
thinks the coded passages are those that refer to the shipping of
various sorts of seeds, the planting of trees around Clarke's house,
the impact of winter frost on cypresses, and the statement 'If I had
your coat of arms in colours, I would get it done in glass to be set
up somewhere at Chipley, being very well acquainted with a good
glass painter here,' for he believes that the 'glass painter' is Argyll,
who was a leading figure in Monmouth's invasion (Ashcraft 1986,
452–3).

As it happens, Locke's letters and private papers are full of
references to seeds and plants, most of which simply reflect his
fascination with gardening. There is nothing inherently suspicious
about a letter from Locke to Clarke about gardening. Even if the
correspondence is suspicious, it seems rash indeed to claim that we
can divine its meaning, for there are simply far too many details
that might be significant. If the trees are supposed to stand for
'forty foot soldiers to be set up in the neighbourhood of Chipley' in
the event of an uprising, as Ashcraft believes, why does Locke also
want to write about turnips and parsnips? Again, if the trees are
soldiers, why must they be twenty feet from the house? And why is
Locke concerned about the unsatisfactory impression they will make
until they are full grown? Or about how many different sorts of
trees are required? These details are entirely unproblematic as long
as we assume Locke was talking about real trees but become incom-

prehensible if we assume that Locke is not writing about trees at all. That Ashcraft's interpretation was arbitrary and unsupported should have been evident even before Mark Goldie confirmed that Clarke was busy planting trees in the winter of 1684–5 (Goldie 1992). Perhaps, too, Locke really did know a glass painter. Ashcraft claimed that references in the correspondence to a Nurse Trent were coded references to a fellow conspirator, John Trenchard, but, thanks to Goldie, we now know there was a real Nurse Trent who had care of Clarke's children.

Of course it is possible that all these realistic details were a blind to distract a suspicious reader's attention from the real nugget of information being conveyed, but the problem is that we need evidence to sort out the background noise from the message, and it is precisely this evidence that is lacking. Ashcraft summarizes the end of the letter as follows: 'After mentioning some other "trees", Locke advises his friend "to examine the gardens and see how many of them were left last summer." That is, after the government's discovery of Argyll's initial plans for an invasion and its arrest of some English radicals.' Perhaps, is the most one can say. For the winter of 1683–4 had been a harsh one, and yew and holly are genuinely hardy. We might as well conclude that Locke was advising Clarke to trust two individuals referred to by the code names 'yew' and 'holly', but not three others, 'phylrea', 'alaternus', 'cypress'. And indeed a host of other explanations would do as well.

What gives Ashcraft's quest for an interpretation its apparent justification is Clarke's annotation referring to 'ciphers'. But this means less than at first appears, for the word 'cipher' is ambiguous: it can refer to a code or, equally, to a diagram or ideogram. It is most improbable that Clarke would label a coded message as containing a code, for up until 1688 he had reason to fear that the authorities might go through his papers, and his practice seems to have been to endorse letters as he received them, for how else would he know the date of receipt? Clarke's reference then ought to be an innocent reference to some sort of diagram or ideogram. Ashcraft makes no mention of the central paragraph of the letter:

I remember Adrian sent me word he could not get the key into the lock of a chest of mine wherein were some clothes. This has sometimes happened to me, for there is a square spike in the lock which goes into the hollow of the key, which if it stands not right the key will not go in, and then the spike in the lock must be turned a little with a pair of nippers or compasses so that the square of it may stand right with the square of the hollow of the key to go into it, and then the key will go in. But when the key is in there requires yet some skill to open the lock, to which purpose I left with him a circle drawn with marks. Pray remember that

    this mark   stands for degrees and
    this   for minutes.

My initial reaction on reading this was to think that Ashcraft had gone far astray. Here are the ideograms or 'ciphers', and, once one has an innocent explanation for Clarke's endorsement, there is no longer any concrete evidence that the letter is in code.

Still there is a puzzle here. We know that Locke had left something he believed to be dangerous in a chest in England (the standard hypothesis is that it was the text of the *Two Treatises*), so that we must have our doubts as to the purpose of any discussion of chests (Yolton 1985, 6–8). Suspicious readers, too, will wonder at the coincidence of Locke discussing locks. But the real problem lies in the illogic of the text. No diagram showing one how to open a lock would need to be marked in minutes of a degree; one is bound to suspect that Adrian has misinterpreted some secret communication, and that Locke is reminding him how to decode it, how to unlock the lock. If so our problem is simple: we do not have the message, or lock, only part of the key or (in Ashcraft's sense) cipher. We may have evidence in our hands that Clarke, Adrian, and Locke were engaged in a common conspiracy, but we have no good evidence as to what that conspiracy was.

A Letter Concerning Toleration

There is a remarkable difference between the literature on *A Letter Concerning Toleration* and that on the *Second Treatise*. Since Laslett, it has been apparent that historical information provides valuable assistance in interpreting the *Second Treatise*, and numerous commentators have felt able to interpret Locke's arguments without constant reference forward to our own views. Nozick and Rawls may mention Locke's *Second Treatise*, but those writing about the *Second Treatise* do not feel under any necessary obligation to mention Nozick and Rawls. But the simple truth is that nobody has been able to provide an adequate treatment of *A Letter Concerning Toleration* within the conventions of the history of ideas.[23] Consequently, almost everybody who writes about it writes in a curiously mixed mode: on the one hand they explain that the text is a survival from another era, written in alien circumstances; but on the other they quickly proceed to compare Locke's arguments to those used here and now.

Locke's *Letter* defies satisfactory historical analysis because we cannot adequately situate it in a biographical, political, or intellectual context. Scholars who try to contextualize it offer not one specific context, but a range of possible contexts. Should we, for example, compare the *Letter* primarily with the *Essay* of 1667, and then trace in it the impact of the political theory which Locke had constructed in the *Second Treatise*? In that case the fact that the letter was written in Holland, in November and December 1685, is irrelevant. But wait: 1685 is the year in which a Catholic, James II, came to the throne in England. To insist, as Locke does in the *Letter*, that there should be toleration, but not toleration for Catholics, is to turn one's back on any possibility of reconciliation with the government in England, which was likely to try (and soon did try) to obtain toleration for both Dissenters and Catholics. William Penn and, indeed, many of Locke's closest Whig associates in England, including Clarke, were soon to reconcile themselves with the government of James, but Locke was not (Goldie 1992). So the *Letter* would seem to have a contemporary English context.

1685 is also the year in which Louis XIV revoked the Edict of Nantes. Subjected to horrifying cruelty in their native land, French Protestants flooded into Holland. Many of them, despite a long Huguenot tradition of insisting on obedience to the civil power, argued that they had a right of resistance against the tyranny of their King. In this context Locke's *Letter* reads as a radical defence of the rights of French Protestants. Locke was also writing in Holland, where there was a state Church, and no formal legislation guaranteeing toleration. But there was a general and informal toleration in practice: toleration not only of Arminians, Lutherans, and Socinians, but also of Jews and Catholics. Read in a Dutch context, Locke's attack on Catholicism seems strangely indifferent to the fact that no harm had come to the Dutch from their extension of toleration to Catholics. Locke's arguments in this context seem almost intolerant.

Thus we have only the loosest of biographical contexts, and a surfeit of divergent political contexts. Matters do not improve when we turn from the political context to the intellectual one. What did Locke read on toleration between 1667 and 1685? Certainly he read a number of Socinian works, but the separation between Church and State on which he insisted in 1685 he did not learn from them, for he had already argued for it in 1667. In the winter of 1685–6 he was reading drafts of Limborch's *Theologia Christiana*, published in 1686: perhaps he read the two chapters in that work on toleration before he wrote his *Letter*. Certainly he was meeting with Limborch at the time, and it was to Limborch (with whom he corresponded in Latin) that the original Latin text, eventually published in Holland in 1689, was addressed, although the identities of both author and addressee were concealed from all but each other, their names replaced by coded initials. But it is hard to see that Limborch had any specific impact on Locke's text.

If only Locke had written the *Letter* in the winter of 1686–7, not that of 1685–6! In 1686 Pierre Bayle, a sceptical Huguenot refugee pretending to write as an unknown Englishman, published his *Commentaire philosophique sur ces paroles de Jésus Christ: 'Contrains-les d'entrer'*. This was the most incisive defence of toleration written in the seventeenth century, better, competent philosophers insist, than Locke's *Letter* (Kilcullen 1988). Locke may have been the author of the review that appeared in the *Bibliothèque Universelle* (Colie 1960, 124–5). Damaris Cudworth wrote to him about the book, praising it to the skies. He certainly bought a copy, and must have enjoyed noting the similarities between Bayle's argument and his own. But we cannot use the *Commentaire philosophique* to explain the *Letter*, nor has anyone shown that the similarities between Locke's position and Bayle's derive from shared assumptions that are peculiarly their own. We might of course argue that Locke had been influenced by Bayle's earlier works, but there is no evidence that he ever read the one that would be most relevant for our purposes, the *Critique générale* directed against the Jesuit Maimbourg.

In short, we cannot (it seems) pin the *Letter* down by establishing Locke's sources, by identifying those specific arguments he is seeking to adopt, transform, or attack. We have to work from the text alone, so that it is not surprising if we quickly find ourselves wondering whether we agree with it, whether it makes sense. Before we know it, the context in which we are reading it has become that of contemporary philosophy. And yet, strangely, this does not necessarily take us far from the work's historical context. The most influential critique of the argument of the *Letter* written by a contemporary philosopher is that by Jeremy Waldron (1988). Waldron insists he is doing philosophy not history, but he ends up admitting that he is simply restating the criticisms of Locke's position published by the Anglican Tory Jonas Proast in 1690 (Proast 1984). His basic claim is that Locke had no answer to those criticisms. Time, one might be forgiven for thinking, has stood still, and the clock has stopped in 1690. It seems futile, as far as this text is concerned, to separate out the tasks of the historian and the philosopher. Both, I think, have missed the true intellectual significance of the *Letter*.

Our question then is 'Does Locke have a valid argument against persecution, and if so what is it?' We need first to note that the *Letter Concerning Toleration* is partly a work about what Christians should believe. Locke insists that toleration is the mark of a true Church; that the clergy should preach peace and love; and that the true Church should not require that its members believe more than is specified in the Gospel as necessary for salvation. He implies that the ceremonies of the Church should be closely based on biblical precedents. He is apparently reluctant in conceding that authority in a Church is properly exercised by bishops or presbyters, and is unhappy at the thought that a convention of clergymen can claim to represent the Church as a whole. He suggests that there may well be more than one 'true' Church, that those issues on which the Churches are in conflict are of secondary importance or 'indifferent'. He insists that the Mosaic law against idolatry no longer applies (although one may wonder whether, on his arguments, it can ever have been just, even if ordained by God). And he claims that there is no commission in the Gospel for persecution (ignoring the parable in which Christ says that his guests should be compelled to come in to the feast). The *Letter* is thus partly a religious tract, and the religion it upholds is very much that which we have come to expect from Locke. Again and again his arguments are at odds with the practices and claims of the Anglican Church. For example, he claims that the only punishment Churches should be able to impose is that of excommunication, and this should have no secular consequences. In England, Church courts had traditionally had extensive jurisdiction in cases involving, for example, adultery, and had been able to impose fines and other punishments.

In 1685 Locke was writing as an anonymous private individual, a member of no Church. When he wrote the *Second Letter Concerning Toleration* (1690) in defence of the *Letter*, he chose, even though he was still writing anonymously, to pretend that he was not its author, but merely someone who approved of its key arguments. And he chose to write as a member of the Church of England. Locke thus distanced himself from the religious radicalism of the *Letter*. This meant that he set to one side the specifically Christian arguments against persecution that he had pressed in the *Letter*. In their place he offered an idealized account of the pastoral role of the clergy that was compatible with Anglicanism.

In Waldron's view Locke's key argument is not Christian at all: it is the claim that the state can shape only behaviour, not belief, through punishments. Punishments do not serve to change beliefs because we cannot change what we think merely because we are told to, not even if we want to. Consequently it is irrational to punish people for what they believe. And therefore the state has no business interfering with beliefs. Having isolated this as Locke's best argument (on the somewhat strange ground that it is his most Weberian), Waldron then claims that the argument is defective. As Proast insisted, social pressures do affect what people think. Government intervention to punish dissent is not irrational or necessarily ineffectual. Censorship, for example, can significantly affect the information we have access to, and the beliefs we consequently come to hold. Locke is wrong to claim that persecution will not work: indeed he admits in his reply to Proast that sometimes it will. His argument is concerned with what is rational behaviour on the part of a government, not with what is right for citizens; with what is effective, not with what is legitimate. As such it is fundamentally misconceived. Locke should have argued, not from the Weberian premise that it is the peculiar attribute of the state to lay claim to a monopoly of force, but from what we might think of as a properly liberal premise, that of the rights of citizens. Locke's argument, in short, is insufficiently Lockean.

If Locke's argument was really open to this attack it would be a poor thing indeed. Waldron admits that he has engaged in inequitable exaggeration. What he does not admit is that Locke three times restates his key arguments, and that each time he appeals not to one argument but three (below, pp. 394–6; 405–6; 407–8 and, the third argument, p. 410). Our task then is to see what the relationship of these three arguments is to each other.

The first argument is not about what is rational for rulers, but about what is rational for subjects. It is not rational for subjects to hand over to their rulers responsibility for deciding what they should believe. And this because they would be placing an obligation on themselves that they could not be confident of fulfilling. The ruler may tell me to be a Hindu, but he cannot make me believe. And I cannot agree that he is doing me any good if he makes me act contrary to my beliefs. Consequently I ought to regard my right to think for myself as inalienable. In no rational original contract will I cede control over belief to the magistrate. Note that this argument does not claim that there may not be all sorts of external factors that will affect what I believe. Locke explicitly discussed in the *Essay Concerning Human Understanding* the way in which censorship warped the judgement of those who were denied information relevant to a decision (Locke 1975, bk IV, ch. 20 §4). He was very clear, as we have seen, in his earliest writings that we are all under strong pressure from public opinion to conform to convention. In his second reply to Proast, the *Third Letter Concerning Toleration*, he recognizes that educators seek to shape the opinions of their charges (Locke 1899, 235). The point is not that these pressures do not usually work; it is simply that if I oblige myself to conform I am entering into an obligation that I may not be able to fulfil, and the price for non-fulfilment is likely to be unacceptably high. His argument, then, is about what sort of state is in the moral interests of its citizens. Locke sees that it makes sense to write a contract for the sale of a house that provides for circumstances in which the contract will be void – e.g. I promise to sell my house to you next year if I do not die in the meantime – but cannot see how one can contract to believe when one cannot control one's own beliefs, nor specify the conditions under which one may, in fact, not believe. A contract to believe in Christianity is superfluous, providing one does believe; oppressive if one does not.

Locke's second argument is the one on which Waldron concentrates his attention. We shall see in a moment if it is open to the objections he makes against it.

His third argument is that it is not rational for a subject to let the magistrate decide for him, even if it is the case that magistrates can make people believe whatever they want. Rulers are not impartial: they, and the clergy who support them, have corrupt interests in furthering their own power and wealth. They are not necessarily learned. Of all the possible ways I might adopt for determining which religion I should hold, that of holding the religion of my ruler is not the most likely to lead to the correct choice. Indeed, there are many rulers in the world, and they uphold many different religions. Consequently if there is only one true religion the odds are that my ruler upholds a false one.[24] I am betting against the odds, and once again the price of losing is too high; I am not just gambling with my worldly wealth (for loss of which the ruler could in any case compensate me) but with my eternal happiness. Note again that this argument does not claim that people do in fact choose their faith on rational grounds. Montaigne and Charron had notoriously argued that we are Protestants and Catholics for the same reason that we are Germans or Frenchmen, because of the accident of where we are born: as Locke puts it, men 'owe their eternal happiness or misery to the places of their nativity' (below, p. 396). The claim is that it is irrational of men to have allowed this situation to occur. They ought to see that it cannot be in their interests to allow their rulers (or their neighbours) to take these decisions for them.

Now this third argument explicitly allows for the possibility that the first two arguments (which Waldron mistakenly elides into one) are false. Even so, allowing a magistrate – or a Church chosen by the magistrate – to decide for me is not rational. Crucial to this argument is a point which Locke turns to again and again: it makes no difference if the magistrate assures me that he will make the right choice for me. For all rulers claim to make the right choice, and perhaps all believe they do in fact do so, and yet most of them must be making the wrong one. Locke's argument is thus a sceptical one based on the simple fact that magistrates do not agree among themselves. Neither the magistrate's assurance that he is right, nor his conviction that he is right, is worth anything unless there is some independent reason for thinking he is right. And there is, in the end, no impartial judge of any such independent reason, so that individuals must ultimately decide for themselves.

Locke's first argument thus depends not on the claim that the state cannot determine what I believe, but on the lesser claim that it may not succeed in doing so. Under what circumstances is it rational for me to commit myself to an action (in this case, the act of believing) that I may not be able to fulfil? Answer: Only under circumstances where I can insure against failure, or the consequences of failure are slight. These circumstances do not obtain as far as religion is concerned. His third argument admits that the state may be able to determine what I believe. Even so, is it rational to give it the opportunity to do so? Answer: Only if it seems likely to make me believe the right thing. But, since I know it is unlikely to choose well, I can scarcely be worse off choosing for myself (or allowing someone more impartial than the government to choose for me).

The conclusion of both of these arguments is that I ought not to agree to the government making religious decisions on my behalf; that this is no proper part of its functions. Now Waldron pushes aside any argument from the state's functions by appealing to Weber: historically states have done anything and everything. Locke of course does not doubt that historically states have sought to make religious decisions for their subjects. Waldron thinks that he is simply claiming that they ought not to have done so. 'Amongst all the tasks that states have undertaken, the question of which fall into the class of the proper functions of government is an important one; but it has to be a matter of argument, not of essentialist definition' (Waldron 1988, 64). What Waldron fails to notice is that it is precisely this complex argument about the proper functions of government, looked at from the point of view of the interests of the citizen, that Locke is concerned with, and that he returns to again and again in his dispute with Proast. Proast and Waldron try to escape the whole issue that Locke is raising – can I trust the government to decide on my behalf? – by saying that of course the state should not compel people to believe a false religion, only the true one (Waldron 1988, 72). Both Locke and Bayle thought that this was the most transparent and ridiculous equivocation, for it presumes that we have the answer to what we are trying to find out, that we know that the state will make the right choice. It is sensible for me to let the state decide conflicts over property for me, because my own decisions in a state of nature would be partial and unenforceable. Moreover it is not too difficult to construct a state that has an interest in getting such decisions right: the state can be made not only powerful, but also impartial.[25] And such decisions can be enforced: property can be forcibly transferred from one party to another, while beliefs cannot be forcibly imposed. There are no comparable arguments, Locke believes, for thinking that I will benefit from giving up my independent right of judgement in matters of religion.

Locke recognizes that it is often sensible to allow others to make decisions for us. If a mathematician tells me I have got my sums wrong, I should try to learn from him, not argue with him. But religious beliefs are not about deductive certainties but, in the end, about the reliability of testimony to matters of fact. Did Christ rise from the dead? What is involved here is a judgement of probability, but one of a peculiar sort. I can entrust my money to an investment company who think the market is going to rise when I happen to think it will fall. If they are right I will profit, and if they are wrong I will lose. But in the case of religion I cannot in this way hand the decision over to someone who I suspect is better informed than I. For in the case of religion, only sincere believers can hope to be rewarded: this was the standard objection of the Protestants to the 'blind faith' they believed was required by Catholicism. It is as if I could profit only when the market's movements and my personal beliefs happened to coincide. In such circumstances it would be dangerous for me to allow my broker to put any pressure on me, for fear that I might end up agreeing with him out of laziness or a desire to please or seem knowledgeable. Religious judgements are thus peculiar ones. Most judgements simply have to be right, but religious judgements also need to be mine, not someone else's; and they need to be sincere, not careless (Mendus 1989).

Locke's first and third arguments are thus explorations of problems in decision-making theory, problems concerning making decisions on the basis of judgements of probabilities, and making decisions that not only have to be correct, but must also be reached in the right way. In this respect their real intellectual context is the intellectual revolution that Ian Hacking has christened 'the emergence of probability' (Hacking 1975). Locke's *Essay Concerning Human Understanding* was intended to be a contribution to that revolution, and we can now begin to see that the *Letter Concerning Toleration* is not just a text that echoes the contractualist political theory and the resistance arguments of the *Second Treatise*; it is also directed to problems central to the discussion of probability and decision-making in the *Essay*.

Proast and Waldron, by trying to sidestep these problems, miss much of the point of Locke's argument. An obvious test is Waldron's claim that Locke has no adequate reply to the argument that it may be rational for rulers, looking at things from their point of view, to persecute if they want to instil sincere belief. Locke has three answers to Proast on this point, but here again Waldron behaves as if he had only one (Waldron 1988, 84). (1) Locke argues that legislation against dissent is not the same as legislation against unbelief, and that all Proast's arguments serve only to justify persecuting unbelievers in general, not dissenters in particular. What of cynical unbelievers who go to church? What of churchgoers who are simply ignorant of the doctrine they are supposed to believe? The problem is that there is no way of identifying the real category with which Proast is concerned – unbelievers – in order to isolate them for punishment. Dissenters are only a subset of unbelievers, and it is unfair to pass a law that is bound to be unenforceable against most of those who break it. This is an argument directed against the legitimacy, not the efficacy, of persecution. It assumes that the government is concerned with saving souls and instilling belief, not (as Locke insists is in fact the case) simply with suppressing dissent. And it assumes that to be legitimate a law must be appropriate to its avowed purpose: a law that is inequitable in its application is inherently illegitimate. (2) Locke argues that legislation intended to make dissenters think again (which was, according to Proast, the purpose of persecution) will affect only a subset of dissenters, those who have not thought hard about the question already. It is unjust to adopt a policy that punishes people for not doing something that they may in fact have done. Those dissenters who have thought hard and long are being punished in order to get at those who have not, and whose views may yet be changed. As Waldron says, this implies that it might be sensible to punish some people, even if it is hard to decide who. But (3) Locke retreats (as one might expect) to the argument that he had formulated in the *Letter* to cover the possibility that his second argument was weak: the fact that the magistrate may succeed in making me adopt his views is no reason to think that he will succeed in making me adopt the right views. He is probably wrong. The fact that he is prepared to resort to force may well be an indication that he is indeed wrong. The end result is that I am likely to be worse off, not better. Thus it is clear that the argument on which Locke finally rests his case is not the one on which Waldron concentrates, but the one from decision-making theory: it is not surprising that he repeats this argument more often in the *Letter* than any other (Locke 1899, 48–51).

I have tried to show that Proast and Waldron miss the heart of Locke's case, which is not about the ineffectiveness of persecution, nor (as Waldron thinks it should be) about the moral evils of intolerance or the pathetic fate of the victims of persecution. Locke's central claim is that there are certain decisions that it is irrational, and perhaps impossible, to allow others to make on our behalf. In the *Essay Concerning Human Understanding* he tried to show how sensible decisions could be reached, but the argument of the *Letter* is neutral as to whether we can get at the truth in religious questions; all Locke seeks to show is that we are not more likely to reach it by submitting to persecution.

Suppose that the core argument of the *Letter* is a good one, what of the other objection often levelled against it, that the concessions Locke makes to persecutors go so far as to make the text intolerant by modern standards? Locke, after all, intends to be intolerant towards the intolerant, and also towards Catholics and atheists. Although he thinks that there should be freedom of thought where what he terms speculative opinions are concerned, he insists that it is right to discriminate against ideas that have anti-social consequences. It is not that the government has a right to step in wherever practical opinions are concerned; it can only do so where public interests (with which alone it is properly concerned) are at stake. Locke's distinction within the sphere of practical opinions thus depends on his being able to draw a line between public concerns and private matters: a line corresponding to his earlier distinction between the realm that is the legitimate concern of the state and that which is properly to be left to the voluntary actions of individuals. Slander should be punished, but not laziness or greed. My laziness or greed do not necessarily injure society or my neighbour; nor is it easy for society to be sure that I am really greedy (as opposed to industrious, cautious, foresightful). Private vices should not be punished (despite what Locke says at the beginning of the *Letter*, where he is talking about what a consistent persecutor would do, not about what he believes should be done).

Locke's argument thus depends on a distinction between what Mill was later to term self-regarding and other-regarding actions, and it obviously runs into the severe problems that bedevil Mill's own version of the argument: it simply is not true that nobody's interests but my own are at stake if (to use Locke's horrifying example) I make my daughter marry someone unsuitable. The solution to this problem is not to have the state step in, but to let my daughter choose for herself. Locke's problem is that he has taken the family as a paradigm of what is private, rather than acknowledging that family life involves conflicts of interest between individuals, other-regarding as much as self-regarding behaviour.

Locke's argument, for all the occasional inconsistencies with which he formulates it, was to become that of classical liberalism. Underlying it, one can surely see the values of a market society. Locke assumes that consumers should have the right to make choices. They may make bad choices or good ones: there is at least no reason to think that they will make worse ones than the state would make on their behalf, and where there is a variety of choices on the market (for example, a variety of medical therapies on offer), there is a prospect for progress. Locke's model is directly hostile to the monopolies that were the norm in the Middle Ages, monopolies often not directly controlled by the state, but by the Guilds and Companies.

But it is quite remarkable, if one compares the *Second Letter* and *Third Letter* with the original *Letter* (or, indeed, with the *Essay Concerning Toleration* of 1667), to see that Locke effectively abandons this crucial distinction between what is properly private and what is public. It is true that he still occasionally insists that it is no part of the magistrate's function to punish vices such as envy or uncharitableness. But the whole balance of his argument has shifted, and he now repeatedly insists that we have no right to make our own moral mistakes in private. Debauchery and lasciviousness, for example, should be rooted out by the state (Cranston 1987, 116–17). The ambiguous passage in the original *Letter*, when he argues that persecutors ought to persecute immorality, not unbelief, becomes his official position. Now he holds that it is 'practicable, just, and useful' for magistrates to force men to a good life (Locke 1899, 43, 286, 324). This is probably the consequence of his efforts to forge an alliance with the latitudinarian wing of the Anglican Church: there was little prospect of his arguments being widely accepted if they appeared to involve tolerating not only schism and heresy, but also vice. It is a retreat that leaves his core argument from decision-making theory intact; but it means that the *Second* and *Third Letters* are no longer able consistently to claim that the state is only properly concerned with worldly, not spiritual, matters. Locke could hardly argue this systematically if he was going to defend a state religion.

The *Second* and *Third Letters* consequently lack much of the radical bite of the first. But there is a further major problem in the argument of the first: Locke makes no distinction between ideas and actions. Dangerous opinions are to be punished because they endanger society. One can see why a distinction between ideas and actions would have been beside the point for his immediate argument (religions involve both beliefs and ceremonies), but there is no doubt that Locke could have formulated such a distinction had he wanted to. He insisted that truth makes its way best when left to itself, and that the resort to force in the course of an argument is often an indication that one is arguing badly. He knew that persecuting people for their beliefs might encourage them to rebel. He could easily have argued that the best way of dealing with mistaken beliefs was not to punish them or censor them, but to refute them.

When Locke wrote the *Letter* he had recently read Bayle's *Pensées diverses sur la comète*. The core argument of that work was that people do not act according to their beliefs. Many prostitutes go to Mass, while many atheists act according to the strictest moral principles. In fact what guides people's behaviour is not their beliefs about comparatively distant events such as the Last Judgement, but their immediate concern for the good opinion of their friends and neighbours. It is social pressure, not intellectual conviction, that shapes our lives. Now this argument corresponded exactly with Locke's own suggestion in the *Essay Concerning Human Understanding* (by now nearing its final form in draft) that public opinion is comparable to a law because it carries with it sanctions – hostility, public censure, refusals of support and assistance – that decisively shape how we behave. Indeed, Locke, just like Bayle, insisted that it was the law of public opinion, not moral principle, that determines how people actually behave.

Moreover, many years before, Locke had translated several essays by a Jansenist theologian, Pierre Nicole, who had much influenced Bayle's argument. Nicole had argued (the argument was to be taken up from Bayle by Mandeville) that vice was what made the world go round. Because men are wicked, it would be hopeless to build a society that depended on mutual affection, charity, and good will. But look at what greed can do! Thanks to it, everywhere I go there are people willing to feed me, to put me up, to clothe me (provided, of course, that I pay them). All these individuals, pursuing their private interests, create a prosperous society. The consequence of competition in the market place is an efficient distribution of resources and expanded productivity, so that the lowest-paid worker in a developed country is better off than a king in an undeveloped one: Locke had paraphrased Nicole's argument on this point in the *Second Treatise* (Wootton 1986, 74–5). Obviously, then, there is no need to punish greed, for it can be channelled into socially useful behaviour. Nor is there any need to worry overmuch about people's beliefs: it is their interests that need to be regulated if we want to shape their behaviour.

Locke could give a perfectly good account of his social contract in terms not of natural law but of the rational calculation of interests (Locke 1899, 349). He knew, however atheists ought in theory to behave, in practice it was not the case that 'the taking away of God, though but even in thought, dissolves all', for it left intact the strong bonds of public opinion and self-interest. He knew too that Dutch Catholics did not act out what he took to be the subversive consequences of their religious beliefs. He could easily have argued that what matters to society is not what people think, not even what they say, but what they do. Given the possible gains that would accompany freedom of speech, Locke could have set out to defend it. He was to have another opportunity in 1694, when he was to write a memorandum against the Licensing Act, which required that books be published only by members of the Stationers' Guild, and provided for the pre-censorship of everything published. Locke's response was that the Act gave a monopoly to the Stationers' Guild that resulted in books being unduly expensive. But he was also opposed to pre-censorship in principle and, like Milton, thought that books should be subject only to the common law post-publication constraints on obscenity, libel, and sedition. Censorship would then take place under the public eye, not in secret. His memorandum implies that the government should be publicly accountable for restrictions on freedom of expression, but it does not, any more than the *Letter Concerning Toleration*, provide a principled defence of freedom of speech (Astbury 1978).

How are we to explain Locke's intolerance towards Catholics and atheists, and his hesitant handling of the question of freedom of speech? Let us take, first, the question of atheism. One view might be that his attack on atheism was simply intended to deflect criticism: despite it, Proast was to accuse him of encouraging atheism and scepticism, and the accusation would have been more telling had Locke not prepared his defences against it (Locke 1899, 285–7). Locke's private manuscripts can be quoted both in support of, and in opposition to, the view expressed in the *Letter*. On the one hand Locke claimed, for example, that a Hobbist (by which he meant an atheist) would not recognize a great many principles of morality (Gauthier 1977); on the other he made a systematic attempt to formulate a set of moral principles that were in no way dependent on religious faith (Locke 1974a).

Another answer might be that Locke had no desire to associate himself with the tradition represented by Hobbes, Nicole, and Bayle (the latter two both being admirers of Hobbes) for the simple reason that there was no way in which one could securely generate rights from interests. In the *Second Treatise* he had carefully set out to argue from natural-law principles, not from the alternative republican tradition represented by the followers of Harrington, such as Moyle and Neville, which depended to a great extent upon arguments from self-interest. He may have believed that such arguments could provide no adequate defence against the interests of the state or the temptations of the moment.

But the real answer, I think, is that Locke (like Bayle, who also thought that atheism should remain illegal) took to heart the notion of a law of opinion. If public opinion governed behaviour, then citizens and magistrates must make use of it to shape that behaviour. There could be no scope for the state adopting a posture of impartial neutrality when it came to ideas. Locke was aware that atheists and Catholics were often in practice good citizens. But in behaving well they were not acting according to their own principles. Atheists could recognize no enduring obligations, for oaths were meaningless to them. And Catholics were under an obligation to obey the pope even if his instructions ran counter to their civil obligations. Such beliefs were pernicious no matter how well individual atheists and Catholics might conduct themselves.

Far from Locke having reached the mistaken conclusion that persecution was irrational because it could not work, his insistence that opinions contrary to the public interest are not to be tolerated is evidence that he knew perfectly well that it could work. Even if men and women could not be made to change their inward judgements, they could be effectively silenced. In the *Letter Concerning Toleration* Locke left considerable scope for state intolerance towards ideas and arguments. The real weakness of the text lies, not in any failure to formulate an adequate argument for religious freedom, but in its failure to argue for freedom of thought (except in the narrow sphere of 'speculative opinion'), and in its failure to argue confidently for freedom of action in some clearly defined sphere of private life. Locke relied on distinctions – between speculative and practical, public and private – which were fragile, and he showed little inclination to stand by them. It was Blount, not Locke, who reiterated the arguments of Milton's *Areopagitica* for freedom of thought and expression; Mandeville, not Locke, who took up Bayle's arguments to insist that individuals should be left to run their own lives as they thought best. Locke's argument does only what it was intended to do: provide an argument in favour of religious freedom. But it does, at least, do that.

Some more equal than others?

We have seen that there is no simple sense in which the *Second Letter Concerning Toleration* is written by the same author as the original *Letter*. One is written in Latin by someone with far from conventional religious views; the other in English by an apparently orthodox Anglican. This raises an important question: Does it really help to think of all the different texts gathered together in this volume as being by the same person? We have seen Locke's political views from 1659 to 1685 traverse a vast range of opinion, and we have already begun to see indications of a shift towards conservatism after 1688. Would it not perhaps be better to see each text as the product of a particular circumstance, rather than a particular author? Or should we be thinking not in terms of authors but in terms of intellectual traditions and conventions? We have seen that Locke's *Second Treatise* has more in common with Tyrrell's *Patriarcha non Monarcha* than it has with anything else written by Locke. Locke's *Letter Concerning Toleration* was published by Limborch in one volume with Samuel Strimesius's *Dissertatio Theologica de Pace Ecclesiastica*: the one a plea for toleration, the other for 'comprehension', the relaxation of Church doctrine to include as many believers within the Church as possible. Should we read Locke and Strimesius together, rather than placing the *Letter Concerning Toleration* alongside the *Essay Concerning Toleration* on the one hand or the *Second Letter* on the other?

One could reach conclusions such as these when approaching Locke's texts from any one of a number of very different intellectual positions. J. G. A. Pocock, for example, has argued that it is the intellectual paradigm, not the author, with which historians of ideas should primarily be concerned. Foucault argued that the 'author function' was a historical peculiarity: novels, for example, have authors in a sense that papers in scientific journals do not. One might question whether there was really a consistent 'author function' present in Locke's works. Locke intends us to be conscious of his presence as author of the *Essay Concerning Human Understanding*. But is it he, or a persona he has adopted, whom we encounter in the *Second Letter Concerning Toleration*? And in the works he wrote with a view to their being approved by a committee, such as the *Constitutions of Carolina*, or the report on poor relief (*Draft of a Representation . . .*, below, pp. 446–61), is there perhaps a collective, not an individual author at work?

I do not introduce these methodological considerations out of a desire to make life complicated: the fact is that we are forced to confront them by the texts themselves. Take, for example, the concept that is central to the *Second Treatise*, that of natural law. Locke published the *Second Treatise* at the same time as he published the *Essay Concerning Human Understanding*. There he maintained that it was possible to have a deductive knowledge of the law of nature, yet at the same time he undermined all the obvious ways in which one might seek to demonstrate the existence of such a law: we have no innate knowledge of it, to begin with, and men and women in diverse societies differ radically about what its contents might be. A law, for Locke, had to carry sanctions with it, otherwise it would merely be a piece of good advice. The sanctions of the law of nature could not simply be natural consequences occurring in this world – the hangover that follows a drink too many – for if so they would not really be sanctions, merely unpleasant consequences a prudent man or woman would avoid. But Locke had, as we have seen, undermined all the available proofs of a life after death in which sanctions might be imposed.

The immediate reaction to the *Essay* was a series of accusations that Locke had undermined the foundations of the law of nature. Newton, for example, told Locke that the *Essay* had caused him to mistake Locke for a Hobbist. By the time he published The *Reason-ableness of Christianity* Locke was prepared to admit that reason could not establish the existence of a divinely ordained set of moral principles, accompanied by other-worldly punishments and re-wards, and he really ought to have been prepared to admit this a decade earlier. The Locke of The *Reasonableness*, and perhaps too the Locke of the *Essay*, is not a natural-law theorist. Yet the same Locke published and republished, revised and eventually acknowl-edged, the *Second Treatise*, a classic text in natural-law theory. It makes a good deal of sense, then, to see the *Second Treatise* as a work designed to develop the potential of the natural-law tradition of Grotius, Pufendorf, and Tyrrell, while at the very same time the *Essay* and *The Reasonableness* questioned the validity of that tra-dition. Locke would seem to have carefully separated the two intel-lectual activities, to the extent that we might as well think of the *Essay* and the *Second Treatise* as having different authors (Laslett in Locke 1967b, 79–91).

One of the central questions we have been exploring in this Introduction is: When and how did Locke become a liberal? Against those scholars who have tried to trace a progressive evolution of liberal positions in Locke's thought, I have stressed that there is a radical difference between the *Second Treatise* and his earlier works: Locke becomes a liberal in June 1681, after reading Tyrrell. We could now reverse this process, and argue that Locke's later works, such as the report on poor relief, are not particularly liberal. Liberal-ism would then be a characteristic of one or two texts written by Locke; it would not be a central aspect of Locke's biography, or of Locke's writing taken as a whole.

In my view there are two fundamental reasons why it would be wrong to proceed in this way, abandoning the notion of Locke as an identifiable persona, a particular author, a liberal philosopher, and replacing it by a series of discrete paradigms or a multitude of anonymous texts.

First, we have the evidence of Locke's behaviour. The *Second Treatise* may have been written at a particular moment in time, 1681. But it must have been revised in 1689; Locke struggled in 1694 and 1698 to bring out more accurate editions; when he died he left behind an extensively revised text that he publicly claimed as his own. None of those revisions blunt the radical arguments in the text, or undermine its natural-law foundations. An indication of Locke's continuing commitment to the argument of the text is the epigraph he chose for it some time between 1698 and 1704, which appears as the epigraph to this Introduction. Locke's commitment to the *Second Treatise* is not momentary, but continuing.

The *Second Treatise* may seem to be difficult to reconcile with the arguments of the *Essay*. But the letters on education repeatedly stress our natural love of liberty, and emphasize the importance of an understanding of property. We even find Locke recommending the *Two Treatises* in 1704 as part of a sound education because of its chapter on property (Locke 1976–89, vol. 8, 58). Similarly, the arguments of the *Second Treatise* reappear in the discussion of tyranny in the *Letter*, and continue to echo through the later *Letters Concerning Toleration*. We cannot neatly separate Locke's political thinking from his educational principles, or from his argument for toleration. We cannot even neatly isolate them from his more narrowly philosophical works: the posthumous *Conduct of the Understanding* firmly asserts that the principle that all men are created equal is the foundational principle for political philosophy. The whole series of Locke's later works thus seems to be inextricably interlinked. An identifiable author seems stubbornly present, even if he is writing in several different conventions and adopts somewhat different personae on different occasions.

But the most important reason for clinging to the category of the author when working on Locke is that Locke himself would have been astonished at the thought that it might not be the right category to use. We have seen that one of the key discussions in the *Essay* (in fact it appears in the second edition, but its argument is to be found in Locke's papers as early as 1683: Ms Locke f 7, 107) is the discussion of personal identity. What is it that makes Locke Locke? Not his physical continuity, for the same mind in another body would be the same person. Not the continuity of his thought processes, for these are interrupted by sleep, even by coma. Not the identity of his mental capacities, for not only do these change over time, but if Locke was reborn in the twentieth century, with no memory of having been Locke, he clearly would not be able to identify himself as the same person as the author of the *Essay*.

Locke's answer is simple: it is memory that constitutes identity, and with memory comes a recognition of responsibility for the things that one has done. The drunk who cannot remember what he did when he wakes the next morning is arguably responsible for having allowed himself to get drunk, not for what he did when drunk. Take away memory and you take away identity, and with it you take away moral responsibility. Without memory and foresight, punishment and reward become irrelevant. Personal identity is a forensic concept, a claim not about mind or body, but about moral responsibility.

Locke's argument was brilliant and novel. It still dominates the philosophy of identity, so that it has been recently said that all later arguments are mere footnotes to it (Noonan 1989, 30). It has a very simple consequence: Locke was committed to the notion of the author function. He was responsible for the arguments in his works; if they were wrong it was his duty to correct them, if they were right it was his responsibility to defend them. He could not see his life as radically compartmentalized into different functions – natural-law theorist, epistemologist, government bureaucrat – because in his view the notion of moral responsibility unified every aspect of an individual's conscious life. Nor would he have wanted to escape responsibility by arguing that the meaning of what he had written was indeterminate: one of the purposes of the *Essay* was to teach people to argue clearly and unambiguously, in order to avoid unnecessary controversy over disputed meanings (Mulligan et al., 1982). If Locke had been sceptical about the concepts of personal identity (as Hume was), of moral responsibility (as fatalists must be), or of linguistic meaning (as Montaigne was) then we might well think that it was wrong to impose the category of 'the author' upon his work. But these were precisely the issues on which he was clear that scepticism was mistaken. Locke is, consequently, the paradigm case of someone to whom it would seem to be appropriate to apply that elusive and seemingly anachronistic concept, the concept of the author, for it was he who did most to construct its philosophical foundations.

Locke knew that there were alternative ways of conceiving of human behaviour, ones markedly at odds with those he presented in his account of identity. In his discussion of the association of ideas he recognized that human beings were often not free agents, but rather environmentally determined mechanisms, often unconscious rather than conscious of their motives and behaviour (Locke 1975, bk II, ch. 33). Sterne's *Tristram Shandy* (1760–67) is perhaps the first major work of literature that is preoccupied with the exploration of the author's own self: it is a straightforward application, as Sterne knew, of Locke's psychology, and again and again Sterne uses the Lockean principle of the association of ideas to undermine Locke's ideas of agency and identity. One of Sterne's primary purposes is to put in question the notion of the responsible author.

So Locke's own psychological theories raise problems comparable to those debated within contemporary theories of interpretation. But Locke, unlike Sterne, did not exploit these problems in order to undermine the notion of personal responsibility. He would have thought us entitled to ask a simple question that some may think hopelessly naïve: Where is the Locke of the *Second Treatise* in the political writings of his later years? The question is peculiarly difficult to answer. The argument of the *Second Treatise* was that there was no reason why men should be bound by the decisions of their ancestors; yet in February 1689 we find Locke calling for the restoration of the ancient constitution (below, p. 437). The argument of the *Second Treatise* was that all men are equal and are entitled to equal representation when the constitution of their government is being determined, but Locke seems to have straightforwardly accepted when he wrote the Preface to the *Two Treatises* that the Convention Parliament was an adequate representative of the people of England, although only a minority had the right to vote. The *Second Treatise* insisted that men in the state of nature were obliged to ensure that they leave enough and as good for others, and it is hard to see how this moral responsibility can simply disappear once commerce has been introduced and political societies have been founded. But in 'Venditio' and the report on poor relief Locke shows no interest in ensuring equal, or even adequate, access to resources: he seems to think the poor should be held responsible for their condition and should pay the maximum price (excluding death by starvation) for their misfortune. The radical, egalitarian, and liberal Locke of the *Second Treatise* seems to have disappeared from view. There are a number of works by scholars claiming that Locke was really a democrat, yet from the moment Locke returns to England in 1689 all trace of democratic arguments seems to disappear from his public statements.

There is, however, one exceptional text that has not received the attention it deserves. 'Labour', an entry in Locke's commonplace book, was probably intended for his eyes alone (below, pp. 440–42). It is evident that it is a commentary upon the discussion of the same theme in More's *Utopia* (1989, 50–55). Locke insists that even the wealthy should work, and that the poorest should have time to think, to read, to relax. In the *Essay* Locke had claimed that it was inevitable that the greater part of mankind would never have the time and resources to inform themselves about the world around them. They were bound to be like cart horses, trudging day by day the same narrow, rutted tracks, blinkered by poverty and overwork (Locke 1975, bk IV, ch. 20 §2). Yet 'Labour' makes clear that Locke did not in fact think there was anything inevitable about this state of affairs: one could perfectly easily imagine, as More had done, a much more egalitarian society, one where both the burden of labour and access to resources would be fairly distributed.

Both the *Essay* and 'Labour' suggest a sympathetic grasp of the plight of the labouring poor. How to reconcile this with Locke's refusal to sympathize with the circumstances of the unemployed? Locke's report on poor relief insists that those who are unemployed are simply lazy and trying to live off the industry of others. They must be harshly punished, and Locke elaborates a whole series of new punishments to add to those already on the statute books. One might think that Locke was expressing the prejudices of the day, or the consensus opinion of the Board of Trade, but one only has to go through the Board of Trade's papers on the problem of poverty to see that this is far from being the case (PRO CO 388). The consensus on the Board was that the poor were unemployed because there was a shortage of jobs, and that the solution was not new punitive measures, but new schemes for state investment in order to create gainful employment. Locke was in a minority on the Board: he was dismayed, but can hardly have been surprised, when his proposals were largely rejected (PRO CO 389.14, 127–38).

The fact that Locke believed that people were under an obligation to act consistently and think coherently does not mean that he always lived up to this obligation. He went on believing that the arguments of the *Second Treatise* were plainly true even after he knew he could not properly ground them in natural law: he continued to believe he could ground them in Revelation, for the moral principles by which one should live had been clearly laid out in the Gospel. To argue, though, that until Christ rose from the dead men had no adequate knowledge of how they should behave towards each other, and could rely only on the guiding principle of self-interest, was to raise a problem in theodicy that could only partially be overcome by maintaining that God had constructed men's interests so that they neatly harmonized with their duties. This was a problem that Locke simply could not solve.

Nor could he necessarily solve the problem of how England and the colonies ought to be governed. The arguments of the *Second Treatise* could easily be developed to support democracy and to demonstrate the illegitimacy of chattel slavery. But Locke's immediate priority lay elsewhere: his concern was to see a secure and wealthy government established that could play a major role in the defeat of Catholicism and absolutism as personified by Louis XIV (Locke 1985). Given this priority, and given the risks he had already taken, the sacrifices he had already made, he may have felt justified in standing idly by while the *Second Treatise* was variously claimed to provide a justification for both the subordination and right to liberty of the Irish Catholics.

It seems to me clear that the argument of the *Second Treatise* made chattel slavery as it existed in the New World illegitimate, and clear too that Locke, who played a role in shaping England's policy towards the colonies, did nothing about it. But in other respects Locke's principles were a great deal less egalitarian than may at first appear. The point of the discussion of property in the *Second Treatise* is to show that economic inequality can be justified by the principles of natural reason. But Locke goes further than that. He argues that agricultural improvement and commercial progress create not only wealth, but also economic opportunities. This key argument he refined and developed in the revision of the text between 1698 and 1704, and it is the key argument employed to justify the punitive measures (so hostile to any respect for individual privacy or dignity) proposed in the report on poor relief. In Locke's view it simply cannot be the case that economic growth could lead to structural unemployment: on the contrary growth must create wealth, not just for a few, but potentially for all. The unemployed must be to blame for their unemployment, for they must be too lazy or shiftless to seek out the opportunities that exist.

Similarly, Locke argues in the *Second Treatise* that money exists before political society; consequently the state may regulate the coinage, but it cannot arbitrarily determine its value. It was this conviction that underlay the economic writings in which he attacked a policy of devaluation (Appleby 1976). The value of a currency was bound to be set by international trade, and could not be controlled by the government. There were sharp natural limits to the extent to which government could profitably intervene to create prosperity or foster equality.

Finally, Locke had argued in the *Second Treatise* that there should be no taxation without representation. Yet indirect taxes fell on the whole of society, and direct taxes on many who had no vote. Did they not have a right to representation? Locke, it would seem, had available two answers to this question. The first was that indirect taxes damaged the economy: taxation ought to be only on landed wealth. On this view there would be nothing wrong with the traditional English franchise in the county constituencies, which confined the vote to those with a freehold worth 40 shillings in rent a year, if a sensible policy of taxation was pursued, where it would be precisely these people who would pay tax. But Locke also held that in practice taxes on commercial wealth and indirect taxes were passed on through the economy until eventually they fell on the landlord: despite appearances, the freeholders were in fact the only ones really paying tax, so that there was no fundamental inequity in allowing them to determine who should be taxed (Locke 1991, 272–9). The principle of no taxation without representation could thus be reconciled with a non-democratic franchise. Locke may also have held that it was the freeholders who were the true members of the body politic: it was they who had the right to sit on juries, and it had once been the case that they and they alone took oaths of allegiance, the acts of explicit consent that alone made individuals members of the political community. Locke's call for the restoration of the ancient constitution, improved where necessary, may well have been a call for the reinforcement, not the erosion, of the legal, constitutional, and economic position of the freeholder. Men who had property only in their lives and liberties were entitled to be treated fairly according to the law of nature, but did they have a claim to be allowed to join the political community and to participate in political decision-making? There is no clear evidence that Locke was ever convinced that they had, although it is certainly strange that he never paused to stress in the *Second Treatise* (as Tyrrell or Ferguson would have done) that they did not.

We do not know how Locke worked out in his own mind these ambiguities and tensions in his thought, and there is little to be gained by trying to impose an artificial and posthumous coherence upon him. Of one thing we can be reasonably certain: that until his dying day he was convinced that the principles of fairness and justice should be applied equally to the weak and to the mighty. There might be considerable room for doubt about what this fundamental principle of equality required in practice, when it came to the details of political institutions or economic policy, but there could be no arguing with its overriding authority. In the end, Locke could not divorce his own sense of personal identity and moral responsibility from the arguments of the *Second Treatise*. He had every opportunity to change or retract them. He could have simply refused to acknowledge that he had written them. Instead he carefully revised them and deliberately took responsibility for them. To this day, Locke and Liberalism go hand in hand, as he intended they should. And the problems that he could not solve – the rational foundation of ethics, political participation, economic equality – are ones that bedevil us too.

Notes

1. Two good accounts of Locke as a liberal political theorist are Seliger (1968) and Grant (1987).
2. The standard biography is Cranston (1957). This should now be supplemented by Ashcraft (1986), read in the light of Goldie (1992). For an account of Locke's place in society, Dunn (1981).
3. Laslett (1960) sought to minimize the influence of Hobbes on Locke. It may

be noted, however, that the claim that Locke possessed no copy of *Leviathan* when working on the *Second Treatise* (Locke 1967b, 74) depends on a rather uncertain interpretation of the 1681 booklist, which includes an untitled work by Hobbes. Laslett presumably assumed that this was not *Leviathan* because it is an $8°$ volume, but there were in fact $8°$ editions of *Leviathan* in 1678 and 1681 (Harrison and Laslett 1965, 272).

4. Locke 1991, 407–9, reproduces Churchill's catalogue.

5. Although there certainly was a consensus among secondhand book dealers that Locke was the author (Ashcraft 1969, 58).

6. '. . . witness the fact that whatever is held to be impious, unjust, disgraceful in one place, is pious, just and honourable in another; one cannot name a single law, custom, or belief which is universally either approved or condemned' (Charron 1783, bk I, ch. 16, p. 132). Contrast Culverwell (1971), ch. 10. The first significant listing of Locke's books, in 1681, includes both Charron and Charron's mentor, Montaigne (Harrison and Laslett 1965, 270–71). In *Some Thoughts Concerning Education* Locke at certain points follows Montaigne so closely that even cautious scholars find it hard to avoid the word plagiarism (Yolton and Yolton in Locke 1989, 12–13).

7. The misdated texts are from Locke's so-called '1661 Common Place Book'. Kraynak follows King (1829) in assuming them to be from around 1661, despite having read the warning of Abrams (in Locke 1967a, 9) that they all date from after 1680. In fact 'Sacerdos', for example, dates to 1698. Kraynak also ignores Abrams's warnings regarding the dangers of assuming that superficially Hobbesian sentiments derive from Hobbes himself (Locke 1967a, 75–7). Torn out of context is, for example, the quotation on p. 58 col. 2 about a state of 'natural liberty' in which things are 'perfectly indifferent'. Locke is in fact denying, not affirming, that there is such a state. For other works to some degree comparable to Kraynak's, see above, pp. 68–71, and the section of the Suggestions for Further Reading devoted to the followers of Leo Strauss, pp. 129–30.

8. Tully thinks the subject is always obliged actively to obey the magistrate's command (in Locke 1983, 6). Ashcraft seems to agree (Ashcraft 1986, 92). But it is clear that Locke recognizes that it would be wrong to obey the magistrate if he commanded one to do something directly contrary to the command of God (below pp. 159, 164–5, 175). On the other hand one could never be justified in resisting.

9. C. M. Andrews seems to me quite wrong to describe them as 'merely copyholders' (Andrews 1937, vol. 3, 215).

10. Public Record Office, 30/24/48pt2/55, f 147 (1675).

11. Haley attributed it, without explanation, to Jones (Haley 1968, 639). Ashcraft accepts Ferguson's claim to have written it (Ashcraft 1986, 317–18). But Worden presented evidence suggesting that Sidney had a hand in it (Worden 1985, 15), and an attribution to Sidney has been accepted by a number of recent authors. A detailed case in favour of its having been largely written by Sidney is presented by Scott, whose arguments at present hold the field (Scott 1991a, 186–95).

12. In fact he purchased it on Tyrrell's behalf to pass on to someone else (Tuck 1979, 169n). Tyrrell had presumably given him a copy of his own shortly before. This copy (LL2999) contained manuscript emendations by Tyrrell, but, if the example quoted by Laslett is typical, then Tyrrell had merely written the errata into the text (Locke 1967b, 334). It should be said that the literature on Tyrrell is surprisingly thin. The correspondence between Tyrrell and Locke can be followed through the pages of Locke (1976–89). Apart from Gough (1976), there are brief discussions in Thompson (1987) and Horne (1990).

13. This manuscript (Ms Locke c 34) is generally described as having been written jointly by Locke and Tyrrell. Marshall provides decisive evidence that it was in fact not a joint effort, but Locke's own composition (Marshall 1992, 277).

14. If Ferguson was one of the authors, he would have been in a good position to know what Shaftesbury knew. But it is also worth wondering whether Somers, whom Burnet thought had a hand in the *Vindication*, was not collaborating with Locke at this time. He is generally accepted as the author of *The Security of Englishmen's Lives*, a 1681 tract on the principles to be followed by grand juries, written with a view to discouraging a jury from bringing in an indictment against Shaftesbury (*State Tracts* 1693). But at several points this pamphlet is reminiscent of Locke: in its definition of government as established to protect the lives, liberties, and properties of Englishmen, in its use of Garcilaso de la Vega, one of the authors Locke relied on in the *Two Treatises*, and in its sophisticated discussion of the meaning of the term 'probability', which is reminiscent of Locke's 1671 drafts of the *Essay*. Is it possible that the collaboration between Locke and Somers began in 1681, not, as is generally assumed, in 1689?

15. See Culverwell for a similar account of legitimate punishment (Culverwell 1971, 44, 52–3).

16. Much more accurate is Dunn's formulation: 'The entire *First Treatise*, which is designed to discredit Filmer's extrapolations from the Old Testament, ends up by making the latter seem almost wholly irrelevant to issues of political right' (Dunn 1969a, 99).

17. Jonathan Scott has argued that the similarities between Sidney's *Discourses* and the *Second Treatise* are so extensive that one probably influenced the other (Scott, 1991b). The dating I propose implies that Locke influenced Sidney, not, as Scott argues, despite Locke's explicit claim never to have read Sidney, that Sidney influenced Locke.

18. John Marshall has demonstrated that fewer radical works were written in 1681 than Ashcraft implies (Marshall 1990, ch. 8). This tends, I think, to reinforce my argument that *Patriarcha non Monarcha* and the *Second Treatise* are exceptional, and exceptionally alike.

19. From this point on I slip into sexist language. To try and suggest that Locke and Tyrrell were talking about men *and* women when they generally refer only to men would be to read them anachronistically. On the other hand it is a feature of their argument – and of many other arguments that Locke employs – that it is easy to conclude from it that men and women are equal. I suspect Locke found this implication attractive, and a number of women sprang to the defence of

Locke's works. Nevertheless I think it would be misleading to present his arguments in non-sexist language, and have instead sought to reproduce the ambiguous and careless formulations of my sources.

20. The Grotian claim that men have a right to punish while in the state of nature had been used by Milton (1991, 9) and by Sexby (Wootton 1986, 373).

21. I have used italics to indicate the pagination of the interpolated section.

22. The model for this argument was presumably Milton's *Tenure of Kings and Magistrates* (Milton 1991, 17–18).

23. This is not true of the *Second* and *Third Letters*, which have been successfully contextualized by Mark Goldie (forthcoming).

24. Locke is paraphrasing a standard argument employed by religious sceptics: it is to be found, for example, in Pomponazzi.

25. Locke, in fact, was very little interested in constitutional measures designed to encourage impartiality, although these lay at the heart of the Harringtonian tradition of analysis. Instead he lays considerable stress on the need for us to trust our governments in secular matters (so long as they do not demonstrate themselves to be manifestly undeserving of our trust), and this underlies his acceptance of the existing constitution. It is to be presumed that, like Shaftesbury's other close associates, Locke wanted exclusion not constitutional reform in 1679–83 (Scott 1991a, 147, 286–7, 291). Dunn has recently emphasized the merits of the theme of trust in Locke's thought (Dunn 1985). I myself have somewhat more sympathy with his earlier criticisms of Locke's 'facile constitutionalism' (Dunn 1969a, 12–13, 55–7, 127–9).

Suggestions for Further Reading

Key Works

The two classic modern studies of Locke's political theory are Peter Laslett's introduction to his edition of Locke's *Two Treatises* (1960; student edition, Cambridge: Cambridge University Press, 1988) and John Dunn's *The Political Thought of John Locke* (Cambridge: Cambridge University Press, 1969). The best detailed commentary on Locke's arguments is Richard Ashcraft's *Locke's 'Two Treatises of Government'* (London: Allen and Unwin, 1987). Three essays provide gateways to large and ever-growing bodies of literature: the chapters on Locke in Leo Strauss's *Natural Right and History* (Chicago: University of Chicago Press, 1953) and C. B. Macpherson's *The Political Theory of Possessive Individualism* (Oxford: Clarendon Press, 1962); and Richard Ashcraft's 'Revolutionary politics and Locke's *Two Treatises of Government*', *Political Theory* 8 (1980), 429–86.

Bibliographies

There are three bibliographies that are indispensable for the older literature. Roland Hall and Roger Woolhouse, *Eighty Years of Locke Scholarship* (Edinburgh: Edinburgh University Press, 1983) is a guide to the secondary literature on Locke, and is updated annually in *The Locke Newsletter*. Jean Yolton and John Yolton, *John Locke: A Reference Guide* (Boston, Mass.: G. K. Hall, 1985) covers the literature on Locke from his own lifetime until 1982. John C. Attig, *The Works of John Locke* (Westport, Conn.: Greenwood Press, 1985) is a sometimes imperfect listing of editions of Locke's works. Suggestions for further reading are to be found in the student version of Laslett's edition of the *Two Treatises*, and in Ashcraft's *Locke's 'Two Treatises'*. The scholarship on Locke is advancing so rapidly that any selection is bound to be rapidly outdated. The suggestions which follow are intended to give an indication of the range of literature in key areas of controversy.

The Political Significance of the *Second Treatise*

The most important recent book on the political significance of the *Second Treatise* is Richard Ashcraft's *Revolutionary Politics and Locke's 'Two Treatises of Government'* (Princeton: Princeton University Press, 1986). Ashcraft's essay of the same title, in *Political Theory* 8 (1980), 429–86, is a more succinct version of broadly the same argument. Ashcraft's account of Locke as a democrat has come under attack: see the debate between Ashcraft and Wootton, which surveys earlier criticisms of Ashcraft, in *Political Studies* 40 (1992), 79–115. Two more recent works have further damaged Ashcraft's case: Mark Goldie, 'John Locke's circle and James II', *Historical Journal* 35 (1992) 557–86; and John Marshall, *John Locke in Context* (Johns Hopkins Ph.D., 1990), ch. 8.

Two other books have presented the *Second Treatise* as an essentially democratic work: James Tully, *A Discourse on Property: John Locke and his Adversaries* (Cambridge: Cambridge University Press, 1980), and Julian Franklin, *John Locke and the Theory of Sovereignty* (Cambridge: Cambridge University Press, 1978). Both, however, are seriously flawed. On this aspect of Tully's book see Joshua Cohen, 'Structure, choice and legitimacy: John Locke's theory of the state', *Philosophy and Public Affairs* 15 (1986), 301–24 (with a reply by Martin Hughes, 'Locke on taxation and suffrage', *History of Political Thought* 11 (1990), 423–42); on Franklin see Conal Condren, 'Resistance and sovereignty in Lawson's *Politica*', *Historical Journal* 24 (1981), 673–81. The best version of the argument for a democratic reading is Judith Richards, Lotte Mulligan and John K. Graham, '"Property" and "people": Political usages of Locke and some contemporaries', *Journal of the History of Ideas* 42 (1981), 29–51.

The Intellectual Context of the *Second Treatise*

The best general account of the natural-law tradition within which Locke's *Second Treatise* is obviously to be placed is Richard Tuck's *Natural Rights Theories: Their Origin and Development* (Cambridge: Cambridge University Press, 1979). The best account of the immediate intellectual context is Martyn Thompson, 'Significant silences in Locke's *Two Treatises of Government*: Constitutional history, contract and law', *Historical Journal* 31 (1987), 275–94. Ever since J. G. A. Pocock's *The Ancient Constitution and the Feudal Law* (Cambridge: Cambridge University Press, 1957) historians have puzzled over Locke's failure to use arguments from history: see, for example, D. Resnick, 'Locke and the rejection of the ancient constitution', *Political Theory* 12 (1984), 97–114. And ever since his *The Machiavellian Moment: Florentine Political Thought and the Atlantic Republican Tradition* (Princeton: Princeton University Press, 1975) they have worried about his relationship to the republican tradition. On republicanism, the best authority is Blair Worden: his latest survey is in *Republicanism, Liberty, and Commercial Society*, ed. David Wootton (Stanford: Stanford University Press, forthcoming).

Locke and Patriarchalism

The best brief introduction to family life and gender relations in seventeenth-century England is Keith Wrightson, *English Society, 1580–1680* (London: Hutchinson, 1982), chapters 3 and 4. These question the views of Lawrence Stone, *The Family, Sex and Marriage in England, 1500–1800* (London: Weidenfeld and Nicolson, 1977), which contains a brief discussion of Locke, and remains fundamental. They provide a context within which to read Gordon J. Schochet, *Patriarchalism in Political Thought* (Oxford: Blackwell, 1975).

For largely negative assessments of Locke's view of women see: L. M. G. Clark, 'Women and John Locke: or Who owns the apples in the Garden of Eden?', *Canadian Journal of Philosophy* 7 (1977), 699–724; T. Brennan and C. Pateman, '"Mere auxiliaries to the commonwealth": Women and the origins of Liberalism', *Political Studies* 27 (1979), 183–200; Hilda L. Smith, *Reasons' Disciples: Seventeenth-Century English Feminists* (Urbana: University of Illinois Press, 1982); Susan M. Okin, *Women in Western Political Thought* (Princeton: Princeton University Press, 1979). For more positive assessments: M. A. Butler, 'Early liberal roots of Feminism', *American Political Science Review* 72 (1978), 135–50: S. M. Shanley, 'Marriage contract and social contract', *Western Political Quarterly*, 32 (1979), 79–91. On female readers of the *Essay*, S. O'Donnell, 'Mr Locke and the ladies: The indelible words on the *tabula rasa*', *Studies in Eighteenth Century Culture* 8 (1979), 151–64. For an overlooked fragment of evidence, see Locke's letter to Stringer of 15 February 1681. There, having mistakenly claimed that *The Character of a Popish Successor* had been written by a woman, Locke roundly declares: 'I am of an opinion she deserves one of the best places in the university.' It would be difficult to find a more straightforwardly feminist sentiment written by a seventeenth-century male.

Locke on Property

Useful brief surveys are Thomas A. Horne, *Property Rights and Poverty* (Chapel Hill: University of North Carolina Press, 1990), Alan Ryan, *Property and Political Theory* (Oxford: Blackwell, 1984), and Andrew Reeve, *Property* (London: Macmillan, 1985). The best philosophical account of Locke's views is now Jeremy Waldron, *The Right to Private Property* (Oxford: Clarendon Press, 1988). The natural-law tradition is surveyed in Stephen Buckle, *Natural Law and the Theory of Property: Grotius to Hume* (Oxford: Clarendon Press, 1991).

In recent years there has been a great deal of debate surrounding James Tully's *A Discourse on Property*, itself a reply to Macpherson's *Possessive Individualism*. Unfortunately, few of Tully's critics have bothered to read each other. Those I have come across are: J. L. Mackie, review, *Philosophical Quarterly*, 23 (1982), 91–4; T. Baldwin, 'Tully, Locke and land', *Locke Newsletter*, 13 (1982), 21–33; Neil Wood, *John Locke and Agrarian Capitalism* (Berkeley:

University of California Press, 1984), ch. 5; G. A. Cohen, 'Marx and Locke on land and labour', *Proceedings of the British Academy*, 71 (1985), 357–88; Ian Shapiro, *The Evolution of Rights in Liberal Theory* (Cambridge: Cambridge University Press, 1986), 90–97, 139–44; N. J. Mitchell, 'John Locke and the rise of capitalism', *History of Political Economy*, 18 (1986), 291–305; J. Isaac, 'Was John Locke a bourgeois theorist?', *Canadian Journal of Political and Social Theory*, 11 (1987), 107–29; G. den Hartogh, 'Tully's Locke', *Political Theory*, 18 (1990), 656–72; and a number of essays by Jeremy Waldron, most recently *The Right to Private Property*, ch. 6. Tully has replied to Baldwin and to an earlier version of Waldron's argument, 'A Reply to Waldron and Baldwin', *Locke Newsletter* 13 (1982), 35–55. For the more recent development of Tully's views see his 'Governing conduct' in *Conscience and Casuistry in Early Modern Europe*, ed. Edmund Leites (Cambridge: Cambridge University Press, 1988), 12–71, and 'Locke' in *The Cambridge History of Political Thought, 1450–1700*, ed. J. H. Burns and M. Goldie (Cambridge: Cambridge University Press, 1991), 616–52.

Locke on Religion and Toleration

The key discussion by a contemporary philosopher of the *Letter Concerning Toleration* is Jeremy Waldron, 'Locke: Toleration and the rationality of persecution', in *Justifying Toleration: Conceptual and Historical Perspectives*, ed. Susan Mendus (Cambridge: Cambridge University Press, 1988), 61–86. In general agreement with Waldron are Susan Mendus, *Toleration and the Limits of Liberalism* (Basingstoke: Macmillan, 1989) and Mark Goldie, 'The theory of religious intolerance in Restoration England', in *From Persecution to Toleration: The Glorious Revolution and Religion in England*, ed. Ole Peter Grell, Jonathan I. Israel and Nicholas Tyacke (Oxford: Clarendon Press, 1991), 331–68. This essay, John Dunn's 'The claim to freedom of conscience', in the same volume, and Goldie's 'John Locke, Jonas Proast, and religious toleration, 1688–1692', in *The Church of England 1689–1833: From Toleration to Tractarianism*, ed. J. Walsh, C. Haydon and S. Taylor (Oxford, forthcoming), give a new context for the *Letters Concerning Toleration*.

Dunn's *Political Thought of John Locke* is the classic statement of the view that Locke was a religious, not a secular, thinker. But it leaves open the question of the exact nature of Locke's religious commitments. A latitudinarian account of Locke's religious thought is to be found in W. M. Spellman, *John Locke and the Problem of Depravity* (Oxford: Clarendon Press, 1988), and in D. D. Wallace, 'Socinianism, justification by faith, and the sources of John Locke's *The Reasonableness of Christianity*', *Journal of the History of Ideas* 45 (1984), 49–66. Locke's relations with the latitudinarians are further explored in John Marshall, 'John Locke and latitudinarianism', in *Philosophy, Science, and Religion in England, 1640–1700*, ed. Richard Ashcraft, Richard Kroll, and Perez Zagorin (Cambridge: Cambridge University Press, 1992), 253–82. In the same volume Ashcraft gives an account of Locke as having views similar to those of the Nonconformists. Marshall shows Locke to have been a Socinian, at least in the 1690s, in 'John Locke and Socinianism', in *Seventeenth-Century Philosophy in Historical Context*, ed. M. A. Steward (Oxford: Clarendon Press, forthcoming). The problem of when his adoption of Socinian principles took place is discussed in David Wootton, 'John Locke: Socinian or natural law theorist?', in *Religion, Secularization and Political Thought*, ed. James Crimmins (London: Routledge, 1989), 39–67. Some, however, particularly those influenced by Leo Strauss, have continued to doubt that Locke was religious. He is portrayed as no Christian in Michael S. Rabich, 'The reasonableness of Locke, or the questionableness of Christianity', *Journal of Politics* 53 (1991), 933–57, and as an atheist in W. T. Bluhm, N. Wintfield and S. Teger, 'Locke's idea of God: Rational truth or political myth?', *Journal of Politics*, 42 (1980), 414–38.

The Reception and Influence of the *Two Treatises*

Two works placed in doubt the traditional picture of the influence of Locke on later political thought: John Dunn's 'The politics of Locke in England and America', in *John Locke: Problems and Perspectives*, ed. John W. Yolton (Cambridge: Cambridge University Press, 1969), 45–80, and J. G. A. Pocock's *The Machiavellian*

Moment. However it does now seem that Locke's influence was greater than they were prepared to admit. For Locke's influence in England, a good starting point is provided by the revised edition of John P. Kenyon's *Revolution Principles: The Politics of Party, 1689–1720* (Cambridge: Cambridge University Press, 1990) and by L. G. Schwoerer, 'Locke, Lockean ideas, and the Glorious Revolution', *Journal of the History of Ideas* 51 (1990), 531–48. The key articles are: Martyn Thompson, 'The reception of Locke's *Two Treatises of Government*', *Political Studies* 24 (1976), 184–91 (with a debate between Thompson and J. M. Nelson in ibid., 26 (1978), 101–8; 28 (1980), 100–108); Richard Ashcraft and M. M. Goldsmith, 'Locke, revolution principles, and the formation of Whig ideology', *Historical Journal* 26 (1983), 773–800; and Ronald Hamowy, 'Cato's *Letters*, John Locke, and the republican paradigm', *History of Political Thought* 11 (1990), 273–94.

An important book for an understanding of Locke's influence in America is Donald S. Lutz, *The Origins of American Constitutionalism* (Baton Rouge: Louisiana State University Press, 1988). The subject is extensively discussed by Thomas Pangle in *The Spirit of Modern Republicanism: The Moral Vision of the American Founders and the Philosophy of Locke* (Chicago: University of Chicago Press, 1988), and by Steven Dworetz in *The Unvarnished Doctrine: Locke, Liberalism and the American Revolution* (Durham: Duke University Press, 1990).

The Straussian Interpretation

There is now a very extensive literature on Locke that takes its inspiration from Leo Strauss's *Natural Right and History*. The methodological principles on which this literature is founded are quite different from those respected in conventional history of ideas and philosophy; see Leo Strauss, *Persecution and the Art of Writing* (2nd edn, Chicago: University of Chicago Press, 1988), and, for critical commentary, Shadia B. Drury, *The Political Ideas of Leo Strauss* (Basingstoke: Macmillan, 1988), and Stephen Holmes, 'Truths for philosophers alone', *Times Literary Supplement*, 1–7 December 1989, 1319–24.

The best of the Straussian studies is Thomas Pangle's *The Spirit of Modern Republicanism*, but Pangle does not give anything like a full bibliography of Straussian work on Locke. There were a number of replies to Strauss's account of Locke between the late fifties and the late sixties, but I know of no sustained discussion of Straussian interpretations of Locke since John Dunn, 'Justice and the interpretation of Locke's political theory', *Political Studies*, 16 (1968), 68–87, and Hans Aarsleff, 'Some observations on recent Locke scholarship', in *John Locke: Problems and Perspectives*, ed. John W. Yolton, 262–71. Since then the followers of Strauss have, at least as far as Locke scholarship is concerned, been left to go their own way largely undisturbed.

A Note on the Texts

In each case (with the exception of the two translations from Latin originals) I have based my own text on the manuscript source, or, where there is no manuscript, on the best published text. I have not bothered to record divergences between my readings and those of previous editors except in the case of the *Two Treatises*: here the published text is so good that it may be worth recording variations, slight as these are.

1. Locke's letter to Stubbe is in Ms Locke c 27, fol. 12. It was first printed, somewhat unreliably, by Abrams (in Locke 1967), and then by de Beer (in Locke 1976–89).

2. Locke's letter to Tom is in Ms Locke c 24, fol. 182. It was first printed by de Beer (in Locke 1976–89). Tom has been variously identified with Locke's brother Thomas and with Locke's friend Thomas Westrowe.

3. Locke's *First Tract on Government* is in Ms Locke e 7. It was first printed by Viano (in Locke 1961); the standard edition is that of Abrams (in Locke 1967a).

4. The Preface to the *First Tract* is in Ms Locke c 28, fols. 1–2. It was first printed by Viano (in Locke 1961); the standard edition is that of Abrams (in Locke 1967a).

5. The *Second Tract* is in Ms Locke c 28. It was first printed by Viano (in Locke 1961). I have translated the text printed by Abrams (in Locke 1967a, 185–209).

6. The *Essays on the Law of Nature* (Ms Locke f 31) were first printed by von Leyden (in Locke 1954). This is likely to remain the standard edition, although there is now also an edition by R. Horwitz, J. Strauss Clay and D. Clay (Locke 1990). I have translated von Leyden's text. Although the other *Essays* probably date to 1663, this one was dated by Locke 1664.

7. There appears to be no surviving manuscript of the letter to Boyle (I am grateful to Michael Hunter for discussing this question with me). The text was first published in Boyle (1744), and reprinted by de Beer (in Locke 1976–82). I have omitted the lengthy postscript to this letter.

8. There is as yet no readily available scholarly edition of the *Essay Concerning Toleration*, of which there are four surviving manuscripts, each differing from the other. I have, unfortunately, not had an opportunity to consult the collation of all four manuscripts prepared by K. Inoue (Locke 1974a). One of the drafts was reprinted in Fox Bourne (1876, vol. 1, 174–94). The present edition is based on what is obviously the last of the four versions: Ms Locke c 28, fols. 21–32. A collation of the differences between these two drafts is to be found in Gough (1956, 197–200).

9. The revised text of *The Fundamental Constitutions of Carolina* was first published in 1670. It appeared in Locke (1720). The original draft, with corrections in Locke's hand, is to be found in PRO CO 1 25.13. It is lovingly reprinted in Locke (1872). The best discussion of authorship is Haley (1968, 242–8). A less than satisfactory account of its place in Locke's political thought is McGuinness (1989).

10. 'Philanthropy, or The Christian Philosophers' is in Locke Ms c 27. It was first published in Locke (1972).

11. 'Obligation of Penal Laws' is in Locke's journal for 1676, Ms Locke f 1. It was first published in King (1829).

12. 'Law' is in Locke's journal for 1678, Ms Locke f 3. It was first published, incorrectly dated, by King (1829).

13. 'Credit, Disgrace' is in Locke's journal for 1678, Ms Locke f 3. It was first published by King (1829).

14. 'The Idea We Have of God' (the title is mine, not Locke's) is in Locke's journal for 1680, Ms Locke f 4. It is published, with incorrect date, in King (1829).

15. 'Inspiration' (again the title is mine) is in Locke's journal for 1681, Ms Locke f 5. It was first published (with incorrect date) by King (1829), and reprinted by Aaron and Gibb (in Locke 1936).

16. 'Virtus' is in Locke's 1661 Commonplace Book. This is in private hands, not, as stated in Long (1959, vii), in Harvard University Library. A microfilm is in the Bodleian Library. It was first published (with incorrect date) in King (1829).

17, 19, 23. There is no surviving manuscript of the *Two Treatises*. The copy text for any scholarly edition must be Locke's own copy in Christ's College, Cambridge, corrected for posterity. This has been brilliantly edited by Peter Laslett (first edition 1960; second edition 1967; student edition 1988). The final version of Laslett's text is the edition of 1988, which also contains his responses to Ashcraft's dating of the text. However, the scholarly apparatus of the 1967 edition must still be consulted. Laslett has emended his edition in at least four separate editions and printings. Nevertheless even the 1988 version is still not a perfect reproduction of the Christ's copy (although it is now near to being so). I have noted the following points at which the 1988 edition differs from the copy text for the passages reproduced here, without it being possible to discover an explanation in the 1967 collation:

1.§90 l. 20: 'their Parents', not 'the Parents'

2.§13 l. 19: 'be endured' has been silently corrected to 'to be endured'

2.§37 l. 26: 'a thousand acres yield', not 'a thousand acres will yield'

2.§42 l. 22: 'increase of lands': this does seem to be the reading of the Ms, but, as Tully has pointed out, the sense seems to require 'hands'. Moreover there are several parallel passages in 'For a General Naturalization: 1693' in which 'hands' is used in this context (Locke 1991, vol. 2, 487–92). The alternative would be 'increase of [the yield of] lands'.

2.§50 l. 7: I do not agree with Laslett's view that the Christ's copy is difficult to follow here; and the copy seems to require 'of the product'

2.§116 l. 17: 'his son', not 'this son'

2.§134, note: *Eccl Pol* l.1 continues to be misprinted in 1988

2.§202 l. 29: 'advantage of' has been silently corrected to 'advantages of'

2.§235 l. 58: 'servicem' has been silently corrected to 'cervicem'

2.§239 l. 53: 'Egyptians' has been silently corrected to 'Egyptian'

Obviously none of these modifications of the text affect the sense, and the majority of them are justified. They can stand as representative of the sorts of differences between my text and previous editions that are to be found in the great majority of texts printed in this edition.

18. 'Two Sorts of Knowledge' (the title is mine) is in Locke's journal for 1681, Ms Locke f 5. It was first printed (with incorrect date) by King (1829). It is also in Aaron and Gibb (Locke 1936).

20, 22. Letters to Edward Clarke: these are in Ms. Locke b 8. They were first published by Rand (in Locke 1927). The standard edition is de Beer's (Locke, 1976–89).

21. The *Letter Concerning Toleration* was published in its original Latin by Limborch in 1689. It is from him that we learn of its original composition in 1685. An English translation by William Popple appeared the same year. The second edition was a carefully corrected version of the first. Most of the corrections are stylistic, and in themselves hardly justify Montuori's hypothesis that the text had been corrected by Locke himself. Clearly, even if the text was only corrected by Popple, the second edition is superior to the first. But in two places there are changes which suggest Locke's own intervention. Near the beginning a quotation from 2 Timothy, introduced by Popple without warrant in his source, is dropped. Most remarkably (and unnoticed by Montuori), one passage (below, p. 409), which reads in the first edition 'our modern English history affords us fresh examples', is corrected to a more literal translation: 'the English history affords us fresher examples'. It is hard to imagine anyone preferring this stilted rendering on stylistic grounds; easy to imagine Locke insisting that the anonymous author must not be identified as English. Some modern scholars have been reluctant to rely on Popple's translation, arguing its unreliability: the case for disagreeing with them has been succinctly put by Ashcraft (1986, 498–9), and need not be repeated here.

There are three modern editions of significance, each with helpful introductions: Klibansky and Gough (in Locke 1968) reprint the Latin *Epistola* with a modern translation; Montuori (in Locke 1963) reproduces the Latin *Epistola* and an English edition based on the second edition of Popple's translation; Tully (in Locke 1983) produces an English text based on the first edition of Popple's translation.

24. 'Labour', like 'Virtus', is in the 1661 Commonplace Book. It was first published by Kelly (in Locke 1991).

25. 'Venditio' is also from the 1661 Commonplace Book. It was first published by Dunn (1968). The standard edition is now that of Kelly (in Locke 1991).

26. There is no modern edition of the Draft Report of the Board of Trade (PRO CO 388.5, fols. 232–49). It was first published in Locke (1789), and reprinted in Fox Bourne (1876). The standard discussion is currently Beier (1988), with some additional information from the Public Record Office manuscripts in Wootton (1989).

JOHN LOCKE
Political Writings

1: Letter to S.H. [Henry Stubbe] (mid–September? 1659)

S.H.

Sir

The same messenger that carried my letter the last week to Bristol returned with your book, which I have read with very much satisfaction, and the only pauses I made in my hasty perusal were to reflect with admiration the strength and vigour of your style, checkered, embellished, seasoned with many poignant passages of wit and sharp sallies, and that clearness of reason and plenty of matter wherewith every page is stuffed. Had some sort of men had but the tithe of so many arguments, they should have been mustered to one and thirtiethly beloved [?], and their numerous though unarmed files should have been marshalled with ostentation.

This is the only deficient I complain of, if I may be permitted to complain after satisfaction, which I do. Not that I think your weapon less sharp, if you do not everywhere show where the point lies, or think you no good champion because you [do not] hold it in that very posture and manage it with that regulated motion which a pedantical fencer would prescribe you. But because that party you more particularly design it against are so blinded with prejudice and ignorance that they will not be able to discover them unless a figure or hand in the margin direct their purblind observation. You must tell them what is argument *ab impossibili*, what *ab incongruo*, if you will have them take notice; and they will never believe you have any forces unless you draw them up into battalions and show them where they lie encamped. They are so generally habituated to that play of primus, secundus, tertius, the only thing one may confidently presume they brought from school, that unless you deal with them in the same method, they will not think themselves concerned. They will not conceive it possible they should be met with by a man that travels not in the same track, and it will fare with you as it did with a gentlewoman who, receiving an address from her servant conned out of the School of Compliments, answered what she thought pertinent, which the overlearned Innamorato finding not to agree with his lesson, nor to be the same he had got without book, told her she answered amiss, and concluded her a very ill courtier because she was not able to maintain the dialogue by rote.

To this I must add that I am sorry that you continued not your history of toleration down to these times, and given us an account of Holland, France, Poland, etc., since nearest examples have the greatest influence, and we are most easily persuaded to tread in those fresh steps which time hath least defaced, and men will travel in that road which is most beaten, though carriers only be their guides. So when you have added to the authority of antiquity the testimony of daily experience that men of different professions may quietly unite under the same government and unanimously carry the same civil interest, and hand in hand march to the same end of peace and mutual society, though they take different ways towards heaven, you will add no small strength to your case, and be very convincing to those to whom what you have already said hath left nothing to doubt but whether it be now practicable. But this I expect from the promise of a second edition. However you must be sure to reserve me one more of this, for I believe the importunity of many here will not let me bring back this to Oxford.

The only scruple I have is how the liberty you grant the Papists can consist with the security of the nation (the end of government), since I cannot see how they can at the same time obey two different authorities carrying on contrary interest, especially where that which is destructive to ours is backed with an opinion of infallibility and holiness supposed by them to be immediately derived from God, founded in the Scripture and their own equally sacred tradition, not limited by any contract and therefore not accountable to anybody, and you know how easy it is under pretence of spiritual jurisdiction to hook in all secular affairs, since in a commonwealth wholly Christian it is no small difficulty to set limits to each and to define exactly where one begins and the other ends. Besides I cannot apprehend, where they have so near a dependency, what security you can take of their fidelity and obedience from all their oaths and protestations, when that other sovereignty they pay homage to is acknowledged by them to be [the] owner of a power that can acquit them of all perfidy and perjury, and that will [be] ready to pardon and court them to it with dispensations and rewards; and you will have but small reason to repose trust in one who, whenever it shall be his interest (which it will always be), shall by deceiving you not only obtain the name of innocent but meritorious, who by throwing off his obligations (whereof he will always keep the key himself) shall not only possess himself of your portion of [the] earth, but purchase additional a title to heaven and be canonized saint at the charge of your life and liberty. And seeing you yourself (if I remember aright) make the apprehensions of interest and the justice of the case the rule and measure of constancy to, activity for, and obedience under any government, you can never hope that they should cordially concur with you to any establishment, whose consciences and concernments both for this world and the other shall always bias them another way.

These are those tares which started up in my thoughts amongst those better seeds you have sown there, and possibly are only owing to the temper of the soil and must grow or wither as you please to order them. Thus you see how I make use of the liberty you allow me out of a belief that you have as much ingenuity as learning, and 'tis in this confidence that I appear perhaps in the head of your assailants, but not with the thoughts of a duellist but doubter, being resolved not to be an opponent but

> your
> Admirer

2: Letter to Tom (20 October 1659)

Dear Tom,

Your errors as well as intentions oblige me, and I am content you should mistake my letters for indictments so long as it gives you occasion to confirm the innocence and integrity of your friendship. 'Twas your guilt that cast blacker upon my paper than my ink. This made you take every messenger for a pursuivant, and suspect every call for a hue and cry. When I complain you conceit I accuse you, and your imagination puts a trick upon you. I cannot blame you for yielding to that which is the great commander of the world, and 'tis fancy that rules us all under the title of reason: this is the great guide both of the wise and the foolish, only the former have the good luck to light upon opinions that are most plausible or most advantageous.

Where is that Great Diana of the world, Reason? Everyone thinks he alone embraces this Juno, whilst others grasp nothing but clouds. We are all Quakers here, and there is not a man but thinks he alone hath this light within and all besides stumble in the dark. 'Tis our passions, that brutish part, that dispose of our thoughts and actions. We are all centaurs, and 'tis the beast that carries us, and everyone's *recta ratio* is but the traverses of his own steps. When did ever any truth settle itself in anyone's mind by the strength and authority of its own evidence? Truths gain admittance to our thoughts as the philosopher did to the tyrant, by their handsome dress and pleasing aspect. They enter us by composition, and are entertained as they suit with our affections, and as they demean themselves towards our imperious passions. When an opinion hath wrought itself into our approbation and is got under the protection of our liking, 'tis not all the assaults of argument and the battery of dispute shall dislodge it.

Men live upon trust, and their knowledge is nothing but opinion moulded up between custom and interest, the two great luminaries of the world, the only lights they walk by. Since, therefore, we are left to the uncertainty of two such fickle guides, let the examples of the bravest men direct our opinions and actions; if custom must guide us, let us tread in those steps that lead to virtue and honour. Let us make it our interest to honour our maker, and be useful to our fellows, and content with ourselves. This, if it will not secure us from error, will keep us from losing ourselves. If we walk not directly straight we shall not be altogether in a maze, and since 'tis not agreed where and what reason is, let us content ourselves with the most beautiful and useful opinions.

The place I am in furnishes me with no relations, and my

affection must say something to you, though it tell you but my own idle thoughts. Though there be no harvest nor gleanings abroad, yet my friendship will needs make you a present, if it be but of the weeds of my own garden. Had I flowers you should have them too, but those I expect in return from your more fruitful and better cultivated mind, where, if there be any remains of reason left amongst men, I may hope to find it, whatever I have said. Bare opinion, methinks, will not serve my turn, for I shall always have reason to be, and you ought always to know that I am, most affectionately,

Sir, your cordial friend

JL

Pensford, 20 October 1659

3: From: 'Question: Whether the civil magistrate may lawfully impose and determine the use of indifferent things in reference to religious worship. Answer: Yes' (*First Tract on Government*, 1660)

[Bradshaw had written:] '*The opposers of liberty have very little else to urge for themselves besides inconveniences.*' But the defenders of the magistrate's power offer something more when they tell you that a man cannot part with his liberty and have it too, convey it by compact to the magistrate and retain it himself.

'*The first inconvenience is the impossibility to fix a point where the imposer will stop. For do but once grant that the magistrate hath a power to impose, and then we lie at his mercy how far he will go.*' An inconvenience as strong against civil as ecclesiastical jurisdiction: do but once grant the magistrate a power to impose taxes and we then lie at this mercy whether he will leave us anything. Grant him a power to confine anyone, and we cannot be long secure of any liberty: who knows how soon he will make our houses our prisons?

Grant him a power to forbid assemblies and conventions, and who knows how long he will allow us the company of our friends, or permit us to enjoy the conversation of our relations? A practice not unknown to the Presbytery of Scotland, who took on them at pleasure to forbid the civil and innocent meeting of friends in any place but the church or market, under pretence to prevent evil and scandal [vid. *Burden of Issachar*]. So far will religious and spiritual jurisdiction be extended even to the most indifferent of common actions when it falls into busy and unskilful hands. Grant once that the magistrate hath a power to command the subject to work, and limit his wages too, and who can secure us that he will not prove rather an Egyptian taskmaster than a Christian ruler, and enforce us to make bricks without straw to erect monuments of his rigour and our slavery [v. *Stat: 5. Eliza. c. 4; 1 Jac. c. 6*].

These are inconveniences whose speculation following from the constitution of polities may often fright but their practice seldom hurt the people. Nor will the largeness of the governor's power appear dangerous or more than necessary if we consider that as occasion requires it is employed upon the multitude that are as impatient of restraint as the sea, and whose tempests and overflows cannot be too well provided against. Would it be thought dangerous or inconvenient that anyone should be allowed to make banks and fences against the waves for fear he should too much encroach upon and straiten the ocean? The magistrate's concernments will always teach him to use no more rigour than the temper of the people and the necessity of the age shall call for, knowing that too great checks as well as too loose a rein may make this untamed beast to cast his rider. Who would decline embarking himself because the pilot hath the sole guiding of the ship, out of fear lest he should be too busy and impertinently troublesome at the helm, and disturb the voyage with the ill-management of his place, who would rather be content to steer the vessel with a gentle than a stiff hand would the winds and waves permit him? He increases his forces and violence only with the increase of the storm and tumult; the tossings and several turns of the ship are from without and not begotten in the steerage or at the helm.

Whence is most danger to be rationally feared, from ignorant or knowing heads? From an orderly council or a confused multitude? To whom are we most like to become a prey, to those whom the Scripture calls gods, or those whom knowing men have always found and therefore called beasts? Who knows but that since the multitude is always craving, never satisfied, that there can be nothing set over them which they will not always be reaching at and endeavouring to pull down? Those constitutions in indifferent things may be erected as the outward fences to secure the more substantial parts of religion which experience tells us they will be sure to be tampering with when these are gone, which are therefore fit to be set up because they may be with least danger assaulted and shaken, and that there may be always something in a readiness to be parted with to their importunity without injuring the indispensable and more sacred parts of religion when their fury and impatience shall make such an indulgence necessary? But I too forwardly intrude myself into the council chamber, and, like an impertinent traveller, which am concerned only which way the hand of the dial points, lose time in searching after the spring and wheels that give it motion. It being our duty not curiously to examine the counsels but cheerfully to obey the commands of the magistrate in all things that God hath left us free.

But to my author's inconvenience I shall oppose another I think greater, I'm sure more to be provided against because more pressing and oftener occurring. Grant the people once free and unlimited in the exercise of their religion, and where will they stop, where will they themselves bound it, and will it not be religion to destroy all that are not of their profession? And will they not think they do God good service to take vengeance on those that they have voted his enemies? Shall not this be the land of promise, and those that join not with them be the Canaanites to be rooted out? Must not Christ reign and they prepare for his coming by cutting off the wicked? Shall we not be all taught of God and the ministry cast off as needless? They that have got the right use of Scripture and the knack of applying it with advantage, who can bring God's word in defence of those practices which his soul abhors and do already tell us we are returning to Egypt, would, were they permitted, as easily find us Egyptians and think it their right to despoil us.

Though I can believe that our author would not make this large use of his liberty, yet if he thinks others would not so far improve his principles, let him look some years back: he will find that a liberty for tender consciences was the first inlet to all those confusions and unheard of and destructive opinions that overspread this nation. The same hearts are still in men, as liable to zealous mistakes and religious furies, there wants but leave for crafty men to inspirit and fire them with such doctrines. I cannot deny but that the sincere and tender-hearted Christians should be gently dealt with, and much might be indulged them, but who shall be able to distinguish them, and if a toleration be allowed as their right, who shall hinder others who shall be ready enough to lay hold on the same plea?

Indeed having observed that almost all those tragical revolutions which have exercised Christendom these many years have turned upon this hinge, that there hath been no design so wicked which hath not worn the vizor of religion, nor rebellion which hath not been so kind to itself as to assume the specious name of reformation, proclaiming a design either to supply the defects or correct the errors of religion, that none ever went about to ruin the *state* but with pretence to build the *temple*, all those disturbers of public quiet being wise enough to lay hold on religion as a shield which if it could not defend their cause was best like to secure their credit, and gain as well pity to their ruin as partisans to their success, men finding no cause that can so rationally draw them to hazard their life, or compound for the dangers of a war, as that which promises them a better; all other arguments, of liberty, country, relations, glory, being to be enjoyed only in this life, can give but small encouragements to a man to endanger that and, to improve their present enjoyments a little, run themselves into the danger of an irreparable loss of all. Hence have the cunning and malice of men taken occasion to pervert the doctrine of peace and charity into a perpetual foundation of war and contention. All those flames that have made such havoc and desolation in Europe, and have not been quenched but with the blood of so many millions, have been at first kindled with coals from the altar, and too much blown with the breath of those that attend the altar, who, forgetting their calling, which is to promote peace and meekness, have proved the trumpeters of strife and sounded a charge with a 'curse ye Meros'. I know not therefore how much it might conduce to the peace and security of mankind if religion were banished the camp and forbid to take arms, at least to use no other sword but that of the word and spirit, if ambition and revenge were disrobed of that so specious outside of reformation and the cause of God, were forced to appear in their own native ugliness and lie open to the eyes and contempt of all the world, if the believer and unbeliever could be content as Paul advises to live together, and use no other weapons to conquer each other's opinions but pity and persuasion (1 Cor. 7), if men would suffer one another to go to heaven every one his own way, and not out of a fond conceit of themselves pretend to a greater knowledge and care of another's soul and eternal concernments than he himself, how much I say if such a temper and tenderness were wrought in the hearts of men our author's doctrine of toleration might promote a quiet in the world, and at last bring those glorious days that men have a great while sought after the wrong way, I shall leave everyone to judge.

But it is like to produce far different effects among a people that are ready to conclude God dishonoured upon every small deviation from that way of his worship which either education or interest hath made sacred to them, and that therefore they ought to vindicate the cause of God with swords in their hands, and rather to fight for his honour than their own; who are apt to judge every other exercise of religion as an affront to theirs, and branding all others with the odious names of idolatry, superstition or will-worship, and so looking on both the persons and practices of others as condemned by God already, are forward to take commission from their own zeal to be their executioners, and so in the actions of the greatest cruelty applaud themselves as good Christians, and think with Paul they do God good service. And here, should not the magistrate's authority interpose itself and put a stop to the secret contrivances of deceivers and the passionate zeal of the deceived, he would certainly neglect his duty of being the great *conservator pacis*, and let the very foundations of government and the end of it lie neglected, and leave the peace of that society [which] is committed to his care open to be torn and rent in pieces by everyone that could but pretend to conscience and draw a sword.

4: 'Preface to the Reader' from the *First Tract on Government* (1661)

Reader

This discourse, which was written many months since, had not been more than *written* now, but had still lain concealed in a secure privacy, had not importunity prevailed against my intention, and forced it into the public. I shall not trouble thee with the history or occasion of its original, though it be certain that thou here receivest from me a present which was not at first designed thee. This confession, how little soever obliging, I the more easily make since I am not very solicitous what entertainment it shall receive, and if truth (which I only aim at) suffer not by this edition, I am very secure as to everything else. To bespeak thy impartial perusal were to expect more from thee than books, especially of this nature, usually meet with; and I should too fondly promise myself the good hap to meet with a temper that this age is scarcely blessed with, wherein truth is seldom allowed a fair hearing, and the generality of men, conducted either by chance or advantage, take to themselves their opinions as they do their wives, which when they have once espoused they think themselves concerned to maintain, though for no other reason but because they are theirs, being as tender of the credit of one as of the other, and if 'twere left to their own choice, 'tis not improbable that this would be the more difficult divorce.

My design being only the clearing a truth in question, I shall be very glad if I have said anything that may satisfy her impartial followers, being otherwise very careless how little soever I gratify the interests or fancies of others. However that I may not give any advantage to this partial humour, I shall take the same way to prevent it that the gentleman whom I trace hath trod before me, and by concealing my name leave thee concerned for nothing but the arguments themselves.

And indeed besides the reasons that persuaded my author to conceal himself there be many other that more strongly oblige me to it. Amongst others, I should be sure to incur the censure of many of my acquaintance. For having always professed myself an enemy to the scribbling of this age and often accused the pens of Englishmen of as much guilt as their swords, judging that the issue of blood from whence such an inundation hath flowed had scarce been opened, or at least not so long unstopped, had men been more sparing of their ink, and that these furies, war, cruelty, rapine, confusion etc., which have so wearied and wasted this poor nation, have been conjured up in private studies and from thence sent abroad to disturb the quiet we enjoyed. This objection, then, will lie against me, that I now run upon the same guilt I condemned in others, disturbing the beginnings of our happy settlement by engaging in a quarrel, and bandying a question which it would be well if it were quite forgotten, and hath been but too loudly disputed already. But I hope I shall deserve no more blame than he that takes arms only to keep the peace, and draws his sword on the same side with the magistrate, with a design to suppress, not begin, a quarrel.

I could heartily wish that all disputes of this nature would cease, that men would rather be content to enjoy the freedom they have, than by such questions increase at once their own suspicions and disquiets, and the magistrate's trouble, such discourses, however cautiously proposed, with desire of search and satisfaction, being understood usually rather to speak discontents than doubts, and increase the one rather than remove the other. And however sincere the author may be, the interested and prejudiced reader not seldom greedily entertains them as the just reproaches of the state, and hence takes the boldness to censure the miscarriages of the magistrate and question the equity and obligation of all laws which have not the good luck to square with his private judgement.

I confess it cannot be thought, but that men should fly from oppression, but disorder will give them but an incommodious sanctuary. 'Tis not without reason that tyranny and anarchy are judged the smartest scourges can fall upon mankind, the plea of authority usually backing the one and of liberty inducing the other: and between these two it is that human affairs are perpetually kept tumbling. Nor is it to be hoped that the prudence of man should provide against these beyond any fear of their return, so long as men have either ambitious thoughts or discontented minds, or till the greatest part of men are well satisfied in their own condition;

which is not to be looked for in this world. All the remedy that can be found is when the prince makes the good of the people the measure of his injunctions, and the people, without examining the reasons of them, pay a ready and entire obedience, and both these founded on a mutual confidence each of other, which is the greatest security and happiness of any people, and a blessing, if ever, to expect now, and to be found amongst those many miracles that have restored, and we hope will continue, his Majesty to us, very pregnant assurances whereof we have received in that great tenderness and affection to his people which his Majesty beyond parallel hath shown in the transactions of the late and the opening of the present Parliament.

As for myself, there is no one can have a greater respect and veneration for authority than I. I no sooner perceived myself in the world but I found myself in a storm, which hath lasted almost hitherto, and therefore cannot but entertain the approaches of a calm with the greatest joy and satisfaction; and this, methinks, obliges me, both in duty and gratitude, to be chary of such a blessing, and what lies in me to endeavour its continuance, by disposing men's minds to obedience to that government which hath brought with it that quiet and settlement which our own giddy folly had put beyond the reach, not only of our contrivance, but hopes. And I would men would be persuaded to be so kind to their religion, their country, and themselves as not to hazard again the substantial blessings of peace and settlement in an over-zealous contention about things which they themselves confess to be little and at most are but indifferent.

Besides the submission I have for authority, I have no less a love of liberty, without which a man shall find himself less happy than a beast. Slavery being a condition which robs us of all the benefits of life, and embitters the greatest blessings, reason itself in slaves (which is the grand privilege of other men) increasing the weight of their chains and joining with their oppressors to torment them. But since I find that a general freedom is but a general bondage, that the popular asserters of public liberty are the greatest engrossers of it too and not unfitly called its keepers, and I know not whether experience (if it may be credited) would not give us some reason to think that were this part of freedom contended for here by our author generally indulged in England, it would prove only a liberty for contention, censure and persecution, and turn us loose to the tyranny of a religious rage. Were every indifferent thing left unlimited nothing would be lawful, and 'twould quickly be found that the practice of indifferent things not approved by dissenting parties would then be judged as anti-Christian and unlawful as their injunction is now, and engage the heads and hands of the zealous partisans in the necessary duty of reformation, and it may well be feared by any that will but consider the conscientious disorders amongst us that the several bands of saints would not want their Venners to animate and lead them on in the work of the Lord:

> Summus utrimque
> Inde furor vulgo, quod numina vicinorum
> Odit uterque locus, quum solos credat habendos
> Esse deos, quos ipse colit.

[Each party is filled with fury against the other, because each hates its neighbours' gods, believing that none can be holy but those that it worships itself. Juvenal, *Satire* XV, ll. 35ff.]

And he must confess himself a stranger to England that thinks that meats and habits, that places and times of worship etc., would not be as sufficient occasions of hatred and quarrels amongst us, as leeks and onions and other trifles described in that satire by Juvenal was amongst them, and be distinctions able to keep us always at a distance, and eagerly ready for like violence and cruelty as often as the teachers should alarm the consciences of their zealous votaries and direct them against the adverse party.

I have not therefore the same apprehensions of liberty that I find some have, or can think the benefits of it to consist in a liberty for men at pleasure to adopt themselves children of God, and from thence assume a title to inheritances here and proclaim themselves heirs of the world; not a liberty for ambition to pull down well-framed constitutions, that out of the ruins they may build themselves fortunes; not a liberty to be Christians so as not to be subjects; nor such a liberty as is like to engage us in perpetual dissension and disorder. All the freedom I can wish my country or myself is to enjoy the protection of those laws which the prudence and providence of our ancestors established and the happy return of his Majesty hath restored: a body of laws so well composed that whilst this nation would be content only to be under them they were always sure to be above their neighbours, which forced from the world this constant acknowledgement, that we were not only the happiest state but the purest Church of the latter age.

'Tis therefore in defence of the authority of these laws that against many reasons I am drawn to appear in public, the preservation whereof as the only security I can yet find of this nation's settlement I think myself concerned in, till I can find other reasons than I have yet met with to show their non-obligation as long as unrepealed, and dispense with my obedience. After this I hope I need not assure thee that neither vanity nor any pique against the author put the pen into my hand, the concealment we both lie under having sufficiently provided against that suspicion. I dare say could his opinion have ever won upon me, it would have been in that handsome dress and those many ornaments his pen hath bestowed upon it with all the advantages it was capable of. But I cannot relinquish the contrary persuasion whilst truth (at least in my apprehension) so strongly declares for it, and I believe he cannot take it ill that whilst he pleads so earnestly for liberty in actions I should be unwilling to have my understanding, the noblest part, imposed on, and will not be so forgetful of his own principles as to deny me the liberty of dissenting. And if he will permit himself to peruse these answers with the same desire of satisfaction wherewith he professes himself to have proposed his doubts, and I assure him I read them, it may be hoped he will be persuaded, if not to alter his judgement, yet at least not to think them blind who cannot see in his spectacles or cannot find themselves by his arguments freed from that obedience to the civil magistrate in all things indifferent, which obedience God in his infinite wisdom hath made necessary and therefore not left free.

I have chose to draw a great part of my discourse from the supposition of the magistrate's power, derived from, or conveyed to him by, the consent of the people, thereby to obviate all objections that might from thence be made by those patrons of liberty, the foundation of their plea being usually an opinion of their natural freedom, which they are apt to think too much entrenched on by impositions in things indifferent. Not that I intend to meddle with that question whether the magistrate's crown drops down on his head immediately from heaven or be placed there by the hands of his subjects, it being sufficient to my purpose that the supreme magistrate of every nation, what way soever created, must necessarily have an absolute and arbitrary power over all the indifferent actions of his people. And if his authority must needs be of so large an extent in the lowest and narrowest way of its original that can be supposed, when derived from the scanty allowance of the people, who are never forward to part with more of their liberty than needs must, I think it will clearly follow, that if he receive his commission immediately from God the people will have little reason thereupon to think it more confined than if he received it from them, until they can produce the charter of their own liberty, or the limitation of his authority, from the same God that gave it. Otherwise, no doubt, that [which] God doth not forbid or command, his vicegerent may, and the people will have but a poor pretence to liberty in indifferent things in a condition wherein they have no liberty at all, but by the appointment of the Great Sovereign of heaven and earth are born subject to the will and pleasure of another.

But I shall not build upon this foundation, but allowing every man by nature as large a liberty as he himself can wish, shall yet make it appear that whilst there is society, government and order in the world, rulers still must have the power of all things indifferent, which I hope (Reader) thou wilt find evident in the following pages whither I remit thee.

Only give me leave first to say that it would be a strange thing if anyone amongst us should question the obligation of those laws which are not ratified nor imposed on him but by his own consent in Parliament.

5: 'Question: Can the civil magistrate specify indifferent things to be included within the order of divine worship, and impose them upon the people? Answer: Yes' (*Second Tract on Government*, *c.* 1662)

This truth is nowadays a matter of controversy. It has been the subject of innumerable bitter disputes, and has been fought over by irreconcilable factions. If only for once people would cease to question it! If it was once acknowledged as it should be by everybody and properly established as beyond doubt it would bring security to individuals and peace to society. Then it would no longer require defence, but merely the recognition of its adherents. Thanks to it, we, worn out as we are by bitter conflicts of pen and sword, could become content with our liberty and tranquillity. But when I remember what disasters have stemmed from mistaken views on this one issue, how it has provoked conflicts both in the political arena and on the battlefield, conflicts which have only recently died down, so that the echo of them has hardly yet died away; when I think how rarely this extraordinarily provocative subject is raised in public without as many armed men as arguments being marshalled on either side of it, so that blows usually follow words; when I realize that it is not a subject for lazy and relaxed discussion, but that it makes people ready to fight, and sets them, furious and enraged, at odds with each other, then I am bound to recognize that I am not embarking on some gentlemanly disagreement or entering into some sporting competition, but that I must prepare to fight, for I am not so much putting forward an argument as giving the signal for battle. There is scarcely anyone who can be even-tempered when discussing this subject, who can participate calmly in disputes of this sort without believing that his own interests are directly involved and must be defended with all his strength, literally as well as metaphorically. Some, excited by their aspirations, their beliefs, their consciences, anxiously complain that too much licence is endangering peace, religion, and the Church; others are driven to the opposite conclusion, bitterly crying out that the liberty of the Gospel, the fundamental entitlement of all Christians, is being tyrannically denied them, and the rights of their consciences trampled upon. This view leads to contempt for the magistrate and disrespect for the laws; nothing, whether secular or spiritual, is taken seriously, for they believe people can do what they like, so long as they defend political freedom and liberty of conscience, two slogans which people are extraordinarily quick to rally around. Indeed the burning zeal of those who discover how to legitimate the rashness and ignorance of the multitude by appealing to conscience often ignites a fire capable of devastating everything. Germany, I need hardly say, is an example of this.

If only we in England, so fortunate in other respects, had in recent times been willing to settle for examples drawn from abroad, and did not have to acknowledge the tragic evidence of our own domestic, self-inflicted wounds, the result of our setting out to experience for ourselves just how many calamities would result if we allowed our passions free rein under the guise of promoting Christian liberty and true religion. The memory of these events would be painful indeed, were it not for our present good fortune. Those days seem now to have passed, and order has been restored. We can now look back upon past miseries as men do when, having recently been tossed about on a stormy sea, they stand safe upon the shore and look with pleasure at the futilely threatening waves. Now God has restored peace to our land, something which could only come about through a long series of miracles, so that the discord of the immediate past makes us delight in it all the more. We must hope that nobody will now be so pig-headed and obstinate as to try once again to destabilize society, or to question the magistrate's authority to legislate on indifferent things. Now that civil strife has died away and religious enthusiasm is on the wane, more sober minds will recognize that civil obedience, even in the indifferent aspects of divine worship, is not one of the least important of Christian obligations, and that our only hope lies in punctilious obedience. Thus it is my hope that in future this controversial subject will give rise to no battles, except mock ones of the sort in which I am now engaged. So that we may the better draw up our battle lines we must explain the issues and define the terms of debate, in particular so that we may be clear about the meaning of the key terms 'magistrate', 'religious worship, and 'indifferent things'.

(1) By the term 'magistrate' we should here be understood to mean the person who has overall responsibility for the welfare of the community, who has the ultimate authority over all individual subjects, and, lastly, to whom is delegated the right to make and to repeal laws. It is this which gives the magistrate that supreme right of command which alone enables him to command others and direct society's affairs to the public good, according to his understanding of it, and employing whatever means he sees fit, and which enables him to order and dispose the people so as to keep them in peace and concord. There is no need to list here all the particular marks of sovereignty, or to enumerate prerogative rights. Among them, however, are the right of final judgement in legal cases, to sentence to death, to declare war and peace, to coin money, to levy tolls and taxes, along with other similar rights, all of which indisputably derive from the right to legislate. The holder of this right may be variously specified in different states according to their particular customs, but there is no need here to go into the various types of constitution, or to define the number of governors who may share in the magistrate's power. For our purposes it is sufficient if we take it to be axiomatic that the magistrate is the individual king or the assembly of whatever sort which can by right impose and enforce laws upon the subjects.

(2) The term 'religious worship' has more than one meaning.

(i) There are some who make no distinction between 'religious worship' and 'religion'. They give both terms an unduly wide meaning, using them to refer to the whole range of obligations imposed on us by divine law. Anything which obliges our consciences, anything which we are responsible for according to God's commands, they quite improperly term 'religion' and a part of 'religious worship'. The result of this is that almost all human actions come to be regarded as part of religious worship, so that we are said to worship God in eating, drinking, and sleeping, since there is scope for virtue and vice in these activities. Surely no one, we can be sure, will deny that if the term is taken in this broad sense, then the magistrate can prescribe indifferent things as part of religious worship and impose them upon his subjects, although if this is conceded it will perhaps be difficult to show why the magistrate must be denied the same right when it comes to matters of Church furnishings or religious ceremonies, for in both cases the same argument from indifferency applies: God, the supreme legislator, has nowhere denied the magistrate authority to concern himself with such matters. But we will return to this question later.

(ii) More properly, the term 'religious worship' is used to refer to all those actions of the inner virtues of which God is the object, such as the love, reverence, fear, trust of God, etc. This is that inner worship of the heart that God demands, in which the life and breath of true religion consists. Take away this, and all the other activities which form part of religious worship serve merely to provoke God, not to propitiate him. On their own, they represent a sacrifice no more pleasing to God than are the mutilated carcasses of slaughtered beasts. This is why the God of the New Testament is unique in insisting, as he does so frequently, that the heart and the spirit must be devoted to him. He calls the hidden recesses of the body temples dedicated to his worship, and demands a spirit obedient to himself as if it were the only form of worship which concerned him. Such worship, however, entirely silent and secret, completely concealed from the eyes and ears of men, is not claimed to be subject to human laws, nor indeed can it be made so. God alone can look into the hearts of men. He alone can inquire into the secret sentiments of the heart, for he alone can have knowledge of the private deliberations of the mind and can pass judgement upon them.

(iii) The outward acts of religion are also termed 'divine worship'. God decided that man should be given a body as well as a soul. The soul is for his service alone, while the body makes possible human society and cooperation, for without its mediation and assistance men cannot make known their sentiments or benefit from their good-will towards each other. God however demands that both should be obedient to him, and requires that each of them render the tribute it is able to pay. Since he expects to be honoured and revered on earth, he is not satisfied with the silent and almost furtive worship of the heart alone, but requires his worshippers openly to proclaim his name, so that by their example the rest of mankind may be taught to worship and reverence the true God. Consequently he demands the performance of those outward actions through which the inner worship of the soul may be expressed, and indeed may even be magnified. These include public prayers, ceremonies of thanksgiving, the singing of psalms, participation in the sacraments, the hearing of the divine word. By these we either publicly testify to our love of, faith in, and obedience to God, or else seek to develop these in the future. This is what is called the outward worship of God, which is required by God throughout his law, and which we are obliged by the Bible to perform. The magistrate has no authority as far as this is concerned, since God's decrees can be altered by none but God himself.

(iv) But since all actions must always be performed in the context of numerous circumstances which necessarily accompany them – circumstances of time, place, behaviour, appearance, and so forth – such circumstances must also accompany religious worship. This context, since it forms a necessary part of religious worship, and because in all times and places it contributes in some degree to the solemn and public ceremonies of religious worship, is generally also understood by the term 'religious worship' and called ritual. However, God in his wisdom and unfailing beneficence has surrendered these ceremonial aspects of religious worship to the discretion of the magistrate, and entrusted them to the discretion of he who holds power and has the right to govern the Church, so that he may change, abolish, renew, or in any other way impose rituals as the circumstances of the time, the customs of the nation, and the needs of the Church may require. God, so long as his injunctions regarding the true and spiritual worship are respected, and so long as the essentials of religion are untouched, permits everything else to be established as seems good to the particular Churches, that is to say to their governors, subject only to this principle and precondition, that dignity, decency, and order be aimed at. In different places these objectives will be realized in different ways, and it would have been impossible for the divine law to decree a single rule and practice which would establish what was proper for each and every nation and what was not. Therefore God in his great mercy, so that the conversion of different peoples to the Christian religion should be made as straightforward as possible, and so that the approach to Christ and the new religion through the Gospel should be free of obstructions, decreed that the Christian religion be embraced privately in the heart and by faith alone, and although he required the true religion to be made known in ceremonies and public gatherings, yet he did not impose so difficult a condition upon new converts as to demand that they should immediately abandon the ceremonies and customs of their nation. These are generally the more beloved the longer they have been respected and have been upheld by public opinion and by education, so that most men would give up their wealth, their liberty, their lives, and everything rather than their veneration for and practice of these customs. How unwillingly, how reluctantly those Jews who converted to Christianity abandoned that heavy and burdensome succession of ceremonies which had become second nature to them as part of the custom of their people; Christ had freed them, but they did not want the heavy yoke of tradition to be lifted off their necks. It has recently been reported how a city in the Far East, located in China, was forced to surrender after a lengthy siege. The gates were opened and the enemy forces let in. All the inhabitants submitted themselves to the will of their triumphant conquerors. They abandoned into their enemies' hands themselves, their wives, their servants, their liberty, their possessions, and indeed everything they possessed, both sacred and secular. But when they were ordered to cut off the pigtail which it was the custom of the country to wear, then they rushed fiercely back into the fray, and fought until they had all been killed. Men who had been willing to hand over all their worldly goods to their enemies would not tolerate the least interference with their hair because they wore it according to the custom of their nation. Thus they easily preferred to life itself and to the concrete benefits afforded by nature something of no significance, of no intrinsic value, a mere excretion of the body, but which they, universally accepting the tradition of their society, happened to regard as sacrosanct. Anyone who thinks back over our own civil conflicts will perhaps admit that even in our country some people on certain occasions have fought against their opponents with as much uncompromising determination and as much savagery when what was at stake was of no greater significance. But we must return to the point.

These ceremonies, these circumstances in which actions are performed, differ so greatly one from another, and vary so much between peoples, that you would look in vain if you hoped to find a common standard of propriety, and you would search through the Gospel to no purpose if that was your aim. You would have great difficulty persuading someone from the East, or a Muslim, to become a Christian if you insisted it involved worshipping God bare-headed and, as they would see it, disrespectfully. This would seem as dreadful to them, because as contrary to custom, as it would seem to us to pray with our heads covered. No one would contemplate converting to a religion whose ceremonies seemed to him to be ridiculous, but of course the customs of every nation seem ridiculous to every other. Consequently God, taking account of human foolishness, made his worship accessible to all, to be adorned with external ceremonies as men thought best, taking account of their own traditions. He no more judges his worshippers according to such things than a king assesses the faith and obedience of his subjects by looking at the quality of their clothes or the cut of their hair. At the same time it must be said, however, that neither Christians nor citizens can expect to be well thought of if they are careless and negligent when it comes to such external matters. It seems then that everybody should agree that the magistrate should be entitled to judge what is orderly and decent, and that he alone can define what is to be considered beautiful and attractive. Nor indeed (despite the claims some people make to the contrary) do I think it the least important part of Christian liberty that it allows the magistrate to consider at the same time both the peace of society and the welfare and dignity of religion, and to provide for them both with a single set of laws. This completes our consideration of the term 'religious worship'.

Next we must explain what we mean when, in this context, we say that the magistrate 'can impose on his subjects'. Among legal theorists it is an axiom that we 'can' do what we are legally entitled to do. But I think two separate things are implied by the phrase we are concerned with. On the one hand it refers to the right of the magistrate and his legal entitlement; on the other to the obligation of the subjects. There is a difference between what the magistrate can do without breaking the law, and what he can do so that in doing it he imposes an obligation upon his subjects. In order to clarify these two types of entitlement we must make some distinctions:

(1) In the sanctions imposed by the magistrate we can identify a

double power which I will call a material power and an injunctive power: one is a power over the subject-matter of the law, the other a right to issue the command in question. Power is material when the thing which is commanded by the magistrate is lawful to be done. It must be an indifferent act which is not contrary to any divine law. Power is injunctive when the particular command is one that the magistrate has a right to issue. For on the one hand the magistrate may commit a sinful action in commanding something which is in principle subject to his determination; on the other it is not legitimate for him to issue commands with regard to anything and everything that is free and indifferent, enclosing everything within legal obligations and leaving the people no freedom of action, for the magistrate is set over the people and governs them only so that he may aim at the public good and the common welfare. He holds the helm so that he may steer the boat into the harbour, not on to the rocks. The extent of the legislator's power is a function of his purpose and intention. The magistrate can impose whatever he thinks is conducive to the safety of the commonwealth, but he cannot (at least not without sin) impose anything which he does not consider to be directed to and determined by this end.

(2) As far as the obligation of subjects is concerned, it needs to be recognized that the authority of the magistrate is on the one hand directive and on the other coercive, and that a double obligation on the part of the subject corresponds to this double authority. In the first place there is an obligation to act, and in the second, if I may so put it, to suffer: that is, in common speech, an obligation to active and to passive obedience.

If this is accepted, I would conclude from it:

(i) That the subject is bound passively to obey any decree of the magistrate whatsoever, whether it is just or unjust. There can be no possible justification for a private citizen's resisting the decrees of the magistrate by force of arms, although if the subject-matter of the decree is unlawful then the magistrate sins in commanding it.

(ii) That if a law is legitimate both materially and injunctively, then the magistrate is entitled to ratify it, and the subject is obliged to obey it in every respect, both actively and passively.

(iii) That if the law is legitimate as to its subject, but illegitimate as concerns its injunction and its intention, in that it is directed not at the public good but private benefit – for example, when a magistrate, acting either out of cruelty, or greed, or vanity, makes a law with the sole purpose of enriching himself, humiliating others, or gratifying himself – then the ruler whose decree it is is certainly guilty, and liable to divine punishment; yet nevertheless the subject is obliged to obey it not only passively but also actively. The reason for this is that where the subject-matter of the law is legitimate it is not the intention of the legislator, which I cannot know with any certainty, which obliges me to obedience but his expressed will, according to which I must shape my actions.

Lastly we must discuss the term 'indifferent things' and establish what they are, since there is a good deal of disagreement on this subject. Things are termed indifferent with respect to moral good and evil, so that all things which are neither good nor bad are said to be morally indifferent. Moral actions presume a law which establishes a standard of good and evil, in the light of which we ought to try and judge our life and actions, for it is certain that if there was no law then all actions and all things would be completely indifferent and equivalent, so that each individual could decide freely for himself whether or not to do them. Consequently if we are to have an adequate understanding of indifferent things we must give some account of law. The judicious Hooker describes it as follows (bk 1, ch. 2): 'That which doth assign the force and power, that which doth appoint the form and measure of working, the same we term a law.' Among other authorities there appear definitions of law which differ in the terms in which they are expressed, but not in their signification, just as they also put forward numerous differing divisions and distinctions, such as those between natural and positive law, divine and human, civil and ecclesiastical, and so on. Leaving these aside, for our present purposes let me distinguish the various types of law in a new way, dividing them into divine or moral; political or human; fraternal or concerned with charity; individual or private. This set of distinctions may be somewhat unfamiliar, and may be less exact than it should be, yet it is probably more useful for our present purposes, and it is certainly helpful in explaining the concept of indifferent things. This method of distinguishing laws depends primarily upon identifying their authors: thus divine law has God as its author; human law is derived from some man in a position of authority. The authors of these laws have an authority which places them above the laws themselves and the subjects over whom they rule. God is also the author of the law of charity, otherwise known as the fraternal law, but we can, and usually do, find ourselves under an obligation to that law because of our relationship to a fellow Christian who is our equal or even inferior. Finally, the type of law we have called 'private' has as its author any private person. He is not superior to that law, for he is subject to it, nor does he have the authority to repeal it once he has imposed it upon himself. The logic of these distinctions will appear more clearly from the following:

(1) The divine law is that which has been given to men by God. It is a rule and pattern of living for them. According as it becomes known by the light of natural reason, implanted in men, or is declared by supernatural revelation it is further divided into natural law and positive divine law. Since both of these are identical in their subject-matter, differing only in the method of their promulgation and the clarity of their injunctions, I call both of them 'moral' as well as 'divine'. For the divine law is the great measure of justice and rectitude, and the eternal foundation of all moral good and evil. Even in indifferent things good and evil can be discovered, but only thanks to the mediation of a subordinate law. Whatever, therefore, this law either orders or forbids is always and of necessity either good or bad; all other things which do not fall within the decrees of this law are left subject to man's free choice and are by their nature indifferent.

(2) Human law is that which is enacted by someone who holds authority over others and has the right to make laws for them. Rather, any instruction given by a superior to an inferior over whom he exercises legitimate authority, for instance the command of a parent to a child, or a master to a servant, can be termed a human law, and requires obedience. However, since the public decrees of a community, issued by a magistrate, are especially important, and since they abolish, confirm, and change private instructions at will, it is these in particular which we mean to refer to by the term human law. The proper subject-matter of this law is those indifferent things which have not been included within the scope of a higher – that is to say, the divine – law, and are thus not yet laid down and determined. It is true that the magistrate may

forbid theft or insist on chastity, but in doing so he is merely recapitulating the divine law: he is not enacting new law so much as disseminating the existing law and requiring obedience to it. Chastity and respect for private property remain necessary even if he does not legislate for them, and the obligation on the consciences of his subjects exists in any case. But since God has made the magistrate responsible for the welfare of society, since it would have been pointless for him to try and guard against all the possible ills which might befall a society by promulgating an infinite number of laws, and since, moreover, it would not have been in the best interests of each nation for them all to have the same legal code, God has left many indifferent things which are not included within his laws to the care of his deputy, the magistrate. It is right that government should concern itself with these indifferent things, for the magistrate can order or forbid them as circumstances require, and by wisely regulating them he can successfully pursue the welfare of his people.

(3) The fraternal law, or law of charity, is the term employed for the law which restricts our liberty within even narrower limits and by which we lose our freedom to do things which are permitted us by both divine and civil law. Thus a brother who lacks strength of character, despite the fact that he has no authority over us, can still have a certain right to restrict our liberty in matters which have been allowed us as indifferent by both God and the magistrate, with the result that something may be forbidden to us 'here and now' (as the phrase goes) which is entirely permissible to someone else under other circumstances. This is generally known as 'the law of scandal', which we obey when, having regard to the welfare and integrity of some Christian who does not have a proper understanding of the extent of his freedom, we choose not to make use in his presence of that freedom which otherwise would properly be ours. For otherwise he might be led astray by our example and, because he did not have a proper understanding of his Christian liberty, do something which he himself was not fully persuaded was permissible, and thereby make himself responsible for a sin. For example, it was permissible for Christians to eat meat offered to idols; nor was there any divine or human law against it. Thus the action was indifferent and fully licit. Since however many were ignorant of

this right, and, as the Apostle Paul says (Corinthians ch. 8, v. 7 et seq.) when he warns that we should abstain from actions which would otherwise be legitimate where there is a chance of our being a stumbling-block to a brother – the upshot of what he says is that indifferent and in every respect licit actions are to be abstained from if there is a fear that a brother might be shaken through our freedom: that is, not a fear that he might be angered, or might take it ill or become indignant that another sins or seems to sin, but a fear that our example might encourage him to do something which he himself ought not to do, because he himself believes it illicit.

(4) Apart from the laws I have spoken about, there remains one other, called the individual or private, which a person imposes on himself. Thus he renders obligatory things which were previously indifferent and were not covered by any pre-existing laws by imposing a new obligation upon himself. This law takes two forms: it can be imposed by the conscience or by an agreement, and thus depends sometimes on one's judgement, and sometimes on one's will. The law of conscience is what we call the final judgement of the practical intellect with regard to the truth of any moral proposition regarding a possible action. For it is not enough that an action should be indifferent in its own nature, unless we are also convinced that it is. God has placed in us a natural light, which he intended should be for us almost a private, ever present law-giver, whose edicts it is wrong to transgress even by a hair's breadth. The result is that our freedom in indifferent matters is highly unstable, and is dependent upon the opinions that each one of us holds, for it is certain that we are not free to do anything which we believe it is wrong to do. This is the point of St Paul's command to the Romans, ch. 14, v. 5: 'Let each man be fully certain in his own mind . . .', and v. 14: 'I know and am persuaded that through the Lord Jesus nothing is impure in itself' – he is talking of things to eat – 'but anything is impure for him who believes it to be impure'; and v. 23: 'He who is uncertain is in the wrong if he eats, because he does not eat out of faith; and whatever is not grounded in faith is sinful': faith here is nothing other than a true opinion as to one's freedom, as the context makes clear.

The other form of the private law results from the will and takes the form of an agreement which we enter into either with God or with our neighbour. In the first case it is called by the particular name of a vow: for example Jacob's vow (Genesis, ch. 28): 'Jacob vowed a vow, saying, If God will be with me, and will support me in the way in which I go, and will give me bread to eat and clothes to wear, then this pile of stones which I have erected will be God's house, and of everything you give me, I will without fail give the tenth of it to you.' Deuteronomy, ch. 23, vv. 21, 22 explains the obligation attached to a vow: 'If you vow a vow to the Lord your God, do not delay to fulfil it, for your God will surely demand full satisfaction of you, and failure will be a sin, where if you had not entered into a vow there would have been no sin'; a vow is there described as a free-will offering. Promises between men have the same obligation. In both cases our liberty is at our own command, to be given up or to be preserved as we choose.

In the light of these distinctions, I would maintain:

(1) That all these laws are in respect of their obligation entirely divine. That is to say, no other law directly and in itself obliges the consciences of men except the divine law. The others oblige men not by their own character and intrinsic strength, but by virtue of the divine precept in which they are grounded. Thus we are not obliged to obey magistrates for any other reason than that God has commanded it, saying 'every soul must be subjected to the higher powers', and 'it is necessary to be under command, not only out of fear, but also for reason of conscience' [Romans 12.1, 5].

(2) That human laws and the others I have just enumerated (with the single exception of the divine law) do not change the nature of indifferent things. They are not, by the authority of these laws, transformed from things indifferent into things which are always and in themselves necessary, but only into things which are necessary as far as we are concerned, here and now, and in the light of the obligation which is temporarily imposed upon us by a new and human command, by which we are required to obey, whether it be to act or to abstain from acting. But when that law is rescinded, or for whatever reason has ceased to apply, we are restored to our former liberty, for the nature of the thing itself is unaltered.

(3) That the subordination of these laws to each other is such that an inferior can in no way remove or diminish the authority or obligation of a superior. This would be to subject the master to the

slave, inverting the proper order of things. It would establish not order and government in the world but anarchy, and would lead to the ultimate authority being placed in the hands of the basest and most ignorant member of the mob. One may not appeal from God's tribunal to man's; nor can a subject's vow or a private error of conscience nullify a magistrate's edict. Otherwise order could nowhere exist, all laws would disappear, and there would disappear from the earth all authority. The beautiful order of nature would be overthrown and the structure of government undermined. Each individual would become his own law-giver, and his own God.

(4) Lastly, that all things which are indifferent as far as a higher law is concerned may be the subject-matter of a lower one; and that the authority of any of the laws is absolute in any matter which no superior law has in any way touched upon. If something has been left, as if evenly poised in a balance, being categorized neither on the one side as good, nor on the other as bad, then the next law down in the hierarchy of laws can establish and define it as being one or the other. Where the authority of the divine law ends, there the authority of the magistrate begins; and everything which is undetermined and indifferent as far as the divine law is concerned is subject to the civil law. Where the commonwealth has given no command, then the law of charity can take over. And if all these laws are silent, the commands of conscience and of the vow are to be listened to. Nor is there anything which is not stipulated by a superior law that a private individual cannot, as master of his own free will, oblige himself to, either by conscience, by vow, or by contract.

It is indeed difficult to see why those same men who in every other matter freely recognize this hierarchical ordering of authority, and this delimiting of inferior laws by superior ones, want to make an exception only in the case of the magistrate and of civil authority, presuming they recognize that public authority is to be preferred to private, and that some sort of authority and political society does, can, or should exist amongst men. In addition to recognizing the ultimate authority of the omnipotent God, these men have not the slightest doubt about the other laws I have enumerated: they cheerfully recognize the authority, as absolute and extensive as you please, of the laws of scandal, conscience, the vow and the contract in determining and restricting indifferent things. But the magistrate, whom they regard as a worthless little man with no more than transitory authority, and not, in the words of the Holy Scriptures, an authority ordained by God, they maintain has no authority when it comes to indifferent matters, at least where they concern the worship of God. The opposite view is the one we endeavour to maintain here, on the basis of comparison with the above-mentioned laws and their hierarchical ordering, and on the basis of the Apostle's instructions, when he commands everyone to be subordinate to the higher powers, or for that matter one could add the Epistle of St Peter, ch. 2, v. 13, 'Therefore be subject to every ordinance of man, or of the king as supreme ruler, on account of the Lord.' From which it would appear that the magistrate certainly has some authority in indifferent things, for where obedience and subjection are required, there authority must necessarily be present, nor can anyone be subjected unless there exists some superior, a person endowed with public authority.

This superior must be able to impose on his subjects not merely (as some would have it) things which are already good or evil by virtue of the divine law, but also indifferent things. This is evident because: (1) The Apostle in the text we have mentioned commands obedience not to God, but to the magistrate. If the magistrate's only duty was to repeat the commands of God, and in the manner of a herald rather than a legislator to repeat and to inculcate the divine instructions, then the magistrate would seem to have no power greater than that of any private citizen. For the divine law has the same force and power to command whether it is made known through a prince or a subject; nor does either one of them so much command as teach. (2) He commands that we be subject by reason of conscience. It would be pointless to add this, unless the magistrate has some authority in indifferent things. For no Christian could doubt that the conscience obliges in necessary things even if the magistrate says nothing, for things are necessary precisely because they oblige the conscience. This passage is to be understood, therefore, as referring to something which is obligatory solely because it is commanded by a superior authority; and this can only be an indifferent thing. (3) The Apostle takes as his example an indifferent thing. 'Tribute,' he says, 'to whom tribute is due,' although it is certain that no tribute is due unless the magistrate commands it. Both ownership and property rights are completely unrestricted. Anyone may choose whether he wishes to conserve his wealth or give his possessions away and as it were transfer them to another, and it is normally absolutely no concern of the law whether they belong to us or to someone else.

But where is this leading us? You may well ask, Is there anyone who denies the authority of the magistrate when it comes to secular indifferent things? My answer is that he who denies the magistrate's authority in one of these areas denies it in the other. Some deny both aspects of the magistrate's authority in so many words; others, under pressure, admit that they have done so; while others dispute the claim that that is what they have done. Nevertheless it is still the case that they stand or fall together. We must start therefore by establishing those principles which, once recognized, will enable us to demonstrate indisputably that indifferent matters, even those relating to the worship of God, ought to be subjected to the authority of the ruler.

All things which are indifferent are so for the same reason; and in both secular and spiritual indifferent matters the logic is the same, and indeed the very same objects are in question, seen only from two different points of view. There is no more difference between them than there is between the jacket I wear on a weekday and the very same jacket when I wear it to church. It follows that the magistrate's authority must embrace both categories of indifferent things, unless God has somewhere decreed that the magistrate's authority should be restricted within narrower limits, and has refused to allow places of worship to be included within the civil jurisdiction.

So that the truth may be still more clearly apparent the question needs to be examined at a little greater length. The sources of civil authority must be uncovered and the very foundations of its jurisdiction must be laid bare. There are however two differing foundations which I find commonly described by authors who treat of this subject. It makes no difference which of these hypotheses is adopted as far as establishing our thesis is concerned, for no matter which one is maintained the argument could scarcely be strengthened.

There are some who claim that men are born to servitude; others that they are born to freedom. The latter affirm that all men are equal according to the law of nature; the former stress that fathers have authority over their children, and claim that this is the origin of political authority. Whether this is true or not, this much is certain: if the ruler is born to exercise authority, and if he occupies the throne by divine institution and by reason of birthright and natural superiority, it follows that he is the sole ruler both of the earth and of its inhabitants, without any contract or limitation, and that he can do whatever is not prohibited by God, to whom alone he is subject, and from whom alone he is obliged to accept restrictions on how he should live and rule. Nor can anyone deny that all indifferent actions, no matter what category they belong to, are under his command, for to his discretion are delivered the liberty, possessions, and life itself of each of his subjects.

On the other hand if men have a right to an equal liberty by virtue of the fact that there is no difference between them at birth and they are therefore entitled to equal rights, it is nevertheless clear that men could establish no cooperation amongst themselves, no social life, no law, no institution of a commonwealth, through which men join together as if they were almost one body, unless each man had first given up that native liberty which the advocates of this hypothesis suppose they are entitled to, and had transferred his rights to another, whether that other be an individual ruler or an assembly, depending on the form of state they wish to establish. It is indispensable that this instituted authority should hold supreme power, for no commonwealth has ever existed or could ever exist without human laws, and laws can only bind if they are imposed by a supreme authority, for who can impose a law upon his superiors, or even upon those who are his equals in freedom? Now a supreme authority is one which does not have to give an account of its actions to any other superior authority upon earth. But such a power cannot be constituted unless each individual hands over to the legislator all his natural liberty, no matter how extensive it may be, and establishes him almost as a proxy, able to act with the authority of all, for each individual's right to consent has been delegated to him, so that he is able to make valid laws for them. The consequence of this is that whatever any individual was entitled to do he can now be commanded to do by the magistrate, for he embodies the authority and natural right of each individual by virtue of their mutual contract. Consequently all indifferent things, whether sacred or secular, are subject to his legislative authority and his right of command.

There may be a third way of accounting for the establishment of civil authority, according to which all authority comes from God, but the choice of who is to exercise that authority depends upon the nomination and designation of the people. The advantage of such an approach is that it overcomes the difficulty that it is hard to show, on the one hand, how a father's authority can develop into a right of sovereignty, or on the other, how the people can establish a ruler with a right to execute offenders. However, I do not intend to defend any one of these approaches, nor is it relevant to our present controversy to establish which of them is true. For in any event this is true: God intends there to be ordered society and government amongst men, or in other words he wants commonwealths to exist. In every commonwealth, however, there must be a supreme authority, for without such an authority a commonwealth cannot exist. That supreme authority is in every state of the same type, for it is always the legislative which is supreme. As we have shown above, the subject-matter of legislative authority is all indifferent things. Let me repeat: the supreme magistrate either has power over these, or he has no power at all. Since it is evident that the magistrate has authority in secular indifferent things, and nearly everyone admits this to be the case, it must follow, according to their own arguments, that if religion did not exist, all indifferent things would be subject to the authority of the magistrate. Since our religion is the Christian one, unless a law can be deduced from the Christian religion itself according to which some aspect of indifferent things must be withdrawn from the authority of the magistrate, a law establishing that one particular sort of indifferent action, carried out in some one particular sort of context, must not be controlled by the magistrate, then the magistrate's power in indifferent things must be (for Christians) identical to what it would be if there was no religion at all. Thus the magistrate's authority in some aspect of indifferent things is to be denied only on the basis of a Christian requirement of this sort. But whether any requirement restricting the magistrate's authority in this manner is indeed to be found in the Gospels will be apparent from the following analysis of the arguments of the differing schools which claim to identify such a requirement:

(1) The first group is that of those who, recognizing the sort of argument required, maintain that the law of the Gospel has withdrawn this authority from the magistrate, and has required the secular ruler to keep his distance from religious affairs. They state that the New Testament forbids him to dare to involve himself and his authority in matters of divine worship. They exult in being emancipated from this sort of slavery, and constantly boast about their Christian liberty. Determined to bolster up their case, they amass quotations from the Holy Scriptures, cite the testimony of the apostles, and deploy an army of precedents. Confident in the forces at their disposal, they look forward to an easy and indisputable victory. But since it would be a lengthy task to enumerate all these citations, let alone to study each one individually and reach a judgement on it, let me briefly respond as follows: it is true that an extensive liberty is given by our Saviour to the human race, and this liberty is often proclaimed in the Gospel, but when one looks a little more closely at the texts one realizes that they are of very little help to their case. For the liberty which is so often mentioned in the Gospels is of two sorts and two sorts only. In the first place, Christ frees his followers from their enslavement to the devil. In the second, he lifted from the necks of the Jews the heavy yoke of the ceremonial law, which neither they nor their fathers had been strong enough to carry, as the Apostle Peter says. He delivered them from that ancient law, under which, constrained and oppressed, they had long groaned, releasing them to share the common heritage of his followers and the happy freedom of his kingdom.

However, the New Testament nowhere makes any mention of restricting or limiting the magistrate's authority, for nowhere either in the Gospels or the Epistles is any instruction directed at the civil magistrate to be found. Indeed for the most part they have nothing to say about the commonwealth and civil government. Christ himself often had opportunities to enter into a discussion of the subject, but refused to involve himself in civil affairs, as if giving up the territory without a struggle. He lays claim to no kingdom as his own other than the spiritual and divine one, and overlooks the unaltered civic laws of the commonwealth. The teacher of the

Gentiles [the Apostle Paul] confirms the point (1 Corinthians, ch. 7) when he teaches that by the Christian religion and Christian freedom the secular condition of men is in no way altered, but that slaves, even when they become followers and subjects of Christ, remain slaves in law, and still owe the same obedience as before to their masters. Obviously the same logic applies to the relationship between princes and their subjects, for there is no hint or suggestion of any command which would diminish the authority of the magistrate in any sort of indifferent matter to be found in the Scriptures.

(2) Others deny that the magistrate is entitled to require particular sorts of indifferent behaviour in religious worship because the Scriptures alone are a perfect rule of life and of conduct. My reply is that this argument from the perfection of Scripture destroys the magistrate's authority as much in secular as in spiritual matters. For if the Scriptures are a perfect rule of conduct as alleged, so that it is a sin to introduce laws controlling and directing people's behaviour, then on this logic all laws would in future be equally illicit, whether they deal with spiritual or secular matters. The magistrate will not be permitted to pass a law on any subject at all, for no law can be introduced which does not seek to regulate people's lives and conduct. Why would he have a better right to prescribe a particular form of dress for judges and lawyers than for priests and ministers of religion? Why should he be free to lay down rules regarding the time, place, and manner in which public lectures are given, but not to regulate the preaching of the Gospel? For the argument applies identically to both cases, and if we already have a perfect rule of life then it will neither require nor permit any additional rule governing public speaking, whether it be on secular or spiritual subjects. There are two senses, however, in which the Gospels can be said to be a perfect rule. Firstly, they can be said to establish general standards of conduct, from which the remaining particular regulations we require derive and can be deduced. In this sense the Scriptures can be said to be a perfect rule, nor can any legitimate command issued by a parent, a master, or a ruler be found which is not contained in and founded upon Scripture. The command, for example, that all things should be done decently and in an orderly fashion authorizes the particular regulations for the conduct of divine worship which are later to be enacted by the

governors of the Church. Secondly, the Scriptures can be said to be a perfect rule of life on the grounds that they detail every individual obligation we are under, and that there is nothing which we ought to do or to avoid doing, in any aspect of our lives, which they do not prescribe. However, there never has been or could be a perfect rule of life of this sort. Even if they prefer to maintain that the Scriptures are a complete and perfect rule for the internal worship of God which is required of us, yet they nowhere lay down or describe the number and type of rites to be adopted in public worship, or the behaviour of the worshippers. These are left to the Churches themselves, so that they can take account of the customs of their country, and establish suitable norms in the light of the needs of the times, local opinion, and the importance of the ceremonies themselves.

(3) It is objected that to introduce human inventions into divine worship is mere superstition; that acts of worship ought to be conducted according to the intentions and commands of God himself, and that man-made ceremonies are inappropriate. It is said that the presumption of men who invade this sacred territory, in which God is the sole legislator, will not go unpunished. If any ceremony is prescribed which they happen not to like, at once they inveigh bitterly against the legislator, and sharply condemn both the ceremony and its author. Because superstition is a word which almost always has negative connotations, those who want either to attack or to change the external worship of God use it as a sort of spectre to frighten the ignorant mob, applying this term to honest and indeed beautiful ceremonies in order to conceal their true character.

In Latin the word superstition properly refers to the worship of the spirits of the dead. It serves to translate the Greek word *daemonia*, which has a number of different meanings: (i) as one would expect, the worship of demons, that is spirits; (ii) the worship of heroes; (iii) fear (of a sort they characterize as slavish) of the one true God, which leads us, abjectly indeed, to portray him as harsh, implacable, and cruel; (iv) each sect and religion has its form of worship called superstitious by others, because the initiates of each sect, condemning all ways of worshipping God other than their own, are inclined to call them superstitious.

Thus (Acts, ch. 25, v. 19) Festus called the Christian religion a superstition: 'They levelled certain accusations against him regarding his superstition, and about a certain Jesus, who was dead, and whom Paul said was alive.' Let us agree therefore that they have as much right as Festus to call the ordinances of the Church, and the religious rites prescribed by law, superstitious, but this term can properly be applied to the true worship of God, and thus is not in itself an indication that it is wrongful. There is no more need to reject a ceremony merely because it has been called superstitious than there was for Paul to abandon Christianity because he had heard the same term applied to it. God is, as they properly say, the only law-giver; but this is to be understood in the same way as the statement that Scripture is the one and perfect rule of life: God alone has authority over men's consciences, laws have their authority only from him, all things legitimately commanded, whether in public or private life, originate in his will and are derived from it. However, the text 'There is only one law-giver, who alone can save and destroy', taken from the Epistle of St James, is completely irrelevant to the present subject, as can be seen when it is read in context.

(4) Objection is made from the law of scandal: the magistrate, it is said, may not impose ceremonies because they will be stumbling-blocks.

I reply (i) that a stumbling-block is not something which annoys another, something which makes him indignant when he sees someone else doing it. Indignation generally characterizes those who are hostile to a ceremony, and generally their sin lies in getting angry, not, as would be required if the law of scandal was to be applicable, in imitating an action they disapprove of.

(ii) Not everything which is called a stumbling-block, over which a man may trip and fall, is necessarily wrong. Christ himself is often called a stumbling-block, and many are said to be offended by him.

(iii) He who takes offence always sins, but he who gives it is sometimes in the right.

(iv) If the magistrate has no right to decree anything which stands any chance of offending somebody, then he can decree nothing at all; for nothing will be approved by everybody, nothing will seem so just and fair to everybody that there will be no one to criticize it and maintain that it is in his judgement illegitimate.

(v) Suppose someone is truly offended by some ceremonies that a magistrate establishes; it does not follow that the law is necessarily unjust and has no binding force; for the ill-will, the private judgement, or the conscientious scruples of a private individual can never invalidate the public authority of the magistrate. It is not possible for the characteristics of an inferior, whatever they may be, to nullify the authority of a superior, for otherwise the obligatory character of the laws would depend not upon the will of the magistrate, but our consent, and any subject could at will abrogate all the laws enacted by the magistrate. The magistrate cannot possibly see into the souls of all his subjects: our weak minds are distorted and bent each one in its own way by corrupt customs, intellectual vanities, seductive pleasures, violent passions and party affiliations. Even if he could, could he or should he take account of the opinions and scruples of each and every one? A law is just and obligatory if it deals with an indifferent matter which has been left to free choice, and if what it establishes is believed by he who has charge of the commonwealth to conduce in some way or other to the welfare of the people and to public order.

(5) Others, in order to escape the authority of the magistrate, and to sidestep their obligation to obey his laws, escape into themselves, and seek asylum where they can safely take refuge, in the sanctuary of their own consciences. They claim the sacred freedom of their consciences must not be violated in any respect by religious rites and regulations. They maintain that liberty of conscience is sacred at all times, and is answerable only to God. If the magistrate claims to have authority over the conscience he is guilty of an affront to the majesty of God himself, as well as of an unjust assault upon his fellow-man. Consequently all laws which in any way constrain and circumscribe the conscience are automatically unjust and invalid.

In order to understand which laws really do threaten freedom of conscience, we need first to remember that all just laws imposed by the magistrate, whether in secular or religious matters, oblige the consciences of subjects. We need therefore to commence by distinguishing the different types of obligation and freedom that are relevant to the conscience.

My first point is that the obligation of human law can be of two forms: material or formal. (i) A material obligation exists when the thing itself which is the subject-matter of the human law is in itself binding upon the conscience; i.e. it was already fully obligatory by reason of divine law before the human law was passed. (ii) A formal obligation exists when something which is otherwise indifferent is imposed on the people by the authority of a legitimate magistrate, by reason of which imposition it obliges the conscience. Some laws therefore oblige by reason of their content, others by reason only of the magistrate's command.

Next, the freedom of which we speak is also of two types: freedom of the judgement, and freedom of the will. (i) Freedom of the judgement exists in circumstances where the approbation of the judgement is not required as to whether this or that is in its nature obligatory; and in this consists the whole of liberty of conscience. (ii) Freedom of the will exists when the consent of the will to this or that action is not required; and this can be removed while the freedom of the conscience is preserved intact.

Given these premises, I argue:

(i) If the magistrate commands something which has already been commanded by God, e.g. that the subject should not commit theft or adultery, the obligation of this law is both material and formal. Consequently it takes away the liberty of both the judgement and the will, and, of course, that of the conscience. This does not make such a law unjust, for it does not bind the conscience in any way it was not bound before. The magistrate has imposed no different or narrower limits upon the conscience than God himself.

(ii) If the magistrate, acting on the basis of the legislative authority which is rightfully his, orders some particular behaviour of his subjects in a matter which is free and indifferent, his decree, the obligation of which is only formal and not material (i.e. its obligation derives not from its content, but only from the secular magistrate's decree), certainly binds the conscience, but it does not destroy its freedom. For it requires the assent of the will only for it to be obeyed; it does not require the approbation of the conscience by claiming that its content is in itself obligatory. I conclude that all laws of the magistrate, whether secular or ecclesiastical, whether dealing with life in society or with divine worship, are just and legitimate if they seek to command not men's judgements but their actions. Looking at such laws from both points of view, one can see they combine an obligation to obedience with freedom of conscience.

(iii) If a magistrate seeks to impose an indifferent matter upon his subjects as if it were materially obligatory (i.e. he commands it as though the matter was by its nature obligatory before his own law was passed, when in fact it was not obligatory but indifferent), then his law entraps the conscience, and he sins in commanding it. But ecclesiastical ordinances are not put forward in this way. By them acts are turned into religious ceremonies; they are not required because they are already obligatory, but are held to be obligatory because they are required.

(6) Last in line hobble those who forebode ill of the magistrate's authority, and who say that so extensive a power is not legitimate and is insupportable, for the reason that it can lead to evil consequences and is full of dangers, for there is no way of knowing where the magistrate will draw the line. What burdensome or ridiculous obligations may not a headstrong magistrate impose upon us, they constantly complain, if he is endowed with such power, which is as good as infinite? Why has God endowed us with reason and revelation, why are we born men and baptized Christians, if neither our reason nor our religion is sufficient to establish the customs which are appropriate to the worship of God? Numerous are the complaints of this sort that they raise, for these foolish men imagine all sorts of things which horrify their simple minds.

Let me first observe that these objections, like the preceding ones, undermine and uproot the magistrate's power as much in secular indifferent matters as in religious. Once again we see how close the affinity and association is between all indifferent things, whether they concern religious ceremonies or secular customs. If the magistrate's authority in one area is successfully denied it collapses at once in the other. But to deal briefly with this argument in particular: in the nature of things there is nothing which is always so perfect and harmless that no evil consequences either in general do or in principle might follow from it, or at least might be feared to do so. There are many just and legitimate things which are regularly felt to be disadvantageous and onerous by some individuals. But those inconveniences which arise or might arise for me as a result of someone exercising their rights in no way constitute legitimate objections to his exercise of his rights.

I have now given a cursory account of the forces mustered by the enemy, and a hasty sketch of the chief arguments they have to offer. It would be a lengthy task to review all their authorities, their examples, and their ambiguities. The weakness of their arguments makes such close attention unnecessary, and the amount of time it would take to deal with each one individually would be prohibitive. Anyone who disagrees with the view I have defended will be found to depend on one or another of the main types of opposing arguments that I have outlined.

6. 'Question: Is each man's private interest the foundation of the law of nature? Answer: No' (*Essays on the Law of Nature*, No. VIII, 1664)

There are some who, having undertaken an assault upon the idea of natural law, have adopted this argument: 'It is in the light of their interests that men have established laws to govern their conduct. These laws vary according to the customs of each nation, and even within each nation they are often changed as circumstances change. There is in fact no law of nature: all creatures, animals as well as men, are bound by nature to pursue their own interests. Consequently there either is no law of nature at all; or if there is one it would be absolutely stupid to obey it, for giving consideration to the welfare of others involves damaging one's own interests.' Long ago, Carneades defended this and other arguments of the same sort in his Academy. The sharpness of his wit and of his tongue left almost no conviction intact, but undermined them all. Ever since there has never been a shortage of people prepared eagerly to defend this view. They have been those who have lacked the moral qualities and the strength of character which might enable them to attain honours and wealth by their own efforts. So they have complained that mankind is treated unfairly, and have maintained that governments act unjustly: the evidence being that they are excluded from the rewards of nature and of society, especially those which exist to serve the common good. They have even declared that the yoke of authority should be thrown off, laying claim to a natural liberty. They have maintained that justice and equity should not be measured by an extraneous law, but should be assessed by each individual in the light of his own interest. However, this unjust view has always been rejected by the wiser amongst mankind, those who retained some sense of common humanity, some concern for the welfare of society. So that we may define the issue between the two groups more accurately we must begin by giving some definition of the terms they employ. What do we mean by the foundation of natural law? And what do we mean by each man's private interest?

First, by the foundation of natural law, we mean that basis and as it were foundation from which all the other less obvious precepts of that law are developed, and upon which they are erected. They are in some way deduced from it, and they obtain all their force and their obligatory character from the fact that they are in line with that primary and fundamental law which is the standard and measure of all the other laws that depend upon it.

Second, when we say that each man's private interest is not the foundation of the law of nature, we do not intend to be understood as saying that there is a fundamental conflict between each man's private interest and the law that should be common to all men. The law of nature is the strongest guarantor of each man's private concerns, and without respect for it no man can have secure possession of his own property or pursue his own advantage. Anyone who carefully considers the human race and its patterns of behaviour will clearly see that nothing contributes as much to the realization of the common interests of all individuals, nothing is as effective in ensuring the safety and security of men's possessions as the observation of the law of nature. But we are denying that each individual is entitled to do what, in the light of the circumstances, he thinks is in his best interests. It is pointless to claim that the private interest of each individual is the measure of equity and right, unless you agree that each individual should be allowed to act as he sees fit, and according to what he himself takes his interests to be. No one can be a fair and impartial judge of someone else's benefit; and you mock him by merely pretending to recognize his interests if you tell him that he can do anything that it is in his interest to do, but at the same time insist that someone else should have the authority to determine what it is that is in his interest. Consequently the real question is this: Is it right, according to the law of nature, for a private individual to do whatever seems to him, in the circumstances, to be most useful for himself and his affairs? Is it not only permissible but also obligatory, according to that law, for him so to act? Is there nothing which one is naturally obliged to do, except in so far as it gives rise to some immediate personal advantage? It is this view which we deny, for the following reasons:

First, it is a necessary characteristic of the foundation of the law of nature that it should be the primary law from which other laws of the same type, but of less universal application, derive their obligatory character. But the binding character of other natural laws does not derive from the principle of self-interest. If you think over all the duties of a man's life, you will not find a single one which derives from self-interest alone, and is obligatory for the sole reason that it is advantageous. Many of the most important virtues consist simply in doing good to others at our own expense. Men who acted in this way were in former times regarded as heroes: they were believed to have their habitation in the heavens and their names were included among those of the gods. They did not buy their way into heaven by accumulating wealth and by never missing an opportunity to make a profit, but earned a place there by hard work, by facing danger, by generously assisting others. They did not pursue their own self-interest, but the welfare of the public and of all mankind. Some earned immortality by their exertions, others by their studies, and others by the circumstances of their deaths; none of them became famous and admirable through avarice, laziness, or cowardice.

But if it were the primary law of nature that each individual ought to look after himself and his own private affairs, then those noble examples of virtue which history has recorded for posterity ought to be consigned to oblivion, so that the memory of so much wickedness and so much folly might be erased. For the very same people whom we now admire as the finest and best of men would have to be regarded not merely as foolish, but as wicked and evil. They spared no effort to show their disregard for themselves and their own interests, thereby acquiring a reputation for infamy at the highest possible price. At the same time as they turned their back on their own affairs they lost their right to a good reputation. When they thought they were working hard, it was only to maximize the injury to themselves and to commit as many crimes as possible. If we think self-interest should be the standard of what is right, then you, Hercules, should have been strung up for your labours, not deified, for you waged a more ferocious war against nature herself than against any monster. Curtius was a madman rather than a hero, since for the sake of his country he plunged into the yawning gulf and buried himself alive lest Rome should be destroyed by the danger he had brought upon her [Livy, bk 7, 6.5]. He said farewell at the same moment to his life and to his good name. He went to his grave at the same moment as he deserved to die. Certainly nature deserves to be thought the kindest mother of all, since she intends our duties to be not only obligations, but sources of pleasure and profit. How kind she has been to mankind in determining that virtue should not be its own reward, but rather the higher the wage the more virtuous the workman should be held to be. Why on earth do we praise the poverty of Fabricius [Cicero, *On Duties*, 3, 22.86], and seek, with elegant turns of phrase, to praise his wicked frugality? He preferred to sacrifice his own wealth and reputation rather than his country. Stupidly, he put his nation before himself, and preferred its welfare to his own. How much more appropriate it would be for us to praise the great Catiline, who grasped perfectly the obligations of natural law, putting his own interests ahead of those of the capital of the world, and not shrinking at the prospect of demolishing her defences [Horace, *Odes* i.16.20], provided he thereby increased his own power. Cicero may have deserved the title of father of his country; but it was Catiline who was a true child of nature, and it was rather he who deserved to be made ruler of the world for attacking Rome than Cicero for defending her.

Anyone who seeks to brand nature with such infamy, and to

attribute such wickedness to her ordinances, ought to be ashamed, for on this view nothing is to be considered so sacred that selfishness will not eventually be entitled to desecrate it. If the logic of virtue is to be identical with that of profit, and if the measure of justice is to be self-interest, what is this than to throw open the door to every species of villainy?

Second, it cannot be the case that it is inevitable that the primary law of nature should be violated. If the private interest of each individual is the foundation of that law, it is inevitable that it should be broken, since it is impossible to act in a way which furthers the interests of each and every individual. The inheritance of the human species as a whole is always one and the same, and it does not increase as the population grows. Nature bestows for the use and convenience of men a fixed profusion of goods. Natural reproduction takes place in a fixed manner and at a predetermined rate. Creatures are not born randomly, nor do they grow in line with the greed or necessities of men. The clothes we need are not born with us, nor do men, like tortoises, have the protection of houses which are born with them and grow as they grow. The boundaries of the world are not extended to keep pace with the growth of men's need or desire for possessions. Food, clothing, ornaments, wealth, and all the other goods of this life are given to mankind in common. When anyone seizes as much as he can for himself, the same amount as he adds to his pile of possessions is subtracted from the possessions of somebody else. Anyone who grows rich does so at the expense of someone else.

Perhaps someone will retort that when we say that each individual's private interest is the foundation of the law of nature, that ought not to be taken to mean that every individual is required to be happy, prosperous, and to have an abundance of worldly goods; but that each individual is obliged, as far as he can, to put himself first: that the standard by which right and wrong are to be measured is one's own self-interest, which is the basis of all the obligations one has in life. Even so, from this premise it follows, first of all, that men are obliged to do that which cannot be done. Each individual is required to obtain for himself, and to hang on to, the greatest possible number of useful possessions. It is a necessary consequence of this behaviour that it leaves to the rest of mankind the smallest possible amount of such goods, since it is clear that you cannot make any gains except at someone else's expense. Quite the contrary happens if we place the foundation of virtue elsewhere: then the virtues are no longer at odds with each other, and they do not put each man into conflict with every other. Rather they support each other and augment each other. If I am just this does not prevent anyone else from being equitable. If a prince is bountiful, that does not prevent his subjects from being generous. A father's integrity does not corrupt the morals of his children. Cato's sobriety does not make Cicero intemperate. Our moral obligations are not in conflict with each other, nor do they arm men against each other, which, I repeat, is the necessary consequence of this premise. If it is adopted then men (as they say) are placed by the law of nature in a state of war; all society is destroyed, and all trust, which is the bond of society. What reason is left for the fulfilment of promises, what protection for the interests of society, what sense of community and common purpose between men, when equity and justice are the same as self-interest? What can social life amongst men consist in, if not fraud, violence, hatred, robbery, murder, and so forth, when every man not only is allowed, but is obliged to grab what he can, by any means, from his neighbour, while his neighbour, for his part, is obliged to hang on to it at all costs?

Thus there emerges a third argument against this view: that the foundation of the law of nature cannot be such that, if it is adopted, all justice, friendship and generosity must disappear from human existence. For what justice is there where there is no property or right of ownership? And what property-right is there when people are entitled, not only to possess what is their own, but also to possess anything that belongs to anybody else, providing it is useful to them? We can briefly observe at this point that the proponents of this view of natural law seek the principles of moral behaviour and a rule to govern their lives not so much in a binding law, as in the natural appetites and instincts of men, as if that was morally the best which most people wanted. It consequently follows that either the law of nature is in no way binding (but no one will say this in so many terms, for then it would be no law), or that human beings are so placed that it is unlawful for a man to give up a right or to do good to someone else unless he has a definite prospect of reward. If the rightness of any action is a function of its expediency, and men are obliged to conform to that standard in their actions, then I cannot see how anyone could give anything to a friend, offer him hospitality or carry out some task on his behalf, or in any other way do him a favour, unless he was prepared to break this law. I leave the reader to judge how unsatisfactory this is, how at odds with reason, human nature, and the idea of a moral life.

Of course a critic might say that if observation of the law of nature and of the duties of one's life always leads to what is beneficial, and if it is impossible for us to act according to the law of nature without our actions proving to be, whether immediately or indirectly, genuinely helpful, then the foundation of the law of nature is each man's self-interest. The minor premise is self-evidently true, he would maintain, for the observation of the law of nature leads to peace, harmony, friendship, security of the person and of property, and, to sum up in one word, happiness. To this argument we can reply as follows: Self-interest is not the foundation of the law of nature, or the reason for obeying it, although it is the consequence of obedience to it. It is one thing for an action to be profitable in and of itself; quite another if it is advantageous solely because it conforms to the law, while if the law were abolished there would be no profit attached to it at all: for example to live up to one's promise, even to one's own disadvantage. One must distinguish between the consequence of the action in itself and the consequences of obedience. An action in itself can be disadvantageous – for example, the repayment of a loan, which leaves us worse off – but obedience to the law may still be self-interested in that it averts the punishment that crime deserves. But this punishment would not be deserved, and there would be no need therefore to avoid it, if the measure of the right was immediate self-interest. Thus the test of the rightness of an action is not whether it is self-interested; but rather a moral action is also self-interested, but only because it is right.

7: Letter to the Hon. Robert Boyle (12/22 December 1665)

Cleve, Dec. 12/22, 1665

Honoured Sir,

      I look upon it as the greatest misfortune of my journey hither that it hath afforded me so little worth your notice; and that after having gone so far, and stayed so long, I should yet send you so empty a letter. But, Sir, it is not unusual, that a man far in debt, after long delays, should pay nothing. And had I travelled through more fruitful places, and been myself better able to observe, I should still have been in the same condition, and not have been able to return anything of what I owe to your many and great favours. We are here in a place very little considerable for anything but its antiquity, which to me seems neither to commend things nor opinions; and I should scarce prefer an old, ruinous and incommodious house, to a new and more convenient, though Julius Caesar built it, as they say he did this the Elector dwells in, which opinion the situation, just on the edge of a precipice, and the oldness of the building seems to favour.

      The town is little, and not very strong or handsome; the buildings and streets irregular; nor is there a greater uniformity in their religion, three professions being publicly allowed: the Calvinists are more than the Lutherans, and the Catholics more than both (but no papist bears any office), besides some few Anabaptists, who are not publicly tolerated. But yet this distance in their Churches gets not into their houses. They quietly permit one another to choose their way to heaven; for I cannot observe any quarrels or animosities amongst them upon the account of religion. This good correspondence is owing partly to the power of the magistrate, and partly to the prudence and good nature of the people, who (as I find by inquiry) entertain different opinions without any secret hatred or rancour.

      I have not yet heard of any person here eminently learned. There is one Dr Scardius, who, I am told, is not altogether a stranger to chemistry. I intend to visit him as soon as I can get an handsome opportunity. The rest of their physicians go the old road, I am told, and also easily guess by their apothecaries' shops, which are unacquainted with chemical remedies. This, I suppose, makes this town so ill-furnished with books of that kind, there being few here curious enough to inquire after chemistry or experimental learning. And as I once heard you say, I find it true here, as well as in other places, that the great cry is ends of gold and silver. A catalogue of those books I have met with, some at Antwerp, and some in this town, I here enclosed send you, and am told by the only bookseller of this place, that he expects others daily from Frankfurt.

The weather is here exceedingly mild, and I have not seen any frost or snow since my coming; but it is an unusual clemency of the air, and the heavens seem to cherish the heat men are in to destroy one another.

I suppose it no news to tell you that the Dutch have forced a surrender of Lochem; there marched out of it two hundred and fifty of the bishop's men. In another rencounter the bishop's men killed and took four hundred Dutch horse, so that this has only shaked the scales, not much inclined them to either side. The States of Cleve and March are met here to raise money for the Elector, and he with that intends to raise men, but as yet declares for neither side. Whether he be willing, or will be able, to keep that neutrality I doubt, since methinks war too is now become infectious, and spreads itself like a contagion, and I fear threatens a great mortality the next summer.

The plague has been very hot at Cologne. There have died there within this quarter of a year above eight thousand. A gentleman that passed by that town last week told me that the week before there died there three hundred and forty-eight.

I know these little trivial things are as far distant from what I ought to send you, as I am from England. For this I do not only blame my own present poverty, but despair of the future, since your great riches in all manner of knowledge forbid me the hopes of ever presenting you with anything new or unknown. I should not therefore take the boldness thus to importune you, did I not know that there is nothing so slight or barren which you cannot force to yield you something, and make an advantageous use of poor common things, which others throw away. This is that, which gives me the confidence to tell you that I am,

> Sir,
>
> your most obedient and most faithful servant,
>
> John Locke

8: *An Essay Concerning Toleration* (1667)

In the question of liberty of conscience, which has for some years been so much bandied amongst us, one thing that hath chiefly perplexed the question, kept up the dispute, and increased the animosity hath been, I conceive, this: that both parties have with equal zeal and mistake too much enlarged their pretensions, whilst one side preach up absolute obedience, and the other claim universal liberty in matters of conscience, without assigning what those things are which have a title to liberty, or showing the boundaries of imposition and obedience.

To clear the way to this I shall lay down this for a foundation which I think will not be questioned or denied, viz.:

That the whole trust, power, and authority of the magistrate is vested in him for no other purpose but to be made use of for the good, preservation, and peace of men in that society over which he is set, and therefore that this alone is and ought to be the standard and measure according to which he ought to square and proportion his laws, model and frame his government. For if men could live peaceably and quietly together without uniting under certain laws and entering into a commonwealth, there would be no need at all of magistrates or polities, which are only made to preserve men in this world from the fraud and violence of one another. So that what was the end of erecting of government ought alone to be the measure of its proceeding.

There are some that tell us that monarchy is *iure divino*. I will not now dispute this opinion, but only mind the asserters of it that if they mean by this (as certainly they must) that the sole, supreme, arbitrary power and disposal of all things is and ought to be by divine right in a single person, 'tis to be suspected they have forgot what country they are born in, under what laws they live, and certainly cannot but be obliged to declare Magna Carta to be downright heresy. If they mean by monarchy *iure divino* not an absolute but limited monarchy (which I think an absurdity if not a contradiction) they ought to show us this charter from heaven, and let us see where God hath given the magistrate a power to do anything but barely in order to the preservation and welfare of his subjects in this life, or else leave us at liberty to believe as we please, since nobody is bound or can allow anyone's pretensions to a power (which he himself confesses limited) further than he shows his title.

There are others who affirm that all the power and authority the magistrate hath is derived from the grant and consent of the people, and to those I say it cannot be supposed the people should give any one or more of their fellow men an authority over them for any other purpose than their own preservation or extend the limits of their jurisdiction beyond the limits of this life.

This being premised – that the magistrate ought to do or meddle with nothing but barely in order to securing the civil peace and property of his subjects – let us next consider the opinions and actions of men, which, in reference to toleration, divide themselves into three sorts. Either they

1. are all such opinions and actions as in themselves concern not government or society at all, and such are all purely speculative opinions and divine worship; or

2. are such as in the[ir] own nature are neither good nor bad, but yet concern society and men's conversations one with another, and these are all practical opinions and actions in matters of indifferency;

3. are such too as concern society, but are also good or bad in their own nature, and these are moral virtues or vices.

1. I say that the first sort only (viz. speculative opinions and divine worship) are those things alone which have an absolute and universal right to toleration. First purely speculative opinions (as the belief of the Trinity, purgatory, transubstantiation, antipodes, Christ's personal reign on earth, etc.): and that in these every man hath his unlimited freedom appears because bare speculations give no bias to my conversation with men nor having any influence on my actions as I am a member of any society, but, being such as would be still the same with all the consequences of them though there were no other person besides myself in the world, cannot by any means either disturb the state or inconvenience my neighbour, and so come not within the magistrate's cognizance. Besides, no man can give another man power (and it would be to no purpose if God should) over that over which he had no power himself. Now

that a man cannot command his own understanding, or positively determine today what opinion he will be of tomorrow, is evident from experience and the nature of the understanding, which can no more apprehend things otherwise than they appear to it than the eye see other colours in the rainbow than it doth, whether those colours be really there or not. [I must only remark before I leave this head of speculative opinions that the belief of a deity is not to be reckoned amongst purely speculative opinions, for it being the foundation of all morality, and that which influence the whole life and actions of men, without which a man is to be considered no other than one of the most dangerous sorts of wild beasts, and so incapable of all society.]¹ The other thing that hath just claim to an unlimited toleration is the place, time, and manner of worshipping my God. Because this is a thing wholly between God and me and of an eternal concernment, above the reach and extent of polities and governments which are but for my well-being in this world. For the magistrate is but umpire between man and man; he can right me against my neighbour but cannot defend me against my God. Whatever evil I suffer by obeying him in other things he can make me amends in this world, but if he force me to a wrong religion he can make me no reparation in the other world, to which let me add that even in things of this world over which the magistrate has an authority he never does, and it would be injustice if he should any further than it concerns the good of the public, enjoin men the care of their private civil concernments, or force them to a prosecution of their own private interests, but only protects them from being invaded and injured in them by others (which is a perfect toleration), and therefore we may well suppose he hath nothing at all to do with my private interest in another world, and that he ought not to prescribe me the way, or require my diligence in the prosecution of that good which is of a far higher concernment to me than anything within his power, having no more certain or more infallible knowledge of the way to attain it than I myself, where we are both equally inquirers, both equally subjects, and wherein he can give me no security that I shall not, nor make me any recompense if I do, miscarry. Can it be reasonable that he that cannot compel me to buy a house should force me his way to venture the purchase of heaven? That he that cannot in justice

prescribe me rules of preserving my health should enjoin me methods of saving my soul? He that cannot choose a wife for me should
choose a religion? But if God (which is the point in question)
would have men forced to heaven, it must not be by the outward
violence of the magistrate on men's bodies, but the inward constraints of his own spirit on their minds, which are not to be
wrought on by any human compulsion. The way to salvation not
being any forced exterior performance, but the voluntary and secret
choice of the mind, and it cannot be supposed that God would
make use of any means which could not reach but would rather
cross the attainment of the end. Nor can it be thought that men
should give the magistrate a power to choose for them their way to
salvation, which is too great to give away, if not impossible to part
with. Since whatsoever the magistrate enjoined in the worship of
God, men must in this necessarily follow what they themselves
thought best, since no consideration could be sufficient to force a
man from or to that which he was fully persuaded was the way to
infinite happiness or infinite misery. Religious worship being that
homage which I pay to that God I adore in a way I judge acceptable
to him, and so being an action or commerce passing only between
God and myself, hath in its own nature no reference at all to my
governor, or to my neighbour, and so necessarily produces no
action which disturbs the community. For kneeling or sitting in the
sacrament can in itself tend no more to the disturbance of the
government or injury of my neighbour than sitting or standing at
my own table; wearing a cope or surplice in the church can no
more in its own nature alarm or threaten the peace of the state than
wearing a cloak or a coat in the market; being rebaptized no more
make a tempest in the commonwealth than it doth in the river, nor
than barely washing myself would do in either. If I observe the
Friday with the Mahometan, or the Saturday with the Jew, or the
Sunday with the Christian, whether I pray with or without a form,
whether I worship God in the various and pompous ceremonies of
the papist or in the plainer way of the Calvinists, I see nothing in
any of these, if they be done sincerely and out of conscience, that
can of itself make me either the worse subject to my prince, or
worse neighbour to my fellow-subject. Unless it be that I will out
of pride or over-weeningness of my own opinion and a secret

conceit of my own infallibility, taking to myself something of a God-like power, force and compel others to be of my mind, or censure or malign them if they be not. This indeed often happens, but 'tis not the fault of the worship, but the men, and is not the consequence of this or that form of devotion, but the product of depraved, ambitious human nature, which successively makes use of all sorts of religion, as Ahab did of keeping a fast, which was not the cause but means and artifice to take away Naboth's vineyard, which miscarriages of some professors do no more discredit any religion (for the same happens in all) than Ahab's rapine does fasting.

['Twill be said that if a toleration shall be allowed as due to all the parts of religious worship it will shut out the magistrate's power from making laws about those things over which it is acknowledged on all hands that he has a power, viz. things indifferent, as many things made use of in religious worship are, viz. wearing a white or a black garment, kneeling or not kneeling, etc. To which I answer that in religious worship nothing is indifferent, for it being the using of those habits, gestures, etc. which I think acceptable to God in my worshipping of him, however they may be in their own nature perfectly indifferent, yet when I am worshipping my God in a way I think he has prescribed and will approve of, I cannot alter, omit, or add any circumstance in that which I think the true way of worship. And therefore if the magistrate permit me to be of a profession or Church different from his, 'tis incongruous that he should prescribe any one circumstance of my worship, and 'tis strange to conceive upon what grounds of uniformity any different profession of Christians can be prohibited in a Christian country where the Jewish religion (which is directly opposite to the principles of Christianity) is tolerated, and would it not be irrational where the Jewish religion is permitted that the Christian magistrate upon pretence of his power in indifferent things should enjoin or forbid anything, or any way interpose in their way or manner of worship.]¹

From what is premised I think will follow:

1. That in speculations and religious worship every man hath a perfect, uncontrollable liberty which he may freely use, without, or contrary to the magistrate's command, without any guilt or sin at

all; provided always that it be all done sincerely and out of conscience to God, according to the best of his knowledge and persuasion. But if there be any ambition, pride, revenge, faction, or any such alloy that mixes itself with [that] which he calls conscience, so much there is of guilt, and so much he shall answer for at the day of judgement.

2. I say all practical principles or opinions by which men think themselves obliged to regulate their actions with one another, as that men may breed their children, or dispose of their estates as they please, that men may work or rest when they think fit, that polygamy and divorce are lawful or unlawful: these opinions and the actions following from them with all other things indifferent have a title also to toleration. But yet only so far as they do not tend to the disturbance of the state, or do not cause greater inconveniences than advantages to the community. For all these opinions, except such of them as are apparently destructive to human society, being things either of indifferency or doubt, and neither the magistrate [n]or subject being on either side infallible, he ought no further to consider them than as the making laws and interposing his authority in such opinions may conduce to the welfare and safety of his people. But yet no such opinion hath any right to toleration on this ground, that it is a matter of conscience, and some men are persuaded that it is either a sin or a duty, because the conscience or persuasion of the subject cannot possibly be a measure by which the magistrate can or ought to frame his laws, which ought to be suited to the good of all his subjects, not the persuasions of a part, which often happening to be contrary one to another must produce contrary laws, and there being nothing so indifferent which the consciences of some or other do not check at, a toleration of men in all that which they pretend, out of conscience, they cannot submit to will wholly take away all the civil laws, and all the magistrate's power; and so there will be no law, nor government, if you deny the magistrate's authority in [in]different things, over which it is acknowledged on all hands that he hath jurisdiction. And therefore the errors or scruples of anyone's conscience, which lead him to, or deter him from, the doing of anything do not destroy the magistrate's power nor alter the nature of the thing, which is still indifferent. For I will not doubt here to call all these

practical opinions in respect of the law-maker indifferent, though perhaps they are not so in themselves. For however the magistrate be persuaded in himself of the reasonableness or absurdity, necessity or unlawfulness of any one of them, and is possibly in the right, yet whilst he acknowledges himself not infallible, he ought to regard them in making of his laws no otherwise than as things indifferent, except only, as that being enjoined, tolerated, or forbidden, they carry with them the good and welfare of the people. Though at the same time he be obliged strictly to suit his personal actions to the dictates of his own conscience and persuasion in these very opinions. For not being made infallible in reference to others by being made a governor over them, he shall hereafter be accountable to God for his actions as a man, according as they are suited to his own conscience and persuasion; but shall be accountable for his laws and administration as a magistrate according as they are intended to the good, preservation, and quiet of all his subjects in this world, as much as is possible, which is a rule so certain and so clear that he can scarce err in it, unless he do it wilfully.

But before I proceed to show the limits of restraint and liberty in reference to those things, it will be necessary to set down the several degrees of imposition that are or may be used in matters of opinion:

(1) The prohibiting to publish or vent any opinion.

(2) Forcing to renounce or abjure any opinion.

(3) Compelling to declare an assent to the contrary opinion.

There are answerable to these the same degrees of toleration. From all which I conclude:

1. That the magistrate may prohibit the publishing of any of these opinions when in themselves they tend to the disturbance of the government, because they are then under his cognizance and jurisdiction.

2. That no man ought to be forced to renounce his opinion or assent to the contrary, because such a compulsion cannot produce any real effect to that purpose for which it is designed. It cannot alter men's minds; it can only force them to be hypocrites, and by this way the magistrate is so far from bringing men to embrace the truth of his opinion of that, as that he only constrains them to lie for their errors; nor doth this injunction at all conduce to the peace

or security of the government, but quite the contrary, because hereby the magistrate does not make anyone to be one jot more of his mind, but to be very much more his enemy.

3. That any actions flowing from any of these opinions, as also in all other indifferent things, the magistrate has a power to command or forbid so far as they tend to the peace, safety or security of his people, whereof though he be judge, yet he ought still to have a great care that no such laws be made, no such restraints established for any other reason but because the necessity of the state and the welfare of the people called for them. And perhaps it will not be sufficient that he barely thinks such impositions and such rigour necessary, or convenient, unless he hath seriously and impartially considered and debated whether they be so or no; and his opinion (if he mistake) will no more justify him in the making of such laws, than the conscience or opinion of the subject will excuse him if he disobey them if consideration and inquiry could have better informed either of them. And I think it will easily be granted that the making of laws to any other end but only for the security of the government and protection of the people in their lives, estates, and liberties, i.e. the preservation of the whole, will meet with the severest doom at the great tribunal, not only because the abuse of that power and trust which is in the law-maker's hand produces greater and more unavoidable mischiefs than anything else to mankind – for whose good only governments were instituted – but also because he is not accountable to any tribunal here, nor can there be a greater provocation to the supreme preserver of mankind than that the magistrate should make use of that power which was given him only for the preservation of all his subjects and every particular person amongst them as far as it is practicable; should misuse it to the service of his pleasure, vanity, or passion, and employ it to the disquieting or oppression of his fellow men, between whom and himself in respect of the king of kings there is but a small and accidental difference.

4. That if the magistrate in these opinions or actions, by laws and impositions, endeavour to restrain or compel men contrary to the sincere persuasions of their own consciences, they ought to do what their consciences require of them, as far as without violence they can; but withal are bound at the same time quietly to submit

to the penalty the law inflicts on such disobedience, for by this means they secure to themselves their grand concernment in another world, and disturb not the peace of this, offend not against their allegiance either to God or the king, but give both their due, the interest of the magistrate and their own being both safe. And certainly he is a hypocrite, and only pretends conscience and aims at something else in this world, who will not, by obeying his conscience and submitting also to the law, purchase heaven for himself and peace for his country, though at the rate of his estate, liberty, or life itself. But here also the private person, as well as the magistrate in the former case, must take great care that his conscience or opinion do not mislead him in the obstinate pursuit or flight of anything as necessary or unlawful which in truth is not so, lest by such an error or wilfulness he come to be punished for the same disobedience in this world and the other too. For liberty of conscience being the great privilege of the subject, as the right of imposing is the great prerogative of the magistrate, they ought the more narrowly to be watched that they do not mislead either magistrate or subject, because of the fair pretences they have. Those wrongs being the most dangerous most carefully are to be avoided, and such as God will most severely punish, which are done under the specious semblances and appearances of right.

5. I say there are besides the two former a third sort of actions which are good or bad in themselves, viz. the duties of the second table or trespasses against it, or the moral virtues and vices of the philosophers. These, though they are the vigorous, active part of religion, and that wherein men's consciences are very much concerned, yet I find that they make but a little part of the disputes of liberty of conscience. I know not whether it be that if men were more zealous for these they would be less contentious about the other, but this is certain, that the countenancing virtue is so necessary a prop to a state, and the allowance of some vices brings so certain a disturbance and ruin to society, that it was never found that any magistrate did, nor can be suspected that he ever will, establish vice by a law or prohibit the practice of virtue, which does by its own authority and the advantages it brings to all governments sufficiently deserve the countenance of the magistrate everywhere.

Yet give me leave to say, however strange it may seem, that the law-maker hath nothing to do with moral virtues and vices, nor ought to enjoin the duties of the second table any otherwise than barely as they are subservient to the good and preservation of mankind under government. For could public societies well subsist, or men enjoy peace and safety without the enforcing of those duties by the injunctions and penalties of laws, it is certain the law-makers ought not to prescribe any rules about them, but leave the practice of them entirely to the discretion and consciences of his people. For could even those moral virtues and vices be separated from the relation they have to the weal of the public, and cease to be a means to settle or disturb men's peace and properties, they would then become only the private and super-political concernment between God and a man's soul, wherein the magistrate's authority is not to interpose. God hath appointed the magistrate his vicegerent in this world with power to command, but 'tis but like other deputies, to command only in the affairs of that place where he is vicegerent. Whoever meddle in the concernments of the other world have no other power but to entreat and persuade. The magistrate, as magistrate, hath nothing to do with the good of men's souls or their concernments in another life, but is ordained and entrusted with his power only for the quiet and comfortable living of men in society, one with another, as hath been already sufficiently proved.

And it is yet further evident that the magistrate commands not the practice of virtues because they are virtues and oblige the conscience, or are the duties of man to God and the way to his mercy and favour, but because they are the advantages of man with man, and most of them the strong ties and bonds of society, which cannot be loosened without shattering the whole frame, for some of them, which have not that influence on the state, and yet are vices and acknowledged to be so as much as any, as covetousness, disobedience to parents, ingratitude, malice, revenge, and several others, the magistrate never draws his sword against; nor can it be said that those are neglected because they cannot be known when the secretest of them, revenge and malice, put the distinction in judicature between manslaughter and murder; [yea, even charity itself, which is certainly the great duty both of a man and a Christian, hath not yet in its full latitude an universal right to toleration, since there are some parts and instances of it which the magistrate hath absolutely forbidden, and that for ought I could ever hear without any offence to the tenderest consciences, for who doubts that to relieve with an alms the poor, though beggars (if one sees them in want), is, if considered absolutely, a virtue and every particular man's duty, yet this is amongst us prohibited by a law, and the rigour of a penalty, and yet nobody in this case complains of the violation of his conscience, or the loss of his liberty, which certainly if it was an unlawful restraint upon the conscience could not be overlooked by so many tender and scrupulous men. God does sometimes (so much does he take care of the preservation of governments) make his law in some degrees submit and comply with man's: his law forbids the vice but the law of man often makes the measure of it. There have been commonwealths that have made theft lawful for such as were not caught in the fact, and perhaps 'twas as guiltless a thing to steal a horse at Sparta as to win a horse race in England. For the magistrate having a power of making rules of transferring properties from one man to another may establish any, so they be universal, equal, and without violence, and suited to the interest and welfare of that society, as this was at Sparta, who, being a warlike people, found this no ill way to teach their citizens vigilance, boldness, and activity. This I only note by the by, to show how much the good of the commonwealth is the standard of all human laws when it seems to limit and alter the obligation even of some of the laws of God, and change the nature of vice and virtue; hence it is that the magistrate who could make theft innocent could not yet make perjury or breach of faith lawful, because destructive to human society.][2] From the power therefore that the magistrate hath over good and bad actions I think it will follow:

(1) That he is not bound to punish all; i.e. he may tolerate some vices, for I would fain know what government in the world doth not.

(2) That he ought not to command the practice of any vice, because such an injunction cannot be subservient to the good of the people, or preservation of the government.

These I suppose are the limits of imposition and liberty, and these three several sorts of things wherein men's consciences are concerned have right to such a latitude of toleration as I have set down and no more, if they are considered separately and abstractly in themselves. But yet there is a case which may still upon the same grounds vary the magistrate's usage of the men that claim this right to toleration.

1. Since men usually take up their religion in gross, and assume to themselves the opinions of their party all at once in a bundle, it often happens that they mix with their religious worship and speculative opinions other doctrines absolutely destructive to the society wherein they live, as is evident in the Roman Catholics that are subjects of any prince but the pope. These, therefore, blending such opinions with their religion, reverencing them as fundamental truths, and submitting to them as articles of their faith, ought not to be tolerated by the magistrate in the exercise of their religion, unless he can be secured that he can allow one part without the spreading of the other, and that those opinions will not be imbibed and espoused by all those who communicate with them in their religious worship, which I suppose is very hard to be done.

[And that which may render them yet more incapable of toleration is when to these doctrines dangerous to government they have the power of a neighbour prince of the same religion at hand to countenance and back them upon any occasion.

The objection usually made against toleration: That the magistrate's great business being to preserve peace and quiet of his government, he is obliged not to tolerate different religions in his country, since they bring distinctions wherein men unite and incorporate into bodies separate from the public, they may occasion disorder, conspiracy, and seditions in the commonwealth and endanger the government.

I answer: If all things that may occasion disorder or conspiracy in a commonwealth must not be endured in it, all discontented and active men must be removed, and whispering must be less tolerated than preaching as much likelier to carry on and foment a conspiracy. And if all numbers of men joined in an union and corporation distinct from the public be not to be suffered, all charters of towns, especially great ones, are presently to be taken away. Men united in religion have as little and perhaps less interest against the government than those united in the privileges of a corporation. This I am sure: they are less dangerous as being more scattered and not formed into that order. And the minds of men are so various in matters of religion, and so nice and scrupulous in things of an eternal concernment, that where men are indifferently tolerated and persecution and force does not drive them together, they are apt to divide and subdivide into so many little bodies, and always with the greatest enmity to those they last parted from or stand nearest to, that they are a guard one upon another, and the public can have no apprehensions of them as long as they have their equal share of common justice and protection. And if the example of old Rome (where so many different opinions, gods, and ways of worship were promiscuously tolerated) be of any weight, we have reason to imagine that no religion can become suspected to the state of ill-intention to it till the government first by a partial usage of them different from the rest of the subjects declare its ill-intentions to its professors, and so make a state business of it. And if any rational man can imagine that force and compulsion can at any time be the right way to get an opinion or religion out of the world, or to break a party of men that unite in the profession of it, this I dare affirm:][5]

[2. Since experience vouches the practice, and men are not all saints that pretend conscience, I think I shall not injure any party if I say that most men – at least factions of men – when they have power sufficient, make use of it, right or wrong, for their own advantage, and the establishment of themselves in authority, few men forbearing to grasp at dominion that have power to seize and hold it. When, therefore, men herd themselves into companies with distinctions from the public, and a stricter confederacy with those of their own denomination and party than other their fellow-subjects, whether the distinction be religious or ridiculous matters not, otherwise than as the ties of religion are stronger, and the pretences fairer and apter to draw partisans, and therefore the more to be suspected and the more heedfully to be watched: when, I say, any such distinct party is grown or growing so numerous as to appear dangerous to the magistrate and seem visibly to threaten the peace of the state, the magistrate may and ought to use all ways, either of policy or power, that shall be convenient to lessen, break, and suppress the party, and so prevent the mischief. For though their separation were really in nothing but religious worship and he should use as the last remedy force and severity against them, who did nothing but worship God in their own way, yet did he not really persecute their religion or punish them for that, more than in a battle the conqueror kills men for wearing white ribbons in their hats, or any other badge about them; but because this was a mark they were enemies and dangerous, religion, i.e. this or that form of worship, being the cause of their union and correspondence, not of their factiousness and turbulency. For the praying to God in this or that posture does no more make men factious or at enmity one with another, nor ought otherwise to be treated, than the wearing of hats or turbans, which yet either of them may do, by being a note of distinction and giving men an opportunity to number their forces, know their strength, be confident of one another, and readily unite upon any occasion. So that they are not restrained because of this or that opinion or worship, but because such a number, of any opinion whatsoever, who dissented would be dangerous. The same thing would happen if any fashion of clothes distinct from that of the magistrate and those that adhere to him should spread itself and become the badge of a very considerable part of the people, who thereupon grow into a very strict correspondency and friendship one with another: might not this well give the magistrate cause of jealousy, and make him with penalties forbid the fashion, not because unlawful but because of the danger it might occasion? Thus a lay cloak may have the same effect with an ecclesiastical cowl or any other religious habit.

And perhaps the Quakers, were they numerous enough to become dangerous to the state, would deserve the magistrate's care and watchfulness to suppress them, were they no other way distinguished from the rest of his subjects but by the bare keeping on their hats, as much as if they had a set form of religion separate from the state; in which case nobody would think that the not standing bare were a thing the magistrate levelled his severity against any otherwise than as it united a great number of men who, though they dissented from him in a very indifferent and trivial circumstance, yet might thereby endanger the government. And in such case he may endeavour to suppress and weaken or dissolve any party of men which religion or any other thing hath united to the manifest danger of his government by all those means that shall be most convenient for that purpose, whereof he is to be judge, nor shall he be accountable in the other world for what he does directly in order to the preservation and peace of his people, according to the best of his knowledge. Whether force and compulsion be the right way to this end I will not here dispute,]⁴ but this I dare affirm, that it is the worst, the last to be used, and with the greatest caution, for these reasons:

(1) Because it brings that upon a man which that he may be fenced from is the only reason why he is a member of the commonwealth, viz. violence, for were there no fear of violence there would be no government in the world, nor any need of it.

(2) Because the magistrate in using of force does in part cross what he pretends to do, which is the safety of all. For the preservation as much as is possible of the property, quiet, and life of every individual being his duty, he is obliged not to disturb or destroy some for the quiet or safety of the rest, till it hath been tried whether there be not ways to save all. For so far as he undoes or destroys any of his subjects for the security of the rest, so far he opposes his own design, which is professed, and ought to be only for the preservation, to which even the meanest have a title. 'Twould be but an uncharitable as well as unskilful way of cure, and such as nobody would use or consent to, to cut off so much as an ulcered toe, though tending to a gangrene, till all other gentler remedies had proved unsuccessful, though it be a part as low as the earth, and far distant from the head.

I can see but one objection that can be made to this, and that is that by the application of gentler remedies such slow methods may make you lose the opportunity of those remedies that if timely would be effectual. Whereas in the faint way of proceeding the malady increases, the faction grows strong, gathers head, and becomes your masters. To this I answer: that parties and factions grow slowly and by degrees, have their time of infancy and weakness as well as full growth and strength, and become not formidable in an instant, but give sufficient time for experimenting other kind of cures without any danger by the delay. But if the magistrate chance to find the dissenters so numerous as to be in a condition to cope with him, I see not what he can gain by force and severity when he thereby gives them the fairer pretence to embody and arm, and make them all unite the firmer against him. But this, bordering something upon that part of the question which concerns more the interest of the magistrate than his duty, I shall refer to a fitter place.

Hitherto I have only traced out the bounds that God hath set to the power of the magistrate and the obedience of the subject, both which are subjects and equally owe obedience to the great king of kings, who expects from them the performance of those duties which are incumbent on them in their several stations and conditions, the sum whereof is that:

1. There are some opinions and actions that are wholly separate from the concernment of the state, and have no direct influence upon men's lives in society, and these are all speculative opinions and religious worship, and these have a clear title to universal toleration which the magistrate ought not to entrench on.

2. There are some opinions and actions which are in their natural tendency absolutely destructive to human society, as that faith may be broken with heretics, that if the magistrate doth not make a public reformation in religion the subjects may, that one is bound publicly to teach and propagate any opinion he believes himself, and such like; and in actions all manner of fraud and injustice, etc. And these the magistrate ought not to tolerate at all.

3. There is a third sort of opinions and actions which in themselves do not inconvenience or advantage human society, but only as the temper of the state and posture of affairs may vary their influence to good or bad, as that polygamy is lawful or unlawful, that flesh and fish is to be eaten or abstained from at certain seasons, and such other practical opinions; and all actions conversant about matters of indifferency have a right to toleration so far only as they do not interfere with the advantages of the public or serve any way to disturb the government.

And thus far of toleration as it concerns the magistrate's duty. Having showed what he is bound in conscience to do, it will not be amiss to consider a little what he ought to do in prudence.

But because the duties of men are contained in general established rules, but their prudence is regulated by circumstances relating to themselves in particular, it will be necessary in showing how much toleration is the magistrate's interest to come to particulars.

To consider, therefore, the state of England at present, there is but this one question in the whole matter, and that is whether toleration or imposition be the readiest way to secure the safety and peace, and promote the welfare, of this kingdom.

As to securing your peace, there is but one way: which is that your friends at home be many and vigorous and your enemies few and contemptible, or at least the inequality of their number make it very dangerous and difficult for malcontents to molest you.

As to promoting the welfare of the kingdom, which consists in riches and power, to this most immediately conduces the number and industry of your subjects.

What influence toleration hath on all these cannot be well seen without considering the different parties now among us, which may well be comprehended under these two: papists and fanatics.

1. As to the papists, 'tis certain that several of their dangerous opinions, which are absolutely destructive to all governments but the pope's, ought not to be tolerated in propagating. Those opinions and whosoever shall spread or publish any of them the magistrate is bound to suppress so far as may be sufficient to restrain it. And this rule reaches not only the papists but any other sort of men amongst us. For such restraint will something hinder the spreading of those doctrines which will always be of ill-consequence, and like serpents never be prevailed on by kind usage to lay by their venom.

2. Papists are not to enjoy the benefit of toleration because where they have power they think themselves bound to deny it to others. For it is unreasonable that any should have a free liberty of their religion who do not acknowledge it as a principle of theirs that nobody ought to persecute or molest another because he dissents from him in religion. For toleration being settled by the magistrate as a foundation whereon to establish the peace and quiet of his people, by tolerating any who enjoy the benefit of this indulgence which at the same time they condemn as unlawful, he only cherishes those who profess themselves obliged to disturb his government as soon as they shall be able.

3. It being impossible either by indulgence or severity to make papists (whilst papists) friends to your government, being enemies to it both in their principles and interest, and therefore considering them as irreconcilable enemies of whose fidelity you can never be secured whilst they owe a blind obedience to any infallible pope who hath the keys of their consciences tied to his girdle and can

upon occasion dispense with all their oaths, promises, and the obligations they have to their prince, especially being (in their sense) an heretic, and arm them to the disturbance of the government, [I] think they ought not to enjoy the benefit of toleration, because toleration can never, but restraint may, lessen their number, or at least not increase it, as it does usually all other opinions which grow and spread by persecution, and recommend themselves to bystanders by the hardships they undergo, men being forward to have compassion for sufferers and esteem for that religion as pure, and the professors of it as sincere, which can stand the test of persecution. But I think it is far otherwise with Catholics, who are less apt to be pitied than others because they receive no other usage than what the[y by the] cruelty of their own principles and practices are known to deserve, most men judging those severities they complain of to be just punishments due to them as enemies to the state, rather than persecutions of conscientious men for their religion, which indeed it is not. Nor can they be thought to be punished merely for their consciences who own themselves at the same time subjects of a foreign enemy prince. Besides the principles and doctrines of that religion are less apt to take inquisitive heads and unstable minds. Men commonly in their voluntary changes do pursue liberty and enthusiasm, wherein they are still free and at their own disposal, rather than give themselves up to the authority and impositions of others. This is certain: that toleration cannot make them divide amongst themselves, nor a severe hand over them (as in other dissenting parties) make them cement with the fanatics (whose principles and worship and tempers are so utterly inconsistent), and by that means increasing the numbers of the united malcontents make the danger greater. Add to this that popery, having been brought in upon the ignorant and zealous world by the art and industry of their clergy, and kept up by the same artifice backed by power and force, it is the most likely of any religion to decay where the secular power handles them severely, or at least takes from them those encouragements and supports they received by their own clergy.

But if restraint of the papists do not lessen the number of our enemies in bringing any of them over to us, yet it increases the number and strengthens the hands of our friends, and knits all the Protestant party firmer to our assistance and defence. For the interest of the king of England as head of the Protestants will be much improved by the discountenancing of popery amongst us. The differing parties will soon unite in a common friendship with us when they find we really separate from and set ourselves against the common enemy, both to our Church and all Protestant professions, and this will be an hostage of our friendship to them, and a security that they shall not be deceived in the confidence they have of us and the sincerity of the accord we make with them.

All the rest of the dissenters come under the opprobrious name of fanatics, which, by the way, I think might with more prudence be laid aside and forgotten than made use of. For what understanding man in a disordered state would find out and fix notes of distinction, a thing to be coveted only by those that are factious, or by giving one common name to different parties teach those to unite whom he is concerned to divide and keep at a distance one among another?

But to come to what is more material: I think it is agreed on all hands that it is necessary the fanatics should be made useful and assisting and as much as possible firm to the government as it now stands, both to secure it from disturbance at home, and defend it against invasions from abroad, which nothing can possibly bring to pass but what is able to alter their minds and bring them over to our[5] profession, or else (if they do not part with their opinions) yet may persuade them to lay by their animosities, and become friends to the state, though they are not sons of the Church. What efficacy force and severity hath to alter the opinions of mankind, though, history be full of examples, and there is scarce an instance to be found of any opinion driven out of the world by persecution, but where the violence of it at once swept away all the professors too. I desire nobody to go further than his own bosom for an experience whether ever violence gained anything upon his opinion, whether even arguments managed with heat do not lose something of their efficacy, and have not made him the more obstinate in his opinion, so chary is human nature to preserve the liberty of that part wherein lies the dignity of a man, which could it be imposed on would make him but little different from a beast. I ask those who in the late times so firmly stood the ineffectual force of persecution themselves, and found how little it obtained on their opinions, and yet are now so forward to try it upon others, whether all the severity in the world could have drawn them one step nearer to a hearty and sincere embracing the opinions that were then uppermost. Let them not say it was because they knew they were in the right, for every man in what he believes has so far this persuasion that he is in the right. But how little his obstinacy or constancy depends upon knowledge may appear in those galley slaves who return from Turkey, who, though they have endured all manner of miseries rather than part with their religion, yet one would guess by the lives and principles of most of them that they had no knowledge of the doctrine and practice of Christianity at all. Who thinks not that those poor captives who, for renouncing a religion they were not ever instructed in, nor during the enjoyment of their freedom at home were ever zealous for, might have regained their liberty for changing their opinion would not, had their chains given them leave, have cut the throats of those cruel patrons who used them so severely, to whom they would yet have done no violence had they been treated civilly, like fair prisoners of war? Whereby we may see it would be an hazardous attempt, if any should design it, to bring this island to the condition of a galley where the greater part shall be reduced to the condition of slaves, be forced with blows to row the vessel, but share in none of the lading, nor have any privilege or protection unless they will make chains for all those who are to be used like Turks, and persuade them to stand still whilst they put them on.

For let divines preach duty as long as they will, 'twas never known that men lay down quietly under the oppression, and submitted their backs to the blows of others when they thought they had strength enough to defend themselves. I say not this to justify such proceedings, which in the former part of this discourse I think I have sufficiently condemned, but to show what the nature and practice of mankind is, and what has usually been the consequence of persecution. Besides the forcible introducing of opinions keeps people off from closing with them by giving men unavoidable jealousies that [it] is not truth that is thus carried on, but interest, and dominion that is sought in making proselytes by compulsion. Who takes this course to convince anyone of the certain truths of mathematics? 'Tis likely, it will be said, that those are truths on which depend not my happiness; I grant it, and am much indebted to the man that takes care I should be happy. But 'tis hard to think that that comes from charity to my soul which brings such ill-usage to my body, or that he is much concerned I should be happy in another world who is pleased to see me miserable in this. I wonder that those who have such a zealous regard to the good of others do not a little more look after the relief of the poor, or think themselves concerned to guard the estates of the rich, which certainly are good things too and make a part of one's happiness, if we may believe the lives of those who tell us of the joys of heaven, but endeavour as much as others for large possessions on earth.

But, after all this, could persecution not only now and then conquer a tender, faint-hearted fanatic (which yet it rarely does, and that usually by the loss of two or three orthodox); could it, I say, at once drive all dissenters within the pale of the Church, it would not thereby secure but more threaten the government, and make the danger as much greater as it is to have a false, secret, but exasperated enemy, rather than a fair, open adversary. For punishment and fear may make men dissemble, but, not convincing anybody's reason, cannot possibly make them assent to the opinion, but will certainly make them hate the person of their persecutor, and give them the greater aversion to both. Such compliers only prefer impunity to the declaring of their opinion, but do not thereby approve of ours.[6] Fear of your power, not love of your government, is that which restrains them, and if that be the chain that ties them to you, it would certainly hold them surer were they open dissenters than secret malcontents, because it would not only be something easier to be worn, but harder to be knocked off. At least this is certain, that compelling men to your opinion any other way than by convincing them of the truth of it makes them no more your friends than forcing the poor Indians by droves into the rivers to be baptized made them Christians.

Though force cannot master the opinions men have, nor plant new ones in their breasts, yet courtesy, friendship, and soft usage may. For several men, whose business or laziness keeps them from examining, take many of their opinions on trust, even in things of religion, but [they] never take them from any man of whose knowledge, friendship, and sincerity they are not well assured, which it's impossible they should be of one that persecutes them. But inquisitive men, though they are not of another's mind, because of his kindness yet they are the more willing to be convinced, and will be apter to search after reasons that may persuade them to be of his opinion whom they are obliged to love.

Since force is a wrong way to bring dissenters off from their persuasions (and by drawing them to your opinion you cement them fast to the state), it will certainly prevail much less with those to be your friends who steadfastly retain their persuasion and continue in an opinion different from you. He that differs in an opinion is only so far at a distance from you, but if you use him ill for that which he believes to be right, he is then at perfect enmity. The one is barely a separation, but the other a quarrel; nor is that all the mischief which severity will do among us as the state of things is at present, for force and harsh usage will not only increase the animosity but number of enemies. For the fanatics taken all together being numerous, and possibly more than the hearty friends to the state religion, are yet crumbled into different parties amongst themselves, and are at as much distance one from another as from you, if you drive them not further off by the ill-treatment they receive from you, for their bare opinions are as inconsistent one with another as with the Church of England. People, therefore, that are so shattered into different factions are best secured by toleration, since being in as good a condition under you as they can hope for under any, 'tis not like[ly] they should join to set up any other, whom they cannot be certain will use them so well. But if you persecute them you make them all of one party and interest against you, tempt them to shake off your yoke and venture for a new government, wherein everyone has hopes to get the dominion themselves or better usage under others who cannot but see that the same severity of the government which helped them to power and partisans to get up will give others the same desire and same strength to pull them down, and therefore may it be expected they will be cautious how they exercise it. But if you think the different parties are already grown to a consistency and formed into one body and interest against you, whether it were the hardships they suffered under you made them unite or no, when they are so many as to equal or exceed you in number, as perhaps they do in England, force will be but an ill and hazardous way to bring them to submission.

If uniformity in England be so necessary as many pretend, and compulsion be the way to it, I demand of those who are so zealous for it whether they really intend by force to have it or no. If they do not it is not only imprudent but malicious under that pretence by ineffectual punishment to disquiet and torment their brethren. For to show how little persecution, if not in the extremest degree, has been able to establish uniformity, I shall ask but this one plain question: Was there ever a free toleration in this kingdom? If there were not, I desire to know of any of the clergy who were once sequestered how they came to be turned out of their livings, and whether impositions and severity were able to preserve the Church of England, and hinder the growth of puritans even before the war. If, therefore, violence be to settle uniformity, 'tis in vain to mince the matter: that severity which must produce it cannot stop short of the total destruction and extirpation of all dissenters at once; and how well this will agree with the doctrine of Christianity, the principles of our Church, and reformation from popery, I leave them to judge who can think the massacre of France worthy their imitation, and desire them to consider if death (for nothing less can make uniformity) were the penalty of not coming to common prayer and joining in all our Church worship how much such a law would settle the quiet and secure the government of the kingdom.

The Romish religion, that had been but a little while planted and taken but small root in Japan (for the poor converts had but a little of the efficacious truths and light of Christianity conveyed to them by those teachers who make ignorance the mother of devotion, and knew very little beyond an Ave Mary or Paternoster), would not be extirpated but by the death of many thousands, which too prevailed not at all to lessen their numbers till they extended the severity beyond the delinquents and made it death not only to the family that entertained a priest, but also to all of both the families that were next neighbours on either hand, though they were strangers or enemies to the new religion, and invented exquisite, lingering torments, worse than a thousand deaths, which, though some had strength enough to endure fourteen days together, yet many renounced their religion, whose names were all registered with a design that when the professors of Christianity were all destroyed those too should be butchered all on a day, never thinking the opinion rooted out beyond possibility of spreading again as long as there were any alive who were the least acquainted with it, or had almost heard anything of Christianity more than the name. Nor are the Christians that trade there to this day suffered to discourse, fold their hands, or use any gesture that may show the difference of their religion. If anyone think uniformity in our Church ought to be restored, though by such a method as this, he will do well to consider how many subjects the king will have left by the time it is done. There is this one thing more observable in the case, which is that it was not to set up uniformity in religion (for they tolerate seven or eight sects, and some so different as is the belief of the mortality or immortality of the soul, nor is the magistrate at all curious or inquisitive what sects his subjects are of, or does in the least force them to his religion), nor any aversion to Christianity, which they suffered a good while quietly to grow up among them, till the doctrines of the popish priests gave them jealousy that religion was but their pretence, but empire their design, and made them fear the subversion of their state, which suspicion their own priests improved all they could to the extirpation of this growing religion.

But to show the danger of establishing uniformity . . .

To give a full prospect of this subject there remain yet these following particulars to be handled:

(1) To show what influence toleration is like to have upon the number and industry of your people, on which depends the power and riches of the kingdom.

(2) That if force must compel all to an uniformity in England, to consider what party alone or what parties are likeliest to unite to make a force able to compel the rest.

(3) To show that all that speak against toleration seem to suppose that severity and force are the only arts of government and way to suppress any faction, which is a mistake.

(4) That for the most part the matters of controversy and distinction between sects are no parts or very inconsiderable ones and appendices of true religion.

(5) To consider how it comes to pass that Christian religion hath made more factions, wars, and disturbances in civil societies than

any other, and whether toleration and latitudinism would prevent those evils.

(6) That toleration conduces no otherwise to the settlement of a government than as it makes the majority of one mind and encourages virtue in all, which is done by making and executing strict laws concerning virtue and vice, but making the terms of Church communion as large as may be, i.e. that your articles in speculative opinions be few and large, and ceremonies in worship few and easy: which is latitudinism.

(7) That the defining and undertaking to prove several doctrines which are confessed to be incomprehensible and to be no otherwise known but by revelation, and requiring men to assent to them in the terms proposed by the doctors of your several Churches, must needs make a great many atheists.

But of these when I have more leisure.

Notes

1. Additions on the facing page.
2. This passage is crossed out in the Ms. It is in the Houghton and Huntingdon copies.
3. This is an addition near the end of the Ms which I have inserted where Locke has indicated it should go.
4. This passage is crossed out in the Ms. It is in the Houghton and Huntingdon copies.
5. 'your' deleted.
6. 'Yours' deleted.

9: *The Fundamental Constitutions of Carolina* (1669)

Our sovereign lord the king having, out of his royal grace and bounty, granted unto us the province of Carolina, with all the royalties, properties, jurisdictions, and privileges of a county palatine, as large and ample as the county palatine of Durham, with other great privileges, for the better settlement of the government of the said place, and establishing the interest of the lords proprietors with equality, and without confusion; and that the government of this province may be made most agreeable to the monarchy under which we live, and of which this province is a part; and that we may avoid erecting a numerous democracy: we, the lords and proprietors of the province aforesaid, have agreed to this following form of government, to be perpetually established amongst us, unto which we do oblige ourselves, our heirs, and successors, in the most binding ways that can be devised.

§1. The eldest of the lords proprietors shall be palatine; and, upon the decease of the palatine, the eldest of the seven surviving proprietors shall always succeed him.

§2. There shall be seven other offices erected, viz. the admiral's, chamberlain's, chancellor's, constable's, chief justice's, high steward's, and treasurer's; which places shall be enjoyed by none but the lords proprietors, to be assigned at first by lot; and upon the vacancy of any one of the seven great offices by death, or otherwise, the eldest proprietor shall have his choice of the said place.

§3. The whole province shall be divided into counties; each county shall consist of eight signories, eight baronies, and four precincts; each precinct shall consist of six colonies.

§4. Each signory, barony, and colony shall consist of twelve thousand acres; the eight signories being the share of the eight proprietors, and the eight baronies of the nobility; both which shares, being each of them one-fifth part of the whole, are to be perpetually annexed, the one to the proprietors, the other to the hereditary nobility, leaving the colonies, being three-fifths, amongst the people: that so, in setting out and planting the lands, the balance of the government may be preserved.

§5. At any time before the year 1701, any of the lords proprietors shall have power to relinquish, alienate, and dispose to any other person his proprietorship, and all the signories, powers, and interest thereunto belonging, wholly and entirely together, and not

otherwise. But after the year 1700, those who are then lords proprietors shall not have power to alienate or make over their proprietorship, with the signories and privileges thereunto belonging, or any
part thereof, to any person whatsoever, otherwise than as in §18,
but it shall all descend unto their heirs male; and for want of heirs
male, it shall all descend on that landgrave, or cassique, of Carolina
who is descended of the next heirs female of the said proprietor;
and, for want of such heirs, it shall descend on the next heir
general; and, for want of such heirs, the remaining seven proprietors
shall, upon the vacancy, choose a landgrave to succeed the deceased
proprietor, who being chosen by the majority of the seven surviving
proprietors, he and his heirs, successively, shall be proprietors, as
fully, to all intents and purposes, as any of the rest.

§6. That the number of eight proprietors may be constantly kept;
if, upon the vacancy of any proprietorship, the seven surviving
proprietors shall not choose a landgrave to be a proprietor before
the second biennial parliament after the vacancy, then the next
biennial parliament but one after such vacancy shall have power to
choose any landgrave to be proprietor.

§7. Whosoever after the year 1700, either by inheritance or choice,
shall succeed any proprietor in his proprietorship, and signories
thereunto belonging, shall be obliged to take the name and arms of
that proprietor whom he succeeds; which from thenceforth shall be
the name and arms of his family and their posterity.

§8. Whatsoever landgrave or cassique shall any way come to be a
proprietor shall take the signories annexed to the said proprietorship; but his former dignity, with the baronies annexed, shall devolve into the hands of the lords proprietors.

§9. There shall be just as many landgraves as there are counties,
and twice as many cassiques, and no more. These shall be the
hereditary nobility of the province, and by right of their dignity be
members of parliament. Each landgrave shall have four baronies,
and each cassique two baronies, hereditarily and unalterably annexed to and settled upon the said dignity.

§10. The first landgraves and cassiques of the twelve first counties to be planted shall be nominated thus: that is to say, of the twelve landgraves, the lords proprietors shall each of them, separately for himself, nominate and choose one; and the remaining four landgraves of the first twelve shall be nominated and chosen by the palatine's court. In like manner, of the twenty-four first cassiques, each proprietor for himself shall nominate and choose two, and the remaining eight shall be nominated and chosen by the palatine's court; and when the twelve first counties shall be planted, the lords proprietors shall again in the same manner nominate and choose twelve more landgraves, and twenty-four cassiques for the twelve next counties to be planted; that is to say two-thirds of each number by the single nomination of each proprietor for himself, and the remaining one-third by the joint election of the palatine's court, and so proceed in the same manner till the whole province of Carolina be set out and planted, according to the proportions in these Fundamental Constitutions.

§11. Any landgrave or cassique at any time before the year 1701 shall have power to alienate, sell, or make over to any other person his dignity, with the baronies thereunto belonging, all entirely together. But after the year 1700, no landgrave or cassique shall have power to alienate, sell, make over, or let the hereditary baronies of his dignity, or any part thereof, otherwise than as in §18; but they shall all entirely, with the dignity thereunto belonging, descend unto his heirs male; and, for want of heirs male, all entirely and undivided to the next heir general; and for want of such heirs shall devolve into the hands of the lords proprietors.

§12. That the due number of landgraves and cassiques may be always kept up; if, upon the devolution of any landgraveship or cassiqueship, the palatine's court shall not settle the devolved dignity, with the baronies thereunto annexed, before the second biennial parliament after such devolution; the next biennial parliament but one after such devolution shall have power to make any one landgrave or cassique, in the room of him, who, dying without heirs, his dignity and baronies devolved.

§13. No one person shall have more than one dignity, with the signories or baronies thereunto belonging. But whensoever it shall happen that anyone, who is already proprietor, landgrave, or cassique, shall have any of these dignities descend to him by inheritance, it shall be at his choice to keep which of the dignities, with the lands annexed, he shall like best; but shall leave the other, with the lands annexed, to be enjoyed by him who, not being his heir apparent, and certain successor to his present dignity, is next of blood.

§14. Whosoever, by right of inheritance, shall come to be landgrave or cassique, shall take the name and arms of his predecessor in that dignity, to be from thenceforth the name and arms of his family and their posterity.

§15. Since the dignity of proprietor, landgrave, or cassique cannot be divided, and the signories or baronies thereunto annexed must for ever all entirely descend with and accompany that dignity; whensoever, for want of heirs male, it shall descend on the issue female, the eldest daughter and her heirs shall be preferred; and in the inheritance of these dignities, and in the signories or baronies annexed, there shall be no co-heirs.

§16. In every signory, barony, and manor, the respective lord shall have power in his own name to hold court-leet there, for trying of all cases both civil and criminal; but where it shall concern any person being no inhabitant, vassal, or leet-man of the said signory, barony, or manor, he, upon paying down of forty shillings to the lords proprietors' use, shall have an appeal from the signory or barony court to the county court, and from the manor court to the precinct court.

§17. Every manor shall consist of not less than three thousand acres, and not above twelve thousand acres in one entire piece and colony: but any three thousand acres or more in one piece, and the possession of one man, shall not be a manor, unless it be constituted a manor by the grant of the palatine's court.

§18. The lords of signories and baronies shall have power only of granting estates not exceeding three lives, or thirty-one years, in two-thirds of the said signories or baronies, and the remaining third shall be always demesne.

§19. Any lord of a manor may alienate, sell, or dispose to any other person and his heirs for ever, his manor, all entirely together, with all the privileges and leet-men thereunto belonging, so far forth as any other colony lands; but no grant of any part thereof, either in fee, or for any longer term than three lives, or one-and-twenty years, shall be good against the next heir.

§20. No manor, for want of issue male, shall be divided amongst co-heirs; but the manor, if there be but one, shall all entirely descend to the eldest daughter and her heirs. If there be more manors than one, the eldest daughter first shall have her choice, the second next, and so on, beginning again at the eldest, till all the manors be taken up; that so the privileges which belong to manors being indivisible, the lands of the manors to which they are annexed may be kept entire, and the manor not lose those privileges which, upon parcelling out to several owners, must necessarily cease.

§21. Every lord of a manor, within his manor, shall have all the powers, jurisdictions, and privileges which a landgrave or cassique hath in his baronies.

§22. In every signory, barony, and manor, all the leet-men shall be under the jurisdiction of the respective lords of the said signory, barony, or manor, without appeal from him. Nor shall any leet-man, or leet-woman, have liberty to go off from the land of their particular lord, and live anywhere else, without licence obtained from the said lord, under hand and seal.

§23. All the children of leet-men shall be leet-men, and so to all generations.

§24. No man shall be capable of having a court-leet, or leet-men, but a proprietor, landgrave, cassique, or lord of a manor.

§25. Whoever shall voluntarily enter himself a leet-man, in the registry of the county court, shall be a leet-man.

§26. Whoever is lord of leet-men shall, upon the marriage of a leet-man or leet-woman of his, give them ten acres of land for their lives; they paying to him therefore not more than one-eighth part of all the yearly produce and growth of the said ten acres.

§27. No landgrave or cassique shall be tried for any criminal case, in any but the chief justice's court, and that by a jury of his peers.

§28. There shall be eight supreme courts. The first called the palatine's court, consisting of the palatine and the other seven proprietors. The other seven courts of the other seven great officers shall consist each of them of a proprietor, and six councillors added to him. Under each of these latter seven courts shall be a college of twelve assistants. The twelve assistants of the several colleges shall be chosen, two out of the landgraves, cassiques, or eldest sons of proprietors, by the palatine's court; two out of the landgraves, by the landgraves' chamber; two out of the cassiques, by the cassiques' chamber; four more of the twelve shall be chosen by the commons' chamber, out of such as have been, or are, members of parliament, sheriffs, or justices of the county court, or the younger sons of proprietors, or eldest sons of landgraves or cassiques; the two other shall be chosen by the palatine's court, out of the same sort of persons out of which the commons' chamber is to choose.

§29. Out of these colleges shall be chosen at first by the palatine's court, six councillors, to be joined with each proprietor in his court; of which six, one shall be of those who were chosen into any of the colleges by the palatine's court, out of the landgraves, cassiques, or eldest sons of proprietors; one out of those who were chosen by the landgraves' chamber; and one out of those who were chosen by the cassiques' chamber; two out of those who were chosen by the commons' chamber; and one out of those who were chosen by the palatine's court, out of the proprietors' younger sons, or eldest sons of landgraves, cassiques, or commons, qualified as aforesaid.

§30. When it shall happen that any councillor dies, and thereby there is a vacancy, the grand council shall have power to remove any councillor that is willing to be removed out of any of the proprietors' courts to fill up the vacancy; provided they take a man of the same degree and choice the other was of, whose vacant place is to be filled up. But if no councillor consent to be removed, or upon such remove the last remaining vacant place, in any of the proprietors' courts, shall be filled up by the choice of the grand council, who shall have power to remove out of any of the colleges any assistant who is of the same degree and choice that councillor was of, into whose vacant place he is to succeed. The grand council also shall have power to remove any assistant, that is willing, out of one college into another, provided he be of the same degree and choice. But the last remaining vacant place in any college shall be filled up by the same choice, and out of the same degree of persons the assistant was of who is dead, or removed. No place shall be vacant in any proprietor's court above six months. No place shall be vacant in any college longer than the next session of parliament.

§31. No man, being a member of the grand council, or of any of the seven colleges, shall be turned out, but for misdemeanor, of which the grand council shall be judge; and the vacancy of the person so put out shall be filled, not by the election of the grand council, but by those who first chose him, and out of the same degree he was of, who is expelled. But it is not hereby to be understood, that the grand council hath any power to turn out any one of the lords proprietors or their deputies, the lords proprietors having in themselves an inherent original right.

§32. All elections in the parliament, in the several chambers of the parliament, and in the grand council, shall be passed by balloting.

§33. The palatine's court shall consist of the palatine and seven proprietors, wherein nothing shall be acted without the presence and consent of the palatine or his deputy, and three others of the proprietors or their deputies. This court shall have power to call parliaments, to pardon all offences, to make elections of all officers in the proprietors' dispose, and to nominate and appoint port towns; and also shall have power, by their order to the treasurer, to dispose of all public treasure, excepting money granted by the parliament, and by them directed to some particular public use; and also shall have a negative upon all acts, orders, votes, and judgements of the grand council and the parliament, except only as in §6 and 12, and shall have all the powers granted to the lords proprietors, by their patent from our sovereign lord the king, except in such things as are limited by these Fundamental Constitutions.

§34. The palatine himself, when he in person shall be either in the army, or in any of the proprietors' courts, shall then have the power of general, or of that proprietor in whose court he is then present; and the proprietor in whose court the palatine then presides, shall during his presence there be but as one of the council.

§35. The chancellor's court, consisting of one of the proprietors and his six councillors, who shall be called vice-chancellors, shall have the custody of the seal of the palatinate, under which all charters (of lands or otherwise), commissions and grants of the palatine's court, shall pass. And it shall not be lawful to put the seal of the palatinate to any writing which is not signed by the palatine or his deputy, and three other proprietors or their deputies. To this court also belongs all state matters, dispatches, and treaties with the neighbour Indians. To this court also belongs all invasions of the law of liberty of conscience, and all disturbances of the public peace upon pretence of religion, as also the licence of printing. The twelve assistants belonging to this court shall be called recorders.

§36. Whatever passes under the seal of the palatinate shall be registered in that proprietor's court to which the matter therein contained belongs.

§37. The chancellor, or his deputy, shall be always speaker in parliament, and president of the grand council; and in his and his deputy's absence, one of his vice-chancellors.

§38. The chief justice's court, consisting of one of the proprietors and his six councillors, who shall be called justices of the bench, shall judge all appeals in cases both civil and criminal, except all such cases as shall be under the jurisdiction and cognizance of any other of the proprietors' courts, which shall be tried in those courts respectively. The government and regulation of the registries of writings and contracts shall belong to the jurisdiction of this court. The twelve assistants of this court shall be called masters.

§39. The constable's court, consisting of one of the proprietors and his six councillors, who shall be called marshals, shall order and determine of all military affairs by land, and all land-forces, arms, ammunition, artillery, garrisons and forts, etc., and whatever belongs unto war. His twelve assistants shall be called lieutenant-generals.

§40. In time of actual war the constable, whilst he is in the army, shall be general of the army; and the six councillors, or such of them as the palatine's court shall for that time or service appoint, shall be the immediate great officers under him, and the lieutenant-generals next to them.

§41. The admiral's court, consisting of one of the proprietors and his six councillors, called consuls, shall have the care and inspection over all ports, moles, and navigable rivers, so far as the tide flows, and also all the public shipping of Carolina, and stores thereunto belonging, and all maritime affairs. This court also shall have the power of the court of admiralty; and shall have power to constitute judges in port towns, to try cases belonging to law-merchant, as shall be most convenient for trade. The twelve assistants belonging to this court shall be called proconsuls.

§42. In time of actual war, the admiral, whilst he is at sea, shall command in chief, and his six councillors, or such of them as the palatine's court shall for that time and service appoint, shall be the immediate great officers under him, and the proconsuls next to them.

§43. The treasurer's court, consisting of a proprietor and his six councillors, called under-treasurers, shall take care of all matters that concern the public revenue and treasury. The twelve assistants shall be called auditors.

§44. The high steward's court, consisting of a proprietor and his six councillors, called comptrollers, shall have the care of all foreign and domestic trade, manufactures, public buildings, work-houses, highways, passages by water above the flood of the tide, drains, sewers, and banks against inundations, bridges, post, carriers, fairs, markets, corruption or infection of the common air or water, and all things in order to the public commerce and health; also setting out and surveying of lands; and also setting out and appointing places for towns to be built on in the precincts, and the prescribing and determining the figure and bigness of the said towns, according to such models as the said court shall order; contrary or differing from which models it shall not be lawful for anyone to build in any town. This court shall have power also to make any public building, or any new highway, or enlarge any old highway, upon any man's land whatsoever; as also to make cuts, channels, banks, locks, and bridges, for making rivers navigable, or for draining fens, or any other public use. The damage the owner of such lands (on or through which any such public thing shall be made) shall receive thereby, shall be valued, and satisfaction made by such ways as the grand council shall appoint. The twelve assistants belonging to this court shall be called surveyors.

§45. The chamberlain's court, consisting of a proprietor and his six councillors, called vice-chamberlains, shall have the care of all ceremonies, precedency, heraldry, reception of public messengers, pedigrees, the registry of all births, burials, and marriages, legitimation, and all cases concerning matrimony or arising from it; and shall also have power to regulate all fashions, habits, badges, games, and sports. To this court also it shall belong to convocate the grand council. The twelve assistants belonging to this court shall be called provosts.

§46. All cases belonging to, or under the jurisdiction of, any of the proprietors' courts shall in them respectively be tried and ultimately determined, without any further appeal.

§47. The proprietors' courts shall have a power to mitigate all fines, and suspend all executions in criminal cases, either before or after sentence, in any of the other inferior courts respectively.

§48. In all debates, hearings, or trials, in any of the proprietors' courts, the twelve assistants belonging to the said courts respectively shall have liberty to be present, but shall not interpose, unless their opinions be required, nor have any vote at all; but their business shall be, by the direction of the respective courts, to prepare such business as shall be committed to them; as also to bear such offices, and dispatch such affairs, either where the court is kept or elsewhere, as the court shall think fit.

§49. In all the proprietors' courts, the proprietor and any three of his councillors shall make a quorum; provided always that for the better dispatch of business, it shall be in the power of the palatine's court to direct what sort of cases shall be heard and determined by a quorum of any three.

§50. The grand council shall consist of the palatine, and seven proprietors, and the forty-two councillors of the several proprietors' courts, who shall have power to determine any controversies that may arise between any of the proprietors' courts about their respective jurisdictions, or between the members of the same court about their manner and methods of proceeding; to make peace and war, leagues, treaties, etc. with any of the neighbour Indians; to issue out their general orders to the constable's and admiral's courts, for the raising, disposing, or disbanding the forces, by land or by sea.

§51. The grand council shall prepare all matters to be proposed in parliament. Nor shall any matter whatsoever be proposed in parliament, but what hath first passed the grand council; which, after having been read three several days in the parliament, shall by majority of votes be passed or rejected.

§52. The grand council shall always be judges of all cases and appeals that concern the palatine, or any of the lords proprietors, or any councillor of any proprietor's court, in any case which otherwise should have been tried in the court in which the said councillor is judge himself.

§53. The grand council, by their warrants to the treasurer's court, shall dispose of all the money given by the parliament, and by them directed to any particular public use.

§54. The quorum of the grand council shall be thirteen, whereof a proprietor, or his deputy, shall be always one.

§55. The grand council shall meet the first Tuesday in every month, and as much oftener as either they shall think fit, or they shall be convocated by the chamberlain's court.

§56. The palatine, or any of the lords proprietors, shall have power, under hand and seal, to be registered in the grand council, to make a deputy, who shall have the same power, to all intents and purposes, as he himself who deputes him, except in confirming acts of parliament, as in §76, and except also in nominating and choosing landgraves and cassiques, as in §10. All such deputations shall cease and determine at the end of four years, and at any time shall be revocable at the pleasure of the deputator.

§57. No deputy of any proprietor shall have any power, whilst the deputator is in any part of Carolina, except the proprietor, whose deputy he is, be a minor.

§58. During the minority of any proprietor, his guardian shall have power to constitute and appoint his deputy.

§59. The eldest of the lords proprietors who shall be personally in Carolina shall of course be the palatine's deputy, and if no proprietor be in Carolina, he shall choose his deputy out of the heirs apparent of any of the proprietors, if any such be there; and if there be no heir apparent of any of the lords proprietors above one and twenty years old in Carolina, then he shall choose for deputy any one of the landgraves of the grand council; and till he have, by deputation, under hand and seal, chosen any one of the forementioned heirs apparent or landgraves to be his deputy, the eldest man of the landgraves, and for want of a landgrave, the eldest man of the cassiques who shall be personally in Carolina shall of course be his deputy.

§60. Each proprietor's deputy shall be always one of his own six councillors respectively; and in case any of the proprietors hath not, in his absence out of Carolina, a deputy, commissioned under his hand and seal, the eldest nobleman of his court shall of course be his deputy.

§61. In every county there shall be a court, consisting of a sheriff and four justices of the county, for every precinct one. The sheriff shall be an inhabitant of the county, and have at least five hundred acres of freehold within the said county; and the justices shall be inhabitants, and have each of them five hundred acres apiece freehold within the precinct for which they serve respectively. These five shall be chosen and commissioned from time to time by the palatine's court.

§62. For any personal cases exceeding the value of two hundred pounds sterling, or in title of land, or in any criminal case, either party, upon paying twenty pounds sterling to the lords proprietors' use, shall have liberty of appeal from the county court unto the respective proprietor's court.

§63. In every precinct there shall be a court, consisting of a steward and four justices of the precinct, being inhabitants, and having three hundred acres of freehold within the said precinct, who shall judge all criminal cases, except for treason, murder, and any other offences punishable with death, and except all criminal cases of the nobility; and shall judge also all civil cases whatsoever; and in all personal actions, not exceeding fifty pounds sterling, without appeal; but where the case shall exceed that value, or concern a title of land, and in all criminal cases, there either party, upon paying five pounds sterling to the lords proprietors' use, shall have liberty of appeal to the county court.

§64. No case shall be twice tried in any one court, upon any reason or pretence whatsoever.

§65. For treason, murder, and all other offences punishable with death, there shall be a commission, twice a year at least, granted unto one or more members of the grand council or colleges, who shall come as itinerant judges to the several counties, and, with the sheriff and four justices, shall hold assizes to judge all such cases; but, upon paying of fifty pounds sterling to the lords proprietors' use, there shall be liberty of appeal to the respective proprietor's court.

§66. The grand jury at the several assizes shall, upon their oaths, and under their hands and seals, deliver in to the itinerant judges a presentment of such grievances, misdemeanors, exigencies, or defects which they think necessary for the public good of the county; which presentment shall, by the itinerant judges, at the end of their circuit, be delivered in to the grand council at their next sitting. And whatsoever therein concerns the execution of laws already made, the several proprietors' courts, in the matters belonging to each of them respectively, shall take cognizance of it, and give such order about it as shall be effectual for the due execution of the laws. But whatever concerns the making of any new law shall be referred to the several respective courts to which that matter belongs, and be by them prepared and brought to the grand council.

§67. For terms, there shall be quarterly such a certain number of days, not exceeding one and twenty at any one time, as the several respective courts shall appoint. The time for the beginning of the term in the precinct court shall be the first Monday in January, April, July, and October; in the county court, the first Monday in February, May, August, and November; and in the proprietors' courts, the first Monday in March, June, September, and December.

§68. In the precinct court, no man shall be a juryman under fifty acres of freehold. In the county court, or at the assizes, no man shall be a grand juryman under three hundred acres of freehold; and no man shall be a petty juryman under two hundred acres of freehold. In the proprietors' courts no man shall be a juryman under five hundred acres of freehold.

§69. Every jury shall consist of twelve men, and it shall not be necessary they should all agree, but the verdict shall be according to the consent of the majority.

§70. It shall be a base and vile thing to plead for money or reward; nor shall anyone (except he be a near kinsman, not further off than cousin-german to the party concerned) be permitted to plead another man's case, till before the judge, in open court, he hath taken an oath that he doth not plead for money or reward, nor hath nor will receive, nor directly nor indirectly bargained with the party whose case he is going to plead for, money or any other reward for pleading his case.

§71. There shall be a parliament, consisting of the proprietors or their deputies, the landgraves and cassiques, and one freeholder out of every precinct, to be chosen by the freeholders of the said precinct respectively. They shall sit all together in one room, and have every member one vote.

§72. No man shall be chosen a member of parliament who hath less than five hundred acres of freehold within the precinct for which he is chosen; nor shall any have a vote in choosing the said member that hath less than fifty acres of freehold within the said precinct.

§73. A new parliament shall be assembled the first Monday of the month of November every second year, and shall meet and sit in the town they last sat in, without any summons, unless, by the palatine's court, they be summoned to meet at any other place. And if there shall be any occasion of a parliament in these intervals, it shall be in the power of the palatine's court to assemble them in forty days' notice, and at such time and place as the said court shall think fit; and the palatine's court shall have power to dissolve the said parliament when they shall think fit.

§74. At the opening of every parliament, the first thing that shall be done shall be the reading of these Fundamental Constitutions, which the palatine and proprietors, and the rest of the members then present, shall subscribe. Nor shall any person whatsoever sit or vote in the parliament, till he hath that session subscribed these Fundamental Constitutions, in a book kept for that purpose by the clerk of the parliament.

§75. In order to the due election of members for the biennial parliament, it shall be lawful for the freeholders of the respective precincts to meet the first Tuesday in September every two years, in the same town or place that they last met in, to choose parliament men; and there choose those members that are to sit the next November following, unless the steward of the precinct shall, by sufficient notice thirty days before, appoint some other place for their meeting, in order to the election.

§76. No act or order of parliament shall be of any force, unless it be ratified in open parliament, during the same session, by the palatine or his deputy, and three more of the lords proprietors or their deputies; and then not to continue longer in force but until the next biennial parliament, unless, in the mean time, it be ratified under the hands and seals of the palatine himself, and three more of the lords proprietors themselves, and by their order published at the next biennial parliament.

§77. Any proprietor, or his deputy, may enter his protestation against any act of the parliament, before the palatine or his deputy's consent be given as aforesaid, if he shall conceive the said act to be contrary to this establishment, or any of these Fundamental Constitutions of the government. And in such case, after a full and free debate, the several estates shall retire into four several chambers:

the palatine and proprietors into one; the landgraves into another; the cassiques into another; and those chosen by the precincts into a fourth; and if the major part of any of the four estates shall vote that the law is not agreeable to this establishment, and these Fundamental Constitutions of the government, then it shall pass no further, but be as if it had never been proposed.

§78. The quorum of the parliament shall be one half of those who are members, and capable of sitting in the house that present session of parliament. The quorum of each of the chambers of parliament shall be one half of the members of that chamber.

§79. To avoid multiplicity of laws, which by degrees always change the right foundations of the original government, all acts of parliament whatsoever, in whatsoever form passed or enacted, shall at the end of a hundred years after their enacting, respectively cease and determine of themselves, and without any repeal become null and void, as if no such acts or laws had ever been made.

§80. Since multiplicity of comments, as well as of laws, have great inconveniences, and serve only to obscure and perplex, all manner of comments and expositions, on any part of these Fundamental Constitutions, or any part of the common or statute law of Carolina, are absolutely prohibited.

§81. There shall be a registry in every precinct, wherein shall be enrolled all deeds, leases, judgements, mortgages, and other conveyances which may concern any of the land within the said precinct; and all such conveyances not so entered or registered shall not be of force against any person not party to the said contract or conveyance.

§82. No man shall be register of any precinct who hath not at least three hundred acres of freehold within the said precinct.

§83. The freeholders of every precinct shall nominate three men, out of which three the chief justice's court shall choose and commission one to be register of the said precinct, whilst he shall well behave himself.

§84. There shall be a registry in every signory, barony, and colony, wherein shall be recorded all the births, marriages, and deaths that shall happen within the respective signories, baronies, and colonies.

§85. No man shall be register of a colony that hath not above fifty acres of freehold within the said colony.

§86. The time of everyone's age, that is born in Carolina, shall be reckoned from the day that his birth is entered in the registry, and not before.

§87. No marriage shall be lawful, whatever contract and ceremony they have used, till both the parties mutually own it before the register of the place where they were married, and he register it, with the names of the father and mother of each party.

§88. No man shall administer to the goods, or have right to them, or enter upon the estate of any person deceased, till his death be registered in the respective registry.

§89. He that doth not enter, in the respective registry, the birth or death of any person that is born or dies in his house or ground, shall pay to the said register one shilling per week for each such neglect, reckoning from the time of each birth or death, respectively, to the time of registering it.

§90. In like manner the births, marriages, and deaths of the lords proprietors, landgraves, and cassiques, shall be registered in the chamberlain's court.

§91. There shall be in every colony one constable, to be chosen annually by the freeholders of the colony; his estate shall be above a hundred acres of freehold within the said colony; and such subordinate officers appointed for his assistance, as the county court shall find requisite, and shall be established by the said county court. The election of the subordinate annual officers shall be also in the freeholders of the colony.

§92. All towns incorporate shall be governed by a mayor, twelve aldermen, and twenty-four of the common council. The said common council shall be chosen by the present householders of the said town; the aldermen shall be chosen out of the common council; and the mayor out of the aldermen, by the palatine's court.

§93. It being of great consequence to the plantation that port towns should be built and preserved, therefore whosoever shall lade or unlade any commodity at any other place but a port town shall forfeit to the lords proprietors, for each tun so laden or unladen, the sum of ten pounds sterling; except only such goods as the palatine's court shall license to be laden or unladen elsewhere.

§94. The first port town upon every river shall be in a colony, and be a port town for ever.

§95. No man shall be permitted to be a freeman of Carolina, or to have any estate or habitation within it, that doth not acknowledge a God; and that God is publicly and solemnly to be worshipped.

§96. As the country comes to be sufficiently planted and distributed into fit divisions, it shall belong to the parliament to take care for the building of churches, and the public maintenance of divines, to be employed in the exercise of religion, according to the Church of England; which being the only true and orthodox, and the national religion of all the king's dominions, is so also of Carolina; and therefore it alone shall be allowed to receive public maintenance by grant of parliament.

§97. But since the natives of that place, who will be concerned in our plantation, are utterly strangers to Christianity, whose idolatry, ignorance, or mistake gives us no right to expel, or use them ill; and those who remove from other parts to plant there, will unavoidably be of different opinions concerning matters of religion, the liberty whereof they will expect to have allowed them, and it will not be reasonable for us on this account to keep them out; that civil peace may be maintained amidst the diversity of opinions, and our agreement and compact with all men may be duly and faithfully observed; the violation whereof, upon what pretence soever, cannot be without great offence to Almighty God, and great scandal to the true religion, which we profess; and also that Jews, heathens, and other dissenters from the purity of Christian religion, may not be scared and kept at a distance from it, but by having an opportunity of acquainting themselves with the truth and reasonableness of its doctrines, and the peaceableness and inoffensiveness of its professors, may by good usage and persuasion, and all those convincing methods of gentleness and meekness, suitable to the rules and design of the gospel, be won over to embrace and unfeignedly receive the truth; therefore any seven or more persons, agreeing in any religion, shall constitute a Church or profession, to which they shall give some name, to distinguish it from others.

§98. The terms of admittance and communion with any Church or profession shall be written in a book, and therein be subscribed by all the members of the said Church or profession; which book shall be kept by the public register of the precinct where they reside.

§99. The time of everyone's subscription and admittance shall be dated in the said book or religious record.

§100. In the terms of communion of every Church or profession, these following shall be three; without which no agreement or assembly of men, upon pretence of religion, shall be accounted a Church or profession within these rules:

1. That there is a God.
2. That God is publicly to be worshipped.
3. That it is lawful, and the duty of every man, being thereunto called by those that govern, to bear witness to truth; and that every Church or profession shall in their terms of communion set down the external way whereby they witness a truth as in the presence of God, whether it be by laying hands on, or kissing the Bible, as in the Church of England, or by holding up the hand, or any other sensible way.

§101. No person above seventeen years of age shall have any benefit or protection of the law, or be capable of any place of profit or honour, who is not a member of some Church or profession, having his name recorded in some one, and but one religious record at once.

§102. No person of any other Church or profession shall disturb or molest any religious assembly.

§103. No person whatsoever shall speak anything in their religious assembly, irreverently or seditiously of the government or governors, or state matters.

§104. Any person subscribing the terms of communion in the record of the said Church or profession, before the precinct register, and any five members of the said Church or profession, shall be thereby made a member of the said Church or profession.

§105. Any person striking out his own name out of any religious record, or his name being struck out by any officer thereunto authorized by each Church or profession respectively, shall cease to be a member of that Church or profession.

§106. No man shall use any reproachful, reviling, or abusive language, against the religion of any Church or profession; that being the certain way of disturbing the peace, and of hindering the conversion of any to the truth, by engaging them in quarrels and animosities, to the hatred of the professors and that profession, which otherwise they might be brought to assent to.

§107. Since charity obliges us to wish well to the souls of all men, and religion ought to alter nothing in any man's civil estate or right, it shall be lawful for slaves, as well as others, to enter themselves, and be of what Church or profession any of them shall think best, and thereof be as fully members as any freeman. But yet no slave shall hereby be exempted from that civil dominion his master hath over him, but be in all other things in the same state and condition he was in before.

§108. Assemblies, upon what pretence soever of religion, not observing and performing the abovesaid rules, shall not be esteemed as Churches, but unlawful meetings, and be punished as other riots.

§109. No person whatsoever shall disturb, molest, or persecute another for his speculative opinions in religion, or his way of worship.

§110. Every freeman of Carolina shall have absolute power and authority over his Negro slaves, of what opinion or religion soever.

§111. No case, whether civil or criminal, of any freeman, shall be tried in any court of judicature, without a jury of his peers.

§112. No person whatsoever shall hold or claim any land in Carolina by purchase or gift, or otherwise, from the natives or any other whatsoever; but merely from and under the lords proprietors; upon pain of forfeiture of all his estate, movable or immovable, and perpetual banishment.

§113. Whosoever shall possess any freehold in Carolina, upon what title or grant soever, shall, at the furthest from and after the year 1689, pay yearly unto the lords proprietors, for each acre of land, English measure, as much fine silver as is at this present in one English penny, or the value thereof, to be as a chief rent and acknowledgement to the lords proprietors, their heirs and successors for ever. And it shall be lawful for the palatine's court by their officers, at any time, to take a new survey of any man's land, not to out him of any part of his possession, but that by such a survey the just number of acres he possesseth may be known, and the rent thereupon due may be paid by him.

§114. All wrecks, mines, minerals, quarries of gems and precious stones, with pearl-fishing, whale-fishing, and one half of all ambergris, by whomsoever found, shall wholly belong to the lords proprietors.

§115. All revenues and profits belonging to the lords proprietors in common shall be divided into ten parts, whereof the palatine shall have three, and each proprietor one; but if the palatine shall govern by a deputy, his deputy shall have one of those three-tenths, and the palatine the other two-tenths.

§116. All inhabitants and freemen of Carolina above seventeen years of age, and under sixty, shall be bound to bear arms, and serve as soldiers whenever the grand council shall find it necessary.

§117. A true copy of these Fundamental Constitutions shall be kept in a great book by the register of every precinct, to be subscribed before the said register. Nor shall any person of what condition or degree soever, above seventeen years old, have any estate or possession in Carolina, or protection or benefit of the law there, who hath not, before a precinct register, subscribed these Fundamental Constitutions in this form:

'I *A.B.* do promise to bear faith and true allegiance to our sovereign lord King Charles the Second; and will be true and faithful to the palatine and lords proprietors of Carolina; and with my utmost power will defend them, and maintain the government according to this establishment in these Fundamental Constitutions.'

§118. Whatsoever alien shall, in this form, before any precinct register, subscribe these Fundamental Constitutions, shall be thereby naturalized.

§119. In the same manner shall every person, at his admittance into any office, subscribe these Fundamental Constitutions.

§120. These Fundamental Constitutions, in number a hundred and twenty, and every part thereof, shall be and remain the sacred and unalterable form and rule of government of Carolina for ever. Witness our hands and seals, the first day of March, 1669.

10: 'Philanthropy, or The Christian Philosophers' (1675)

Mankind is supported in the ways of virtue or vice by the society he is of, and the conversation he keeps, example and fashion being the great governors of this world. The first question every man ought to ask in all things he doth, or undertakes, is: How is this acceptable to God? But the first question most men ask is: How will this render me to my company, and those whose esteem I value? He that asks neither of those questions is a melancholy rogue, and always of the most dangerous and worst of men. This is the foundation of all the sects and orders, either of religion or philosophy, that have been in the world. Men are supported and delighted with the friendship and protection they enjoy from all the rest of the same way; and as these are more or less really performed amongst them, so the party increaseth or diminisheth. The Protestant religion, whilst it was a sect and a party, cherished and favoured each other; increased strangely against all the power and persecution of the Church of Rome. But since the warmth of that is over, and 'tis embraced only as a truer doctrine, this last 40 years [it] hath hardly produced as many converts from the Romish fopperies, the greater clergy plainly inclining to go back to their interest, which is highest exalted in that religion, but the greatest part of the laity, having an abhorrence to their cruelty and ambition as well as their interests contrary [to the clergy's], have divided themselves into sects and Churches of new and different names and ways, that they may keep up some warmth and heat in opposition to the common enemy, who otherwise was like to find us all asleep. The Quakers are a great instance, how little truth and reason operates upon mankind, and how great force society and conversation hath amongst those that maintain an inviolable friendship and concern for all of their way. 'Tis a true proverb, what is every man's business is no man's. This befalls truth, she hath no sect, no corporation, 'tis made no man's interest to own her. There is no body of men, no council sitting, that should take care of him that suffers for her; the clergy have pretended to that care for many hundreds of years past, but how well they have performed it the world knows: they have found a mistress, called the priest power, that pays them much better than truth can. Whatever truth she enjoins, they offer us to be worshipped as this great goddess; and their impudence hath been so great, that though they vary it as often as the priest power itself changeth, yet they affirm it still to be the same goddess, Truth. Neither is it possible that the greatest part of that sort of men should not either flatter the magistrate or the people: in both truth suffers. Learning is a trade that most men apply themselves to with pains and charge, that they may hereafter live and make advantage by it. 'Tis natural for trade to go to the best market: truth and money, truth and hire did never yet long agree. These thoughts moved us to endeavour to associate ourselves with such as are lovers of truth and virtue, that we may encourage, assist, and support each other in the ways of them, and may possibly become some help in the preserving truth, religion, and virtue amongst us, whatever deluge of misery and mischief may overrun this part of the world. We intermeddle not with anything that concerns the just and legal power of the civil magistrate; the government and laws of our country cannot be injured by such as love truth, virtue, and justice; we think ourselves obliged to lay down our lives and fortunes in the defence of it. No man can say he loves God that loves not his neighbour; no man can love his neighbour that loves not his country. 'Tis the greatest charity to preserve the laws and rights of the nation whereof we are. A good man, and a charitable man, is to give to every man his due. From the king upon the throne to the beggar in the street.

11: 'Obligation of Penal Laws' (Journal, 25 February 1676)

There are virtues and vices antecedent to, and abstract from, society, e.g. love of God, unnatural lust: other virtues and vices there are that suppose society and laws, as obedience to magistrates, or dispossessing a man of his heritage; in both these the rule and obligation is antecedent to human laws, though the matter about which that rule is may be consequent to them, as property in land, distinction, and power of persons.

All things not commanded or forbidden by the law of God are indifferent, nor is it in the power of man to alter their nature; and so no human law can lay any new obligation on the conscience, and therefore all human laws are purely penal, i.e. have no other obligation but to make the transgressors liable to punishment in this life. All divine laws oblige the conscience, i.e. render the transgressors liable to answer at God's tribunal, and receive punishment at his hands; but because very frequently both these obligations concur, and the same action comes to be commanded or forbidden by both laws together, and so in these cases men's consciences are obliged, men have thought that civil laws oblige their consciences to active obedience. Whereas in things in their own nature indifferent the conscience is obliged only to active or passive obedience, and that not by virtue of that human law which the man either practises or is punished by, but by that law of God which forbids disturbance or dissolution of governments.

The Gospel alters not in the least civil affairs, but leaves husband

and wife, master and servant, magistrate and subject, every one of them with the very same power and privileges that it found them [with], neither more nor less. And therefore, when the New Testament says 'obey your superiors in all things', it cannot be thought that it laid any new obligation upon the Christians after their conversion, other than what they were under before; nor that the magistrate had any other extent of jurisdiction over them than over his heathen subjects: so that the magistrate has the same power still over his Christian as he had [over] his heathen subjects; so that, where he had power to command, they had still, notwithstanding the liberties and privileges of the Gospel, obligation to obey.

Now to heathen polities (which cannot be supposed to be instituted by God for the preservation and propagation of true religion) there can be no other end assigned, but the preservation of the members of that society in peace and safety together: this being found to be the end, will give us the rule of civil obedience. For if the end of civil society be civil peace, the immediate obligation of every subject must be to preserve that society or government which was ordained to produce it; and no member of any society can possibly have any obligation of conscience beyond this. So that he that obeys the magistrate to the degree as not to endanger or disturb the government, under what form of government soever he lives, fulfils all the law of God concerning government, i.e. obeys to the utmost that the magistrate or society can oblige his conscience, which can be supposed to have no other rule set it by God in this matter but this – the end of the institution being always the measure of operation. The obligation of conscience then upon every subject being to preserve the government, 'tis plain that when any law made with a penalty is submitted to, i.e. the penalty is quietly undergone without other obedience, the government cannot be disturbed or endangered; for whilst the magistrate hath power to increase the penalty, even to loss of life, and the subject submits patiently to the penalty, which he in conscience is obliged to do, the government can never be in danger, nor can the public want active obedience in any case when it hath power to require it under pain of death. For no man can be supposed to refuse his active obedience in a lawful or indifferent thing where the refusal will cost him his life, and lose all his civil rights at once for want of performing one civil action; for civil laws have only to do with civil actions.

This, thus stated, clears a man from that infinite number of sins that otherwise he must unavoidably be guilty of, if all penal laws oblige the conscience further than this.

One thing further is to be considered, that all human laws are penal, for where the penalty is not expressed, it is by the judge to be proportioned to the consequence and circumstances of the fault. See the practice of the King's Bench. Penalties are so necessary to civil laws, that God found it necessary to annex them even to the civil laws he gave the Jews.

12: 'Law' (Journal, 21 April 1678)

A civil law is nothing but the agreement of a society of men, either by themselves, or one or more authorized by them, determining the rights, and appointing rewards and punishments, to certain actions of all within that society.

13: 'Credi, Disgrace' (Journal, 12 December 1678)

The principal spring from which the actions of men take their rise, the rule they conduct them by, and the end to which they direct them, seems to be credit and reputation, and that which at any rate they avoid, is in the greatest part shame and disgrace. This makes the Hurons and other people of Canada with such constancy endure inexpressible torments; this makes merchants in one country and soldiers in another; this puts men upon school divinity in one country, and physic or mathematics in another; this cuts out the dresses for the women, and makes the fashions for the men; and makes them endure the inconveniences of all. This makes men drunkards and sober, thieves and honest, and robbers themselves true to one another. Religions are upheld by this, and factions maintained, and the shame of being disesteemed by those with whom one hath lived, and to whom one would recommend oneself, is the great source and director of most of the actions of men. Where riches is in credit, knavery and injustice that produce them is not out of countenance, because the state being got, esteem follows it, and, as it is said in some countries, the crown ennobles the blood. Where power, and not the good exercise of it, gives reputation, all the injustice, falsehood, violence and oppression that attains that [i.e. power] goes for wisdom and ability. Where love of one's country is the thing in credit, there we shall see a race of brave Romans; and when being a favourite at court was the only thing in fashion, one may observe the same race of Romans all turned flatterers and informers. He, therefore, that would govern the world well, had need consider rather what fashions he makes than what laws; and to bring anything into use he need only give it reputation.

14: 'The Idea We Have of God' (Journal, 1 August 1680)

Whatsoever carries any excellency with it, and includes not imperfection, that must needs make a part of the idea we have of God. So that with being, and the continuation of it, or perpetual duration, power and wisdom and goodness must be ingredients of the perfect or super-excellent being which we call God, and that in the utmost or an infinite degree. But yet that unlimited power cannot be an excellency without it be regulated by wisdom and goodness; for since God is eternal and perfect in his own being, he cannot make use of that power to change his own being into a better or another state; and therefore all the exercise of that power must be in and upon his creatures, which cannot but be employed for their good and benefit, as much as the order and perfection of the whole can allow to each individual in its particular rank and station. And, therefore, looking on God as a being infinite in goodness as well as power, we cannot imagine he hath made anything with a design that it should be miserable, but that he hath afforded it all the means of being happy that its nature and state is capable of. And though justice be also a perfection which we must necessarily ascribe to the Supreme Being, yet we cannot suppose the exercise of it should extend further than his goodness has need of it for the preservation of his creatures in the order and beauty of that state that he has placed each of them in; for since our actions cannot reach unto him, or bring him any profit or damage, the punishments he inflicts on any of his creatures, i.e. the misery or destruction he brings upon them, can be nothing else but to preserve the greater or more considerable part, and so being only for preservation, his justice is nothing but a branch of his goodness, which is fain by severity to restrain the irregular and destructive parts from doing harm; for to imagine God under a necessity of punishing for any other reason but this, is to make his justice a great imperfection, and to suppose a power over him that necessitates him to operate contrary to the rules of his wisdom and goodness, which cannot be supposed to make anything so idly as that it should be purposely destroyed or be put in a worse state than destruction (misery being as much a worse state than annihilation, as pain is than insensibility, or the torments of the rack less eligible than quiet sound sleeping): the justice then of God can be supposed to extend itself no further than infinite goodness shall find it necessary for the preservation of his works.

15: 'Inspiration' (Journal, 3 April 1681)

Religion being that homage and obedience which man pays immediately to God, it supposes that man is capable of knowing that there is a God, and what is required by and will be acceptable to him, thereby to avoid his anger and procure his favour. That there is a God, and what that God is, nothing can discover to us, nor judge in us, but natural reason. For whatever discovery we receive any other way must come originally from inspiration, which is an opinion or persuasion in the mind whereof a man knows not the rise nor reason, but is received there as a truth coming from an unknown, and therefore a supernatural, cause, and not founded upon those principles, nor observations, nor way of reasoning which makes the understanding admit other things for truths. But no such inspiration concerning God, or his worship, can be admitted for truth by him that thinks himself thus inspired, much less by any other whom he would persuade to believe him inspired, any further than it is conformable to his reason. Not only because where reason is not, [I] judge it is impossible for a man himself to distinguish betwixt inspiration and fancy, truth and error. But also it is impossible to have such a notion of God as to believe that he should make a creature to whom the knowledge of himself was necessary, and yet not to be discovered by that way which discovers everything else that concerns us, but was to come into the minds of men only by such a way by which all manner of errors come in, and is more likely to let in falsehoods than truths, since nobody can doubt, from the contradiction and strangeness of opinions concerning God and religion in the world, that men are likely to have more fancies than inspirations.

Inspiration then, barely in itself, cannot be a ground to receive any doctrine not conformable to reason. In the next place let us see how far inspiration can enforce on the mind any opinion concerning God or his worship, when accompanied with a power to do a miracle; and here too, I say, the last determination must be that of reason.

1st. Because reason must be the judge what is a miracle and what is not; which not knowing how far the power of natural causes do extend themselves, and what strange effects they may produce, is very hard to determine.

2nd. It will always be as great a miracle that God should alter the course of natural things to overturn the principles of knowledge and understanding in a man, by setting up anything to be received by him as a truth which his reason cannot assent to, as the miracle itself; and so, at best, it will be but one miracle against another, and the greater still on reason's side; it being harder to believe that God should alter and put out of its ordinary course some phenomenon of the great world for once, and make things act contrary to their ordinary rule, purposely that the mind of man might do so always afterwards, than that this is some fallacy or natural effect, of which he knows not the cause, let it look never so strange.

3rd. Because man does not know whether there be not several sorts of creatures above him, and between him and the Supreme, amongst which there may be some that have the power to produce in nature such extraordinary effects as we call miracles, and may have the will to do it for other reasons than the confirmation of truth. For 'tis certain the magicians of Egypt turned their rods into serpents as well as Moses; and since so great a miracle as that was done in opposition to the true God, and the revelation sent by him, what miracle can have certainty and assurance greater than that of a man's reason?

And if inspiration have so much the disadvantage of reason in the man himself who is inspired, it has much more so in him who receives this revelation only from another, and that too very remote in time and place.

I do not hereby deny in the least that God can [do], or hath done, miracles for the confirmation of truths; but I only say that we cannot think he should do them to enforce doctrines, or notions of himself, or any worship of him not conformable to reason, or that we can receive such for truths for the miracle's sake: and even in those books which have the greatest proof of revelation from God, and the attestation of miracles to confirm their being so, the miracles were to be judged by the doctrine, and not the doctrine by the miracles, v. Deut. xiii 1; Matt. xiv 24. And St Paul says, 'If an angel from heaven should teach any other doctrine . . .'

16: 'Virtus' (1681; from the 1661 Commonplace Book)

Virtue, as in its obligation it is the will of God, discovered by natural reason, and thus has the force of a law; so in the matter of it, it is nothing else but doing of good, either to oneself or others; and the contrary hereunto, vice, is nothing else but doing of harm. Thus the bounds of temperance are prescribed by the health, estates, and the use of our time: justice, truth, and mercy by the good or evil they are likely to produce; since everybody allows one may with justice deny another the possession of his own sword, when there is reason to believe he would make use of it to his own harm.

But since men in society are in a far different estate than when considered single and alone, the instances and measures of virtue and vice are very different under these two considerations; for though, as I said before, the measures of temperance, to a solitary man, be none but those above-mentioned, yet if he be a member of a society, it may, according to the station he has in it, receive measures from reputation and example; so that which would be no vicious excess in a retired obscurity may be a very great one amongst people who think ill of such excess because, by lessening his esteem amongst them, it makes a man incapable of having the authority, and doing the good, which otherwise he might. For esteem and reputation being a sort of moral strength, whereby a man is enabled to do, as it were, by an augmented force, that which others, of equal natural parts and natural power, cannot do without it; he that by any intemperance weakens this his moral strength, does himself as much harm as if by intemperance he weakened the natural strength either of his mind or body, and so is equally vicious by doing harm to himself.

This, if well considered, will give us better boundaries of virtue and vice than curious questions stated with the nicest distinctions; that being always the greatest vice whose consequences draw after it the greatest harm; and therefore the injuries and mischiefs done to societies are much more culpable than those done to private men, though with greater personal aggravations. And so many things naturally become vices amongst men in society, which without that would be innocent actions. Thus for a man to cohabit and have children by one or more women, who are at their own disposal, and, when they think fit, to part again, I see not how it can be condemned as a vice, since nobody is harmed, supposing it done amongst persons considered as separate from the rest of mankind. But yet this hinders not but it is a vice of deep dye when the same thing is done in a society wherein modesty, the great virtue of the weaker sex, has often other rules and bounds set by custom and reputation, than what it has by direct instances of the law of nature in a solitude or an estate separate from the opinion of this or that society. For if a woman, by transgressing those bounds which the received opinion of her country or religion, and not nature or reason, have set to modesty, has drawn any blemish on her reputation, she may run the risk of being exposed to infamy, and other mischiefs, amongst which the least is not the danger of losing the comforts of a conjugal settlement, and therewith the chief end of her being, the propagation of mankind.

17: From *The First Treatise of Government* (*c.* 1681)

CHAPTER FIVE: Of Adam's Title to Sovereignty by the Subjection of Eve

44. The next place of Scripture we find our author [Filmer] builds his monarchy of Adam on, is 3 Genesis 16: 'And thy desire shall be to thy husband, and he shall rule over thee.' 'Here we have,' says he, 'the original grant of government,' from whence he concludes, in the following part of the page (O. [*Observations upon Mr Hunton's Treatise of Monarchy*] 244), 'that the supreme power is settled in the fatherhood, and limited to one kind of government, that is to monarchy.' For let his premises be what they will, this is always the conclusion; let 'rule' in any text be but once named, and presently absolute monarchy is by divine right established. If anyone will but carefully read our author's own reasoning from these words (O. 244), and consider among other things the line and posterity of Adam as he there brings them in, he will find some difficulty to make a sense of what he says. But we will allow this at present to his peculiar way of writing, and consider the force of the text in hand. The words are the curse of God upon the woman, for having

been the first and forwardest in the disobedience, and if we will consider the occasion of what God says here to our first parents, that he was denouncing judgement, and declaring his wrath against them both, for their disobedience, we cannot suppose that this was the time, wherein God was granting Adam prerogatives and privileges, investing him with dignity and authority, elevating him to dominion and monarchy. For though as a helper in the temptation, as well as a partner in the transgression, Eve was laid below him, and so he had accidentally a superiority over her, for her greater punishment, yet he too had his share in the fall, as well as the sin, and was laid lower, as may be seen in the following verses, and 'twould be hard to imagine, that God, in the same breath, should make him universal monarch over all mankind, and a day labourer for his life, turn him out of Paradise to till the ground (verse 23), and at the same time advance him to a throne, and all the privileges and ease of absolute power.

45. This was not a time when Adam could expect any favours, any grant of privileges, from his offended maker. If this be 'the original grant of government', as our author tells us, and Adam was now made monarch, whatever Sir Robert would have him, 'tis plain God made him but a very poor monarch, such an one as our author himself would have counted it no great privilege to be. God sets him to work for his living, and seems rather to give him a spade into his hand, to subdue the earth, than a sceptre, to rule over its inhabitants. 'In the sweat of thy face thou shalt eat thy bread,' says God to him (verse 19). This was unavoidable, may it perhaps be answered, because he was yet without subjects, and had no body to work for him, but afterwards, living as he did above 900 years, he might have people enough, whom he might command to work for him; no, says God, not only whilst thou art without other help, save thy wife, but as long as thou livest, shalt thou live by thy labour. 'In the sweat of thy face, shalt thou eat thy bread, till thou return unto the ground, for out of it wast thou taken, for dust thou art, and unto dust shalt thou return' (verse 19). It will perhaps be answered again in favour of our author, that these words are not spoken personally to Adam, but in him, as their representative, to all mankind, this being a curse upon mankind, because of the fall.

46. God, I believe, speaks differently from men, because he speaks with more truth, more certainty; but when he vouchsafes to speak to men, I do not think he speaks differently from them, in crossing the rules of language in use amongst them. This would not be to condescend to their capacities, when he humbles himself to speak to them, but to lose his design in speaking what, thus spoken, they could not understand. And yet thus must we think of God, if the interpretations of Scripture necessary to maintain our author's doctrine, must be received for good. For by the ordinary rules of language, it will be very hard to understand what God says if what he speaks here in the singular number to Adam must be understood to be spoken to all mankind, and what he says in the plural number (1 Genesis 26 and 28) must be understood of Adam alone, exclusive of all others, and what he says to Noah and his sons jointly must be understood to be meant to Noah alone (Genesis 9).

47. Further, it is to be noted that these words here of 3 Genesis 16, which our author calls 'the original grant of government', were not spoken to Adam, neither indeed was there any grant in them made to Adam, but a punishment laid upon Eve: and if we will take them as they were directed in particular to her, or in her, as their representative, to all other women, they will at most concern the female sex only, and import no more but that subjection they should ordinarily be in to their husbands. But there is here no more law to oblige a woman to such a subjection, if the circumstances either of her condition or contract with her husband should exempt her from it, than there is, that she should bring forth her children in sorrow and pain, if there could be found a remedy for it, which is also a part of the same curse upon her: for the whole verse runs thus: 'Unto the woman he said, "I will greatly multiply thy sorrow and thy conception; in sorrow thou shalt bring forth children, and thy desire shall be to thy husband, and he shall rule over thee."' 'Twould, I think, have been a hard matter for anybody but our author to have found out a grant of monarchical government to Adam in these words, which were neither spoke to, nor of, him. Neither will anyone, I suppose, by these words, think the weaker sex, as by a law so subjected to the curse contained in them, that 'tis their duty not to endeavour to avoid it. And will anyone say, that Eve, or any other woman, sinned, if she were brought to bed

without those multiplied pains God threatens her here with? Or that either of our Queens Mary or Elizabeth, had they married any of their subjects, had been by this text put into a political subjection to him? Or that he thereby should have had monarchical rule over her? God, in this text, gives not, that I see, any authority to Adam over Eve, or to men over their wives, but only foretells what should be the woman's lot, how by his providence he would order it so, that she should be subject to her husband, as we see that generally the laws of mankind and customs of nations have ordered it so; and there is, I grant, a foundation in nature for it.

48. Thus when God says of Jacob and Esau, that 'the elder should serve the younger' (25 Genesis 23), nobody supposes that God hereby made Jacob Esau's sovereign, but foretold what should *de facto* come to pass.

But if these words here spoke to Eve must needs be understood as a law to bind her and all other women to subjection, it can be no other subjection than what every wife owes her husband, and then if this be the 'original grant of government' and the 'foundation of monarchical power', there will be as many monarchs as there are husbands. If, therefore, these words give any power to Adam, it can be only a conjugal power, not political: the power that every husband hath to order the things of private concernment in his family, as proprietor of the goods and land there, and to have his will take place before that of his wife in all things of their common concernment; but not a political power of life and death over her, much less over anybody else.

49. This I am sure: If our author will have this text to be a grant, 'the original grant of government', political government, he ought to have proved it by some better arguments than by barely saying that 'thy desire shall be unto thy husband' was a law whereby Eve 'and all that should come of her' were subjected to the absolute monarchical power of Adam and his heirs. 'Thy desire shall be to thy husband' is too doubtful an expression, of whose signification interpreters are not agreed, to build so confidently on, and in a matter of such moment, and so great and general concernment. But our author, according to his way of writing, having once named the text, concludes presently without any more ado, that the meaning is as he would have it. Let the words rule and subject be but found in

the text or margin, and it immediately signifies the duty of a subject to his prince, the relation is changed, and though God says 'husband', Sir Robert will have it 'king'; Adam has presently absolute monarchical power over Eve, and not only over Eve, but 'all that should come of her', though the Scripture says not a word of it, nor our author a word to prove it. But Adam must for all that be an absolute monarch, and so down to the end of the chapter. And here I leave my reader to consider, whether my bare saying, without offering any reasons to evince it, that this text gave not Adam that absolute monarchical power our author supposes, be not as sufficient to destroy that power, as his bare assertion is to establish it, since the text mentions neither prince nor people, speaks nothing of absolute or monarchical power, but the subjection of Eve to Adam, a wife to her husband. And he that would trace our author so all through, would make a short and sufficient answer to the greatest part of the grounds he proceeds on, and abundantly confute them by barely denying, it being a sufficient answer to assertions without proof to deny them without giving a reason. And therefore should I have said nothing, but barely denied that by this text 'the supreme power was settled and founded by God himself in the fatherhood, limited to monarchy, and that to Adam's person and heirs', all which our author notably concludes from these words, as may be seen in the same page (O. 244), it had been a sufficient answer; should I have desired any sober man only to have read the text, and considered to whom and on what occasion it was spoken, he would no doubt have wondered how our author found out 'monarchical absolute power' in it, had he not had an exceeding good faculty to find it himself where he could not show it others. And thus we have examined the two places of Scripture, all that I remember our author brings to prove Adam's sovereignty, that supremacy which, he says, 'it was God's ordinance should be unlimited in Adam, and as large as all the acts of his will' (O. 245), viz. 1 Genesis 28 and 3 Genesis 16, one whereof signifies only the subjection of the inferior ranks of creatures to mankind, and the other the subjection that is due from a wife to her husband, both far enough from that which subjects owe the governors of political societies.

CHAPTER NINE: Of Monarchy by Inheritance from Adam

81. Though it be never so plain that there ought to be government in the world, nay, should all men be of our author's mind, that divine appointment had ordained it to be monarchical, yet since men cannot obey anything that cannot command, and ideas of government in the fancy, though never so perfect, though never so right, cannot give laws, nor prescribe rules to the actions of men, it would be of no behoof for the settling of order, and establishment of government in its exercise and use amongst men, unless there were a way also taught how to know the person to whom it belonged to have this power, and exercise this dominion over others. 'Tis in vain then to talk of subjection and obedience, without telling us whom we are to obey. For were I never so fully persuaded that there ought to be magistracy and rule in the world, yet I am nevertheless at liberty still, till it appears who is the person that hath right to my obedience: since if there be no marks to know him by, and distinguish him that hath right to rule from other men, it may be myself as well as any other. And therefore, though submission to government be everyone's duty, yet since that signifies nothing but submitting to the direction and laws of such men as have authority to command, 'tis not enough to make a man a subject, to convince him that there is regal power in the world, but there must be ways of designing and knowing the person to whom this regal power of right belongs; and a man can never be obliged in conscience to submit to any power, unless he can be satisfied who is the person who has a right to exercise that power over him. If this were not so, there would be no distinction between pirates and lawful princes, he that has force is without any more ado to be obeyed, and crowns and sceptres would become the inheritance only of violence and rapine. Men too might as often and as innocently change their governors as they do their physicians, if the person cannot be known who has a right to direct me, and whose prescriptions I am bound to follow. To settle therefore men's consciences under an obligation to obedience, 'tis necessary that they know, not only that there is a power somewhere in the world, but the person who by right is vested with this power over them.

82. How successful our author has been in his attempts to set up a monarchical absolute power in Adam the reader may judge by what has been already said. But were that absolute monarchy as clear as our author would desire it, as I presume it is the contrary, yet it could be of no use to the government of mankind now in the world, unless he also make out these two things:

First, that this power of Adam was not to end with him, but was upon his decease conveyed entire to some other person, and so on to posterity.

Secondly, that the princes and rulers now on earth are possessed of this power of Adam by a right way of conveyance derived to them.

83. If the first of these fail, the power of Adam, were it never so great, never so certain, will signify nothing to the present governments and societies in the world, but we must seek out some other original of power for the government of polities than this of Adam, or else there will be none at all in the world. If the latter fail, it will destroy the authority of the present governors, and absolve the people from subjection to them, since they having no better a claim than others to that power which is alone the fountain of all authority, can have no title to rule over them.

84. Our author, having fancied an absolute sovereignty in Adam, mentions several ways of its conveyance to princes that were to be his successors, but that which he chiefly insists on is that of inheritance, which occurs so often in his several discourses, and I having in the foregoing chapter quoted several of these passages, I shall not need here again to repeat them. This sovereignty he erects, as has been said, upon a double foundation, viz. that of property, and that of fatherhood. One was the right he was supposed to have in all creatures, a right to possess the earth with the beasts and other inferior ranks of things in it for his private use, exclusive of all other men. The other was the right he was supposed to have to rule and govern men, all the rest of mankind.

85. In both these rights, there being supposed an exclusion of all other men, it must be upon some reason peculiar to Adam that they must both be founded.

That of his property our author supposes to arise from God's immediate donation (Genesis 1.28), and that of fatherhood from the act of begetting. Now in all inheritance, if the heir succeed not to the reason upon which his father's right was founded, he cannot succeed to the right which followeth from it. For example, Adam had a right of property in the creatures, upon the donation and grant of God almighty, who was lord and proprietor of them all. Let this be so as our author tells us, yet upon his death his heir can have no title to them, no such right of property in them, unless the same reason, viz. God's donation, vested a right in the heir too. For if Adam could have had no property in, nor use of, the creatures without this positive donation from God, and this donation were only personally to Adam, his heir could have no right by it, but upon his death it must revert to God the lord and owner again: for positive grants give no title further than the express words convey it, and by which only it is held. And thus, if as our author himself contends, that donation (Genesis 1.28), were made only to Adam personally, his heir could not succeed to his property in the creatures; and if it were a donation to any but Adam, let it be shown that it was to his heir in our author's sense, i.e. to one of his children exclusive of all the rest.

86. But not to follow our author too far out of the way, the plain of the case is this: God having made man, and planted in him, as in all other animals, a strong desire of self-preservation, and furnished the world with things fit for food and raiment and other necessaries of life, subservient to his design that man should live and abide for some time upon the face of the earth, and not that so curious and wonderful a piece of workmanship by its own negligence, or want of necessaries, should perish again, presently, after a few moments continuance; God, I say, having made man and the world thus, spoke to him, (that is) directed him by his senses and reason, as he did the inferior animals by their sense and instinct, which he had placed in them to that purpose, to the use of those things which were serviceable for his subsistence, and given him as means of his preservation. And therefore I doubt not, but before these words were pronounced (1 Genesis 28, 29) (if they must be understood literally to have been spoken) and without any such verbal donation, man had a right to a use of the creatures by the will and grant of God. For the desire, strong desire of preserving his life and being having been planted in him as a principle of action by God himself,

reason, which was the voice of God in him, could not but teach him and assure him, that pursuing that natural inclination he had to preserve his being, he followed the will of his maker, and therefore had a right to make use of those creatures which by his reason or senses he could discover would be serviceable thereunto. And thus man's property in the creatures was founded upon the right he had to make use of those things that were necessary or useful to his being.

87. This being the reason and foundation of Adam's property gave the same title, on the same ground, to all his children, not only after his death, but in his lifetime. So that here was no privilege of his heir above his other children which could exclude them from an equal right to the use of the inferior creatures for the comfortable preservation of their beings, which is all the property man hath in them: and so Adam's sovereignty built on property, or, as our author calls it, private dominion, comes to nothing. Every man had a right to the creatures by the same title Adam had, viz. by the right everyone had to take care of, and provide for, their subsistence. And thus men had a right in common, Adam's children in common with him. But if anyone had begun, and made himself a property in any particular thing (which how he, or anyone else, could do, shall be shown in another place), that thing, that possession, if he disposed not otherwise of it by his positive grant, descended naturally to his children, and they had a right to succeed to it, and possess it.

88. It might reasonably be asked here how come children by this right of possessing, before any other, the properties of their parents upon their decease. For it being personally the parents', when they die, without actually transferring their right to another, why does it not return again to the common stock of mankind? 'Twill perhaps be answered that common consent hath disposed of it to the children. Common practice, we see, indeed does so dispose of it, but we cannot say that it is the common consent of mankind; for that hath never been asked, nor actually given: and if common tacit consent hath established it, it would make but a positive and not natural right of children to inherit the goods of their parents. But where the practice is universal, 'tis reasonable to think the cause is natural. The ground, then, I think to be this. The first and strongest

desire God planted in men, and wrought into the very principles of their nature, being that of self-preservation, that is the foundation of a right to the creatures for the particular support and use of each individual person himself. But next to this, God planted in men a strong desire also of propagating their kind, and continuing themselves in their posterity, and this gives children a title to share in the property of their parents, and a right to inherit their possessions. Men are not proprietors of what they have merely for themselves, their children have a title to part of it, and have their kind of right joined with their parents', in the possession which comes to be wholly theirs, when death having put an end to their parents' use of it, hath taken them from their possessions, and this we call inheritance. Men being by a like obligation bound to preserve what they have begotten as to preserve themselves, their issue come to have a right in the goods they are possessed of. That children have such a right is plain from the laws of God, and that men are convinced that children have such a right is evident from the law of the land, both which laws require parents to provide for their children.

89. For children being by the course of nature born weak, and unable to provide for themselves, they have by the appointment of God himself, who hath thus ordered the course of nature, a right to be nourished and maintained by their parents, nay a right not only to a bare subsistence but to the conveniences and comforts of life, as far as the conditions of their parents can afford it. Hence it comes that when their parents leave the world, and so the care due to their children ceases, the effects of it are to extend as far as possibly they can, and the provisions they have made in their lifetime are understood to be intended as nature requires they should, for their children, whom after themselves they are bound to provide for. Though the dying parents, by express words, declare nothing about them, nature appoints the descent of their property to their children, who thus come to have a title and natural right of inheritance to their father's goods, which the rest of mankind cannot pretend to.

90. Were it not for this right of being nourished and maintained by their parents, which God and nature has given to children, and obliged parents to, as a duty, it would be reasonable that the father should inherit the estate of his son, and be preferred in the

inheritance before his grandchild. For to the grandfather there is due a long score of care and expenses laid out upon the breeding and education of his son, which one would think in justice ought to be paid. But that having been done in obedience to the same law, whereby he received nourishment and education from his own parents, this score of education received from a man's father is paid by taking care and providing for his own children; is paid, I say, as much as is required of payment by alteration of property, unless present necessity of the parents require a return of goods for their necessary support and subsistence. For we are not now speaking of that reverence, acknowledgement, respect and honour that is always due from children to their parents, but of possessions and commodities of life valuable by money. But though it be incumbent on parents to bring up and provide for their children, yet this debt to the children does not quite cancel the score due to their parents, but only is made by nature preferable to it. For the debt a man owes his father takes place, and gives the father a right to inherit the son's goods, where for want of issue the right of children doth not exclude that title. And therefore a man having a right to be maintained by his children where he needs it, and to enjoy also the comforts of life from them, when the necessary provision due to them and their children will afford it, if his son die without issue, the father has a right in nature to possess his goods and inherit his estate (whatever the municipal laws of some countries may absurdly direct otherwise), and so again his children and their issue from him, or, for want of such, his father and his issue. But where no such are to be found, i.e. no kindred, there we see the possessions of a private man revert to the community, and so in politic societies come into the hands of the public magistrate: but in the state of nature become again perfectly common, nobody having a right to inherit them, nor can anyone have a property in them, otherwise than in other things common by nature, of which I shall speak in its due place.

91. I have been the larger in showing upon what ground children have a right to succeed to the possession of their fathers' properties, not only because by it it will appear that if Adam had a property (a titular insignificant useless property; for it could be no better, for he was bound to nourish and maintain his children and posterity

out of it) in the whole earth and its product, yet all his children coming to have by the law of nature and right of inheritance a joint title and right of property in it after his death, it could convey no right of sovereignty to any one of his posterity over the rest: since everyone having a right of inheritance to his portion, they might enjoy their inheritance, or any part of it, in common, or share it, or some parts of it, by division, as it best liked them. But no one could pretend to the whole inheritance, or any sovereignty supposed to accompany it, since a right of inheritance gave every one of the rest, as well as any one, a title to share in the goods of his father. Not only upon this account, I say, have I been so particular in examining the reason of children's inheriting the property of their fathers, but also because it will give us further light in the inheritance of rule and power, which in countries where their particular municipal laws give the whole possession of land entirely to the first born, and descent of power has gone so to men by this custom, some have been apt to be deceived into an opinion that there was a natural or divine right of primogeniture to both estate and power; and that the inheritance of both rule over men and property in things sprang from the same original, and were to descend by the same rules.

92. Property, whose original is from the right a man has to use any of the inferior creatures for the subsistence and comfort of his life, is for the benefit and sole advantage of the proprietor, so that he may even destroy the thing that he has property in by his use of it, where need requires; but government, being for the preservation of every man's right and property, by preserving him from the violence or injury of others, is for the good of the governed. For the magistrate's sword being for a terror to evil doers, and by that terror to enforce men to observe the positive laws of the society, made (conformable to the laws of nature) for the public good, i.e. the good of every particular member of that society, as far as by common rules it can be provided for, the sword is not given the magistrate for his own good alone.

93. Children, therefore, as has been showed, by the dependence they have on their parents for subsistence, have a right of inheritance to their father's property, as that which belongs to them for their proper good and behoof, and therefore are fitly termed goods,

wherein the first born has not a sole or peculiar right by any law of God and nature, the younger children having an equal title with him founded on that right they all have to maintenance, support and comfort from their parents, and nothing else. But government being for the benefit of the governed, and not the sole advantage of the governors (but only for theirs with the rest, as they make a part of that politic body, each of whose parts and members are taken care of, and directed in its peculiar functions for the good of the whole, by the laws of the society), cannot be inherited by the same title that children have to the goods of their father. The right a son has to be maintained and provided with the necessaries and conveniences of life out of his father's stock gives him a right to succeed to his father's property for his own good, but this can give him no right to succeed also to the rule which his father had over other men. All that a child has right to claim from his father is nourishment and education, and the things nature furnishes for the support of life; but he has no right to demand rule or dominion from him. He can subsist and receive from him the portion of good things, and advantages of education, naturally due to him without empire and dominion. That (if his father hath any) was vested in him for the good and behoof of others, and therefore the son cannot claim or inherit it by a title which is founded wholly on his private good and advantage.

94. We must know how the first ruler from whom anyone claims came by his authority, upon what ground anyone has empire, what his title is to it, before we can know who has a right to succeed him in it, and inherit it from him. If the agreement and consent of men first gave a sceptre into anyone's hand, or put a crown on his head, that also must direct its descent and conveyance. For the same authority that made the first a lawful ruler, must make the second too, and so give right of succession. In this case inheritance or primogeniture can in itself have no right, no pretence to it, any further than that consent which established the form of the government hath so settled the succession. And thus we see the succession of crowns in several countries places it on different heads, and he comes by right of succession to be a prince in one place, who would be a subject in another.

95. If God, by his positive grant and revealed declaration, first

gave rule and dominion to any man, he that will claim by that title must have the same positive grant of God for his succession. For if that has not directed the course of its descent and conveyance down to others, nobody can succeed to this title of the first ruler; children have no right of inheritance to this, and primogeniture can lay no claim to it, unless God the author of this constitution hath so ordained it. Thus we see the pretensions of Saul's family, who received his crown from the immediate appointment of God, ended with his reign, and David, by the same title that Saul reigned, viz. God's appointment, succeeded in his throne, to the exclusion of Jonathan and all pretensions of paternal inheritance. And if Solomon had a right to succeed his father, it must be by some other title than that of primogeniture. A cadet, or sister's son, must have the preference in succession, if he has the same title the first lawful prince had. And in dominion that has its foundation only in the positive appointment of God himself, Benjamin, the youngest, must have the inheritance of the crown if God so direct as well as one of that tribe had the first possession.

96. If paternal right, the act of begetting, give a man rule and dominion, inheritance or primogeniture can give no title. For he that cannot succeed to his father's title, which was begetting, cannot succeed to that power over his brethren, which his father had by paternal right over them. But of this I shall have occasion to say more in another place. This is plain in the meantime, that any government, whether supposed to be at first founded in paternal right, consent of the people, or the positive appointment of God himself (which can supersede either of the other, and so begin a new government upon a new foundation): I say, any government begun upon either of these, can by right of succession come to those only who have the title of him they succeed to. Power founded on contract can descend only to him who has right by that contract; power founded on begetting, he only can have that begets; and power founded on the positive grant or donation of God, he only can have by right of succession, to whom that grant directs it.

97. From what I have said, I think this is clear, that a right to the use of the creatures, being founded originally in the right a man has to subsist and enjoy the conveniences of life; and the natural right children have to inherit the goods of their parents, being

founded in the right they have to the same subsistence and commodities of life, out of the stock of their parents, who are therefore taught by natural love and tenderness to provide for them, as a part of themselves – and all this being only for the good of the proprietor, or heir – it can be no reason for children's inheriting of rule and dominion, which has another original and a different end. Nor can primogeniture have any pretence to a right of solely inheriting either property or power, as we shall, in its due place, see more fully. 'Tis enough to have showed here that Adam's property, or private dominion, could not convey any sovereignty or rule to his heir, who, not having a right to inherit all his father's possessions, could not thereby come to have any sovereignty over his brethren. And therefore if any sovereignty on account of his property had been vested in Adam, which in truth there was not, yet it would have died with him.

98. As Adam's sovereignty, if, by virtue of being proprietor of the whole world, he had any authority over men, could not have been inherited by any of his children over the rest, because they had the same title to divide the inheritance, and everyone had a right to a portion of his father's possessions, so neither could Adam's sovereignty by right of fatherhood, if any such he had, descend to any one of his children. For it being, in our author's account, a right, acquired by begetting, to rule over those he had begotten, it was not a power possible to be inherited, because the right being consequent to, and built on, an act perfectly personal, made that power so too, and impossible to be inherited. For paternal power, being a natural right rising only from the relation of father and son, is as impossible to be inherited as the relation itself, and a man may pretend as well to inherit the conjugal power the husband, whose heir he is, had over his wife, as he can to inherit the paternal power of a father over his children. For the power of the husband being founded on contract, and the power of the father on begetting, he may as well inherit the power obtained by the conjugal contract, which was only personal, as he may the power obtained by begetting, which could reach no further than the person of the begetter, unless begetting can be a title to power in him that does not beget.

99. Which makes it a reasonable question to ask, whether Adam, dying before Eve, his heir (suppose Cain, or Seth) should have had,

by right of inheriting Adam's fatherhood, sovereign power over Eve his mother. For Adam's fatherhood being nothing but a right he had to govern his children, because he begot them, he that inherits Adam's fatherhood inherits nothing, even in our author's sense, but the right Adam had to govern his children because he begot them. So that the monarchy of the heir would not have taken in Eve, or, if it did, it being nothing but the fatherhood of Adam descended by inheritance, the heir must have right to govern Eve because Adam begot her; for fatherhood is nothing else.

100. Perhaps it will be said with our author that a man can alien his power over his child, and what may be transferred by compact may be possessed by inheritance. I answer, a father cannot alien the power he has over his child; he may perhaps to some degrees forfeit it, but cannot transfer it. And if any other man acquire it, 'tis not by the father's grant, but by some act of his own. For example, a father, unnaturally careless of his child, sells or gives him to another man; and he again exposes him. A third man finding him, breeds up, cherishes, and provides for him as his own. I think in this case, nobody will doubt but that the greatest part of filial duty and subjection was here owing, and to be paid, to this foster-father. And if anything could be demanded from the child by either of the other, it could be only due to his natural father, who, perhaps, might have forfeited his right to much of that duty comprehended in the command 'honour your parents', but could transfer none of it to another. He that purchased, and neglected, the child, got, by his purchase and grant of the father, no title to duty or honour from the child, but only he acquired it who by his own authority, performing the office and care of a father to the forlorn and perishing infant, made himself, by paternal care, a title to proportionable degrees of paternal power. This will be more easily admitted upon consideration of the nature of paternal power, for which I refer my reader to the Second Book.

101. To return to the argument in hand: This is evident, that paternal power arising only from begetting, for in that our author places it alone, can neither be transferred nor inherited. And he that does not beget, can no more have paternal power which arises from thence, than he can have a right to anything who performs not the condition to which only it is annexed. If one should ask 'By

what law has a father power over his children?' it will be answered, no doubt, 'By the law of nature, which gives such a power over them to him that begets them.' If one should ask, likewise, 'By what law does our author's heir come by a right to inherit?' I think it would be answered 'By the law of nature' too. For I find not that our author brings one word of Scripture to prove the right of such an heir he speaks of. Why then, the law of nature gives fathers paternal power over their children because they did beget them, and the same law of nature gives the same paternal power to the heir over his brethren, who did not beget them. Whence it follows, that either the father has not his paternal power by begetting, or else that the heir has it not at all. For 'tis hard to understand how the law of nature, which is the law of reason, can give the paternal power to the father over his children for the only reason of begetting, and to the first born over his brethren without this only reason, i.e. for no reason at all. And if the eldest, by the law of nature, can inherit this paternal power, without the only reason that gives a title to it, so may the youngest as well as he, and a stranger as well as either. For where there is no reason for anyone, as there is not, but for him that begets, all have an equal title. I am sure our author offers no reason, and when anybody does, we shall see whether it will hold or no.

102. In the meantime, 'tis as good sense to say that by the law of nature a man has right to inherit the property of another because he is of kin to him, and is known to be of his blood, and therefore by the same law of nature an utter stranger to his blood has right to inherit his estate, as to say that by the law of nature he that begets them has paternal power over his children, and therefore by the law of nature the heir that begets them not has this paternal power over them. Or supposing the law of the land gave absolute power over their children to such only who nursed them, and fed their children themselves, could anybody pretend that this law gave anyone who did no such thing absolute power over those who were not his children?

103. When, therefore, it can be showed that conjugal power can belong to him that is not an husband, it will also, I believe, be proved that our author's paternal power, acquired by begetting, may be inherited by a son, and that a brother, as heir to his father's

power, may have paternal power over his brethren, and, by the same rule, conjugal power too. But, till then, I think we may rest satisfied that the paternal power of Adam, this sovereign authority of fatherhood, were there any such, could not descend to, nor be inherited by, his next heir. Fatherly power, I easily grant our author, if it will do him any good, can never be lost, because it will be as long in the world as there are fathers; but none of them will have Adam's paternal power, or derive theirs from him, but every one will have his own, by the same title Adam had his, viz. by begetting, but not by inheritance or succession, no more than husbands have their conjugal power by inheritance from Adam. And thus we see, as Adam had no such property, no such paternal power, as gave him sovereign jurisdiction over mankind, so likewise his sovereignty built upon either of these titles, if he had any such, could not have descended to his heir, but must have ended with him. Adam, therefore, as has been proved, being neither monarch, nor his imaginary monarchy hereditable, the power which is now in the world is not that which was Adam's, since all that Adam could have upon our author's grounds, either of property or fatherhood, necessarily died with him, and could not be conveyed to posterity by inheritance. In the next place we will consider whether Adam had any such heir, to inherit his power, as our author talks of.

18: 'Two Sorts of Knowledge' (Journal, 26 June 1681)

There are two sorts of knowledge in the world, general and particular, founded upon two different principles: i.e. true ideas, and matter of fact, or history. All general knowledge is founded only upon true ideas; and so far as we have these we are capable of demonstration, or certain knowledge. For he that has the true idea of a triangle or circle is capable of knowing any demonstration concerning these figures; but if he have not the true idea of a scalenon, he cannot know anything concerning a scalenon, though he may have some confused or imperfect opinion concerning a scalenon, upon a confused or imperfect idea of it; or, when he believes what he hath heard others say concerning a scalenon, he may have some uncertain opinion concerning its properties, but this is belief and not knowledge. Upon the same reason, he that has a true idea of God, of himself as his creature, or the relation he stands in to God and his fellow-creatures, and of justice, goodness, law, happiness, etc., is capable of knowing moral things, or having a demonstrative certainty in them.

But though I say a man that hath such ideas is capable of certain knowledge in them, yet I do not say that presently he hath thereby that certain knowledge, no more than that he that hath a true idea of a triangle and a right angle, doth presently thereby know that three angles of a triangle are equal to two right ones. He may believe others that tell him so, but know it not till he himself hath employed his thoughts on it and seen the connection and agreement of these ideas, and so made to himself the demonstration; i.e. upon examination seen it to be so.

The first and great step, therefore, to knowledge is to get the mind furnished with true ideas, which the mind being capable of having of moral things as well as figures, I cannot but think morality as well as mathematics capable of demonstration, if men would employ their understandings to think more about it, and not give themselves up to the lazy, traditional way of talking one after another. By [contrast] the knowledge of natural bodies and their operations reaching little further than bare matter-of-fact, without having perfect ideas of the ways and manner they are produced, nor the concurrent causes they depend on; and also the well-management of public or private affairs depending upon the various and unknown humours, interests, and capacities of men we have to do with in the world, and not upon any settled ideas of things, physic, polity, and prudence are not capable of demonstration, but a man is principally helped in them by the history of matter-of-fact, and a sagacity of inquiring into probable causes, and finding out an analogy in their operations and effects.

Knowledge then depends upon right and true ideas; opinion, upon history and matter-of-fact. And hence it comes to pass that our knowledge of general things are *aeternae veritates*, and depend not upon the existence or accidents of things, for the truths of mathematics and morality are certain, whether men make true mathematical figures, or suit their actions to the rules of morality or no. For that the three angles of a triangle are equal to two right ones, is infallibly true, whether there be any such figure as a triangle existing in the world or no. And it is true, that it is every man's duty to be just, whether there be any such thing as a just man in the world or no. But whether this course in public or private affairs will succeed well, whether rhubarb will purge, or quinquina cure an ague, is only known by experience; and there is but probability grounded upon experience or analogical reasoning, but no certain knowledge or demonstration.

19: *The Second Treatise of Government: An Essay Concerning the True Original, Extent, and End of Civil Government* (*c.* 1681)

CHAPTER ONE

1. It having been shown in the foregoing discourse:

1: that Adam had not either by natural right of fatherhood, or by positive donation from God, any such authority over his children, or dominion over the world as is pretended.

2: that if he had, his heirs, yet, had no right to it.

3: that if his heirs had, there being no law of nature nor positive law of God that determines which is the right heir in all cases that may arise, the right of succession, and consequently of bearing rule, could not have been certainly determined.

4: that if even that had been determined, yet the knowledge of which is the eldest line of Adam's posterity, being so long since utterly lost, that in the races of mankind and families of the world there remains not to one above another the least pretence to be the eldest house, and to have the right of inheritance.

All these premises having, as I think, been clearly made out, it

is impossible that the rulers now on earth should make any benefit, or derive any the least shadow of authority, from that which
is held to be the fountain of all power, Adam's private dominion
and paternal jurisdiction, so that he that will not give just occasion to think that all government in the world is the product
only of force and violence, and that men live together by no other
rules but that of beasts, where the strongest carries it, and so lay
a foundation for perpetual disorder and mischief, tumult, sedition,
and rebellion (things that the followers of that hypothesis so
loudly cry out against), must of necessity find out another rise of
government, another original of political power, and another way
of designing and knowing the persons that have it than what Sir
Robert F[ilmer] hath taught us.

2. To this purpose, I think it may not be amiss to set down what
I take to be political power, that the power of a magistrate over a
subject may be distinguished from that of a father over his children,
a master over his servant, a husband over his wife, and a lord over
his slave. All which distinct powers happening sometimes together
in the same man, if he be considered under these different relations,
it may help us to distinguish these powers one from another, and
show the difference betwixt a ruler of a commonwealth, a father of
a family, and a captain of a galley.

3. Political power, then, I take to be a right of making laws with
penalties of death, and consequently all less penalties, for the regulating and preserving of property, and of employing the force of the
community in the execution of such laws, and in the defence of the
commonwealth from foreign injury, and all this only for the public
good.

CHAPTER TWO: Of the State of Nature

4. To understand political power right, and derive it from its
original, we must consider what state all men are naturally in, and
that is a state of perfect freedom to order their actions and dispose
of their possessions and persons as they think fit, within the bounds
of the law of nature, without asking leave, or depending upon the
will of any other man.

A state also of equality, wherein all the power and jurisdiction is reciprocal, no one having more than another: there being nothing more evident than that creatures of the same species and rank promiscuously born to all the same advantages of nature, and the use of the same faculties, should also be equal one amongst another without subordination or subjection, unless the lord and master of them all should by any manifest declaration of his will set one above another, and confer on him by an evident and clear appointment an undoubted right to dominion and sovereignty.

5. This equality of men by nature, the judicious Hooker looks upon as so evident in itself, and beyond all question, that he makes it the foundation of that obligation to mutual love amongst men on which he builds the duties they owe one another, and from whence he derives the great maxims of justice and charity. His words are

The like natural inducement hath brought men to know that it is no less their duty to love others than themselves, for, seeing those things which are equal must needs all have one measure, if I cannot but wish to receive good, even as much at every man's hands as any man can wish unto his own soul, how should I look to have any part of my desire herein satisfied, unless myself be careful to satisfy the like desire, which is undoubtedly in other men, being of one and the same nature? To have anything offered them repugnant to this desire must needs in all respects grieve them as much as me, so that if I do harm I must look to suffer, there being no reason that others should show greater measure of love to me than they have by me showed unto them. My desire therefore to be loved of my equals in nature, as much as possible may be, imposeth upon me a natural duty of bearing to themward fully the like affection; from which relation of equality between ourselves and them that are as ourselves, what several rules and canons natural reason hath drawn for direction of life, no man is ignorant. (*Ecclesiastical Polity*, lib. 1)

6. But though this be a state of liberty, yet it is not a state of licence, though man in that state have an uncontrollable liberty to dispose of his person or possessions, yet he has not liberty to destroy himself, or so much as any creature in his possession, but where some nobler use than its bare preservation calls for it. The state of nature has a law of nature to govern it, which obliges everyone. And reason, which is that law, teaches all mankind who

will but consult it that, being all equal and independent, no one ought to harm another in his life, health, liberty, or possessions. For men being all the workmanship of one omnipotent and infinitely wise maker, all the servants of one sovereign master, sent into the world by his order and about his business, they are his property whose workmanship they are, made to last during his, not one another's, pleasure. And being furnished with like faculties, sharing all in one community of nature, there cannot be supposed any such subordination among us that may authorize us to destroy one another, as if we were made for one another's uses, as the inferior ranks of creatures are for ours. Everyone, as he is bound to preserve himself, and not to quit his station wilfully, so by the like reason, when his own preservation comes not in competition, ought he, as much as he can, to preserve the rest of mankind, and may not, unless it be to do justice on an offender, take away or impair the life, or what tends to the preservation of the life, liberty, health, limb, or goods of another.

7. And that all men may be restrained from invading others' rights, and from doing hurt to one another, and the law of nature be observed, which willeth the peace and preservation of all mankind, the execution of the law of nature is in that state put into every man's hands, whereby everyone has a right to punish the transgressors of that law to such a degree as may hinder its violation. For the law of nature would, as all other laws that concern men in this world, be in vain, if there were nobody that in the state of nature had a power to execute that law, and thereby preserve the innocent and restrain offenders, and if anyone in the state of nature may punish another, for any evil he has done, everyone may do so. For in that state of perfect equality, where naturally there is no superiority or jurisdiction of one over another, what any may do in prosecution of that law, everyone must needs have a right to do.

8. And thus in the state of nature, one man comes by a power over another; but yet no absolute or arbitrary power to use a criminal, when he has got him in his hands, according to the passionate heats, or boundless extravagancy of his own will, but only to retribute to him, so far as calm reason and conscience dictates, what is proportionate to his transgression, which is so much as may serve for reparation and restraint. For these two are

the only reasons why one man may lawfully do harm to another, which is what we call *punishment*. In transgressing the law of nature the offender declares himself to live by another rule than that of reason and common equity, which is that measure God has set to the actions of men for their mutual security; and so he becomes dangerous to mankind, the tie which is to secure them from injury and violence being slighted and broken by him. Which, being a trespass against the whole species, and the peace and safety of it provided for by the law of nature, every man upon this score, by the right he hath to preserve mankind in general, may restrain, or, where it is necessary, destroy things noxious to them, and so may bring such evil on anyone who hath transgressed that law as may make him repent the doing of it, and thereby deter him, and by his example others, from doing the like mischief. And, in this case and upon this ground, every man hath a right to punish the offender, and be executioner of the law of nature.

9. I doubt not but this will seem a very strange doctrine to some men; but before they condemn it I desire them to resolve me, by what right any prince or state can put to death, or punish, an alien, for any crime he commits in their country. 'Tis certain their laws, by virtue of any sanction they receive from the promulgated will of the legislative, reach not a stranger. They speak not to him, nor, if they did, is he bound to hearken to them. The legislative authority, by which they are in force over the subjects of that commonwealth, hath no power over him. Those who have the supreme power of making laws in England, France, or Holland are to an Indian but like the rest of the world, men without authority; and therefore if by the law of nature every man hath not a power to punish offences against it, as he soberly judges the case to require, I see not how the magistrates of any community can punish an alien of another country, since in reference to him they can have no more power than what every man naturally may have over another.

10. Besides the crime which consists in violating the law, and varying from the right rule of reason, whereby a man so far becomes degenerate, and declares himself to quit the principles of human nature, and to be a noxious creature, there is commonly injury done to some person or other, and some other man receives damage by his transgression, in which case he who hath received any

damage has, besides the right of punishment common to him with other men, a particular right to seek reparation from him that has done it. And any other person who finds it just may also join with him that is injured, and assist him in recovering from the offender so much as may make satisfaction for the harm he has suffered.

11. From these two distinct rights, the one of punishing the crime for restraint, and preventing the like offence, which right of punishing is in everybody; the other of taking reparation, which belongs only to the injured party, comes it to pass that the magistrate, who by being magistrate hath the common right of punishing put into his hands, can often, where the public good demands not the execution of the law, remit the punishment of criminal offences by his own authority, but yet cannot remit the satisfaction due to any private man for the damage he has received. That, he who has suffered the damage has a right to demand in his own name, and he alone can remit. The damnified person has this power of appropriating to himself the goods or service of the offender by right of self-preservation, as every man has a power to punish the crime, to prevent its being committed again, by the right he has of preserving all mankind, and doing all reasonable things he can in order to that end. And thus it is that every man in the state of nature has a power to kill a murderer, both to deter others from doing the like injury, which no reparation can compensate, by the example of the punishment that attends it from everybody, and also to secure men from the attempts of a criminal who, having renounced reason, the common rule and measure God hath given to mankind, hath, by the unjust violence and slaughter he hath committed upon one, declared war against all mankind, and therefore may be destroyed as a lion or a tiger, one of those wild savage beasts with whom men can have no society nor security. And upon this is grounded the great law of nature 'Who so sheddeth man's blood, by man shall his blood be shed' [Genesis 9.6]. And Cain was so fully convinced that everyone had a right to destroy such a criminal that after the murder of his brother he cries out 'Every one that findeth me shall slay me' [Genesis 4.14]; so plain was it writ in the hearts of all mankind.

12. By the same reason may a man in the state of nature punish the lesser breaches of that law. It will perhaps be demanded: With

death? I answer: Each transgression may be punished to that degree, and with so much severity, as will suffice to make it an ill bargain to the offender, give him cause to repent, and terrify others from doing the like. Every offence that can be committed in the state of nature may in the state of nature be also punished, equally and as far forth as it may in a commonwealth; for though it would be besides my present purpose to enter here into the particulars of the law of nature, or its measures of punishment, yet it is certain there is such a law, and that too as intelligible and plain to a rational creature, and a studier of that law, as the positive laws of commonwealths; nay possibly plainer, as much as reason is easier to be understood than the fancies and intricate contrivances of men following contrary and hidden interests put into words. For so, truly, are a great part of the municipal laws of countries, which are only so far right as they are founded on the law of nature, by which they are to be regulated and interpreted.

13. To this strange doctrine, viz. that in the state of nature everyone has the executive power of the law of nature, I doubt not but it will be objected that it is unreasonable for men to be judges in their own cases, that self-love will make men partial to themselves and their friends. And, on the other side, that ill-nature, passion, and revenge will carry them too far in punishing others. And hence nothing but confusion and disorder will follow, and that therefore God hath certainly appointed government to restrain the partiality and violence of men. I easily grant that civil government is the proper remedy for the inconveniences of the state of nature, which must certainly be great where men may be judges in their own case, since 'tis easily to be imagined that he who was so unjust as to do his brother an injury will scarce be so just as to condemn himself for it. But I shall desire those who make this objection to remember that absolute monarchs are but men, and if government is to be the remedy of those evils which necessarily follow from men's being judges in their own cases, and the state of nature is therefore not [to] be endured, I desire to know what kind of government that is, and how much better it is than the state of nature, where one man commanding a multitude has the liberty to be judge in his own case, and may do to all his subjects whatever he pleases, without the least liberty to anyone to question or control those who execute

his pleasure? And in whatsoever he doth, whether led by reason, mistake, or passion, must be submitted to? Much better it is in the state of nature, wherein men are not bound to submit to the unjust will of another, and if he that judges judges amiss in his own or any other case, he is answerable for it to the rest of mankind.

14. 'Tis often asked as a mighty objection: Where are or ever were there any men in such a state of nature? To which it may suffice as an answer at present: That since all princes and rulers of independent governments all through the world are in a state of nature, 'tis plain the world never was, nor ever will be, without numbers of men in that state. I have named all governors of independent communities, whether they are, or are not, in league with others. For 'tis not every compact that puts an end to the state of nature between men, but only this one of agreeing together mutually to enter into one community, and make one body politic; other promises and compacts men may make one with another, and yet still be in the state of nature. The promises and bargains for truck etc. between the two men in the desert island mentioned by Garcilaso de la Vega, in his history of Peru, or between a Swiss and an Indian in the woods of America, are binding to them, though they are perfectly in a state of nature in reference to one another. For truth and keeping of faith belongs to men as men, and not as members of society.

15. To those that say there were never any men in the state of nature, I will not only oppose the authority of the judicious Hooker (*Ecclesiastical Polity*, lib. 1, sect. 10) where he says

The laws which have been hitherto mentioned (i.e. the laws of nature) do bind men absolutely, even as they are men, although they have never any settled fellowship, never any solemn agreement amongst themselves what to do or not to do, but for as much as we are not by ourselves sufficient to furnish ourselves with competent store of things needful for such a life as our nature doth desire, a life fit for the dignity of man, therefore to supply those defects and imperfections which are in us, as living singly and solely by ourselves, we are naturally induced to seek communion and fellowship with others: this was the cause of men's uniting themselves at first in politic societies.

But I moreover affirm that all men are naturally in that state, and remain so, till by their own consents they make themselves members of some politic society; and I doubt not in the sequel of this discourse to make it very clear.

CHAPTER THREE: Of the State of War

16. The state of war is a state of enmity and destruction. And, therefore, declaring by word or action, not a passionate and hasty, but a sedate, settled design upon another man's life puts him in a state of war with him against whom he has declared such an intention, and so has exposed his life to the other's power, to be taken away by him, or anyone that joins with him in his defence and espouses his quarrel: it being reasonable and just I should have a right to destroy that which threatens me with destruction. For by the fundamental law of nature – man being to be preserved, as much as possible – when all cannot be preserved the safety of the innocent is to be preferred. And one may destroy a man who makes war upon him, or has discovered an enmity to his being, for the same reason that he may kill a wolf or a lion: because such men are not under the ties of the common law of reason, have no other rule but that of force and violence, and so may be treated as beasts of prey, those dangerous and noxious creatures, that will be sure to destroy him whenever he falls into their power.

17. And hence it is that he who attempts to get another man into his absolute power does thereby put himself into a state of war with him, it being to be understood as a declaration of a design upon his life. For I have reason to conclude that he who would get me into his power without my consent would use me as he pleased when he had got me there, and destroy me too when he had a fancy to it; for nobody can desire to have me in his absolute power, unless it be to compel me by force to that which is against the right of my freedom, i.e. make me a slave. To be free from such force is the only security of my preservation, and reason bids me look on him as an enemy to my preservation, who would take away that freedom which is the fence to it. So that he who makes an attempt to enslave me thereby puts himself into a state of war with me. He that in the state of nature would take away the freedom that belongs to anyone

in that state must necessarily be supposed to have a design to take away everything else, that freedom being the foundation of all the rest; as he that in the state of society would take away the freedom belonging to those of that society or commonwealth must be supposed to design to take away from them everything else, and so be looked on as in a state of war.

18. This makes it lawful for a man to kill a thief who has not in the least hurt him, nor declared any design upon his life, any further than by the use of force so to get him in his power as to take away his money, or what he pleases, from him. Because using force, where he has no right, to get me into his power, let his pretence be what it will, I have no reason to suppose that he, who would take away my liberty, would not when he had me in his power take away everything else. And therefore it is lawful for me to treat him as one who has put himself into a state of war with me, i.e. kill him if I can; for to that hazard does he justly expose himself, whoever introduces a state of war, and is aggressor in it.

19. And here we have the plain difference between the state of nature and the state of war, which, however some men have confounded, are as far distant as a state of peace, good-will, mutual assistance, and preservation, and a state of enmity, malice, violence, and mutual destruction are one from another. Men living together according to reason, without a common superior on earth with authority to judge between them, is properly the state of nature. But force, or a declared design of force upon the person of another, where there is no common superior on earth to appeal to for relief, is the state of war; and 'tis the want of such an appeal gives a man the right of war even against an aggressor, though he be in society and a fellow-subject. Thus a thief, whom I cannot harm but by appeal to the law for having stolen all that I am worth, I may kill when he sets on me to rob me but of my horse or coat. Because the law, which was made for my preservation, where it cannot interpose to secure my life from present force, which, if lost, is capable of no reparation, permits me my own defence, and the right of war, a liberty to kill the aggressor, because the aggressor allows not time to appeal to our common judge, nor the decision of the law for remedy in a case where the mischief may be irreparable. Want of a common judge with authority puts all men in a state of nature;

force without right upon a man's person makes a state of war, both where there is and is not a common judge.

20. But when the actual force is over, the state of war ceases between those that are in society and are equally on both sides subjected to the fair determination of the law, because then there lies open the remedy of appeal for the past injury, and to prevent future harm. But where no such appeal is, as in the state of nature, for want of positive laws and judges with authority to appeal to, the state of war, once begun, continues, with a right to the innocent party to destroy the other whenever he can, until the aggressor offers peace and desires reconciliation on such terms as may repair any wrongs he has already done, and secure the innocent for the future. Nay, where an appeal to the law and constituted judges lies open, but the remedy is denied by a manifest perverting of justice, and a barefaced wresting of the laws, to protect or indemnify the violence or injuries of some men or party of men, there it is hard to imagine anything but a state of war. For wherever violence is used, and injury done, though by hands appointed to administer justice, it is still violence and injury, however coloured with the name, pretences, or forms of law, the end whereof being to protect and redress the innocent, by an unbiased application of it to all who are under it, wherever that is not *bona fide* done, war is made upon the sufferers, who having no appeal on earth to right them, they are left to the only remedy in such cases, an appeal to heaven.

21. To avoid this state of war (wherein there is no appeal but to heaven, and wherein every the least difference is apt to end, where there is no authority to decide between the contenders) is one great reason of men's putting themselves into society, and quitting the state of nature. For where there is an authority, a power on earth from which relief can be had by appeal, there the continuance of the state of war is excluded, and the controversy is decided by that power. Had there been any such court, any superior jurisdiction on earth, to determine the right between Jephtha and the Ammonites, they had never come to a state of war, but we see he was forced to appeal to heaven. 'The Lord the Judge,' says he, 'be judge this day between the children of Israel and the children of Ammon' (Judges 11.27), and then prosecuting, and relying on his appeal, he leads out his army to battle. And therefore in such controversies, where

the question is put: 'Who shall be judge?', it cannot be meant 'Who shall decide the controversy?'; everyone knows what Jephtha here tells us, that the Lord the Judge shall judge. Where there is no judge on earth, the appeal lies to God in heaven. That question then cannot mean 'Who shall judge whether another hath put himself in a state of war with me, and whether I may, as Jephtha did, appeal to heaven in it?' Of that I myself can only be judge in my own conscience, as I will answer it at the great day, to the supreme judge of all men.

CHAPTER FOUR: Of Slavery

22. The natural liberty of man is to be free from any superior power on earth, and not to be under the will or legislative authority of man, but to have only the law of nature for his rule. The liberty of man, in society, is to be under no other legislative power but that established, by consent, in the commonwealth, nor under the dominion of any will, or restraint of any law, but what the legislative shall enact, according to the trust put in it. Freedom, then, is not what Sir R. F. tells us, *O[bservations on] A[ristotle]*, [p.]55: 'A liberty for everyone to do what he lists, to live as he pleases, and not to be tied by any laws.' But freedom of men under government is to have a standing rule to live by, common to everyone of that society, and made by the legislative power erected in it; a liberty to follow my own will in all things where the rule prescribes not; and not to be subject to the inconstant, uncertain, unknown, arbitrary will of another man. As freedom of nature is to be under no other restraint but the law of nature.

23. This freedom from absolute, arbitrary power is so necessary to, and closely joined with, a man's preservation, that he cannot part with it but by what forfeits his preservation and life together. For a man, not having the power of his own life, cannot, by compact or his own consent, enslave himself to anyone, nor put himself under the absolute, arbitrary power of another, to take away his life when he pleases. Nobody can give more power than he has himself; and he that cannot take away his own life cannot give another power over it. Indeed having, by his fault, forfeited his own life by some act that deserves death, he to whom he has forfeited it may (when he has him in his power) delay to take it, and make use of him to his own service, and he does him no injury by it. For whenever he finds the hardship of his slavery outweigh the value of his life, 'tis in his power, by resisting the will of his master, to draw on himself the death he desires.

24. This is the perfect condition of slavery, which is nothing else but the state of war continued between a lawful conqueror and a captive. For if once compact enter between them, and make an agreement for a limited power on the one side, and obedience on the other, the state of war and slavery ceases, as long as the compact endures. For, as has been said, no man can, by agreement, pass over to another that which he hath not in himself, a power over his own life.

I confess, we find among the Jews, as well as other nations, that men did sell themselves; but, 'tis plain, this was only to drudgery, not to slavery. For, it is evident, the person sold was not under an absolute, arbitrary, despotical power. For the master could not have power to kill him at any time whom, at a certain time, he was obliged to let go free out of his service; and the master of such a servant was so far from having an arbitrary power over his life that he could not, at pleasure, so much as maim him, but the loss of an eye, or tooth, set him free (Exodus 21).

CHAPTER FIVE: Of Property

25. Whether we consider natural reason, which tells us that men, being once born, have a right to their preservation, and consequently to meat and drink, and such other things as nature affords for their subsistence; or revelation, which gives us an account of those grants God made of the world to Adam, and to Noah and his sons, 'tis very clear that God, as King David says (Psalm 115.16), 'has given the earth to the children of men', given it to mankind in common. But this being supposed, it seems to some a very great difficulty how anyone should ever come to have a property in anything. I will not content myself to answer, that if it be difficult to make out property upon a supposition that God gave the world to Adam

and his posterity in common, it is impossible that any man, but one universal monarch, should have any property upon a supposition that God gave the world to Adam and his heirs in succession, exclusive of all the rest of his posterity. But I shall endeavour to show how men might come to have a property in several parts of that which God gave to mankind in common, and that without any express compact of all the commoners.

26. God, who hath given the world to men in common, hath also given them reason to make use of it to the best advantage of life and convenience. The earth, and all that is therein, is given to men for the support and comfort of their being. And though all the fruits it naturally produces, and beasts it feeds, belong to mankind in common, as they are produced by the spontaneous hand of nature, and nobody has originally a private dominion, exclusive of the rest of mankind, in any of them, as they are thus in their natural state; yet, being given for the use of men, there must of necessity be a means to appropriate them some way or other before they can be of any use, or at all beneficial to any particular man. The fruit or venison which nourishes the wild Indian, who knows no enclosure, and is still a tenant in common, must be his, and so his (i.e. a part of him) that another can no longer have any right to it, before it can do him any good for the support of his life.

27. Though the earth and all inferior creatures be common to all men, yet every man has a property in his own person. This nobody has any right to but himself. The labour of his body, and the work of his hands, we may say, are properly his. Whatsoever, then, he removes out of the state that nature hath provided and left it in, he hath mixed his labour with, and joined to it something that is his own, and thereby makes it his property. It being by him removed from the common state nature placed it in, it hath by this labour something annexed to it that excludes the common right of other men. For this labour being the unquestionable property of the labourer, no man but he can have a right to what that is once joined to, at least where there is enough and as good left in common for others.

28. He that is nourished by the acorns he picked up under an oak, or the apples he gathered from the trees in the wood, has

certainly appropriated them to himself. Nobody can deny but the nourishment is his. I ask then, When did they begin to be his? When he digested? Or when he ate? Or when he boiled? Or when he brought them home? Or when he picked them up? And 'tis plain if the first gathering made them not his, nothing else could. That labour put a distinction between them and common. That added something to them more than nature, the common mother of all, had done; and so they became his private right. And will anyone say he had no right to those acorns or apples he thus appropriated, because he had not the consent of all mankind to make them his? Was it a robbery thus to assume to himself what belonged to all in common? If such a consent as that was necessary, man had starved, notwithstanding the plenty God had given him. We see in commons, which remain so by compact, that 'tis the taking any part of what is common, and removing it out of the state nature leaves it in, which begins the property; without which the common is of no use. And the taking of this or that part does not depend on the express consent of all the commoners. Thus the grass my horse has bit, the turfs my servant has cut, and the ore I have digged in any place where I have a right to them in common with others become my property, without the assignation or consent of anybody. The labour that was mine, removing them out of that common state they were in, hath fixed my property in them.

29. By making an explicit consent of every commoner necessary to anyone's appropriating to himself any part of what is given in common, children or servants could not cut the meat which their father or master had provided for them in common, without assigning to everyone his peculiar part. Though the water running in the fountain be everyone's, yet who can doubt but that in the pitcher is his only who drew it out? His labour hath taken it out of the hands of nature, where it was common, and belonged equally to all her children, and hath thereby appropriated it to himself.

30. Thus this law of reason makes the deer that Indian's who hath killed it; 'tis allowed to be his goods who hath bestowed his labour upon it, though before it was the common right of everyone. And amongst those who are counted the civilized part of mankind, who have made and multiplied positive laws to determine property, this original law of nature for the beginning of property in what was

before common, still takes place; and by virtue thereof, what fish anyone catches in the ocean, that great and still remaining common of mankind, or what ambergris anyone takes up here is by the labour that removes it out of that common state nature left it in, made his property who takes that pains about it. And even amongst us, the hare that anyone is hunting is thought his who pursues her during the chase. For being a beast that is still looked upon as common, and no man's private possession, whoever has employed so much labour about any of that kind as to find and pursue her has thereby removed her from the state of nature, wherein she was common, and hath begun a property.

31. It will perhaps be objected to this that if gathering the acorns, or other fruits of the earth, etc. makes a right to them, then anyone may engross as much as he will. To which I answer: Not so. The same law of nature that does by this means give us property, does also bound that property too. 'God has given us all things richly' (1 Tim. 6.17) is the voice of reason confirmed by inspiration. But how far has he given it us? To enjoy. As much as anyone can make use of to any advantage of life before it spoils, so much he may by his labour fix a property in. Whatever is beyond this, is more than his share, and belongs to others. Nothing was made by God for man to spoil or destroy. And thus, considering the plenty of natural provisions there was a long time in the world, and the few spenders, and to how small a part of that provision the industry of one man could extend itself, and engross it to the prejudice of others; especially keeping within the bounds, set by reason, of what might serve for his use; there could be then little room for quarrels or contentions about property so established.

32. But the chief matter of property being now not the fruits of the earth, and the beasts that subsist on it, but the earth itself, as that which takes in and carries with it all the rest, I think it is plain that property in that too is acquired as the former. As much land as a man tills, plants, improves, cultivates, and can use the product of, so much is his property. He by his labour does, as it were, enclose it from the common. Nor will it invalidate his right to say 'Everybody else has an equal title to it, and therefore he cannot appropriate, he cannot enclose, without the consent of all his fellow-commoners, all mankind.' God, when he gave the world in

common to all mankind, commanded man also to labour, and the penury of his condition required it of him. God and his reason commanded him to subdue the earth, i.e. improve it for the benefit of life, and therein lay out something upon it that was his own, his labour. He that, in obedience to this command of God, subdued, tilled and sowed any part of it, thereby annexed to it something that was his property, which another had no title to, nor could without injury take from him.

33. Nor was this appropriation of any parcel of land, by improving it, any prejudice to any other man, since there was still enough – and as good – left; and more than the yet unprovided could use. So that, in effect, there was never the less left for others because of his enclosure for himself. For he that leaves as much as another can make use of, does as good as take nothing at all. Nobody could think himself injured by the drinking of another man, though he took a good draught, who had a whole river of the same water left him to quench his thirst. And the case of land and water, where there is enough of both, is perfectly the same.

34. God gave the world to men in common; but since he gave it them for their benefit, and the greatest conveniences of life they were capable to draw from it, it cannot be supposed he meant it should always remain common and uncultivated. He gave it to the use of the industrious and rational (and labour was to be his title to it); not to the fancy or covetousness of the quarrelsome and contentious. He that had as good left for his improvement as was already taken up needed not complain, ought not to meddle with what was already improved by another's labour. If he did, 'tis plain he desired the benefit of another's pains, which he had no right to, and not the ground which God had given him in common with others to labour on, and whereof there was as good left as that already possessed, and more than he knew what to do with, or his industry could reach to.

35. 'Tis true, in land that is common, in England, or any other country where there is plenty of people under government, who have money and commerce, no one can enclose or appropriate any part without the consent of all his fellow-commoners: because this is left common by compact, i.e. by the law of the land, which is not to be violated. And though it be common in respect of some men, it

is not so to all mankind, but is the joint property of this country, or this parish. Besides, the remainder, after such enclosure, would not be as good to the rest of the commoners as the whole was when they could all make use of the whole; whereas in the beginning and first peopling of the great common of the world, it was quite otherwise. The law man was under was rather *for* appropriating. God commanded, and his wants forced him, to labour. That was his property which could not be taken from him wherever he had fixed it. And hence, subduing or cultivating the earth and having dominion, we see are joined together. The one gave title to the other. So that God, by commanding to subdue, gave authority so far to appropriate. And the condition of human life, which requires labour and materials to work on, necessarily introduces private possessions.

36. The measure of property, nature has well set, by the extent of men's labour and the conveniency of life: no man's labour could subdue or appropriate all, nor could his enjoyment consume more than a small part; so that it was impossible for any man, this way, to entrench upon the right of another, or acquire to himself a property to the prejudice of his neighbour, who would still have room for as good and as large a possession (after the other had taken out his) as before it was appropriated. This measure did confine every man's possession to a very moderate proportion, and such as he might appropriate to himself without injury to anybody, in the first ages of the world when men were more in danger to be lost by wandering from their company in the then vast wilderness of the earth, than to be straitened for want of room to plant in. And the same measure may be allowed still, without prejudice to anybody, as full as the world seems. For supposing a man, or family, in the state they were at first peopling of the world by the children of Adam or Noah; let him plant in some inland, vacant places of America, we shall find that the possessions he could make himself, upon the measures we have given, would not be very large, nor even to this day, prejudice the rest of mankind, or give them reason to complain, or think themselves injured by this man's encroachment, though the race of men have now spread themselves to all the corners of the world, and do infinitely exceed the small number [which] was at the beginning. Nay, the extent of ground is of so

little value, without labour, that I have heard it affirmed that in Spain itself a man may be permitted to plough, sow, and reap without being disturbed, upon land he has no other title to, but only his making use of it. But, on the contrary, the inhabitants think themselves beholden to him, who, by his industry on neglected and consequently waste land, has increased the stock of corn, which they wanted. But be this as it will, which I lay no stress on; this I dare boldly affirm, that the same rule of property, viz. that every man should have as much as he could make use of, would hold still in the world, without straitening anybody, since there is land enough in the world to suffice double the inhabitants, had not the invention of money, and the tacit agreement of men to put a value on it, introduced (by consent) larger possessions, and a right to them; which, how it has done, I shall, by and by, show more at large.

37. This is certain, that in the beginning, before the desire of having more than men needed had altered the intrinsic value of things, which depends only on their usefulness to the life of man; or [men] had agreed that a little piece of yellow metal, which would keep without wasting or decay, should be worth a great piece of flesh, or a whole heap of corn, though men had a right to appropriate by their labour, each one to himself, as much of the things of nature as he could use; yet this could not be much, nor to the prejudice of others, where the same plenty was still left to those who would use the same industry. *To which let me add, that he who appropriates land to himself by his labour, does not lessen but increase the common stock of mankind. For the provisions serving to the support of human life produced by one acre of enclosed and cultivated land are (to speak much within compass) ten times more than those which are yielded by an acre of land, of an equal richness, lying waste in common. And, therefore, he that encloses land and has a greater plenty of the conveniences of life from ten acres than he could have from an hundred left to nature may truly be said to give ninety acres to mankind. For his labour now supplies him with provisions out of ten acres which were but the product of an hundred lying in common. I have here rated the improved land very low in making its product but as ten to one, when it is much nearer an hundred to one. For I ask whether in the wild woods and uncultivated waste of America, left to nature, without any*

improvement, tillage or husbandry, a thousand acres yield the needy and wretched inhabitants as many conveniences of life as ten acres of equally fertile land do in Devonshire, where they are well-cultivated.[1]

Before the appropriation of land, he who gathered as much of the wild fruit, killed, caught, or tamed as many of the beasts as he could, he that so employed his pains about any of the spontaneous products of nature as any way to alter them from the state which nature put them in by placing any of his labour on them, did thereby acquire a property in them. But if they perished in his possession, without their due use; if the fruits rotted or the venison putrified before he could spend it, he offended against the common law of nature, and was liable to be punished; he invaded his neighbour's share, for he had no right further than his use called for any of them and they might serve to afford him conveniences of life.

38. The same measures governed the possession of land too: whatsoever he tilled and reaped, laid up and made use of, before it spoiled, that was his peculiar right; whatsoever he enclosed and could feed and make use of, the cattle and product was also his. But if either the grass of his enclosure rotted on the ground, or the fruit of his planting perished without gathering, and laying up, this part of the earth, notwithstanding his enclosure, was still to be looked on as waste, and might be the possession of any other. Thus, at the beginning, Cain might take as much ground as he could till, and make it his own land, and yet leave enough to Abel's sheep to feed on; a few acres would serve for both their possessions. But as families increased, and industry enlarged their stocks, their possessions enlarged with the need of them; but yet it was commonly without any fixed property in the ground they made use of, till they incorporated, settled themselves together, and built cities; and then, by consent, they came in time to set out the bounds of their distinct territories, and agree on limits between them and their neighbours, and, by laws within themselves, settled the properties of those of the same society. For we see that in that part of the world which was first inhabited, and therefore like to be best peopled, even as low down as Abraham's time, they wandered with their flocks and their herds, which was their substance, freely up and down; and this Abraham did, in a country where he was a stranger. Whence it is plain that at least a great part of the land lay in common; that the

inhabitants valued it not, nor claimed property in any more than they made use of. But when there was not room enough in the same place for their herds to feed together, they, by consent, as Abraham and Lot did (Genesis 13.5), separated, and enlarged their pasture where it best liked them. And for the same reason Esau went from his father and his brother, and planted in Mount Seir (Genesis 36.6).

39. And thus, without supposing any private dominion and property in Adam over all the world, exclusive of all other men, which can no way be proved, nor anyone's property be made out from it, but supposing the world given as it was to the children of men in common, we see how labour could make men distinct titles to several parcels of it, for their private uses; wherein there could be no doubt of right, no room for quarrel.

40. Nor is it so strange as perhaps before consideration it may appear that the property of labour should be able to overbalance the community of land. For 'tis labour indeed that puts the difference of value on everything; and let anyone consider what the difference is between an acre of land planted with tobacco or sugar, sown with wheat or barley; and an acre of the same land lying in common, without any husbandry upon it, and he will find that the improvement of labour makes the far greater part of the value. I think it will be but a very modest computation to say that of the products of the earth useful to the life of man, nine-tenths are the effects of labour; nay, if we will rightly estimate things as they come to our use, and cast up the several expenses about them, what in them is purely owing to nature, and what to labour, we shall find that in most of them 99/100 are wholly to be put on the account of labour.

41. There cannot be a clearer demonstration of anything than several nations of the Americans are of this, who are rich in land, and poor in all the comforts of life; whom nature having furnished as liberally as any other people with the materials of plenty, i.e. a fruitful soil, apt to produce in abundance what might serve for food, raiment, and delight, yet, for want of improving it by labour, have not one-hundredth part of the conveniences we enjoy; and a king of a large and fruitful territory there feeds, lodges, and is clad worse than a day-labourer in England.

42. To make this a little clearer, let us but trace some of the ordinary provisions of life through their several progresses, before they come to our use, and see how much they receive of their value from human industry. Bread, wine, and cloth are things of daily use and great plenty, yet notwithstanding, acorns, water, and leaves or skins must be our bread, drink, and clothing, did not labour furnish us with these more useful commodities. For whatever bread is more worth than acorns, wine than water, and cloth or silk than leaves, skins, or moss, that is wholly owing to labour and industry. The one of these being the food and raiment which unassisted nature furnishes us with; the other provisions which our industry and pains prepare for us, which how much they exceed the other in value, when anyone hath computed, he will then see how much labour makes the far greater part of the value of things we enjoy in this world; and the ground which produces the materials is scarcely to be reckoned in as any, or at most but a very small part, of it. So little, that even amongst us land that is left wholly to nature, that hath no improvement of pasturage, tillage, or planting, is called, as indeed it is, *waste*; and we shall find the benefit of it amount to little more than nothing. *This shows how much numbers of men are to be preferred to largeness of dominions, and that the increase of lands [i.e. 'hands'?] and the right employing of them is the great art of government. And that prince who shall be so wise and godlike as by established laws of liberty to secure protection and encouragement to the honest industry of mankind against the oppression of power and narrowness of party, will quickly be too hard for his neighbours. But this bye the bye. To return to the argument in hand:*[1]

43. An acre of land that bears here twenty bushels of wheat, and another in America which, with the same husbandry, would do the like, are without doubt of the same natural, intrinsic value. But yet the benefit mankind receives from the one, in a year, is worth £5, and from the other possibly not worth a penny, if all the profit an Indian received from it were to be valued and sold here; at least I may truly say, not 1/1000. 'Tis labour then which puts the greatest part of value upon land, without which it would scarcely be worth anything; 'tis to that we owe the greatest part of all its useful products, for all that the straw, bran, bread of that acre of wheat is more worth than the product of an acre of as good land which lies

waste is all the effect of labour. For 'tis not barely the plough-man's pains, the reaper's and thresher's toil, and the baker's sweat is to be counted into the bread we eat; the labour of those who broke the oxen, who digged and wrought the iron and stones, who felled and framed the timber employed about the plough, mill, oven, or any other utensils, which are a vast number, requisite to this corn, from its being seed to be sown to its being made bread, must all be charged on the account of labour, and received as an effect of that; nature and the earth furnished only the almost worthless materials, as in themselves. 'Twould be a strange cata-logue of things that industry provided and made use of about every loaf of bread before it came to our use, if we could trace them: iron, wood, leather, bark, timber, stone, bricks, coals, lime, cloth, dying-drugs, pitch, tar, masts, ropes, and all the materials made use of in the ship that brought any of the commodities made use of by any of the workmen to any part of the work, all which 'twould be almost impossible, at least too long, to reckon up.

44. From all which it is evident that, though the things of nature are given in common, yet man (by being master of himself, and proprietor of his own person and the actions or labour of it) had still in himself the great foundation of property, and that which made up the great part of what he applied to the support or comfort of his being, when invention and arts had improved the conveniences of life, was perfectly his own, and did not belong in common to others.

45. Thus labour, in the beginning, gave a right of property wherever anyone was pleased to employ it upon what was common, which remained a long while the far greater part, and is yet more than mankind makes use of. Men at first, for the most part, con-tented themselves with what unassisted nature offered to their necessities; and though afterwards, in some parts of the world (where the increase of people and stock, with the use of money, had made land scarce, and so of some value), the several communities settled the bounds of their distinct territories, and by laws within themselves regulated the properties of the private men of their society, and so, by compact and agreement, settled the property which labour and industry began; and the leagues that have been made between several states and kingdoms, either expressly or

tacitly disowning all claim and right to the land in the other's possession, have, by common consent, given up their pretences to their natural common right which originally they had to those countries, and so have, by positive agreement, settled a property amongst themselves in distinct parts and parcels of the earth. Yet there are still great tracts of ground to be found which (the inhabitants thereof not having joined with the rest of mankind in the consent of the use of their common money) lie waste, and are more than the people who dwell on it do or can make use of, and so still lie in common. Tho' this can scarce happen amongst that part of mankind that have consented to the use of money.

46. The greatest part of things really useful to the life of man, and such as the necessity of subsisting made the first commoners of the world look after, as it doth the Americans now, are generally things of short duration, such as, if they are not consumed by use, will decay and perish of themselves. Gold, silver, and diamonds are things that fancy or agreement hath put the value on, more than real use and the necessary support of life. Now of those good things which nature hath provided in common, everyone had a right (as hath been said) to as much as he could use, and had a property in all that he could affect with his labour. All that his industry could extend to, to alter from the state nature had put it in, was his. He that gathered a hundred bushels of acorns or apples had thereby a property in them; they were his goods as soon as gathered. He was only to look that he used them before they spoiled; else he took more than his share and robbed others. And indeed it was a foolish thing, as well as dishonest, to hoard up more than he could make use of. If he gave away a part to anybody else, so that it perished not uselessly in his possession, these he also made use of. And if he also bartered away plums that would have rotted in a week for nuts that would last good for his eating a whole year, he did no injury; he wasted not the common stock, destroyed no part of the portion of goods that belonged to others, so long as nothing perished uselessly in his hands. Again, if he would give his nuts for a piece of metal, pleased with its colour, or exchange his sheep for shells, or wool for a sparkling pebble or a diamond, and keep those by him all his life, he invaded not the right of others: he might heap up as much of these durable things as he pleased; the exceeding of the

bounds of his just property not lying in the largeness of his possession, but the perishing of anything uselessly in it.

47. And thus came in the use of money, some lasting thing that men might keep without spoiling, and that by mutual consent men would take in exchange for truly useful but perishable supports of life.

48. And as different degrees of industry were apt to give men possessions in different proportions, so this invention of money gave them the opportunity to continue and enlarge them. For supposing an island separate from all possible commerce with the rest of the world, wherein there were but a hundred families, but there were sheep, horses, and cows, with other useful animals, wholesome fruits, and land enough for corn for a hundred thousand times as many, but nothing in the island, either because of its commonness, or perishableness, fit to supply the place of money: what reason could anyone have there to enlarge his possessions beyond the use of his family, and a plentiful supply to its consumption, either in what their own industry produced or they could barter for like perishable, useful commodities with others? Where there is not something both lasting and scarce, and so valuable to be hoarded up, there men will not be apt to enlarge their possessions of land, were it never so rich, never so free for them to take. For I ask, what would a man value ten thousand or an hundred thousand acres of excellent land, ready cultivated and well-stocked too with cattle, in the middle of the inland parts of America, where he had no hopes of commerce with other parts of the world, to draw money to him by the sale of the product? It would not be worth the enclosing, and we should see him give up again to the wild common of nature whatever was more than would supply the conveniences of life to be had there for him and his family.

49. Thus in the beginning all the world was America, and more so than that is now, for no such thing as money was anywhere known. Find out something that hath the use and value of money amongst his neighbours, you shall see the same man will begin presently to enlarge his possessions.

50. But since gold and silver, being little useful to the life of man in proportion to food, raiment, and carriage, has its value only from the consent of men, whereof labour yet makes, in great part, the

measure, it is plain that men have agreed to disproportionate and unequal possession of the earth, they having by a tacit and voluntary consent found out a way how a man may fairly possess more land than he himself can use of the product, by receiving in exchange for the overplus gold and silver, which may be hoarded up without injury to anyone, these metals not spoiling or decaying in the hands of the possessor. This partage of things in an inequality of private possessions, men have made practicable out of the bounds of society, and without compact, only by putting a value on gold and silver and tacitly agreeing in the use of money. For in governments the laws regulate the right of property, and the possession of land is determined by positive constitutions.

51. And thus, I think, it is very easy to conceive without any difficulty how labour could at first begin a title of property in the common things of nature, and how the spending it upon our uses bounded it. So that there could then be no reason of quarrelling about title, nor any doubt about the largeness of possession it gave. Right and conveniency went together, for as a man had a right to all he could employ his labour upon, so he had no temptation to labour for more than he could make use of. This left no room for controversy about the title, nor for encroachment on the right of others; what portion a man carved to himself was easily seen, and it was useless as well as dishonest to carve himself too much, or take more than he needed.

Note

1. Passages in italics added in the Christ's College, Cambridge, copy.

CHAPTER SIX: Of Paternal Power

52. It may perhaps be censured as an impertinent criticism in a discourse of this nature to find fault with words and names that have obtained in the world. And yet possibly it may not be amiss to offer new ones when the old are apt to lead men into mistakes, as this of 'paternal power' probably has done, which seems so to place

the power of parents over their children wholly in the father, as if the mother had no share in it, whereas if we consult reason or revelation, we shall find she hath an equal title. This may give one reason to ask whether this might not be more properly called 'parental power'. For whatever obligation nature and the right of generation lays on children, it must certainly bind them equal[ly] to both the concurrent causes of it. And, accordingly, we see the positive law of God everywhere joins them together without distinction when it commands the obedience of children: 'Honour thy father and thy mother' (Exodus 20.12); 'Whosoever curseth his father or his mother' (Leviticus 20.9); 'Ye shall fear every man his mother and his father' (Leviticus 19.3); 'Children obey your parents', etc. (Ephesians 6.1) is the style of the Old and New Testament.

53. Had but this one thing been well considered without looking any deeper into the matter, it might perhaps have kept men from running into those gross mistakes they have made about this power of parents. Which, however it might, without any great harshness, bear the name of absolute dominion, and regal authority, when under the title of paternal power it seemed appropriated to the father, would yet have sounded but oddly, and in the very name shown the absurdity, if this supposed absolute power over children had been called parental, and thereby have discovered that it belonged to the mother too; for it will but very ill serve the turn of those men who contend so much for the absolute power and authority of the fatherhood, as they call it, that the mother should have any share in it. And it would have but ill supported the monarchy they contend for, when by the very name it appeared that that fundamental authority from whence they would derive their government of a single person only was not placed in one, but two persons jointly. But to let this of names pass.

54. Though I have said above, chapter two, that 'all men by nature are equal,' I cannot be supposed to understand all sorts of equality. Age or virtue may give men a just precedency; excellency of parts and merit may place others above the common level; birth may subject some, and alliance or benefits others, to pay an observance to those to whom nature, gratitude or other respects may have made it due; and yet all this consists with the equality which all

men are in, in respect of jurisdiction or dominion one over another, which was the equality I there spoke of, as proper to the business in hand, being that equal right that every man hath to his natural freedom, without being subjected to the will or authority of any other man.

55. Children, I confess, are not born in this full state of equality, though they are born to it. Their parents have a sort of rule and jurisdiction over them when they come into the world, and for some time after, but 'tis but a temporary one. The bonds of this subjection are like the swaddling cloths they are wrapped up in, and supported by, in the weakness of their infancy. Age and reason, as they grow up, loosen them till at length they drop quite off, and leave a man at his own free disposal.

56. Adam was created a perfect man, his body and mind in full possession of their strength and reason, and so was capable from the first instant of his being to provide for his own support and preservation, and govern his actions according to the dictates of the law of reason which God had implanted in him. From him the world is peopled with his descendants, who are all born infants, weak and helpless, without knowledge or understanding. But to supply the defects of this imperfect state, till the improvement of growth and age hath removed them, Adam and Eve, and after them all parents, were by the law of nature under an obligation to preserve, nourish, and educate the children they had begotten, not as their own workmanship, but the workmanship of their own maker, the Almighty, to whom they were to be accountable for them.

57. The law that was to govern Adam was the same that was to govern all his posterity, the law of reason. But his offspring having another way of entrance into the world, different from him, by a natural birth that produced them ignorant and without the use of reason, they were not presently under that law, for nobody can be under a law which is not promulgated to him; and this law being promulgated or made known by reason only, he that is not come to the use of his reason cannot be said to be under this law; and Adam's children being not presently as soon as born under this law of reason, were not presently free. For law, in its true notion, is not so much the limitation as the direction of a free and intelligent

agent to his proper interest, and prescribes no further than is for the general good of those under that law. Could they be happier without it, the law, as an useless thing, would of itself vanish, and that ill deserves the name of confinement which hedges us in only from bogs and precipices. So that, however it may be mistaken, the end of law is not to abolish or restrain, but to preserve and enlarge freedom. For in all the states of created beings capable of laws, where there is no law there is no freedom. For liberty is to be free from restraint and violence from others, which cannot be where there is no law. But freedom is not, as we are told, 'a liberty for every man to do what he lists', for who could be free when every other man's humour might domineer over him? But a liberty to dispose and order as he lists his person, actions, possessions, and his whole property, within the allowance of those laws under which he is; and therein not to be subject to the arbitrary will of another, but freely follow his own.

58. The power, then, that parents have over their children arises from that duty which is incumbent on them to take care of their offspring during the imperfect state of childhood. To inform the mind, and govern the actions of their yet ignorant nonage, till reason shall take its place, and ease them of that trouble, is what the children want, and the parents are bound to. For God, having given man an understanding to direct his actions, has allowed him a freedom of will, and liberty of acting as properly belonging thereunto, within the bounds of that law he is under. But whilst he is in an estate wherein he has not understanding of his own to direct his will, he is not to have any will of his own to follow. He that understands for him must will for him too; he must prescribe to his will, and regulate his actions; but when he comes to the estate that made his father a freeman, the son is a freeman too.

59. This holds in all the laws a man is under, whether natural or civil. Is a man under the law of nature? What made him free of that law? What gave him a free disposing of his property according to his own will, within the compass of that law? I answer: State of maturity, wherein he might be supposed capable to know that law, that so he might keep his actions within the bounds of it. When he has acquired that state he is presumed to know how far that law is to be his guide, and how far he may make use of his freedom, and

so comes to have it; till then somebody else must guide him, who is presumed to know how far the law allows a liberty. If such a state of reason, such an age of discretion made him free, the same shall make his son free too. Is a man under the law of England? What made him free of that law? That is, to have the liberty to dispose of his actions and possessions according to his own will, within the permission of that law? A capacity of knowing that law. Which is supposed by that law at the age of one and twenty years, and in some cases sooner. If this made the father free, it shall make the son free too. Till then we see the law allows the son to have no will, but he is to be guided by the will of his father or guardian, who is to understand for him. And if the father die, and fail to substitute a deputy in this trust, if he hath not provided a tutor to govern his son during his minority, during his want of understanding, the law takes care to do it; some other must govern him, and be a will to him, till he hath attained to a state of freedom, and his understanding be fit to take the government of his will. But after that the father and son are equally free as much as tutor and pupil after nonage, equally subjects of the same law together, without any dominion left in the father over the life, liberty or estate of his son, whether they be only in the state and under the law of nature, or under the positive laws of an established government.

60. But if, through defects that may happen out of the ordinary course of nature, anyone comes not to such a degree of reason, wherein he might be supposed capable of knowing the law, and so living within the rules of it, he is never capable of being a free man, he is never let loose to the disposure of his own will (because he knows no bounds to it, has not understanding, its proper guide) but is continued under the tuition and government of others, all the time his own understanding is incapable of that charge. And so lunatics and idiots are never set free from the government of their parents; 'children, who are not as yet come unto those years whereat they may have; and innocents which are excluded by a natural defect from ever having; thirdly, madmen, which for the present cannot possibly have the use of right reason to guide themselves, have for their guide the reason that guideth other men which are tutors over them, to seek and procure their good for them,' says Hooker (*Ecclesiastical Polity*, lib. 1, sect. 7). All which seems no

more than that duty which God and nature has laid on man as well as other creatures to preserve their offspring till they can be able to shift for themselves, and will scarce amount to an instance or proof of parent's regal authority.

61. Thus we are born free, as we are born rational: not that we have actually the exercise of either; age that brings one, brings with it the other too. And thus we see how natural freedom and subjection to parents may consist together, and are both founded on the same principle. A child is free by his father's title, by his father's understanding, which is to govern him till he hath it of his own. The freedom of a man at years of discretion, and the subjection of a child to his parents, whilst yet short of that age, are so consistent and so distinguishable that the most blinded contenders for monarchy by right of fatherhood cannot miss this difference, the most obstinate cannot but allow their consistency. For were their doctrine all true, were the right heir of Adam now known, and by that title settled a monarch in his throne, invested with all the absolute, unlimited power Sir R.F. talks of, if he should die as soon as his heir was born, must not the child, notwithstanding he were never so free, never so much sovereign, be in subjection to his mother and nurse, to tutors and governors, till age and education brought him reason and ability to govern himself, and others? The necessities of his life, the health of his body, and the information of his mind would require him to be directed by the will of others and not his own; and yet will anyone think that this restraint and subjection were inconsistent with, or spoiled him of, that liberty or sovereignty he had a right to, or gave away his empire to those who had the government of his nonage? This government over him only prepared him the better and sooner for it. If anybody should ask me 'When my son is of age to be free?' I shall answer 'Just when his monarch is of age to govern'. 'But at what time,' says the judicious Hooker (*Ecclesiastical Polity*, lib. 1, sect. 6), 'a man may be said to have attained so far forth the use of reason as sufficeth to make him capable of those laws whereby he is then bound to guide his actions; this is a great deal more easy for sense to discern, than for anyone by skill and learning to determine.'

62. Commonwealths themselves take notice of and allow that there is a time when men are to begin to act like free men, and

therefore till that time require not oaths of fealty, or allegiance, or other public owning of, or submission to, the government of their countries.

63. The freedom, then, of man, and liberty of acting according to his own will, is grounded on his having reason, which is able to instruct him in that law he is to govern himself by, and make him know how far he is left to the freedom of his own will. To turn him loose to an unrestrained liberty, before he has reason to guide him, is not the allowing him the privilege of his nature, to be free; but to thrust him out amongst brutes, and abandon him to a state as wretched, and as much beneath that of a man, as theirs. This is that which puts the authority into the parents' hands to govern the minority of their children. God hath made it their business to employ this care on their offspring, and hath placed in them suitable inclinations of tenderness and concern to temper this power, to apply it as his wisdom designed it, to the children's good, as long as they should need to be under it.

64. But what reason can hence advance this care of the parents due to their offspring into an absolute, arbitrary dominion of the father, whose power reaches no further than by such a discipline as he finds most effectual to give such strength and health to their bodies, such vigour and rectitude to their minds, as may best fit his children to be most useful to themselves and others; and, if it be necessary to his condition, to make them work when they are able for their own subsistence? But in this power the mother too has her share with the father.

65. Nay, this power so little belongs to the father by any peculiar right of nature, but only as he is guardian of his children, that when he quits his care of them he loses his power over them, which goes along with their nourishment and education, to which it is inseparably annexed, and it belongs as much to the foster-father of an exposed child as to the natural father of another: so little power does the bare act of begetting give a man over his issue, if all his care ends there, and this be all the title he hath to the name and authority of a father. And what will become of this paternal power in that part of the world where one woman hath more than one husband at a time? Or in those parts of America where when the husband and wife part, which happens frequently, the children are

all left to the mother, follow her, and are wholly under her care and provision? If the father die whilst the children are young, do they not naturally everywhere owe the same obedience to their mother, during their minority, as to their father were he alive? And will anyone say that the mother hath a legislative power over her children? That she can make standing rules which shall be of perpetual obligation, by which they ought to regulate all the concerns of their property, and bound their liberty all the course of their lives? Or can she enforce the observation of them with capital punishments? For this is the proper power of the magistrate, of which the father hath not so much as the shadow. His command over his children is but temporary, and reaches not their life or property. It is but a help to the weakness and imperfection of their nonage, a discipline necessary to their education; and though a father may dispose of his own possessions as he pleases, when his children are out of danger of perishing for want, yet his power extends not to the lives or goods which either their own industry or another's bounty has made theirs; not to their liberty neither, when they are once arrived to the enfranchisement of the years of discretion. The father's empire then ceases, and he can from thence forwards no more dispose of the liberty of his son than that of any other man; and it must be far from an absolute or perpetual jurisdiction from which a man may withdraw himself, having licence from divine authority to 'leave father and mother, and cleave to his wife' [Genesis 2.24; Matthew 19.5].

66. But though there be a time when a child comes to be as free from subjection to the will and command of his father as the father himself is free from subjection to the will of anybody else, and they are each under no other restraint but that which is common to them both, whether it be the law of nature, or municipal law of their country; yet this freedom exempts not a son from that honour which he ought, by the law of God and nature, to pay his parents. God having made the parents instruments in his great design of continuing the race of mankind, and the occasions of life to their children, as he hath laid on them an obligation to nourish, preserve and bring up their offspring, so he has laid on the children a perpetual obligation of honouring their parents, which containing in it an inward esteem and reverence to be shown by all outward

expressions, ties up the child from anything that may ever injure or affront, disturb or endanger the happiness or life of those from whom he received his; and engages him in all actions of defence, relief, assistance and comfort of those by whose means he entered into being and has been made capable of any enjoyments of life. From this obligation no state, no freedom can absolve children. But this is very far from giving parents a power of command over their children, or an authority to make laws and dispose as they please of their lives or liberties. 'Tis one thing to owe honour, respect, gratitude, and assistance; another to require an absolute obedience and submission. The honour due to parents, a monarch in his throne owes his mother, and yet this lessens not his authority, nor subjects him to her government.

67. The subjection of a minor places in the father a temporary government which terminates with the minority of the child; and the honour due from a child places in the parents a perpetual right to respect, reverence, support, and compliance too, more or less as the father's care, cost, and kindness in his education has been more or less. This ends not with minority, but holds in all parts and conditions of a man's life. The want of distinguishing these two powers, viz. that which the father hath in the right of tuition, during minority, and the right of honour all his life, may perhaps have caused a great part of the mistakes about this matter. For, to speak properly of them, the first of these is rather the privilege of children, and duty of parents, than any prerogative of paternal power. The nourishment and education of their children is a charge so incumbent on parents for their children's good that nothing can absolve them from taking care of it. And though the power of commanding and chastising them go along with it, yet God hath woven into the principles of human nature such a tenderness for their offspring that there is little fear that parents should use their power with too much rigour; the excess is seldom on the severe side, the strong bias of nature drawing the other way. And therefore God Almighty, when he would express his gentle dealing with the Israelites, he tells them that though he chastened them, 'he chastened them as a man chastens his son' (Deuteronomy 8.5), i.e. with tenderness and affection, and kept them under no severer discipline than what was absolutely best for them, and had been less

kindness to have slackened. This is that power to which children are commanded obedience, that the pains and care of their parents might not be increased, or ill-rewarded.

68. On the other side, honour and support, all that which gratitude requires to return for the benefits received by and from them, is the indispensable duty of the child, and the proper privilege of the parents. This is intended for the parents' advantage, as the other is for the child's; though education, the parents' duty, seems to have most power because the ignorance and infirmities of childhood stand in need of restraint and correction, which is a visible exercise of rule, and a kind of dominion. And that duty which is comprehended in the word 'honour' requires less obedience, though the obligation be stronger on grown than younger children. For who can think the command 'Children, obey your parents' requires in a man that has children of his own the same submission to his father as it does in his yet young children to him? And that by this precept he were bound to obey all his father's commands, if out of a conceit of authority he should have the indiscretion to treat him still as a boy?

69. The first part, then, of paternal power, or rather duty, which is education, belongs so to the father that it terminates at a certain season; when the business of education is over it ceases of itself, and is also alienable before. For a man may put the tuition of his son in other hands; and he that has made his son an apprentice to another has discharged him, during that time, of a great part of his obedience both to himself and to his mother. But all the duty of honour, the other part, remains nevertheless entire to them; nothing can cancel that. It is so inseparable from them both that the father's authority cannot dispossess the mother of this right, nor can any man discharge his son from honouring her that bore him. But both these are very far from a power to make laws, and enforcing them with penalties that may reach estate, liberty, limbs and life. The power of commanding ends with nonage; and though after that honour and respect, support and defence, and whatsoever gratitude can oblige a man to, for the highest benefits he is naturally capable of, be always due from a son to his parents, yet all this puts no sceptre into the father's hand, no sovereign power of commanding. He has no dominion over his son's property or actions, nor any

right that his will should prescribe to his son's in all things; however it may become his son in many things, not very inconvenient to him and his family, to pay a deference to it.

70. A man may owe honour and respect to an ancient or wise man, defence to his child or friend, relief and support to the distressed, and gratitude to a benefactor to such a degree that all he has, all he can do, cannot sufficiently pay it. But all these give no authority, no right to anyone of making laws over him from whom they are owing. And, 'tis plain, all this is due not to the bare title of father, not only because, as has been said, it is owing to the mother too, but because these obligations to parents, and the degrees of what is required of children, may be varied by the different care and kindness, trouble and expense, which is often employed upon one child more than another.

71. This shows the reason how it comes to pass that parents in societies where they themselves are subjects, retain a power over their children, and have as much right to their subjection as those who are in the state of nature, which could not possibly be if all political power were only paternal, and that in truth they were one and the same thing; for then, all paternal power being in the prince, the subject could naturally have none of it. But these two powers, political and paternal, are so perfectly distinct and separate, are built upon so different foundations, and given to so different ends, that every subject that is a father has as much a paternal power over his children as the prince has over his; and every prince that has parents owes them as much filial duty and obedience as the meanest of his subjects do to theirs; and can therefore contain not any part or degree of that kind of dominion which a prince or magistrate has over his subject.

72. Though the obligation on the parents to bring up their children, and the obligation on children to honour their parents, contain all the power on the one hand, and submission on the other, which are proper to this relation; yet there is another power ordinarily in the father, whereby he has a tie on the obedience of his children; which, though it be common to him with other men, yet the occasions of showing it almost constantly happening to fathers in their private families, and the instances of it elsewhere being rare, and less taken notice of, it passes in the world for a part

of paternal jurisdiction. And this is the power men generally have to bestow their estates on those who please them best. The possession of the father being the expectation and inheritance of the children ordinarily in certain proportions, according to the law and custom of each country, yet it is commonly in the father's power to bestow it with a more sparing or liberal hand, according as the behaviour of this or that child hath comported with his will and humour.

73. This is no small tie on the obedience of children; and there being always annexed to the enjoyment of land a submission to the government of the country of which that land is a part, it has been commonly supposed that a father could oblige his posterity to that government of which he himself was a subject, and that his compact held them, whereas, it being only a necessary condition annexed to the land, and the inheritance of an estate which is under that government, reaches only those who will take it on that condition, and so is no natural tie or engagement, but a voluntary submission. For every man's children being by nature as free as himself, or any of his ancestors ever were, may, whilst they are in that freedom, choose what society they will join themselves to, what commonwealth they will put themselves under. But if they will enjoy the inheritance of their ancestors, they must take it on the same terms their ancestors had it, and submit to all the conditions annexed to such a possession. By this power, indeed, fathers oblige their children to obedience to themselves, even when they are past minority, and most commonly, too, subject them to this or that political power. But neither of these by any peculiar right of fatherhood, but by the reward they have in their hands to enforce and recompense such a compliance; and is no more power than what a Frenchman has over an Englishman who, by the hopes of an estate he will leave him, will certainly have a strong tie on his obedience. And if, when it is left him, he will enjoy it, he must certainly take it upon the conditions annexed to the possession of land in that country where it lies, whether it be France or England.

74. To conclude, then, though the father's power of commanding extends no further than the minority of his children, and to a degree only fit for the discipline and government of that age; and though that honour and respect, and all that which the Latins called

'piety', which they indispensably owe to their parents all their lifetimes, and in all estates, with all that support and defence [which] is due to them, gives the father no power of governing, i.e. making laws and enacting penalties on his children; though by all this he has no dominion over the property or actions of his son; yet 'tis obvious to conceive how easy it was in the first ages of the world, and in places still where the thinness of people gives families leave to separate into unpossessed quarters, and they have room to remove and plant themselves in yet vacant habitations, for the father of the family to become the prince of it;* he had been a ruler from the beginning of the infancy of his children; and since without some government it would be hard for them to live together, it was likeliest it should, by the express or tacit consent of the children, when they were grown up, be in the father, where it seemed without any change barely to continue; when indeed nothing more was required to it than the permitting the father to exercise alone in his family that executive power of the law of nature which every free man naturally hath, and by that permission resigning up to him a monarchical power, whilst they remained in it. But that this was not by any paternal right, but only by the consent of his children, is evident from hence, that nobody doubts but if a stranger, whom chance or business had brought to his family, had there killed any of his children, or committed any other fact, he might condemn and put him to death, or otherwise have punished him as well as any of his children: which it was impossible he

---

*'It is no improbable opinion, therefore, which the arch-philosopher was of, that the chief person in every household was always, as it were, a king. So when numbers of households joined themselves in civil societies together, kings were the first kind of governors amongst them, which is also, as it seemeth, the reason why the name of fathers continued still in them, who, of fathers, were made rulers; as also the ancient custom of governors to do as Melchizedec, and, being kings, to exercise the office of priests, which fathers did, at the first grew perhaps by the same occasion. Howbeit, this is not the only kind of regiment that has been received in the world. The inconveniences of one kind have caused sundry other to be devised; so that, in a word, all public regiment of what kind soever, seemeth evidently to have risen from the deliberate advice, consultation, and composition between men, judging it convenient, and behoveful; there being no impossibility in nature considered by itself, but that man might have lived without any public regiment.' Hooker's *Ecclesiastical Polity*, lib. 1, sect. 10.

should do by virtue of any paternal authority over one who was not his child, but by virtue of that executive power of the law of nature, which, as a man, he had a right to. And he alone could punish him in his family, where the respect of his children had laid by the exercise of such a power, to give way to the dignity and authority they were willing should remain in him, above the rest of his family.

75. Thus 'twas easy and almost natural for children by a tacit and scarce avoidable consent to make way for the father's authority and government. They had been accustomed in their childhood to follow his direction, and to refer their little differences to him, and when they were men, who fitter to rule them? Their little properties and less covetousness seldom afforded greater controversies; and, when any should arise, where could they have a fitter umpire than he, by whose care they had every one been sustained and brought up, and who had a tenderness for them all? 'Tis no wonder that they made no distinction betwixt minority and full age, nor looked after one and twenty, or any other age, that might make them the free disposers of themselves and fortunes, when they could have no desire to be out of their pupillage. The government they had been under, during it, continued still to be more their protection than restraint; and they could nowhere find a greater security to their peace, liberties and fortunes than in the rule of a father.

76. Thus the natural fathers of families, by an insensible change, became the politic monarchs of them too, and, as they chanced to live long, and leave able and worthy heirs, for several successions, or otherwise, so they laid the foundations of hereditary or elective kingdoms, under several constitutions and manners, according as chance, contrivance, or occasions happened to mould them. But if princes have their titles in the father's right, and it be a sufficient proof of the natural right of fathers to political authority, because they commonly were those in whose hands we find, *de facto*, the exercise of government: I say, if this argument be good, it will as strongly prove that all princes, nay princes only, ought to be priests, since 'tis as certain that in the beginning the father of the family was priest as that he was ruler in his own household.

CHAPTER SEVEN: Of Political or Civil Society

77. God having made man such a creature that, in his own judge-ment, it was not good for him to be alone, put him under strong obligations of necessity, convenience and inclination to drive him into society, as well as fitted him with understanding and language to continue and enjoy it. The first society was between man and wife, which gave beginning to that between parents and children; to which, in time, that between master and servant came to be added. And though all these might, and commonly did, meet to-gether and make up but one family, wherein the master or mistress of it had some sort of rule proper to a family, each of these, or all together, came short of political society, as we shall see if we consider the different ends, ties, and bounds of each of these.

78. Conjugal society is made by a voluntary compact between man and woman; and though it consist chiefly in such a communion and right in one another's bodies as is necessary to its chief end, procreation, yet it draws with it mutual support and assistance, and a communion of interest too, as necessary not only to unite their care and affection, but also necessary to their common off-spring, who have a right to be nourished and maintained by them till they are able to provide for themselves.

79. For the end of conjunction between male and female, being not barely procreation, but the continuation of the species, this conjunction betwixt male and female ought to last, even after pro-creation, so long as is necessary to the nourishment and support of the young ones, who are to be sustained by those that got them, till they are able to shift and provide for themselves. This rule which the infinite wise maker hath set to the works of his hands, we find the inferior creatures steadily obey. In those viviparous animals which feed on grass, the conjunction between male and female lasts no longer than the very act of copulation, because the teat of the dam being sufficient to nourish the young till it be able to feed on grass, the male only begets, but concerns not himself for the female or young, to whose sustenance he can contribute nothing. But in beasts of prey the conjunction lasts longer, because the dam not being able well to subsist herself and nourish her numerous

offspring by her own prey alone, a more laborious, as well as more dangerous way of living than by feeding on grass, the assistance of the male is necessary to the maintenance of their common family, which cannot subsist till they are able to prey for themselves but by the joint care of male and female. The same is to be observed in all birds (except some domestic ones, where plenty of food excuses the cock from feeding and taking care of the young brood) whose young needing food in the nest, the cock and hen continue mates till the young are able to use their wing and provide for themselves.

80. And herein, I think, lies the chief, if not the only, reason why the male and female in mankind are tied to a longer conjunction than other creatures, viz. because the female is capable of conceiving, and *de facto* is commonly with child again, and brings forth too a new birth long before the former is out of a dependency for support on his parents' help, and able to shift for himself, and has all the assistance is due to him from his parents, whereby the father, who is bound to take care for those he hath begot, is under an obligation to continue in conjugal society with the same woman longer than other creatures, whose young being able to subsist of themselves, before the time of procreation returns again, the conjugal bond dissolves of itself, and they are at liberty, till Hymen, at his usual anniversary season, summons them again to choose new mates. Wherein one cannot but admire the wisdom of the great creator, who, having given to man foresight and an ability to lay up for the future, as well as to supply the present necessity, hath made it necessary that society of man and wife should be more lasting than of male and female amongst other creatures; that so their industry might be encouraged, and their interest better united, to make provision and lay up goods for their common issue, which uncertain mixture, or easy and frequent solutions of conjugal society would mightily disturb.

81. But though these are ties upon mankind, which make the conjugal bonds more firm and lasting in man than the other species of animals; yet it would give one reason to inquire why this compact, where procreation and education are secured, and inheritance taken care for, may not be made determinable, either by consent, or at a certain time, or upon certain conditions, as well as any other voluntary compacts, there being no necessity in the nature of the thing,

nor to the ends of it, that it should always be for life; I mean to such as are under no restraint of any positive law, which ordains all such contracts to be perpetual.

82. But the husband and wife, though they have but one common concern, yet having different understandings, will unavoidably sometimes have different wills too; it therefore being necessary that the last determination, i.e. the rule, should be placed somewhere, it naturally falls to the man's share, as the abler and the stronger. But this, reaching but to the things of their common interest and property, leaves the wife in the full and free possession of what by contract is her peculiar right, and gives the husband no more power over her life than she has over his. The power of the husband being so far from that of an absolute monarch that the wife has, in many cases, a liberty to separate from him, where natural right or their contract allows it, whether that contract be made by themselves in the state of nature, or by the customs or laws of the country they live in; and the children upon such separation fall to the father or mother's lot, as such contract does determine.

83. For all the ends of marriage being to be obtained under politic government, as well as in the state of nature, the civil magistrate doth not abridge the right or power of either naturally necessary to those ends, viz. procreation and mutual support and assistance whilst they are together, but only decides any controversy that may arise between man and wife about them. If it were otherwise, and that absolute sovereignty and power of life and death naturally belonged to the husband, and were necessary to the society between man and wife, there could be no matrimony in any of those countries where the husband is allowed no such absolute authority. But the ends of matrimony requiring no such power in the husband, the condition of conjugal society put it not in him, it being not at all necessary to that state. Conjugal society could subsist and obtain its ends without it; nay community of goods and the power over them, mutual assistance and maintenance, and other things belonging to conjugal society, might be varied and regulated by that contract which unites man and wife in that society, as far as may consist with procreation and bringing up of children till they could shift for themselves; nothing being necessary to any society that is not necessary to the ends for which it is made.

84. The society betwixt parents and children, and the distinct rights and powers belonging respectively to them, I have treated of so largely in the foregoing chapter that I shall not here need to say anything of it. And I think it is plain that it is far different from a politic society.

85. Master and servant are names as old as history, but given to those of far different condition; for a free man makes himself a servant to another by selling him for a certain time the service he undertakes to do, in exchange for wages he is to receive. And though this commonly puts him into the family of his master, and under the ordinary discipline thereof, yet it gives the master but a temporary power over him, and no greater than what is contained in the contract between 'em. But there is another sort of servants, which by a peculiar name we call slaves, who, being captives taken in a just war, are by the right of nature subjected to the absolute dominion and arbitrary power of their masters. These men having, as I say, forfeited their lives, and with it their liberties, and lost their estates, and being in the state of slavery not capable of any property, cannot in that state be considered as any part of civil society, the chief end whereof is the preservation of property.

86. Let us therefore consider a master of a family with all these subordinate relations of wife, children, servants, and slaves united under the domestic rule of a family; which what resemblance soever it may have in its order, offices, and number too with a little commonwealth, yet is very far from it, both in its constitution, power and end. Or, if it must be thought a monarchy, and the paterfamilias the absolute monarch in it, absolute monarchy will have but a very shattered and short power, when 'tis plain, by what has been said before, that the master of the family has a very distinct and differently limited power, both as to time and extent, over those several persons that are in it; for, excepting the slave (and the family is as much a family, and his power as paterfamilias as great, whether there be any slaves in his family or no), he has no legislative power of life and death over any of them, and none too but what a mistress of a family may have as well as he. And he certainly can have no absolute power over the whole family, who has but a very limited one over every individual in it. But how a family, or any other society of men, differ from that which is

properly political society, we shall best see by considering wherein political society itself consists.

87. Man being born, as has been proved, with a title to perfect freedom, and an uncontrolled enjoyment of all the rights and privileges of the law of nature, equally with any other man or number of men in the world, hath by nature a power not only to preserve his property, that is his life, liberty and estate, against the injuries and attempts of other men, but to judge of and punish the breaches of that law in others as he is persuaded the offence deserves, even with death itself in crimes where the heinousness of the fact, in his opinion, requires it. But because no political society can be, nor subsist, without having in itself the power to preserve the property, and in order thereunto punish the offences, of all those of that society; there and there only is political society where every one of the members hath quitted this natural power, resigned it up into the hands of the community in all cases that exclude him not from appealing for protection to the law established by it. And thus all private judgement of every particular member being excluded, the community comes to be umpire, by settled standing rules, indifferent and the same to all parties; and, by men having authority from the community for the execution of those rules, decides all the differences that may happen between any members of that society concerning any matter of right; and punishes those offences which any member hath committed against the society with such penalties as the law has established. Whereby it is easy to discern who are and who are not in political society together. Those who are united into one body, and have a common established law and judicature to appeal to, with authority to decide controversies between them, and punish offenders, are in civil society one with another; but those who have no such common appeal, I mean on earth, are still in the state of nature, each being, where there is no other, judge for himself and executioner; which is, as I have before showed it, the perfect state of nature.

88. And thus the commonwealth comes by a power to set down what punishment shall belong to the several transgressions which they think worthy of it, committed amongst the members of that society (which is the power of making laws), as well as it has the power to punish any injury done unto any of its members by

anyone that is not of it (which is the power of war and peace); and all this for the preservation of the property of all the members of that society, as far as is possible. But though every man who has entered into civil society, and is become a member of any commonwealth, has thereby quitted his power to punish offences against the law of nature in prosecution of his own private judgement, yet with the judgement of offences which he has given up to the legislative, in all cases where he can appeal to the magistrate, he has given a right to the commonwealth to employ his force for the execution of the judgements of the commonwealth whenever he shall be called to it; which indeed are his own judgements, they being made by himself, or his representative. And herein we have the original of the legislative and executive power of civil society, which is to judge by standing laws how far offences are to be punished when committed within the commonwealth; and also to determine, by occasional judgements founded on the present circumstances of the fact, how far injuries from without are to be vindicated, and in both these to employ all the force of all the members when there shall be need.

· 89. Wherever, therefore, any number of men are so united into one society as to quit every one his executive power of the law of nature, and to resign it to the public, there and there only is a political or civil society. And this is done wherever any number of men, in the state of nature, enter into society to make one people, one body politic under one supreme government, or else when anyone joins himself to and incorporates with any government already made. For hereby he authorizes the society, or, which is all one, the legislative thereof, to make laws for him as the public good of the society shall require; to the execution whereof his own assistance (as to his own decrees) is due. And this puts men out of a state of nature into that of a commonwealth, by setting up a judge on earth with authority to determine all the controversies and redress the injuries that may happen to any member of the commonwealth; which judge is the legislative, or magistrates appointed by it. And wherever there are any number of men, however associated, that have no such decisive power to appeal to, there they are still in the state of nature.

90. Hence it is evident that absolute monarchy, which by some

men is counted the only government in the world, is indeed inconsistent with civil society, and so can be no form of civil government at all. For the end of civil society being to avoid and remedy those inconveniences of the state of nature which necessarily follow from every man's being judge in his own case, by setting up a known authority to which everyone of that society may appeal upon any injury received, or controversy that may arise, and which everyone of the society ought to obey,* wherever any persons are who have not such an authority to appeal to for the decision of any difference between them, there those persons are still in the state of nature. And so is every absolute prince in respect of those who are under his dominion.

91. For he being supposed to have all, both legislative and executive power in himself alone, there is no judge to be found, no appeal lies open to anyone who may fairly and indifferently, and with authority, decide, and from whose decision relief and redress may be expected of any injury or inconveniency that may be suffered from the prince or by his order. So that such a man, however entitled – Czar, or Grand Signor, or how you please – is as much in the state of nature with all under his dominion as he is with the rest of mankind. For wherever any two men are who have no standing rule and common judge to appeal to on earth for the determination of controversies of right betwixt them, there they are still in the state of nature, and under all the inconveniences of it,†

---

*'The public power of all society is above every soul contained in the same society; and the principal use of that power is to give laws unto all that are under it, which laws in such cases we must obey, unless there be reason showed which may necessarily enforce that the law of reason, or of God, doth enjoin the contrary.' Hooker, *Ecclesiastical Polity*, lib. 1, sect. 16.

†'To take away all such mutual grievances, injuries and wrongs (i.e. such as attend men in the state of nature), there was no way but only by growing into composition and agreement amongst themselves, by ordaining some kind of government public, and by yielding themselves subject thereunto, that unto whom they granted authority to rule and govern, by them the peace, tranquillity, and happy estate of the rest might be procured. Men always knew that where force and injury was offered they might be defenders of themselves; they knew that however men may seek their own commodity, yet if this were done with injury unto others it was not to be suffered, but by all men and all good means to be withstood. Finally, they knew that no man might in reason take upon him to determine his

with only this woeful difference to the subject, or rather slave, of an absolute prince, that whereas in the ordinary state of nature he has a liberty to judge of his right and, according to the best of his power, to maintain it, now whenever his property is invaded by the will and order of his monarch, he has not only no appeal, as those in society ought to have, but, as if he were degraded from the common state of rational creatures, is denied a liberty to judge of or to defend his right, and so is exposed to all the misery and inconveniences that a man can fear from one who, being in the unrestrained state of nature, is yet corrupted with flattery, and armed with power.

92. For he that thinks absolute power purifies men's bloods, and corrects the baseness of human nature, need read but the history of this or any other age to be convinced of the contrary. He that would have been insolent and injurious in the woods of America would not probably be much better in a throne, where, perhaps, learning and religion shall be found out to justify all that he shall do to his subjects, and the sword presently silence all those that dare question it. For what the protection of absolute monarchy is, what kind of fathers of their countries it makes princes to be, and to what a degree of happiness and security it carries civil society where this sort of government is grown to perfection, he that will look into the late relation of Ceylon may easily see.

93. In absolute monarchies, indeed, as well as other governments of the world, the subjects have an appeal to the law, and judges to decide any controversies and restrain any violence that may happen betwixt the subjects themselves, one amongst another. This everyone thinks necessary, and believes he deserves to be thought a declared enemy to society and mankind who should go about to take it away. But whether this be from a true love of mankind and society, and such a charity as we owe all one to another, there is reason to doubt. For this is no more than what every man who

own right, and according to his own determination proceed in maintenance thereof, in as much as every man is towards himself, and them whom he greatly affects, partial; and therefore that strifes and troubles would be endless, except they gave their common consent all to be ordered by some whom they should agree upon, without which consent there would be no reason that one man should take upon him to be lord or judge over another.' Hooker's *Ecclesiastical Polity*, lib. 1, sect. 10.

loves his own power, profit, or greatness may, and naturally must, do, keep those animals from hurting or destroying one another who labour and drudge only for his pleasure and advantage, and so are taken care of, not out of any love the master has for them, but love of himself, and the profit they bring him. For if it be asked, what security, what fence is there in such a state against the violence and oppression of this absolute ruler, the very question can scarce be born. They are ready to tell you that it deserves death only to ask after safety. Betwixt subject and subject, they will grant, there must be measures, laws and judges, for their mutual peace and security. But as for the ruler, he ought to be absolute, and is above all such circumstances; because he has power to do more hurt and wrong, 'tis right when he does it. To ask how you may be guarded from harm or injury on that side where the strongest hand is to do it is presently the voice of faction and rebellion. As if when men, quitting the state of nature, entered into society, they agreed that all of them but one should be under the restraint of laws, but that he should still retain all the liberty of the state of nature, increased with power, and made licentious by impunity. This is to think that men are so foolish that they take care to avoid what mischiefs may be done them by polecats or foxes, but are content, nay think it safety, to be devoured by lions.

94. But whatever flatterers may talk to amuse people's understandings, it hinders not men from feeling: and when they perceive that any man, in what station soever, is out of the bounds of the civil society which they are of, and that they have no appeal on earth against any harm they may receive from him, they are apt to think themselves in the state of nature in respect of him whom they find to be so; and to take care as soon as they can to have that safety and security in civil society for which it was first instituted, and for which only they entered into it. And therefore, though perhaps at first (as shall be showed more at large hereafter in the following part of this discourse) some one good and excellent man, having got a pre-eminence amongst the rest, had this deference paid to his goodness and virtue, as to a kind of natural authority, that the chief rule, with arbitration of their differences, by a tacit consent devolved into his hands, without any other caution but the assurance they had of his uprightness and wisdom; yet when time, giving authority and (as some men would persuade us) sacredness

to customs which the negligent and unforeseeing innocence of the first ages began, had brought in successors of another stamp, the people finding their properties not secure under the government as then it was (whereas government has no other end but the preservation of property) could never be safe nor at rest, nor think themselves in civil society, till the legislature was placed in collective bodies of men, call them senate, parliament, or what you please.* By which means every single person became subject equally with other the meanest men to those laws which he himself, as part of the legislative, had established; nor could anyone, by his own authority, avoid the force of the law when once made, nor by any pretence of superiority plead exemption, thereby to license his own, or the miscarriages of any of his dependants. No man in civil society can be exempted from the laws of it.† For if any man may do what he thinks fit, and there be no appeal on earth for redress or security against any harm he shall do, I ask whether he be not perfectly still in the state of nature, and so can be no part or member of that civil society: unless anyone will say the state of nature and civil society are one and the same thing, which I have never yet found anyone so great a patron of anarchy as to affirm.

CHAPTER EIGHT: Of the Beginning of Political Societies

95. Men being, as has been said, by nature all free, equal and independent, no man can be put out of this estate and subjected to the political power of another without his own consent. The only way whereby anyone divests himself of his natural liberty and puts

---

*'At the first, when some certain kind of regiment was once appointed, it may be that nothing was then further thought upon for the manner of governing, but all permitted unto their wisdom and discretion, which were to rule, till by experience they found this for all parts very inconvenient, so as the thing which they had devised for a remedy did indeed but increase the sore which it should have cured. They saw that to live by one man's will became the cause of all men's misery. This constrained them to come unto laws wherein all men might see their duty beforehand, and know the penalties of transgressing them.' Hooker's *Ecclesiastical Polity*, lib. 1, sect. 10.

†'Civil law being the act of the whole body politic, doth therefore over-rule each several part of the same body.' Hooker, ibid.

on the bonds of civil society is by agreeing with other men to join and unite into a community for their comfortable, safe, and peaceable living one amongst another in a secure enjoyment of their properties, and a greater security against any that are not of it. This any number of men may do, because it injures not the freedom of the rest; they are left as they were, in the liberty of the state of nature. When any number of men have so consented to make one community or government, they are thereby presently incorporated, and make one body politic, wherein the majority have a right to act and conclude the rest.

96. For when any number of men have, by the consent of every individual, made a community, they have thereby made that community one body, with a power to act as one body, which is only by the will and determination of the majority. For that which acts any community being only the consent of the individuals of it, and it being necessary to that which is one body to move one way, it is necessary the body should move that way whither the greater force carries it, which is the consent of the majority; or else it is impossible it should act or continue one body, one community, which the consent of every individual that united into it agreed that it should; and so everyone is bound by that consent to be concluded by the majority. And therefore we see that in assemblies empowered to act by positive laws where no number is set by that positive law which empowers them, the act of the majority passes for the act of the whole, and of course determines, as having by the law of nature and reason the power of the whole.

97. And thus every man, by consenting with others to make one body politic under one government, puts himself under an obligation to everyone of that society to submit to the determination of the majority, and to be concluded by it; or else this original compact, whereby he with others incorporates into one society, would signify nothing, and be no compact, if he be left free, and under no other ties than he was in before, in the state of nature. For what appearance would there be of any compact? What new engagement if he were no further tied by any decrees of the society than he himself thought fit and did actually consent to? This would still be as great a liberty as he himself had before his compact, or anyone else in the state of nature hath, who may submit himself and consent to any acts of it if he thinks fit.

98. For if the consent of the majority shall not, in reason, be received as the act of the whole, and conclude every individual, nothing but the consent of every individual can make anything to be the act of the whole. But such a consent is next impossible ever to be had, if we consider the infirmities of health and avocations of business which, in a number though much less than that of a commonwealth, will necessarily keep many away from the public assembly. To which if we add the variety of opinions, and contrariety of interests, which unavoidably happen in all collections of men, the coming into society upon such terms would be only like Cato's coming into the theatre, only to go out again. Such a constitution as this would make the mighty Leviathan of a shorter duration than the feeblest creatures, and not let it outlast the day it was born in; which cannot be supposed till we can think that rational creatures should desire and constitute societies only to be dissolved. For where the majority cannot conclude the rest, there they cannot act as one body, and consequently will be immediately dissolved again.

99. Whosoever, therefore, out of a state of nature unite into a community, must be understood to give up all the power necessary to the ends for which they unite into society to the majority of the community, unless they expressly agreed in any number greater than the majority. And this is done by barely agreeing to unite into one political society, which is all the compact that is, or needs be, between the individuals that enter into or make up a commonwealth. And thus that which begins and actually constitutes any political society is nothing but the consent of any number of freemen capable of a majority to unite and incorporate into such a society. And this is that, and that only, which did or could give beginning to any lawful government in the world.

100. To this I find two objections made. First, that there are no instances to be found in story of a company of men, independent and equal one amongst another, that met together and in this way began and set up a government.

Secondly, 'tis impossible of right that men should do so, because all men being born under government, they are to submit to that, and are not at liberty to begin a new one.

101. To the first there is this to answer: That it is not at all to be wondered that history gives us but a very little account of men that

lived together in the state of nature. The inconveniences of that condition, and the love and want of society, no sooner brought any number of them together, but they presently united and incorporated, if they designed to continue together. And if we may not suppose men ever to have been in the state of nature because we hear not much of them in such a state, we may as well suppose the armies of Salmanasser or Xerxes were never children because we hear little of them till they were men, and embodied in armies. Government is everywhere antecedent to records, and letters seldom come in amongst a people till a long continuation of civil society has by other more necessary arts provided for their safety, ease and plenty. And then they begin to look after the history of their founders, and search into their original, when they have out-lived the memory of it. For 'tis with commonwealths as with particular persons, they are commonly ignorant of their own births and infancies. And if they know anything of their original, they are beholding for it to the accidental records that others have kept of it. And those that we have of the beginning of any polities in the world, excepting that of the Jews, where God himself immediately interposed, and which favours not at all paternal dominion, are all either plain instances of such a beginning as I have mentioned, or at least have manifest footsteps of it.

102. He must show a strange inclination to deny evident matter of fact when it agrees not with his hypothesis who will not allow that the beginning of Rome and Venice were by the uniting together of several men free and independent one of another, amongst whom there was no natural superiority or subjection. And if Josephus Acosta's word may be taken, he tells us that in many parts of America there was no government at all. 'There are great and apparent conjectures,' says he, 'that these men,' speaking of those of Peru, 'for a long time had neither kings nor commonwealths, but lived in troops, as they do this day in Florida, the Cheriquanas, those of Brasil, and many other nations which have no certain kings, but, as occasion is offered in peace or war, they choose their captains as they please' (lib. I, c. 25). If it be said that every man there was born subject to his father, or the head of his family, [I reply] that the subjection due from a child to a father took not away his freedom of uniting into what political society he thought fit has

been already proved. But be that as it will, these men, 'tis evident, were actually free; and whatever superiority some politicians now would place in any of them, they themselves claimed it not; but by consent were all equal, till by the same consent they set rulers over themselves. So that their politic societies all began from a voluntary union, and the mutual agreement of men freely acting in the choice of their governors and forms of government.

103. And I hope those who went away from Sparta with Palantus, mentioned by Justin (lib. 3, c. 4), will be allowed to have been freemen independent one of another, and to have set up a government over themselves by their own consent. Thus I have given several examples out of history of people free and in the state of nature that being met together incorporated and began a commonwealth. And if the want of such instances be an argument to prove that government were not, nor could not be, so begun, I suppose the contenders for paternal empire were better let it alone, than urge it against natural liberty. For if they can give so many instances out of history of governments begun upon paternal right, I think (though at best an argument from what has been to what should of right be has no great force) one might, without any great danger, yield them the cause. But if I might advise them in the case, they would do well not to search too much into the original of governments, as they have begun *de facto*, lest they should find at the foundation of most of them something very little favourable to the design they promote, and such a power as they contend for.

104. But to conclude, reason being plain on our side, that men are naturally free, and the examples of history showing that the governments of the world, that were begun in peace, had their beginning laid on that foundation, and were made by the consent of the people, there can be little room for doubt, either where the right is, or what has been the opinion or practice of mankind about the first erecting of governments.

105. I will not deny that if we look back as far as history will direct us towards the original of commonwealths, we shall generally find them under the government and administration of one man. And I am also apt to believe that where a family was numerous enough to subsist by itself, and continued entire together, without mixing with others, as it often happens where there is much land

and few people, the government commonly began in the father. For the father having, by the law of nature, the same power with every man else to punish, as he thought fit, any offences against that law, might thereby punish his transgressing children even when they were men, and out of their pupillage; and they were very likely to submit to his punishment, and all join with him against the offender, in their turns, giving him thereby power to execute his sentence against any transgression, and so in effect make him the law-maker and governor over all that remained in conjunction with his family. He was fittest to be trusted; paternal affection secured their property and interest under his care; and the custom of obeying him in their childhood made it easier to submit to him rather than to any other. If therefore they must have one to rule them, as government is hardly to be avoided amongst men that live together, who so likely to be the man as he that was their common father; unless negligence, cruelty, or any other defect of mind or body made him unfit for it? But when either the father died, and left his next heir, for want of age, wisdom, courage, or any other qualities, less fit for rule; or where several families met and consented to continue together: there, 'tis not to be doubted, but they used their natural freedom to set up him whom they judged the ablest, and most likely, to rule well over them. Conformable hereunto we find the people of America who (living out of the reach of the conquering swords and spreading domination of the two great empires of Peru and Mexico) enjoyed their own natural freedom, though, *caeteris paribus*, they commonly prefer the heir of their deceased king, yet if they find him any way weak or uncapable, they pass him by and set up the stoutest and bravest man for their ruler.

106. Thus, though looking back as far as records give us any account of peopling the world and the history of nations we commonly find the government to be in one hand, yet it destroys not that which I affirm, viz. that the beginning of politic society depends upon the consent of the individuals to join into and make one society; who, when they are thus incorporated, might set up what form of government they thought fit. But this having given occasion to men to mistake, and think that by nature government was monarchical, and belonged to the father, it may not be amiss here to consider why people in the beginning generally pitched upon this

form, which though perhaps the father's pre-eminence might in the first institution of some commonwealths give a rise to, and place, in the beginning, the power in one hand, yet it is plain that the reason that continued the form of government in a single person was not any regard or respect to paternal authority, since all petty monarchies, that is, almost all monarchies near their original, have been commonly, at least upon occasion, elective.

107. First then, in the beginning of things the father's government of the childhood of those sprung from him having accustomed them to the rule of one man, and taught them that where it was exercised with care and skill, with affection and love to those under it, it was sufficient to procure and preserve to men all the political happiness they sought for in society, it was no wonder that they should pitch upon and naturally run into that form of government which from their infancy they had been all accustomed to; and which, by experience, they had found both easy and safe. To which, if we add, that monarchy being simple, and most obvious to men whom neither experience had instructed in forms of government, nor the ambition or insolence of empire had taught to beware of the encroachments of prerogative, or the inconveniences of absolute power, which monarchy, in succession, was apt to lay claim to and bring upon them, it was not at all strange that they should not much trouble themselves to think of methods of restraining any exorbitances of those to whom they had given the authority over them, and of balancing the power of government by placing several parts of it in different hands. They had neither felt the oppression of tyrannical dominion, nor did the fashion of the age, nor their possessions or way of living (which afforded little matter for covetousness or ambition) give them any reason to apprehend or provide against it; and therefore 'tis no wonder they put themselves into such a frame of government as was not only, as I said, most obvious and simple, but also best suited to their present state and condition, which stood more in need of defence against foreign invasions and injuries, than of multiplicity of laws. The equality of a simple poor way of living confining their desires within the narrow bounds of each man's small property made few controversies, and so no need of many laws to decide them. And there wanted not of justice where there were but few trespasses, and few

offenders. Since then those who liked one another so well as to join into society cannot but be supposed to have some acquaintance and friendship together, and some trust one in another, they could not but have greater apprehensions of others than of one another. And therefore their first care and thought cannot but be supposed to be how to secure themselves against foreign force. 'Twas natural for them to put themselves under a frame of government which might best serve to that end, and choose the wisest and bravest man to conduct them in their wars, and lead them out against their enemies, and in this chiefly be their ruler.

108. Thus we see that the kings of the Indians in America, which is still a pattern of the first ages in Asia and Europe, whilst the inhabitants were too few for the country, and want of people and money gave men no temptation to enlarge their possessions of land, or contest for wider extent of ground, are little more than generals of their armies; and though they command absolutely in war, yet at home and in time of peace they exercise very little dominion, and have but a very moderate sovereignty, the resolutions of peace and war being ordinarily either in the people, or in a council. Though the war itself, which admits not of plurality of governors, naturally devolves the command into the king's sole authority.

109. And thus in Israel itself, the chief business of their judges and first kings seems to have been to be captains in war and leaders of their armies; which (besides what is signified by 'going out and in before the people', which was to march forth to war and home again in the heads of their forces) appears plainly in the story of Jephtha. The Ammonites making war upon Israel, the Gileadites in fear send to Jephtha, a bastard of their family whom they had cast off, and article with him, if he will assist them against the Ammonites, to make him their ruler; which they do in these words: 'And the people made him head and captain over them' (Judges 11.11), which was, as it seems, all one as to be judge. 'And he judged Israel' (Judges 12.7), that is, was their captain-general, 'six years'. So when Jotham upbraids the Shechemites with the obligation they had to Gideon, who had been their judge and ruler, he tells them, 'He fought for you, and adventured his life far, and delivered you out of the hands of Midian' (Judges 9.17). Nothing mentioned of

him but what he did as a general, and indeed that is all is found in his history, or in any of the rest of the judges. And Abimelech particularly is called 'king', though at most he was but their general. And when, being weary of the ill-conduct of Samuel's sons, the children of Israel desired a king, 'like all the nations, to judge them, and to go out before them, and to fight their battles' (1 Samuel 8.20), God, granting their desire, says to Samuel, 'I will send thee a man, and thou shalt anoint him to be captain over my people Israel, that he may save my people out of the hands of the Philistines' (c. 9, v. 16). As if the only business of a king had been to lead out their armies and fight in their defence; and, accordingly, at his inauguration, pouring a vial of oil upon him, declares to Saul that 'the Lord had anointed him to be captain over his inheritance' (c. 10, v. 1). And therefore those who, after Saul's being solemnly chosen and saluted king by the tribes at Mispah, were unwilling to have him their king, make no other objection but this, 'How shall this man save us?' (v. 27), as if they should have said, 'This man is unfit to be our king, not having skill and conduct enough in war to be able to defend us.' And when God resolved to transfer the government to David, it is in these words: 'But now thy kingdom shall not continue: The Lord hath sought him a man after his own heart, and the Lord hath commanded him to be captain over his people' (c. 13, v. 14), as if the whole kingly authority were nothing else but to be their general. And therefore the tribes who had stuck to Saul's family, and opposed David's reign, when they came to Hebron with terms of submission to him, they tell him, amongst other arguments they had to submit to him as to their king, that he was in effect their king in Saul's time, and therefore they had no reason but to receive him as their king now. 'Also,' say they, 'in time past, when Saul was king over us, thou wast he that leddest out and broughtest in Israel, and the Lord said unto thee, "Thou shalt feed my people Israel, and thou shalt be a captain over Israel."'

110. Thus whether a family by degrees grew up into a commonwealth, and the fatherly authority being continued on to the elder son, everyone in his turn growing up under it, tacitly submitted to it, and the easiness and equality of it not offending anyone, everyone acquiesced, till time seemed to have confirmed it, and settled a

right of succession by prescription; or whether several families, or the descendants of several families, whom chance, neighbourhood, or business brought together, uniting into society, the need of a general whose conduct might defend them against their enemies in war, and the great confidence the innocence and sincerity of that poor but virtuous age (such as are almost all those which begin governments, that ever come to last in the world) gave men one of another, made the first beginners of commonwealths generally put the rule into one man's hand, without any other express limitation or restraint, but what the nature of the thing, and the end of government required: whichever of these it was that at first put the rule into the hands of a single person, certain it is that nobody was ever entrusted with it but for the public good and safety, and to those ends in the infancies of commonwealths those who had it, commonly used it. And unless they had done so, young societies could not have subsisted; without such nursing fathers, tender and careful of the public weal, all governments would have sunk under the weakness and infirmities of their infancy, and the prince and the people had soon perished together.

111. But though the golden age (before vain ambition, and *amor sceleratus habendi*, evil concupiscence, had corrupted men's minds into a mistake of true power and honour) had more virtue, and consequently better governors, as well as less vicious subjects, and there was then no stretching prerogative on the one side to oppress the people, nor consequently on the other any dispute about privilege to lessen or restrain the power of the magistrate;* and so no contest betwixt rulers and people about governors or government, yet, when ambition and luxury in future ages would retain and increase the power, without doing the business for which it was

---

*'At first, when some certain kind of regiment was once approved, it may be nothing was then further thought upon for the manner of governing, but all permitted unto their wisdom and discretion which were to rule, till by experience they found this for all parts very inconvenient, so as the thing which they had devised for a remedy did indeed but increase the sore which it should have cured. They saw that to live by one man's will became the cause of all men's misery. This constrained them to come unto laws wherein all men might see their duty beforehand, and know the penalties of transgressing them.' Hooker's *Ecclesiastical Polity*, lib. 1, sect. 10.

given, and, aided by flattery, taught princes to have distinct and separate interests from their people, men found it necessary to examine more carefully the original and rights of government, and to find out ways to restrain the exorbitances and prevent the abuses of that power which they having entrusted in another's hands only for their own good, they found was made use of to hurt them.

112. Thus we may see how probable it is that people that were naturally free, and by their own consent either submitted to the government of their father, or united together out of different families to make a government, should generally put the rule into one man's hands, and choose to be under the conduct of a single person, without so much as by express conditions limiting or regulating his power, which they thought safe enough in his honesty and prudence. Though they never dreamed of monarchy being *iure divino*, which we never heard of among mankind till it was revealed to us by the divinity of this last age; nor ever allowed paternal power to have a right to dominion, or to be the foundation of all government. And thus much may suffice to show that as far as we have any light from history, we have reason to conclude that all peaceful beginnings of government have been laid in the consent of the people. I say peaceful, because I shall have occasion in another place to speak of conquest, which some esteem a way of beginning of governments.

The other objection I find urged against the beginning of polities in the way I have mentioned is this, viz.:

113. That all men being born under government, some or other, it is impossible any of them should ever be free, and at liberty to unite together and begin a new one, or ever be able to erect a lawful government.

If this argument be good, I ask, how came so many lawful monarchies into the world? For if anybody, upon this supposition, can show me any one man in any age of the world free to begin a lawful monarchy, I will be bound to show him ten other free men at liberty, at the same time, to unite and begin a new government under a regal, or any other, form. It being demonstration that if anyone, born under the dominion of another, may be so free as to have a right to command others in a new and distinct empire, everyone that is born under the dominion of another may be so free too, and may become a ruler, or subject, of a distinct separate government. And so by this their own principle, either all men, however born, are free, or else there is but one lawful prince, one lawful government in the world. And then they have nothing to do but barely to show us which that is. Which when they have done, I doubt not but all mankind will easily agree to pay obedience to him.

114. Though it be a sufficient answer to their objection to show that it involves them in the same difficulties that it doth those they use it against, yet I shall endeavour to discover the weakness of this argument a little further.

'All men,' say they, 'are born under government, and therefore they cannot be at liberty to begin a new one. Everyone is born a subject to his father, or his prince, and is therefore under the perpetual tie of subjection and allegiance.' 'Tis plain mankind never owned nor considered any such natural subjection that they were born in, to one or to the other, that tied them, without their own consents, to a subjection to them and their heirs.

115. For there are no examples so frequent in history, both sacred and profane, as those of men withdrawing themselves, and their obedience, from the jurisdiction they were born under, and the family or community they were bred up in, and setting up new governments in other places; from whence sprang all that number of petty commonwealths in the beginning of ages, and which always multiplied, as long as there was room enough, till the stronger or more fortunate swallowed the weaker; and, those great ones again breaking to pieces, dissolved into lesser dominions. All which are so many testimonies against paternal sovereignty, and plainly prove that it was not the natural right of the father, descending to his heirs, that made governments in the beginning, since it was imposs- ible, upon that ground, there should have been so many little kingdoms; all must have been but only one universal monarchy if men had not been at liberty to separate themselves from their families, and the government, be it what it will, that was set up in it, and go and make distinct commonwealths and other governments, as they thought fit.

116. This has been the practice of the world from its first begin- ning to this day. Nor is it now any more hindrance to the freedom of of mankind that they are born under constituted and ancient poli-

ties, that have established laws and set forms of government, than if they were born in the woods, amongst the unconfined inhabitants that ran loose in them. For those who would persuade us that by being born under any government we are naturally subjects to it, and have no more any title or pretence to the freedom of the state of nature, have no other reason (bating that of paternal power, which we have already answered) to produce for it, but only because our fathers or progenitors passed away their natural liberty, and thereby bound up themselves and their posterity to a perpetual subjection to the government which they themselves submitted to. 'Tis true that whatever engagements or promises anyone has made for himself, he is under the obligation of them, but cannot by any compact whatsoever bind his children or posterity. For his son, when a man, being altogether as free as the father, any act of the father can no more give away the liberty of the son, than it can of anybody else. He may indeed annex such conditions to the land he enjoyed as a subject of any commonwealth as may oblige his son to be of that community if he will enjoy those possessions which were his father's; because that estate being his father's property, he may dispose or settle it as he pleases.

117. And this has generally given the occasion to mistake in this matter, because commonwealths not permitting any part of their dominions to be dismembered, nor to be enjoyed by any but those of their community, the son cannot ordinarily enjoy the possessions of his father, but under the same terms his father did, by becoming a member of the society; whereby he puts himself presently under the government he finds there established, as much as any other subject of that commonwealth. And thus the consent of freemen, born under government, which only makes them members of it, being given separately in their turns, as each comes to be of age, and not in a multitude together, people take no notice of it, and thinking it not done at all, or not necessary, conclude they are naturally subjects as they are men.

118. But, 'tis plain, governments themselves understand it otherwise; they claim no power over the son because of that they had over the father; nor look on children as being their subjects by their fathers being so. If a subject of England have a child by an English woman in France, whose subject is he? Not the king of England's,

for he must have leave to be admitted to the privileges of it; nor the king of France's, for how then has his father a liberty to bring him away, and breed him as he pleases? And whoever was judged a traitor or deserter if he left, or warred against a country, for being barely born in it of parents that were aliens there? 'Tis plain then, by the practice of governments themselves, as well as by the law of right reason, that a child is born a subject of no country or government. He is under his father's tuition and authority till he come to age of discretion; and then he is a free man, at liberty what government he will put himself under, what body politic he will unite himself to. For if an Englishman's son, born in France, be at liberty, and may do so, 'tis evident there is no tie upon him by his father being a subject of this kingdom; nor is he bound up, by any compact of his ancestors. And why then hath not his son, by the same reason, the same liberty, though he be born anywhere else? Since the power that a father hath naturally over his children is the same, wherever they be born; and the ties of natural obligations are not bounded by the positive limits of kingdoms and commonwealths.

119. Every man being, as has been showed, naturally free, and nothing being able to put him into subjection to any earthly power, but only his own consent; it is to be considered, what shall be understood to be a sufficient declaration of a man's consent, to make him subject to the laws of any government. There is a common distinction of an express and a tacit consent, which will concern our present case. Nobody doubts but an express consent, of any man, entering into any society, makes him a perfect member of that society, a subject of that government. The difficulty is what ought to be looked upon as a tacit consent, and how far it binds, i.e. how far anyone shall be looked on to have consented, and thereby submitted to any government, where he has made no expressions of it at all. And to this I say that every man that hath any possession, or enjoyment, of any part of the dominions of any government, doth thereby give his tacit consent, and is as far forth obliged to obedience to the laws of that government, during such enjoyment, as anyone under it; whether this his possession be of land, to him and his heirs for ever, or a lodging only for a week; or whether it be barely travelling freely on the highway; and, in effect, it reaches as

far as the very being of anyone within the territories of that government.

120. To understand this the better, it is fit to consider that every man, when he, at first, incorporates himself into any commonwealth, he, by his uniting himself thereunto, annexed also and submits to the community those possessions which he has, or shall acquire, that do not already belong to any other government. For it would be a direct contradiction for anyone to enter into society with others for the securing and regulating of property, and yet to suppose his land, whose property is to be regulated by the laws of the society, should be exempt from the jurisdiction of that government to which he himself, the proprietor of the land, is a subject. By the same act, therefore, whereby anyone unites his person, which was before free, to any commonwealth, by the same he unites his possessions, which were before free, to it also; and they become, both of them, person and possession, subject to the government and dominion of that commonwealth, as long as it hath a being. Whoever, therefore, from thenceforth, by inheritance, purchase, permission, or otherways enjoys any part of the land so annexed to and under the government of that commonwealth, must take it with the condition it is under, that is, of submitting to the government of the commonwealth under whose jurisdiction it is, as far forth as any subject of it.

121. But since the government has a direct jurisdiction only over the land, and reaches the possessor of it (before he has actually incorporated himself in the society) only as he dwells upon, and enjoys that, the obligation anyone is under, by virtue of such enjoyment, to submit to the government, begins and ends with the enjoyment. So that whenever the owner who has given nothing but such a tacit consent to the government will, by donation, sale, or otherwise, quit the said possession, he is at liberty to go and incorporate himself into any other commonwealth, or to agree with others to begin a new one, *in vacuis locis*, in any part of the world they can find free and unpossessed. Whereas he that has once by actual agreement and any express declaration given his consent to be of any commonwealth, is perpetually and indispensably obliged to be and remain unalterably a subject to it, and can never be again in the liberty of the state of nature, unless by any calamity the

government he was under comes to be dissolved; or else by some public act cuts him off from being any longer a member of it.

122. But submitting to the laws of any country, living quietly, and enjoying privileges and protection under them, makes not a man a member of that society. This is only a local protection and homage due to, and from, all those who, not being in a state of war, come within the territories belonging to any government, to all parts whereof the force of its law extends. But this no more makes a man a member of that society, a perpetual subject of that commonwealth, than it would make a man a subject to another in whose family he found it convenient to abide for some time; though, whilst he continued in it, he were obliged to comply with the laws, and submit to the government he found there. And thus we see that foreigners, by living all their lives under another government, and enjoying the privileges and protection of it, though they are bound, even in conscience, to submit to its administration, as far forth as any denizen, yet do not thereby come to be subjects or members of that commonwealth. Nothing can make any man so, but his actually entering into it by positive engagement, and express promise and compact. This is that which I think concerning the beginnings of political societies and that consent which makes anyone a member of any commonwealth.

CHAPTER NINE: Of the Ends of Political Society and Government

123. If man in the state of nature be so free as has been said; if he be absolute lord of his own person and possessions, equal to the greatest, and subject to nobody, why will he part with his freedom? Why will he give up this empire, and subject himself to the dominion and control of any other power? To which 'tis obvious to answer that, though in the state of nature he hath such a right, yet the enjoyment of it is very uncertain, and constantly exposed to the invasion of others. For all being kings as much as he, every man his equal, and the greater part no strict observers of equity and justice, the enjoyment of the property he has in this state is very unsafe, very insecure. This makes him willing to quit this condition which,

however free, is full of fears and continual dangers. And 'tis not without reason that he seeks out, and is willing to join in society with others who are already united, or have a mind to unite, for the mutual preservation of their lives, liberties, and estates, which I call by the general name *property*.

124. The great and chief end, therefore, of men's uniting into commonwealths, and putting themselves under government, is the preservation of their property, to which in the state of nature there are many things wanting.

First, there wants an established, settled, known law, received and allowed by common consent to be the standard of right and wrong, and the common measure to decide all controversies between them. For though the law of nature be plain and intelligible to all rational creatures, yet men being biased by their interest, as well as ignorant for want of study of it, are not apt to allow of it as a law binding to them in the application of it to their particular cases.

125. Secondly, in the state of nature there wants a known and indifferent judge, with authority to determine all differences according to the established law. For everyone in that state being both judge and executioner of the law of nature, men being partial to themselves, passion and revenge is very apt to carry them too far, and with too much heat, in their own cases; as well as negligence and unconcernedness to make them too remiss in other men's.

126. Thirdly, in the state of nature there often wants power to back and support the sentence when right, and to give it due execution. They who by any injustice offended, will seldom fail, where they are able, by force to make good their injustice. Such resistance many times makes the punishment dangerous, and frequently destructive, to those who attempt it.

127. Thus mankind, notwithstanding all the privileges of the state of nature, being but in an ill condition while they remain in it, are quickly driven into society. Hence it comes to pass that we seldom find any number of men live any time together in this state. The inconveniences that they are therein exposed to, by the irregular and uncertain exercise of the power every man has of punishing the transgressions of others, make them take sanctuary under the established laws of government, and therein seek the preservation of their property. 'Tis this makes them so willingly give up every

one his single power of punishing to be exercised by such alone as shall be appointed to it amongst them; and by such rules as the community, or those authorized by them to that purpose, shall agree on. And in this we have the original right and rise of both the legislative and executive power, as well as of the governments and societies themselves.

128. For in the state of nature, to omit the liberty he has of innocent delights, a man has two powers:

The first is to do whatsoever he thinks fit for the preservation of himself and others within the permission of the law of nature; by which law, common to them all, he and all the rest of mankind are one community, make up one society distinct from all other creatures. And were it not for the corruption and viciousness of degenerate men, there would be no need of any other; no necessity that men should separate from this great and natural community, and by positive agreements combine into smaller and divided associations.

The other power a man has in the state of nature is the power to punish the crimes committed against that law. Both these he gives up when he joins in a private, if I may so call it, or particular political society, and incorporates into any commonwealth, separate from the rest of mankind.

129. The first power, viz. of doing whatsoever he thought fit for the preservation of himself, and the rest of mankind, he gives up to be regulated by laws made by the society, so far forth as the preservation of himself and the rest of that society shall require. Which laws of the society in many things confine the liberty he had by the law of nature.

130. Secondly, the power of punishing he wholly gives up, and engages his natural force (which he might before employ in the execution of the law of nature, by his own single authority, as he thought fit) to assist the executive power of the society, as the law thereof shall require. For being now in a new state, wherein he is to enjoy many conveniences from the labour, assistance, and society of others in the same community, as well as protection from its whole strength, he is to part also with as much of his natural liberty in providing for himself as the good, prosperity, and safety of the society shall require: which is not only necessary, but just, since the other members of the society do the like.

131. But though men when they enter into society give up the

equality, liberty, and executive power they had in the state of nature into the hands of the society, to be so far disposed of by the legislative as the good of the society shall require; yet it being only with an intention in everyone the better to preserve himself his liberty and property (for no rational creature can be supposed to change his condition with an intention to be worse), the power of the society, or legislative constituted by them, can never be supposed to extend further than the common good; but is obliged to secure everyone's property by providing against those three defects above-mentioned that made the state of nature so unsafe and uneasy. And so whoever has the legislative or supreme power of any commonwealth is bound to govern by established standing laws, promulgated and known to the people, and not by extemporary decrees; by indifferent and upright judges, who are to decide controversies by those laws; and to employ the force of the community at home only in the execution of such laws, or abroad to prevent or redress foreign injuries, and secure the community from inroads and invasion. And all this to be directed to no other end, but the peace, safety, and public good of the people.

CHAPTER TEN: Of the Forms of a Commonwealth

132. The majority having, as has been showed, upon men's first uniting into society, the whole power of the community naturally in them, may employ all that power in making laws for the community from time to time, and executing those laws by officers of their own appointing; and then the form of the government is a perfect democracy. Or else may put the power of making laws into the hands of a few select men, and their heirs or successors, and then it is an oligarchy. Or else into the hands of one man, and then it is a monarchy; if to him and his heirs, it is an hereditary monarchy; if to him only for life, but upon his death the power only of nominating a successor to return to them, an elective monarchy. And so accordingly of these the community may make compounded and mixed forms of government, as they think good. And if the legislative power be at first given by the majority to one or more persons only for their lives, or any limited time, and then the supreme

power to revert to them again, when it is so reverted the community may dispose of it again anew into what hands they please, and so constitute a new form of government. For the form of government depending upon the placing the supreme power, which is the legislative, it being impossible to conceive that an inferior power should prescribe to a superior, or any but the supreme make laws, according as the power of making laws is placed, such is the form of the commonwealth.

133. By commonwealth I must be understood all along to mean, not a democracy, or any form of government, but any independent community, which the Latins signified by the word *civitas*, to which the word which best answers in our language is commonwealth, and most properly expresses such a society of men, which community or city in English does not, for there may be subordinate communities in a government; and city amongst us has a quite different notion from commonwealth. And therefore, to avoid ambiguity, I crave leave to use the word commonwealth in that sense, in which I find it used by king James the First, and I take it to be its genuine signification; which if anybody dislike, I consent with him to change it for a better.

CHAPTER ELEVEN: Of the Extent of the Legislative Power

134. The great end of men's entering into society being the enjoyment of their properties in peace and safety, and the great instrument and means of that being the laws established in that society, the first and fundamental positive law of all commonwealths is the establishing of the legislative power; as the first and fundamental natural law, which is to govern even the legislative itself, is the preservation of the society, and (as far as will consist with the public good) of every person in it. This legislative is not only the supreme power of the commonwealth, but sacred and unalterable in the hands where the community have once placed it; nor can any edict of anybody else, in what form soever conceived, or by what power soever backed, have the force and obligation of a law which has not its sanction from that legislative which the public has

chosen and appointed. For without this the law could not have that which is absolutely necessary to its being a law, the consent of the society, over whom nobody can have a power to make laws, but by their own consent,* and by authority received from them; and therefore all the obedience which by the most solemn ties anyone can be obliged to pay ultimately terminates in this supreme power, and is directed by those laws which it enacts; nor can any oaths to any foreign power whatsoever, or any domestic subordinate power, discharge any member of the society from his obedience to the legislative, acting pursuant to their trust, nor oblige him to any obedience contrary to the laws so enacted, or further than they do allow; it being ridiculous to imagine one can be tied ultimately to obey any power in the society which is not the supreme.

135. Though the legislative, whether placed in one or more, whether it be always in being or only by intervals, though it be the supreme power in every commonwealth, yet:

First, it is not, nor can possibly be, absolutely arbitrary over the lives and fortunes of the people. For it being but the joint power of every member of the society given up to that person, or assembly, which is legislator, it can be no more than those persons had in a state of nature before they entered into society, and gave up to the community. For nobody can transfer to another more power than he has in himself; and nobody has an absolute arbitrary power over himself, or over any other, to destroy his own life, or take away the life or property of another. A man, as has been proved, cannot

---

*'The lawful power of making laws to command whole politic societies of men belonging so properly unto the same entire societies that for any prince or potentate of what kind soever upon earth to exercise the same of himself, and not by express commission immediately and personally received from God, or else by authority derived at the first from their consent upon whose persons they impose laws, it is no better than mere tyranny. Laws they are not, therefore, which public approbation hath not made so.' Hooker's *Ecclesiastical Polity*, lib. 1, sect. 10. 'Of this point therefore we are to note, that sith [i.e. since] men naturally have no full and perfect power to command whole politic multitudes of men, therefore, utterly without our consent, we could in such sort be at no man's commandment living. And to be commanded we do consent when that society, whereof we be a part, hath at any time before consented, without revoking the same after by the like universal agreement.

'Laws, therefore, human, of what kind soever, are available by consent.' Ibid.

subject himself to the arbitrary power of another; and having in the state of nature no arbitrary power over the life, liberty, or possession of another, but only so much as the law of nature gave him for the preservation of himself and the rest of mankind, this is all he doth, or can give up to the commonwealth, and by it to the legislative power, so that the legislative can have no more than this. Their power, in the utmost bounds of it, is limited to the public good of the society. It is a power that hath no other end but preservation, and therefore can never have a right to destroy, enslave, or designedly to impoverish the subjects.* The obligations of the law of nature cease not in society, but only in many cases are drawn closer, and have by human laws known penalties annexed to them to enforce their observation. Thus the law of nature stands as an eternal rule to all men, legislators as well as others. The rules that they make for other men's actions must, as well as their own and other men's actions, be conformable to the law of nature, i.e. to the will of God, of which that is a declaration. And the fundamental law of nature being the preservation of mankind, no human sanction can be good or valid against it.

136. Secondly, the legislative, or supreme authority, cannot assume to itself a power to rule by extemporary arbitrary decrees,† but is bound to dispense justice and decide the rights of the subject by promulgating standing laws, and known authorized judges. For

---

*'Two foundations there are which bear up public societies, the one a natural inclination, whereby all men desire sociable life and fellowship; the other an order, expressly or secretly agreed upon, touching the manner of their union in living together; the latter is that which we call the law of a commonwealth, the very soul of a politic body, the parts whereof are by law animated, held together, and set on work in such actions as the common good requireth. Laws politic, ordained for external order and regiment amongst men, are never framed as they should be, unless presuming the will of man to be inwardly obstinate, rebellious, and averse from all obedience to the sacred laws of his nature; in a word, unless presuming man to be, in regard of his depraved mind, little better than a wild beast, they do accordingly provide notwithstanding so to frame his outward actions that they be no hindrance unto the common good for which societies are instituted. Unless they do this they are not perfect.' Hooker's *Ecclesiastical Polity*, lib. 1, sect. 10.

†'Human laws are measures in respect of men, whose actions they must direct, howbeit such measures they are as have also their higher rules to be measured by, which rules are two: the law of God and the law of nature; so that laws human

the law of nature being unwritten, and so nowhere to be found but in the minds of men, they who through passion or interest shall mis-cite or misapply it cannot so easily be convinced of their mistake where there is no established judge; and so it serves not, as it ought, to determine the rights and fence the properties of those that live under it, especially where everyone is judge, interpreter, and executioner of it too, and that in his own case; and he that has right on his side, having ordinarily but his own single strength, hath not force enough to defend himself from injuries, or to punish delinquents. To avoid these inconveniences which disorder men's properties in the state of nature, men unite into societies, that they may have the united strength of the whole society to secure and defend their properties, and may have standing rules to bound it, by which everyone may know what is his. To this end it is that men give up all their natural power to the society which they enter into, and the community put the legislative power into such hands as they think fit, with this trust, that they shall be governed by declared laws, or else their peace, quiet, and property will still be at the same uncertainty as it was in the state of nature.

137. Absolute arbitrary power, or governing without settled standing laws, can neither of them consist with the ends of society and government, which men would not quit the freedom of the state of nature for, and tie themselves up under, were it not to preserve their lives, liberties, and fortunes; and by stated rules of right and property to secure their peace and quiet. It cannot be supposed that they should intend, had they a power so to do, to give to any one, or more, an absolute arbitrary power over their persons and estates, and put a force into the magistrate's hand to execute his unlimited will arbitrarily upon them. This were to put themselves into a worse condition than the state of nature, wherein they had a liberty to defend their right against the injuries of others, and were upon equal terms of force to maintain it, whether invaded by a single man or many in combination. Whereas by supposing they have given up themselves to the absolute arbitrary

must be made according to the general laws of nature, and without contradiction to any positive law of Scripture, otherwise they are ill-made.' Ibid. lib. 3, sect. 9.

'To constrain men to anything inconvenient doth seem unreasonable.' Ibid. lib. 1, sect. 10.

power and will of a legislator, they have disarmed themselves, and armed him to make a prey of them when he pleases. He being in a much worse condition who is exposed to the arbitrary power of one man who has the command of 100,000 than he that is exposed to the arbitrary power of 100,000 single men, nobody being secure that his will who has such a command is better than that of other men, though his force be 100,000 times stronger. And therefore, whatever form the commonwealth is under, the ruling power ought to govern by declared and received laws, and not by extemporary dictates and undetermined resolutions. For then mankind will be in a far worse condition than in the state of nature, if they shall have armed one or a few men with the joint power of a multitude, to force them to obey at pleasure the exorbitant and unlimited decrees of their sudden thoughts, or unrestrained and till that moment unknown wills, without having any measures set down which may guide and justify their actions. For all the power the government has being only for the good of the society, as it ought not to be arbitrary and at pleasure, so it ought to be exercised by established and promulgated laws, that both the people may know their duty, and be safe and secure within the limits of the law, and the rulers too kept within their due bounds, and not to be tempted by the power they have in their hands to employ it to such purposes, and by such measures, as they would not have known, and own not willingly.

138. Thirdly, the supreme power cannot take from any man any part of his property without his own consent. For the preservation of property being the end of government, and that for which men enter into society, it necessarily supposes and requires that the people should have property, without which they must be supposed to lose that by entering into society which was the end for which they entered into it, too gross an absurdity for any man to own. Men therefore in society having property, they have such a right to the goods which by the law of the community are theirs, that nobody hath a right to take their substance, or any part of it, from them without their own consent; without this they have no property at all. For I have truly no property in that which another can by right take from me when he pleases, against my consent. Hence it is a mistake to think that the supreme or legislative power of any

commonwealth can do what it will, and dispose of the estates of the subject arbitrarily, or take any part of them at pleasure. This is not much to be feared in governments where the legislative consists, wholly or in part, in assemblies which are variable, whose members upon the dissolution of the assembly are subjects under the common laws of their country, equally with the rest. But in governments where the legislative is in one lasting assembly always in being, or in one man, as in absolute monarchies, there is danger still that they will think themselves to have a distinct interest from the rest of the community, and so will be apt to increase their own riches and power by taking, when they think fit, from the people. For a man's property is not at all secure, though there be good and equitable laws to set the bounds of it, between him and his fellow-subjects, if he who commands those subjects have power to take from any private man what part he pleases of his property, and use and dispose of it as he thinks good.

139. But government, into whatsoever hands it is put, being as I have before showed entrusted with this condition and for this end, that men might have and secure their properties, the prince or senate, however it may have power to make laws for the regulating of property between the subjects one amongst another, yet can never have a power to take to themselves the whole or any part of the subject's property, without their own consent. For this would be in effect to leave them no property at all. And to let us see that even absolute power, where it is necessary, is not arbitrary by being absolute, but is still limited by that reason and confined to those ends which required it in some cases to be absolute, we need look no further than the common practice of martial discipline. For the preservation of the army, and in it of the whole commonwealth, requires an absolute obedience to the command of every superior officer, and it is justly death to disobey or dispute the most dangerous or unreasonable of them: but yet we see that neither the Sargent that would command a soldier to march up to the mouth of a cannon, or stand in a breach where he is almost sure to perish, can command that soldier to give him one penny of his money; nor the general, that can condemn him to death for deserting his post, or for not obeying the most desperate orders, can yet, with all his absolute power of life and death, dispose of one farthing of that

soldier's estate, or seize one jot of his goods; whom yet he can command anything, and hang for the least disobedience. Because such a blind obedience is necessary to that end for which the commander has his power, viz. the preservation of the rest; but the disposing of his goods has nothing to do with it.

140. 'Tis true, governments cannot be supported without great charge, and 'tis fit everyone who enjoys his share of the protection should pay out of his estate his proportion for the maintenance of it. But still it must be with his own consent, i.e. the consent of the majority, giving it either by themselves or their representatives chosen by them. For if anyone shall claim a power to lay and levy taxes on the people by his own authority, and without such consent of the people, he thereby invades the fundamental law of property, and subverts the end of government. For what property have I in that which another may by right take, when he pleases, to himself?

141. Fourthly, the legislative cannot transfer the power of making laws to any other hands. For it being but a delegated power from the people, they who have it cannot pass it over to others. The people alone can appoint the form of the commonwealth, which is by constituting the legislative, and appointing in whose hands that shall be. And when the people have said: We will submit to rules, and be governed by laws made by such men, and in such forms, nobody else can say other men shall make laws for them, nor can the people be bound by any laws but such as are enacted by those whom they have chosen and authorized to make laws for them. The power of the legislative being derived from the people by a positive voluntary grant and institution, can be no other than what that positive grant conveyed, which being only to make laws, and not to make legislators, the legislative can have no power to transfer their authority of making laws, and place it in other hands.

142. These are the bounds which the trust that is put in them by the society, and the law of God and nature, have set to the legislative power of every commonwealth, in all forms of government.

First, they are to govern by promulgated, established laws, not to be varied in particular cases, but to have one rule for rich and poor, for the favourite at court and the country man at plough.

Secondly, these laws also ought to be designed for no other end ultimately but the good of the people.

Thirdly, they must not raise taxes on the property of the people without the consent of the people, given by themselves or their deputies. And this properly concerns only such governments where the legislative is always in being, or at least where the people have not reserved any part of the legislative to deputies, to be from time to time chosen by themselves.

Fourthly, the legislative neither must nor can transfer the power of making laws to anybody else, or place it anywhere but where the people have.

CHAPTER TWELVE: Of the Legislative, Executive, and Federative Power of the Commonwealth

143. The legislative power is that which has a right to direct how the force of the commonwealth shall be employed for preserving the community and the members of it. But because those laws which are constantly to be executed, and whose force is always to continue, may be made in a little time, therefore there is no need that the legislative should be always in being, not having always business to do. And because it may be too great a temptation to human frailty, apt to grasp at power, for the same persons who have the power of making laws to have also in their hands the power to execute them, whereby they may exempt themselves from obedience to the laws they make, and suit the law, both in its making and execution, to their own private advantage, and thereby come to have a distinct interest from the rest of the community, contrary to the end of society and government, therefore in well-ordered commonwealths, where the good of the whole is so considered as it ought, the legislative power is put into the hands of diverse persons who, duly assembled, have by themselves, or jointly with others, a power to make laws, which when they have done, being separated again, they are themselves subject to the laws they have made; which is a new and near tie upon them to take care that they make them for the public good.

144. But because the laws, that are at once and in a short time

made, have a constant and lasting force, and need a perpetual execution, or an attendance thereunto, therefore 'tis necessary there should be a power always in being, which should see to the execution of the laws that are made, and remain in force. And thus the legislative and executive power come often to be separated.

145. There is another power in every commonwealth which one may call natural, because it is that which answers to the power every man naturally had before he entered into society. For though in a commonwealth the members of it are distinct persons still in reference to one another, and as such are governed by the laws of the society; yet in reference to the rest of mankind they make one body, which is, as every member of it before was, still in the state of nature with the rest of mankind. Hence it is that the controversies that happen between any man of the society with those that are out of it are managed by the public, and an injury done to a member of their body engages the whole in the reparation of it. So that under this consideration the whole community is one body in the state of nature in respect of all other states or persons out of its community.

146. This therefore contains the power of war and peace, leagues and alliances, and all the transactions with all persons and communities without the commonwealth, and may be called federative, if anyone pleases. So the thing be understood, I am indifferent as to the name.

147. These two powers, executive and federative, though they be really distinct in themselves, yet one comprehending the execution of the municipal laws of the society within itself, upon all that are parts of it; the other the management of the security and interest of the public without, with all those that it may receive benefit or damage from, yet they are always (almost) united. And though this federative power in the well- or ill-management of it be of great moment to the commonwealth, yet it is much less capable to be directed by antecedent, standing, positive laws than the executive; and so must necessarily be left to the prudence and wisdom of those whose hands it is in, to be managed for the public good. For the laws that concern subjects one amongst another, being to direct their actions, may well enough precede them. But what is to be

done in reference to foreigners, depending much upon their actions, and the variation of designs and interests, must be left in great part to the prudence of those who have this power committed to them, to be managed by the best of their skill, for the advantage of the commonwealth.

148. Though, as I said, the executive and federative power of every community be really distinct in themselves, yet they are hardly to be separated, and placed, at the same time, in the hands of distinct persons. For both of them requiring the force of the society for their exercise, it is almost impracticable to place the force of the commonwealth in distinct and not subordinate hands; or that the executive and federative power should be placed in persons that might act separately, whereby the force of the public would be under different commands; which would be apt sometime or other to cause disorder and ruin.

CHAPTER THIRTEEN: Of the Subordination of the Powers of the Commonwealth

149. Though in a constituted commonwealth, standing upon its own basis, and acting according to its own nature, that is, acting for the preservation of the community, there can be but one supreme power, which is the legislative, to which all the rest are and must be subordinate, yet the legislative being only a fiduciary power to act for certain ends, there remains still in the people a supreme power to remove or alter the legislative when they find the legislative act contrary to the trust reposed in them. For all power given with trust for the attaining an end being limited by that end, whenever that end is manifestly neglected or opposed the trust must necessarily be forfeited, and the power devolve into the hands of those that gave it, who may place it anew where they shall think best for their safety and security. And thus the community perpetually retains a supreme power of saving themselves from the attempts and designs of anybody, even of their legislators, whenever they shall be so foolish, or so wicked, as to lay and carry on designs against the liberties and properties of the subject. For no man, or society of men, having a power to deliver up their preservation, or

consequently the means of it, to the absolute will and arbitrary dominion of another, whenever anyone shall go about to bring them into such a slavish condition, they will always have a right to preserve what they have not a power to part with; and to rid themselves of those who invade this fundamental, sacred, and unalterable law of self-preservation for which they entered into society. And thus the community may be said in this respect to be always the supreme power, but not as considered under any form of government, because this power of the people can never take place till the government be dissolved.

150. In all cases, whilst the government subsists, the legislative is the supreme power. For what can give laws to another must needs be superior to him; and since the legislative is no otherwise legislative of the society but by the right it has to make laws for all the parts and for every member of the society, prescribing rules to their actions and giving power of execution where they are transgressed, the legislative must needs be the supreme, and all other powers in any members or parts of the society, derived from and subordinate to it.

151. In some commonwealths, where the legislative is not always in being, and the executive is vested in a single person who has also a share in the legislative, there that single person in a very tolerable sense may also be called supreme, not that he has in himself all the supreme power, which is that of law-making, but because he has in him the supreme execution, from whom all inferior magistrates derive all their several subordinate powers, or at least the greatest part of them; having also no legislative superior to him, there being no law to be made without his consent, which cannot be expected should ever subject him to the other part of the legislative, he is properly enough, in this sense, supreme. But yet it is to be observed, that though oaths of allegiance and fealty are taken to him, 'tis not to him as supreme legislator, but as supreme executor of the law, made by a joint power of him with others; allegiance being nothing but an obedience according to law, which when he violates, he has no right to obedience, nor can claim it otherwise than as the public person vested with the power of the law, and so is to be considered as the image, phantom, or representative of the common-

wealth, acted by the will of the society declared in its laws; and thus he has no will, no power, but that of the law. But when he quits this representation, this public will, and acts by his own private will, he degrades himself, and is but a single private person without power, and without will that has any right to obedience; the members owing no obedience but to the public will of the society.

152. The executive power placed anywhere but in a person that has also a share in the legislative is visibly subordinate and accountable to it, and may be at pleasure changed and displaced; so that it is not the supreme executive power that is exempt from subordination, but the supreme executive power vested in one who, having a share in the legislative, has no distinct superior legislative to be subordinate and accountable to, further than he himself shall join and consent: so that he is no more subordinate than he himself shall think fit, which one may certainly conclude will be but very little. Of other ministerial and subordinate powers in a commonwealth we need not speak, they being so multiplied with infinite variety, in the different customs and constitutions of distinct commonwealths, that it is impossible to give a particular account of them all. Only thus much, which is necessary to our present purpose, we may take notice of concerning them, that they have no manner of authority, any of them, beyond what is, by positive grant and commission, delegated to them, and are all of them accountable to some other power in the commonwealth.

153. It is not necessary, no nor so much as convenient, that the legislative should be always in being. But absolutely necessary that the executive power should, because there is not always need of new laws to be made, but always need of execution of the laws that are made. When the legislative hath put the execution of the laws they make into other hands, they have a power still to resume it out of those hands when they find cause, and to punish for any maladministration against the laws. The same holds also in regard of the federative power, that and the executive being both ministerial and subordinate to the legislative, which, as has been showed, in a constituted commonwealth is the supreme. The legislative also in this case being supposed to consist of several persons (for if it be a

single person it cannot but be always in being, and so will, as supreme, naturally have the supreme executive power together with the legislative) may assemble and exercise their legislature at the times that either their original constitution or their own adjournment appoints, or when they please if neither of these hath appointed any time, or there be no other way prescribed to convoke them. For the supreme power being placed in them by the people, 'tis always in them, and they may exercise it when they please, unless by their original constitution they are limited to certain seasons, or by an act of their supreme power they have adjourned to a certain time, and when that time comes they have a right to assemble and act again.

154. If the legislative, or any part of it, be made up of representatives chosen for that time by the people, which afterwards return into the ordinary state of subjects, and have no share in the legislature but upon a new choice, this power of choosing must also be exercised by the people, either at certain appointed seasons, or else when they are summoned to it; and in this latter case the power of convoking the legislative is ordinarily placed in the executive, and has one of these two limitations in respect of time: that either the original constitution requires their assembling and acting at certain intervals, and then the executive power does nothing but ministerially issue directions for their electing and assembling, according to due forms; or else it is left to his prudence to call them by new elections when the occasions or exigencies of the public require the amendment of old or making of new laws, or the redress or prevention of any inconveniences that lie on or threaten the people.

155. It may be demanded here, What if the executive power, being possessed of the force of the commonwealth, shall make use of that force to hinder the meeting and acting of the legislative when the original constitution or the public exigencies require it? I say: Using force upon the people without authority, and contrary to the trust put in him that does so, is a state of war with the people, who have a right to reinstate their legislative in the exercise of their power. For having erected a legislative with an intent they should exercise the power of making laws, either at certain set times, or when there is need of it, when they are

hindered by any force from what is so necessary to the society, and wherein the safety and preservation of the people consists, the people have a right to remove it by force. In all states and conditions the true remedy of force without authority is to oppose force to it. The use of force without authority always puts him that uses it into a state of war, as the aggressor, and renders him liable to be treated accordingly.

156. The power of assembling and dismissing the legislative, placed in the executive, gives not the executive a superiority over it, but is a fiduciary trust, placed in him for the safety of the people, in a case where the uncertainty and variableness of human affairs could not bear a steady fixed rule. For it not being possible that the first framers of the government should, by any foresight, be so much masters of future events as to be able to prefix so just periods of return and duration to the assemblies of the legislative, in all times to come, that might exactly answer all the exigencies of the commonwealth, the best remedy could be found for this defect was to trust this to the prudence of one who was always to be present, and whose business it was to watch over the public good. Constant frequent meetings of the legislative, and long continuations of their assemblies, without necessary occasion, could not but be burdensome to the people, and must necessarily in time produce more dangerous inconveniencies, and yet the quick turn of affairs might be sometimes such as to need their present help. Any delay of their convening might endanger the public; and sometimes too their business might be so great that the limited time of their sitting might be too short for their work, and rob the public of that benefit which could be had only from their mature deliberation. What then could be done, in this case, to prevent the community from being exposed sometime or other to eminent hazard, on one side or the other, by fixed intervals and periods, set to the meeting and acting of the legislative, but to entrust it to the prudence of some who, being present and acquainted with the state of public affairs, might make use of this prerogative for the public good? And where else could this be so well placed as in his hands who was entrusted with the execution of the laws, for the same end? Thus, supposing the regulation of times for the assembling and sitting of the legislative not settled by the original constitution, it naturally fell into the

hands of the executive, not as an arbitrary power depending on his good pleasure, but with this trust always to have it exercised only for the public weal, as the occurrences of times and change of affairs might require. Whether settled periods of their convening, or a liberty left to the prince for convoking the legislative, or perhaps a mixture of both hath the least inconvenience attending it, 'tis not my business here to inquire, but only to show that though the executive power may have the prerogative of convoking and dissolving such conventions of the legislative, yet it is not thereby superior to it.

157. Things of this world are in so constant a flux that nothing remains long in the same state. Thus people, riches, trade, power change their stations; flourishing mighty cities come to ruin and prove in time neglected, desolate corners, whilst other unfrequented places grow into populous countries, filled with wealth and inhabitants. But things not always changing equally, and private interest often keeping up customs and privileges when the reasons of them are ceased, it often comes to pass that in governments where part of the legislative consists of representatives chosen by the people, that in tract of time this representation becomes very unequal and disproportionate to the reasons it was at first established upon. To what gross absurdities the following of custom, when reason has left it, may lead, we may be satisfied when we see the bare name of a town, of which there remains not so much as the ruins, where scarce so much housing as a sheepcot, or more inhabitants than a shepherd is to be found, sends as many representatives to the grand assembly of law-makers as a whole county numerous in people and powerful in riches. This strangers stand amazed at, and everyone must confess needs a remedy. Though most think it hard to find one, because the constitution of the legislative being the original and supreme act of the society, antecedent to all positive laws in it, and depending wholly on the people, no inferior power can alter it. And therefore the people, when the legislative is once constituted, having in such a government as we have been speaking of no power to act as long as the government stands, this inconvenience is thought incapable of a remedy.

158. *Salus populi suprema lex* is certainly so just and fundamental a rule that he who sincerely follows it cannot dangerously err. If,

therefore, the executive, who has the power of convoking the legislative, observing rather the true proportion than fashion of representation, regulates, not by old custom but true reason, the number of members in all places that have a right to be distinctly represented, which no part of the people however incorporated can pretend to, but in proportion to the assistance which it affords to the public, it cannot be judged to have set up a new legislative, but to have restored the old and true one, and to have rectified the disorders which succession of time had insensibly, as well as inevitably, introduced. For it being the interest as well as intention of the people to have a fair and equal representative, whoever brings it nearest to that is an undoubted friend to and establisher of the government, and cannot miss the consent and approbation of the community. Prerogative being nothing but a power in the hands of the prince to provide for the public good, in such cases which, depending upon unforeseen and uncertain occurrences, certain and unalterable laws could not safely direct, whatsoever shall be done manifestly for the good of the people, and the establishing the government upon its true foundations, is, and always will be, just prerogative. The power of erecting new corporations, and therewith new representatives, carries with it a supposition that in time the measures of representation might vary, and those places have a just right to be represented which before had none, and, by the same reason, those cease to have a right, and be too inconsiderable for such a privilege, which before had it. 'Tis not a change from the present state, which perhaps corruption or decay has introduced, that makes an inroad upon the government, but the tendency of it to injure or oppress the people, and to set up one part, or party, with a distinction from, and an unequal subjection of, the rest. Whatsoever cannot but be acknowledged to be of advantage to the society and people in general, upon just and lasting measures, will always, when done, justify itself; and whenever the people shall choose their representatives upon just and undeniably equal measures suitable to the original frame of the government, it cannot be doubted to be the will and act of the society, whoever permitted or caused them so to do.

CHAPTER FOURTEEN: Of Prerogative

159. Where the legislative and executive power are in distinct hands (as they are in all moderated monarchies, and well-framed governments), there the good of the society requires that several things should be left to the discretion of him that has the executive power. For the legislators not being able to foresee, and provide by laws for, all that may be useful to the community, the executor of the laws having the power in his hands, has by the common law of nature a right to make use of it for the good of the society in many cases where the municipal law has given no direction, till the legislative can conveniently be assembled to provide for it. Many things there are which the law can by no means provide for, and those must necessarily be left to the discretion of him that has the executive power in his hands, to be ordered by him as the public good and advantage shall require; nay, 'tis fit that the laws themselves should in some cases give way to the executive power, or rather to this fundamental law of nature and government, viz. that, as much as may be, all the members of the society are to be preserved. For since many accidents may happen, wherein a strict and rigid observation of the laws may do harm (as not to pull down an innocent man's house to stop the fire, when the next to it is burning), and a man may come sometimes within the reach of the law, which makes no distinction of persons, by an action that may deserve reward and pardon, 'tis fit the ruler should have a power, in many cases, to mitigate the severity of the law, and pardon some offenders; for the end of government being the preservation of all, as much as may be, even the guilty are to be spared, where it can prove no prejudice to the innocent.

160. This power to act according to discretion, for the public good, without the prescription of the law, and sometimes even against it, is that which is called prerogative. For since in some governments the law-making power is not always in being, and is usually too numerous, and so too slow, for the dispatch requisite to execution, and because also it is impossible to foresee, and so by laws to provide for, all accidents and necessities that may concern the

public, or to make such laws as will do no harm if they are executed with an inflexible rigour, on all occasions, and upon all persons that may come in their way, therefore there is a latitude left to the executive power, to do many things of choice which the laws do not prescribe.

161. This power whilst employed for the benefit of the community, and suitably to the trust and ends of the government, is undoubted prerogative, and never is questioned. For the people are very seldom, or never, scrupulous or nice in the point: they are far from examining prerogative whilst it is in any tolerable degree employed for the use it was meant; that is, for the good of the people, and not manifestly against it. But if there comes to be a question between the executive power and the people about a thing claimed as a prerogative, the tendency of the exercise of such prerogative to the good or hurt of the people will easily decide that question.

162. It is easy to conceive that in the infancy of governments, when commonwealths differed little from families in number of people, they differed from them too but little in number of laws; and the governors, being as the fathers of them, watching over them for their good, the government was almost all prerogative. A few established laws served the turn, and the discretion and care of the ruler supplied the rest. But when mistake, or flattery, prevailed with weak princes to make use of this power for private ends of their own, and not for the public good, the people were fain by express laws to get prerogative determined in those points wherein they found disadvantage from it; and thus declared limitations of prerogative were by the people found necessary in cases which they and their ancestors had left in the utmost latitude, to the wisdom of those princes who made no other but a right use of it, that is, for the good of their people.

163. And therefore they have a very wrong notion of government, who say that the people have encroached upon the prerogative when they have got any part of it to be defined by positive laws. For in so doing they have not pulled from the prince anything that of right belonged to him, but only declared that that power which they indefinitely left in his, or his ancestors', hands to be exercised for their good was not a thing which they

intended him when he used it otherwise. For the end of government being the good of the community, whatsoever alterations are made in it, tending to that end, cannot be an encroachment upon anybody, since nobody in government can have a right tending to any other end. And those only are encroachments which prejudice or hinder the public good. Those who say otherwise speak as if the prince had a distinct and separate interest from the good of the community, and was not made for it, the root and source from which spring almost all those evils and disorders which happen in kingly governments. And indeed if that be so, the people under his government are not a society of rational creatures entered into a community for their mutual good; they are not such as have set rulers over themselves to guard and promote that good; but are to be looked on as an herd of inferior creatures, under the dominion of a master who keeps them, and works them for his own pleasure or profit. If men were so void of reason, and brutish, as to enter into society upon such terms, prerogative might indeed be, what some men would have it, an arbitrary power to do things hurtful to the people.

164. But since a rational creature cannot be supposed, when free, to put himself into subjection to another for his own harm (though where he finds a good and wise ruler he may not perhaps think it either necessary or useful to set precise bounds to his power in all things), prerogative can be nothing but the people's permitting their rulers to do several things of their own free choice, where the law was silent, and sometimes too against the direct letter of the law, for the public good; and their acquiescing in it when so done. For as a good prince, who is mindful of the trust put into his hands, and careful of the good of his people, cannot have too much prerogative, that is, power to do good; so a weak and ill prince, who would claim that power which his predecessors exercised without the direction of the law as a prerogative belonging to him by right of his office, which he may exercise at his pleasure, to make or promote an interest distinct from that of the public, gives the people an occasion to claim their right, and limit that power which, while it was exercised for their good, they were content should be tacitly allowed.

165. And therefore he that will look into the history of England

will find that prerogative was always largest in the hands of our wisest and best princes, because the people observing the whole tendency of their actions to be the public good contested not what was done without law to that end; or if any human frailty or mistake (for princes are but men, made as others) appeared in some small declinations from that end, yet 'twas visible the main of their conduct tended to nothing but the care of the public. The people therefore, finding reason to be satisfied with these princes, whenever they acted without or contrary to the letter of the law, acquiesced in what they did, and, without the least complaint, let them enlarge their prerogative as they pleased, judging rightly that they did nothing herein to the prejudice of their laws, since they acted conformable to the foundation and end of all laws, the public good.

166. Such god-like princes indeed had some title to arbitrary power, by that argument that would prove absolute monarchy the best government, as that which God himself governs the universe by, because such kings partake of his wisdom and goodness. Upon this is founded that saying, that the reigns of good princes have been always most dangerous to the liberties of their people, for when their successors, managing the government with different thoughts, would draw the actions of those good rulers into precedent, and make them the standard of their prerogative, as if what had been done only for the good of the people was a right in them to do for the harm of the people, if they so pleased, it has often occasioned contest, and sometimes public disorders, before the people could recover their original right, and get that to be declared not to be prerogative which truly was never so, since it is impossible that anybody in the society should ever have a right to do the people harm; though it be very possible and reasonable that the people should not go about to set any bounds to the prerogative of those kings or rulers who themselves transgressed not the bounds of the public good. For prerogative is nothing but the power of doing public good without a rule.

167. The power of calling parliaments in England, as to precise time, place, and duration, is certainly a prerogative of the king, but still with this trust, that it shall be made use of for the good of the nation, as the exigencies of the times and variety of occasions shall

require. For it being impossible to foresee which should always be the fittest place for them to assemble in, and what the best season, the choice of these was left with the executive power, as might be most subservient to the public good, and best suit the ends of parliaments.

168. The old question will be asked in this matter of prerogative: But who shall be judge when this power is made a right use of? I answer: Between an executive power in being, with such a prerogative, and a legislative that depends upon his will for their convening, there can be no judge on earth; as there can be none between the legislative and the people, should either the executive or the legislative, when they have got the power in their hands, design or go about to enslave or destroy them. The people have no other remedy in this, as in all other cases where they have no judge on earth, but to appeal to heaven. For the rulers, in such attempts, exercising a power the people never put into their hands (who can never be supposed to consent that anybody should rule over them for their harm), do that which they have not a right to do. And where the body of the people, or any single man, is deprived of their right, or is under the exercise of a power without right, and have no appeal on earth, there they have a liberty to appeal to heaven whenever they judge the cause of sufficient moment. And therefore, though the people cannot be judge, so as to have by the constitution of that society any superior power to determine and give effective sentence in the case, yet they have, by a law antecedent and paramount to all positive laws of men, reserved that ultimate determination to themselves, which belongs to all mankind, where there lies no appeal on earth, viz. to judge whether they have just cause to make their appeal to heaven. And this judgement they cannot part with, it being out of a man's power so to submit himself to another as to give him a liberty to destroy him; God and nature never allowing a man so to abandon himself as to neglect his own preservation; and, since he cannot take away his own life, neither can he give another power to take it. Nor let anyone think this lays a perpetual foundation for disorder: for this operates not, till the inconvenience is so great that the majority feel it, and are weary of it, and find a necessity to have it amended. But

this the executive power, or wise princes, never need come in the danger of; and 'tis the thing of all others they have most need to avoid, as of all others the most perilous.

CHAPTER FIFTEEN: Of Paternal, Political, and Despotical Power Considered Together

169. Though I have had occasion to speak of these separately before, yet the great mistakes of late about government having, as I suppose, arisen from confounding these distinct powers one with another, it may not, perhaps, be amiss to consider them here together.

170. First, then, paternal or parental power is nothing but that which parents have over their children, to govern them for the children's good till they come to the use of reason, or a state of knowledge wherein they may be supposed capable to understand that rule, whether it be the law of nature or the municipal law of their country they are to govern themselves by: capable, I say, to know it, as well as several others who live, as free men, under that law. The affection and tenderness which God hath planted in the breasts of parents towards their children, makes it evident that this is not intended to be a severe, arbitrary government, but only for the help, instruction, and preservation of their offspring. But happen it as it will, there is, as I have proved, no reason why it should be thought to extend to life and death, at any time, over their children, more than over anybody else, neither can there be any pretence why this parental power should keep the child, when grown to a man, in subjection to the will of his parents any further than the having received life and education from his parents obliges him to respect, honour, gratitude, assistance, and support all his life to both father and mother. And thus, 'tis true, the paternal is a natural government, but not at all extending itself to the ends and jurisdictions of that which is political. The power of the father doth not reach at all to the property of the child, which is only in his own disposing.

171. Secondly, political power is that power which every man, having in the state of nature, has given up into the hands of the society, and therein to the governors whom the society hath set

over itself, with this express or tacit trust, that it shall be employed for their good, and the preservation of their property. Now this power, which every man has in the state of nature, and which he parts with to the society in all such cases where the society can secure him, is to use such means for the preserving of his own property as he thinks good, and nature allows him; and to punish the breach of the law of nature in others so as (according to the best of his reason) may most conduce to the preservation of himself and the rest of mankind. So that the end and measure of this power, when in every man's hands in the state of nature, being the preservation of all of his society, that is, all mankind in general, it can have no other end or measure, when in the hands of the magistrate, but to preserve the members of that society in their lives, liberties, and possessions; and so cannot be an absolute, arbitrary power over their lives and fortunes, which are as much as possible to be preserved, but a power to make laws, and annex such penalties to them, as may tend to the preservation of the whole, by cutting off those parts, and those only, which are so corrupt that they threaten the sound and healthy, without which no severity is lawful. And this power has its original only from compact and agreement, and the mutual consent of those who make up the community.

172. Thirdly, despotical power is an absolute, arbitrary power one man has over another, to take away his life whenever he pleases. This is a power which neither nature gives, for it has made no such distinction between one man and another; nor compact can convey, for man, not having such an arbitrary power over his own life, cannot give another man such a power over it; but it is the effect only of forfeiture, which the aggressor makes of his own life when he puts himself into the state of war with another. For having quitted reason, which God hath given to be the rule betwixt man and man, and the common bond whereby human kind is united into one fellowship and society; and having renounced the way of peace, which that teaches, and made use of the force of war to compass his unjust ends upon another, where he has no right, and so revolting from his own kind to that of beasts by making force, which is theirs, to be his rule of right, he renders himself liable to be destroyed by the injured

person and the rest of mankind, that will join with him in the execution of justice, as any other wild beast or noxious brute with whom mankind can have neither society nor security. And thus captives, taken in a just and lawful war, and such only, are subject to a despotical power, which as it arises not from compact, so neither is it capable of any, but is the state of war continued. For what compact can be made with a man that is not master of his own life? What condition can he perform? And if he be once allowed to be master of his own life, the despotical, arbitrary power of his master ceases. He that is master of himself and his own life has a right too to the means of preserving it, so that as soon as compact enters, slavery ceases, and he so far quits his absolute power, and puts an end to the state of war, who enters into conditions with his captive.

173. Nature gives the first of these, viz. paternal power, to parents for the benefit of their children during their minority, to supply their want of ability and understanding how to manage their property. (By property I must be understood here, as in other places, to mean that property which men have in their persons as well as goods.) Voluntary agreement gives the second, viz. political power, to governors for the benefit of their subjects, to secure them in the possession and use of their properties. And forfeiture gives the third, despotical power, to lords for their own benefit over those who are stripped of all property.

174. He that shall consider the distinct rise and extent, and the different ends, of these several powers will plainly see that paternal power comes as far short of that of the magistrate as despotical exceeds it; and that absolute dominion, however placed, is so far from being one kind of civil society that it is as inconsistent with it as slavery is with property. Paternal power is only where minority makes the child incapable to manage his property; political where men have property in their own disposal; and despotical over such as have no property at all.

CHAPTER SIXTEEN: Of Conquest

175. Though governments can originally have no other rise than that before mentioned, nor polities be founded on anything but the consent of the people; yet such has been the disorders ambition has filled the world with, that in the noise of war, which makes so great a part of the history of mankind, this consent is little taken notice of; and therefore many have mistaken the force of arms for the consent of the people, and reckon conquest as one of the originals of government. But conquest is as far from setting up any government as demolishing an house is from building a new one in the place. Indeed it often makes way for a new frame of a commonwealth by destroying the former; but, without the consent of the people, can never erect a new one.

176. That the aggressor, who puts himself into the state of war with another, and unjustly invades another man's right, can, by such an unjust war, never come to have a right over the conquered, will be easily agreed by all men, who will not think that robbers and pirates have a right of empire over whomsoever they have force enough to master; or that men are bound by promises which unlawful force extorts from them. Should a robber break into my house, and, with a dagger at my throat, make me seal deeds to convey my estate to him, would this give him any title? Just such a title by his sword has an unjust conqueror who forces me into submission. The injury and the crime is equal, whether committed by the wearer of a crown or some petty villain. The title of the offender, and the number of his followers, make no difference in the offence, unless it be to aggravate it. The only difference is, great robbers punish little ones, to keep them in their obedience, but the great ones are rewarded with laurels and triumphs, because they are too big for the weak hands of justice in this world, and have the power in their own possession which should punish offenders. What is my remedy against a robber that so broke into my house? Appeal to the law for justice. But perhaps justice is denied, or I am crippled and cannot stir, robbed and have not the means to do it. If God has taken away all means of seeking remedy, there is nothing left but patience. But my son, when able, may seek the relief of the law, which I am

denied. He, or his son, may renew his appeal, till he recover his right. But the conquered, or their children, have no court, no arbitrator on earth to appeal to. Then they may appeal, as Jephtha did, to heaven, and repeat their appeal till they have recovered the native right of their ancestors, which was to have such a legislative over them as the majority should approve and freely acquiesce in. If it be objected this would cause endless trouble, I answer: No more than justice does, where she lies open to all that appeal to her. He that troubles his neighbour without a cause is punished for it by the justice of the court he appeals to. And he that appeals to heaven must be sure he has right on his side; and a right too that is worth the trouble and cost of the appeal, as he will answer at a tribunal that cannot be deceived, and will be sure to retribute to everyone according to the mischiefs he hath created to his fellow-subjects; that is, any part of mankind. From whence, 'tis plain, that he that conquers in an unjust war can thereby have no title to the subjection and obedience of the conquered.

177. But supposing victory favours the right side, let us consider a conqueror in a lawful war, and see what power he gets, and over whom.

First, 'tis plain he gets no power by his conquest over those that conquered with him. They that fought on his side cannot suffer by the conquest, but must at least be as much freemen as they were before. And most commonly they serve upon terms, and on condition to share with their leader, and enjoy a part of the spoil, and other advantages that attend the conquering sword; or at least have a part of the subdued country bestowed upon them. And the conquering people are not, I hope, to be slaves by conquest, and wear their laurels only to show they are sacrifices to their leader's triumph. They that found absolute monarchy upon the title of the sword make their heroes, who are the founders of such monarchies, arrant draw-can-sirs, and forget they had any officers and soldiers that fought on their side in the battles they won, or assisted them in the subduing, or shared in possessing the countries they mastered. We are told by some that the English monarchy is founded in the Norman Conquest, and that our princes have thereby a title to absolute dominion. Which, if it were true (as by the history it appears otherwise), and that William had a right to make war on this island, yet his dominion by conquest could reach no further than to the Saxons and Britons that were then inhabitants of this country. The Normans that came with him, and helped to conquer, and all descended from them, are free men, and no subjects by conquest, let that give what dominion it will. And if I, or anybody else, shall claim freedom, as derived from them, it will be very hard to prove the contrary. And 'tis plain the law, that has made no distinction between the one and the other, intends not there should be any difference in their freedom or privileges.

178. But supposing, which seldom happens, that the conquerors and conquered never incorporate into one people, under the same laws and freedom. Let us see next what power a lawful conqueror has over the subdued; and that I say is purely despotical. He has an absolute power over the lives of those who by an unjust war have forfeited them; but not over the lives or fortunes of those who engaged not in the war, nor over the possessions even of those who were actually engaged in it.

179. Secondly, I say then the conqueror gets no power but only over those who have actually assisted, concurred, or consented to that unjust force that is used against him. For the people having given to their governors no power to do an unjust thing, such as is to make an injust war (for they never had such a power in themselves), they ought not to be charged, as guilty of the violence and injustice that is committed in an unjust war, any further than they actually abet it. No more than they are to be thought guilty of any violence or oppression their governors should use upon the people themselves, or any part of their fellow-subjects, they having empowered them no more to the one than to the other. Conquerors, 'tis true, seldom trouble themselves to make the distinction, but they willingly permit the confusion of war to sweep all together; but yet this alters not the right: for the conqueror's power over the lives of the conquered being only because they have used force to do or maintain an injustice, he can have that power only over those who have concurred in that force. All the rest are innocent, and he has no more title over the people of that country who have done him no injury, and so have made no forfeiture of their lives, than he has over any other who, without any injuries or provocations, have lived upon fair terms with him.

180. Thirdly, the power a conqueror gets over those he overcomes in a just war is perfectly despotical: he has an absolute power over the lives of those who, by putting themselves in a state of war, have forfeited them; but he has not thereby a right and title to their possessions. This, I doubt not, but at first sight will seem a strange doctrine, it being so quite contrary to the practice of the world, there being nothing more familiar in speaking of the dominion of countries than to say: Such an one conquered it. As if conquest, without any more ado, conveyed a right of possession. But when we consider that the practice of the strong and powerful, how universal soever it may be, is seldom the rule of right, however it be one part of the subjection of the conquered not to argue against the conditions cut out to them by the conquering sword.

181. Though in all war there be usually a complication of force and damage, and the aggressor seldom fails to harm the estate when he uses force against the persons of those he makes war upon; yet 'tis the use of force only that puts a man into the state of war. For whether by force he begins the injury, or else, having quietly and by fraud done the injury, he refuses to make reparation and by force maintains it (which is the same thing as at first to have done it by force) 'tis the unjust use of force that makes the war. For he that breaks open my house, and violently turns me out of doors, or, having peaceably got in, by force keeps me out, does in effect the same thing; supposing we are in such a state that we have no common judge on earth whom I may appeal to, and to whom we are both obliged to submit: for of such I am now speaking. 'Tis the unjust use of force, then, that puts a man into the state of war with another, and thereby he that is guilty of it makes a forfeiture of his life. For, quitting reason, which is the rule given between man and man, and using force the way of beasts, he becomes liable to be destroyed by him he uses force against, as any savage ravenous beast that is dangerous to his being.

182. But because the miscarriages of the father are no faults of the children, and they may be rational and peaceable, notwithstanding the brutishness and injustice of the father, the father, by his miscarriages and violence, can forfeit but his own life, but involves not his children in his guilt or destruction. His goods, which nature, that willeth the preservation of all mankind as much as is possible,

hath made to belong to the children to keep them from perishing, do still continue to belong to his children. For supposing them not to have joined in the war, either through infancy, absence, or choice, they have done nothing to forfeit them; nor has the conqueror any right to take them away by the bare title of having subdued him that by force attempted his destruction; though perhaps he may have some right to them to repair the damages he has sustained by the war, and the defence of his own right, which how far it reaches to the possessions of the conquered we shall see by and by. So that he that by conquest has a right over a man's person to destroy him if he pleases, has not thereby a right over his estate to possess and enjoy it. For it is the brutal force the aggressor has used that gives his adversary a right to take away his life, and destroy him if he pleases, as a noxious creature; but 'tis damage sustained that alone gives him title to another man's goods. For though I may kill a thief that sets on me in the highway, yet I may not (which seems less) take away his money and let him go; this would be robbery on my side. His force, and the state of war he put himself in, made him forfeit his life, but gave me no title to his goods. The right then of conquest extends only to the lives of those who joined in the war, not to their estates, but only in order to make reparation for the damages received, and the charges of the war, and that too with reservation of the right of the innocent wife and children.

183. Let the conqueror have as much justice on his side as could be supposed, he has no right to seize more than the vanquished could forfeit; his life is at the victor's mercy, and his service and goods he may appropriate to make himself reparation; but he cannot take the goods of his wife and children: they too had a title to the goods he enjoyed, and their shares in the estate he possessed. For example, I, in the state of nature (and all commonwealths are in the state of nature one with another), have injured another man, and, refusing to give satisfaction, it comes to a state of war, wherein my defending by force what I had gotten unjustly makes me the aggressor. I am conquered. My life, 'tis true, as forfeit, is at mercy, but not my wife's and children's. They made not the war, nor assisted in it. I could not forfeit their lives, they were not mine to forfeit. My wife had a share in my estate, that neither could I forfeit. And

my children also, being born of me, had a right to be maintained out of my labour or substance. Here then is the case: the conqueror has a title to reparation for damages received, and the children have a title to their father's estate for their subsistence. For as to the wife's share, whether her own labour or compact gave her a title to it, 'tis plain her husband could not forfeit what was hers. What must be done in the case? I answer: The fundamental law of nature being that all, as much as may be, should be preserved, it follows that if there be not enough fully to satisfy both, viz. for the conqueror's losses and children's maintenance, he that hath, and to spare, must remit something of his full satisfaction, and give way to the pressing and preferable title of those who are in danger to perish without it.

184. But supposing the charge and damages of the war are to be made up to the conqueror, to the utmost farthing, and that the children of the vanquished, spoiled of all their father's goods, are to be left to starve and perish: yet the satisfying of what shall on this score be due to the conqueror will scarce give him a title to any country he shall conquer. For the damages of war can scarce amount to the value of any considerable tract of land, in any part of the world where all the land is possessed and none lies waste. And if I have not taken away the conqueror's land, which, being vanquished, it is impossible I should, scarce any other spoil I have done him can amount to the value of mine, supposing it equally cultivated and of an extent any way coming near what I had overrun of his. The destruction of a year's product or two (for it seldom reaches four or five) is the utmost spoil that usually can be done. For as to money, and such riches and treasure taken away, these are none of nature's goods, they have but a fantastical imaginary value: nature has put no such upon them; they are of no more account by her standard than the wampompeke [wampum] of the Americans to an European prince, or the silver money of Europe would have been formerly to an American. And five years' product is not worth the perpetual inheritance of land where all is possessed and none remains waste to be taken up by him that is disseised: which will be easily granted, if one do but take away the imaginary value of money, the disproportion being more than between five and five hundred. Though, at the same time, half a year's product is more

worth than the inheritance where, there being more land than the inhabitants possess and make use of, anyone has liberty to make use of the waste: but there conquerors take little care to possess themselves of the lands of the vanquished. No damage, therefore, that men in the state of nature (as all princes and governments are in reference to one another) suffer from one another can give a conqueror power to dispossess the posterity of the vanquished and turn them out of their inheritance, which ought to be the possession of them and their descendants to all generations. The conqueror indeed will be apt to think himself master, and 'tis the very condition of the subdued not to be able to dispute their right. But if that be all, it gives no other title than what bare force gives to the stronger over the weaker. And, by this reason, he that is strongest will have a right to whatever he pleases to seize on.

185. Over those then that joined with him in the war, and over those of the subdued country that opposed him not, and the posterity even of those that did, the conqueror, even in a just war, hath, by his conquest, no right of dominion: they are free from any subjection to him, and if their former government be dissolved, they are at liberty to begin and erect another to themselves.

186. The conqueror, 'tis true, usually, by the force he has over them, compels them, with a sword at their breasts, to stoop to his conditions, and submit to such a government as he pleases to afford them. But the inquiry is, What right he has to do so? If it be said they submit by their own consent, then this allows their own consent to be necessary to give the conqueror a title to rule over them. It remains only to be considered whether promises, extorted by force, without right, can be thought consent, and how far they bind. To which I shall say they bind not at all, because whatsoever another gets from me by force, I still retain the right of, and he is obliged presently to restore. He that forces my horse from me ought presently to restore him, and I have still a right to retake him. By the same reason, he that forced a promise from me ought presently to restore it, i.e. quit me of the obligation of it, or I may resume it myself, i.e. choose whether I will perform it. For the law of nature laying an obligation on me only by the rules she prescribes, cannot oblige me by the violation of her rules. Such is the extorting anything from me by force. Nor does it at all alter the case to say I

gave my promise, no more than it excuses the force, and passes the right, when I put my hand in my pocket and deliver my purse myself to a thief who demands it with a pistol at my breast.

187. From all which it follows that the government of a conqueror, imposed by force on the subdued, against whom he had no right of war, or who joined not in the war against him, where he had right, has no obligation upon them.

188. But let us suppose that all the men of that community, being all members of the same body politic, may be taken to have joined in that unjust war wherein they are subdued, and so their lives are at the mercy of the conqueror.

189. I say: This concerns not their children, who are in their minority. For since a father hath not, in himself, a power over the life or liberty of his child, no act of his can possibly forfeit it. So that the children, whatever may have happened to the fathers, are free men, and the absolute power of the conqueror reaches no further than the persons of the men that were subdued by him, and dies with them; and, should he govern them as slaves, subjected to his absolute, arbitrary power, he has no such right of dominion over their children. He can have no power over them but by their own consent, whatever he may drive them to say, or do; and he has no lawful authority, whilst force and not choice compels them to submission.

190. Every man is born with a double right: first, a right of freedom to his person, which no other man has a power over, but the free disposal of it lies in himself. Secondly, a right, before any other man, to inherit, with his brethren, his father's goods.

191. By the first of these, a man is naturally free from subjection to any government, though he be born in a place under its jurisdiction. But if he disclaim the lawful government of the country he was born in, he must also quit the right that belonged to him by the laws of it, and the possessions there descending to him from his ancestors, if it were a government made by their consent.

192. By the second, the inhabitants of any country who are descended and derive a title to their estates from those who are subdued, and had a government forced upon them against their free consents, retain a right to the possession of their ancestors, though they consent not freely to the government, whose hard

conditions were by force imposed on the possessors of that country. For the first conqueror never having had a title to the land of that country, the people who are the descendants of, or claim under, those who were forced to submit to the yoke of a government by constraint, have always a right to shake it off, and free themselves from the usurpation, or tyranny, which the sword hath brought in upon them, till their rulers put them under such a frame of government as they willingly, and of choice, consent to. Who doubts but the Grecian Christians, descendants of the ancient possessors of that country, may justly cast off the Turkish yoke which they have so long groaned under whenever they have a power to do it? For no government can have a right to obedience from a people who have not freely consented to it: which they can never be supposed to do till either they are put in a full state of liberty to choose their government and governors, or at least till they have such standing laws, to which they have by themselves or their representatives given their free consent, and also till they are allowed their due property, which is so to be proprietors of what they have that nobody can take away any part of it without their own consent, without which men under any government are not in the state of free men, but are direct slaves under the force of war.

193. But granting that the conqueror in a just war has a right to the estates, as well as power over the persons of the conquered (which, 'tis plain, he hath not), nothing of absolute power will follow from hence in the continuance of the government. Because the descendants of these being all free men, if he grants them estates and possessions to inhabit his country (without which it would be worth nothing), whatsoever he grants them, they have, so far as it is granted, property in. The nature whereof is, that without a man's own consent it cannot be taken from him.

194. Their persons are free by a native right, and their properties, be they more or less, are their own, and at their own disposal, and not at his; or else it is no property. Supposing the conqueror gives to one man a thousand acres, to him and his heirs for ever; to another he lets a thousand acres for his life, under the rent of £50 or £500 per annum. Has not the one of these a right to his thousand acres for ever, and the other during his life, paying the said rent? And hath not the tenant for life a property in all that he

gets, over and above his rent, by his labour and industry during the said term, supposing it be double the rent? Can anyone say: The king or conqueror, after his grant, may by his power of conqueror take away all or part of the land from the heirs of one, or from the other during his life, he paying the rent? Or can he take away from either the goods or money they have got upon the said land, at his pleasure? If he can, then all free and voluntary contracts cease and are void, in the world. There needs nothing to dissolve them at any time but power enough. And all the grants and promises of men in power are but mockery and collusion. For can there be anything more ridiculous than to say: I give you and yours this for ever, and that in the surest and most solemn way of conveyance can be devised, and yet it is to be understood that I have right, if I please, to take it away from you again tomorrow?

195. I will not dispute now whether princes are exempt from the laws of their country; but this I am sure, they owe subjection to the laws of God and nature. Nobody, no power, can exempt them from the obligations of that eternal law. Those are so great, and so strong, in the case of promises, the omnipotency itself can be tied by them. Grants, promises and oaths are bonds that hold the Almighty – whatever some flatterers say to princes of the world, who all together, with all their people joined to them, are in comparison of the great God but as a drop of the bucket, or a dust on the balance, inconsiderable nothing!

196. The short of the case in conquest is this: the conqueror, if he have a just cause, has a despotical right over the persons of all that actually aided and concurred in the war against him, and a right to make up his damage and cost out of their labour and estates, so he injure not the right of any other. Over the rest of the people, if there were any that consented not to the war, and over the children of the captives themselves, or the possessions of either, he has no power; and so can have, by virtue of conquest, no lawful title himself to dominion over them, or derive it to his posterity; but is an aggressor if he attempts upon their properties, and thereby puts himself in a state of war against them; and has no better a right of principality, he, nor any of his successors, than Ingware or Ubba, the Danes, had here in England, or Spartacus, had he conquered Italy, would have had; which is to have their yoke cast

off as soon as God shall give those under their subjection courage and opportunity to do it. Thus, notwithstanding whatever title the kings of Assyria had over Judah by the sword, God assisted Hezekiah to throw off the dominion of that conquering empire. 'And the Lord was with Hezekiah and he prospered; wherefore he went forth, and he rebelled against the king of Assyria, and served him not' (2 Kings 18.7). Whence it is plain that shaking off a power which force and not right hath set over anyone, though it hath the name of rebellion, yet is no offence before God, but is that which he allows and countenances, though even promises and covenants, when obtained by force, have intervened. For 'tis very probable to anyone that reads the story of Ahaz and Hezekiah attentively that the Assyrians subdued Ahaz and deposed him, and made Hezekiah king in his father's lifetime, and that Hezekiah by agreement had done him homage and paid him tribute all this time.

CHAPTER SEVENTEEN: Of Usurpation

197. As conquest may be called a foreign usurpation, so usurpation is a kind of domestic conquest, with this difference, that an usurper can never have right on his side, it being no usurpation but where one is got into the possession of what another has right to. This, so far as it is usurpation, is a change only of persons, but not of the forms and rules of the government; for if the usurper extend his power beyond what of right belonged to the lawful princes or governors of the commonwealth, 'tis tyranny added to usurpation.

198. In all lawful governments the designation of the persons who are to bear rule is as natural and necessary a part as the form of the government itself, and is that which had its establishment originally from the people. Hence all commonwealths with the form of government established have rules also of appointing those who are to have any share in the public authority; and settled methods of conveying the right to them. For the anarchy is much alike to have no form of government at all, or to agree that it shall be monarchical, but to appoint no way to know or design the person that shall have the power and be the monarch. Whoever gets into the exercise of any part of the power by other ways than what the

laws of the community have prescribed hath no right to be obeyed, though the form of the commonwealth be still preserved, since he is not the person the laws have appointed, and consequently not the person the people have consented to. Nor can such an usurper, or any deriving from him, ever have a title till the people are both at liberty to consent and have actually consented to allow and confirm in him the power he hath till then usurped.

CHAPTER EIGHTEEN: Of Tyranny

199. As usurpation is the exercise of power which another hath a right to, so tyranny is the exercise of power beyond right, which nobody can have a right to. And this is making use of the power anyone has in his hands, not for the good of those who are under it, but for his own private, separate advantage. When the governor, however entitled, makes not the law but his will the rule, and his commands and actions are not directed to the preservation of the properties of his people, but the satisfaction of his own ambition, revenge, covetousness, or any other irregular passion.

200. If one can doubt this to be truth or reason because it comes from the obscure hand of a subject, I hope the authority of a king will make it pass with him. King James the first, in his speech to the Parliament (1603), tells them thus:

I will ever prefer the weal of the public, and of the whole commonwealth, in making of good laws and constitutions to any particular and private ends of mine. Thinking ever the wealth and weal of the commonwealth to be my greatest weal and worldly felicity; a point wherein a lawful king doth directly differ from a tyrant. For I do acknowledge that the special and greatest point of difference that is between a rightful king and an usurping tyrant is this: that whereas the proud and ambitious tyrant doth think his kingdom and people are only ordained for satisfaction of his desires and unreasonable appetites, the righteous and just king doth by the contrary acknowledge himself to be ordained for the procuring of the wealth and property of his people.

And again in his speech to the Parliament (1609), he hath these words:

The king binds himself by a double oath to the observation of the fundamental laws of his kingdom. Tacitly, as by being a king, and so bound to protect as well the people as the laws of his kingdom, and expressly by his oath at his coronation; so as every just king in a settled kingdom is bound to observe that paction made to his people by his laws in framing his government agreeable thereunto, according to that paction which God made with Noah after the deluge: hereafter seed-time and harvest, and cold and heat, and summer and winter, and day and night shall not cease while the earth remaineth. And therefore a king governing in a settled kingdom leaves to be a king, and degenerates into a tyrant, as soon as he leaves off to rule according to his laws.

And a little after:

Therefore all kings that are not tyrants, or perjured, will be glad to bound themselves within the limits of their laws. And they that persuade them the contrary are vipers and pests, both against them and the commonwealth.

Thus that learned king, who well understood the notions of things, makes the difference betwixt a king and a tyrant to consist only in this: that one makes the laws the bounds of his power, and the good of the public the end of his government; the other makes all give way to his own will and appetite.

201. 'Tis a mistake to think this fault is proper only to monarchies. Other forms of government are liable to it, as well as that. For wherever the power that is put in any hands for the government of the people and the preservation of their properties is applied to other ends, and made use of to impoverish, harass, or subdue them to the arbitrary and irregular commands of those that have it, there it presently becomes tyranny, whether those that thus use it are one or many. Thus we read of the thirty tyrants at Athens, as well as one at Syracuse; and the intolerable dominion of the decemviri at Rome was nothing better.

202. Wherever law ends tyranny begins (if the law be transgressed to another's harm). And whosoever in authority exceeds the power given him by the law, and makes use of the force he has under his command to compass that upon the subject which the law allows not, ceases in that to be a magistrate, and, acting without

authority, may be opposed, as any other man who by force invades the right of another. This is acknowledged in subordinate magistrates. He that hath authority to seize my person in the street may be opposed as a thief and a robber if he endeavours to break into my house to execute a writ, notwithstanding that I know he has such a warrant and such a legal authority as will empower him to arrest me abroad. And why this should not hold in the highest as well as in the most inferior magistrate I would gladly be informed. Is it reasonable that the eldest brother, because he has the greatest part of his father's estate, should thereby have a right to take away any of his younger brother's portions? Or that a rich man, who possessed a whole country, should from thence have a right to seize, when he pleased, the cottage and garden of his poor neighbour? The being rightfully possessed of great power and riches exceedingly beyond the greatest part of the sons of Adam is so far from being an excuse, much less a reason, for rapine and oppression, which the endamaging another without authority is, that it is a great aggravation of it. For the exceeding the bounds of authority is no more a right in a great than a petty officer, no more justifiable in a king than a constable. But is so much the worse in him, in that he has more trust put in him, has already a much greater share than the rest of his brethren, and is supposed from the advantage of education, employment, and councillors to be more knowing in the measures of right or wrong.

203. May the commands then of a prince be opposed? May he be resisted as often as anyone shall find himself aggrieved, and but imagine he has not right done him? This will unhinge and overturn all polities, and instead of government and order leave nothing but anarchy and confusion.

204. To this I answer: That force is to be opposed to nothing but to unjust and unlawful force. Whoever makes any opposition in any other case draws on himself a just condemnation both from God and man, and so no such danger or confusion will follow as is often suggested, for:

205. First, as in some countries the person of the prince by the law is sacred, and so, whatever he commands or does, his person is still free from all question or violence, not liable to force or any judicial censure or condemnation. But yet opposition may be made

to the illegal acts of any inferior officer, or other commissioned by him; unless he will, by actually putting himself into a state of war with his people, dissolve the government, and leave them to that defence which belongs to everyone in the state of nature. For of such things who can tell what the end will be? And a neighbour kingdom has showed the world an odd example. In all other cases the sacredness of the person exempts him from all inconveniences whereby he is secure, whilst the government stands, from all violence and harm whatsoever: than which there cannot be a wiser constitution. For the harm he can do in his own person not being likely to happen often, nor to extend itself far; nor being able by his single strength to subvert the laws, nor oppress the body of the people, should any prince have so much weakness and ill-nature as to be willing to do it, the inconveniency of some particular mischiefs that may happen sometimes, when a heady prince comes to the throne, are well recompensed by the peace of the public and security of the government, in the person of the chief magistrate, thus set out of the reach of danger: it being safer for the body that some few private men should be sometimes in danger to suffer than that the head of the republic should be easily, and upon slight occasions, exposed.

206. Secondly, but this privilege, belonging only to the king's person, hinders not but they may be questioned, opposed, and resisted who use unjust force, though they pretend a commission from him, which the law authorizes not. As is plain in the case of him that has the king's writ to arrest a man, which is a full commission from the king; and yet he that has it cannot break open a man's house to do it, nor execute this command of the king upon certain days, nor in certain places, though this commission have no such exception in it, but they are the limitations of the law, which if anyone transgresses, the king's commission excuses him not. For the king's authority being given him only by the law, he cannot empower anyone to act against the law, or justify him by his commission in so doing. The commission or command of any magistrate, where he has no authority, being as void and insignificant as that of any private man. The difference between the one and the other being that the magistrate has some authority so far, and to such ends, and the private man has none at all. For 'tis not

the commission, but the authority, that gives the right of acting; and against the laws there can be no authority. But, notwithstanding such resistance, the king's person and authority are still both secured, and so no danger to governor or government.

207. Thirdly, supposing a government wherein the person of the chief magistrate is not thus sacred, yet this doctrine of the lawfulness of resisting all unlawful exercises of his power will not upon every slight occasion endanger him, or embroil the government. For where the injured party may be relieved, and his damages repaired by appeal to the law, there can be no pretence for force, which is only to be used where a man is intercepted from appealing to the law. For nothing is to be accounted hostile force but where it leaves not the remedy of such an appeal. And 'tis such force alone that puts him that uses it into a state of war, and makes it lawful to resist him. A man with a sword in his hand demands my purse in the highway, when perhaps I have not 12d. in my pocket. This man I may lawfully kill. To another I deliver £100 to hold only whilst I alight, which he refuses to restore me when I am got up again, but draws his sword to defend the possession of it by force if I endeavour to retake it. The mischief this man does me is a hundred, or possibly a thousand times more than the other perhaps intended me (whom I killed before he really did me any), and yet I might lawfully kill the one, and cannot so much as hurt the other lawfully. The reason whereof is plain: because the one using force, which threatened my life, I could not have time to appeal to the law to secure it; and when it was gone 'twas too late to appeal. The law could not restore life to my dead carcass: the loss was irreparable; which to prevent, the law of nature gave me a right to destroy him who had put himself into a state of war with me, and threatened my destruction. But in the other case, my life not being in danger, I may have the benefit of appealing to the law, and have reparation for my £100 that way.

208. Fourthly, but if the unlawful acts done by the magistrate be maintained (by the power he has got) and the remedy which is due by law be by the same power obstructed, yet the right of resisting, even in such manifest acts of tyranny, will not suddenly, or on slight occasions, disturb the government. For if it reach no further than some private men's cases, though they have a right to defend

themselves, and to recover by force what by unlawful force is taken from them, yet the right to do so will not easily engage them in a contest wherein they are sure to perish; it being as impossible for one or a few oppressed men to disturb the government, where the body of the people do not think themselves concerned in it, as for a raving madman or heady malcontent to overturn a well-settled state, the people being as little apt to follow the one as the other.

209. But if either these illegal acts have extended to the majority of the people, or if the mischief and oppression has light only on some few but in such cases as the precedent and consequences seem to threaten all, and they are persuaded in their consciences that their laws, and with them their estates, liberties, and lives are in danger, and perhaps their religion too, how they will be hindered from resisting illegal force used against them I cannot tell. This is an inconvenience, I confess, that attends all governments whatsoever, when the governors have brought it to this pass, to be generally suspected of their people – the most dangerous state which they can possibly put themselves in; wherein they are the less to be pitied because it is so easy to be avoided, it being as impossible for a governor, if he really means the good of his people, and the preservation of them and their laws together, not to make them see and feel it, as it is for the father of a family not to let his children see he loves and takes care of them.

210. But if all the world shall observe pretences of one kind and actions of another, arts used to elude the law and the trust of prerogative (which is an arbitrary power in some things left in the prince's hand to do good not harm to the people) employed contrary to the end for which it was given; if the people shall find the ministers and subordinate magistrates chosen suitable to such ends, and favoured or laid by proportionably as they promote or oppose them; if they see several experiments made of arbitrary power, and that religion underhand favoured (though publicly proclaimed against) which is readiest to introduce it, and the operators in it supported as much as may be; and when that cannot be done, yet approved still, and liked the better: if a long train of actings show the councils all tending that way, how can a man any more hinder himself from being persuaded in his own mind which way things are going, or from casting about how to save himself, than he could

from believing the captain of the ship he was in was carrying him and the rest of the company to Algiers when he found him always steering that course, though crosswinds, leaks in his ship, and want of men and provisions did often force him to turn his course another way for some time, which he steadily returned to again, as soon as the wind, weather, and other circumstances would let him?

CHAPTER NINETEEN: Of the Dissolution of Government

211. He that will with any clearness speak of the dissolution of government ought, in the first place, to distinguish between the dissolution of the society and the dissolution of the government. That which makes the community, and brings men out of the loose state of nature into one politic society, is the agreement which everyone has with the rest to incorporate and act as one body, and so be one distinct commonwealth. The usual, and almost only, way whereby this union is dissolved is the inroad of foreign force making a conquest upon them. For in that case (not being able to maintain and support themselves as one entire and independent body) the union belonging to that body which consisted therein must necessarily cease, and so everyone return to the state he was in before, with a liberty to shift for himself, and provide for his own safety as he thinks fit in some other society. Whenever the society is dissolved, 'tis certain the government of that society cannot remain. Thus conquerors' swords often cut up governments by the roots, and mangle societies to pieces, separating the subdued or scattered multitude from the protection of, and dependence on, that society which ought to have preserved them from violence. The world is too well instructed in, and too forward to allow of, this way of dissolving of governments to need any more to be said of it; and there wants not much argument to prove that where the society is dissolved the government cannot remain, that being as impossible as for the frame of an house to subsist when the materials of it are scattered and dissipated by a whirlwind, or jumbled into a confused heap by an earthquake.

212. Besides this overturning from without, governments are dissolved from within.

First, when the legislative is altered. Civil society being a state of peace amongst those who are of it, from whom the state of war is excluded by the umpirage which they have provided in their legislative for the ending all differences that may arise amongst any of them, 'tis in their legislative that the members of a commonwealth are united and combined together into one coherent living body. This is the soul that gives form, life, and unity to the commonwealth. From hence the several members have their mutual influence, sympathy, and connection; and therefore when the legislative is broken, or dissolved, dissolution and death follows. For the essence and union of the society consisting in having one will, the legislative, when once established by the majority, has the declaring, and as it were keeping, of that will. The constitution of the legislative is the first and fundamental act of society, whereby provision is made for the continuation of their union, under the direction of persons, and bonds of laws made by persons authorized thereunto, by the consent and appointment of the people, without which no one man, or number of men, amongst them can have authority of making laws that shall be binding to the rest. When any one, or more, shall take upon them to make laws, whom the people have not appointed so to do, they make laws without authority, which the people are not therefore bound to obey; by which means they come again to be out of subjection, and may constitute to themselves a new legislative, as they think best, being in full liberty to resist the force of those who, without authority, would impose anything upon them. Everyone is at the disposure of his own will when those who had by the delegation of the society the declaring of the public will are excluded from it, and others usurp the place who have no such authority or delegation.

213. This being usually brought about by such in the commonwealth who misuse the power they have, it is hard to consider it aright, and know at whose door to lay it, without knowing the form of government in which it happens. Let us suppose then the legislative placed in the concurrence of three distinct persons.

1. A single hereditary person having the constant, supreme executive power, and with it the power of convoking and dissolving the other two within certain periods of time.

2. An assembly of hereditary nobility.

3. An assembly of representatives chosen *pro tempore* by the people. Such a form of government supposed, it is evident:

214. First, that when such a single person or prince sets up his own arbitrary will in place of the laws, which are the will of the society, declared by the legislative, then the legislative is changed. For that being in effect the legislative whose rules and laws are put in execution and required to be obeyed, when other laws are set up, and other rules pretended and enforced, than what the legislative, constituted by the society, have enacted, 'tis plain that the legislative is changed. Whoever introduces new laws, not being thereunto authorized by the fundamental appointment of the society, or subverts the old, disowns and overturns the power by which they were made, and so sets up a new legislative.

215. Secondly, when the prince hinders the legislative from assembling in its due time, or from acting freely pursuant to those ends for which it was constituted, the legislative is altered. For 'tis not a certain number of men, no, nor their meeting, unless they have also freedom of debating, and leisure of perfecting, what is for the good of the society wherein the legislative consists: when these are taken away or altered, so as to deprive the society of the due exercise of their power, the legislative is truly altered. For it is not names that constitute governments, but the use and exercise of those powers that were intended to accompany them, so that he who takes away the freedom, or hinders the acting of the legislative in its due seasons, in effect takes away the legislative, and puts an end to the government.

216. Thirdly, when by the arbitrary power of the prince the electors or ways of election are altered, without the consent and contrary to the common interest of the people, there also the legislative is altered. For if others than those whom the society has authorized thereunto do choose, or in another way than what the society hath prescribed, those chosen are not the legislative appointed by the people.

217. Fourthly, the delivery also of the people into the subjection of a foreign power, either by the prince, or by the legislative, is certainly a change of the legislative, and so a dissolution of the government. For the end why people entered into society being to be preserved one entire, free, independent society, to be governed

by its own laws, this is lost whenever they are given up into the power of another.

218. Why, in such a constitution as this, the dissolution of the government in these cases is to be imputed to the prince is evident: because he having the force, treasure, and offices of the state to employ, and often persuading himself, or being flattered by others, that as supreme magistrate he is incapable of control, he alone is in a condition to make great advances towards such changes under pretence of lawful authority, and has it in his hands to terrify or suppress opposers as factious, seditious, and enemies to the government; whereas no other part of the legislative or people is capable by themselves to attempt any alteration of the legislative without open and visible rebellion, apt enough to be taken notice of; which, when it prevails, produces effects very little different from foreign conquest. Besides the prince, in such a form of government, having the power of dissolving the other parts of the legislative, and thereby rendering them private persons, they can never, in opposition to him or without his concurrence, alter the legislative by a law, his consent being necessary to give any of their decrees that sanction. But yet so far as the other parts of the legislative any way contribute to any attempt upon the government, and do either promote, or not (what lies in them) hinder such designs, they are guilty, and partake in this which is certainly the greatest crime men can be guilty of one towards another.

219. There is one way more whereby such a government may be dissolved, and that is when he who has the supreme executive power neglects and abandons that charge, so that the laws already made can no longer be put in execution. This is demonstratively to reduce all to anarchy, and so effectually to dissolve the government. For laws not being made for themselves, but to be by their execution the bonds of the society, to keep every part of the body politic in its due place and function, when that totally ceases the government visibly ceases, and the people become a confused multitude, without order or connection. Where there is no longer the administration of justice for the securing of men's rights, nor any remaining power within the community to direct the force or provide for the necessities of the public, there certainly is no government left. Where the laws cannot be executed, it is all one as if there were no laws, and a

government without laws is, I suppose, a mystery in politics, inconceivable to human capacity, and inconsistent with human society.

220. In these and the like cases, when the government is dissolved the people are at liberty to provide for themselves by erecting a new legislative, differing from the other by the change of persons, or form, or both as they shall find it most for their safety and good. For the society can never, by the fault of another, lose the native and original right it has to preserve itself, which can only be done by a settled legislative, and a fair and impartial execution of the laws made by it. But the state of mankind is not so miserable that they are not capable of using this remedy till it be too late to look for any. To tell people they may provide for themselves by erecting a new legislative when, by oppression, artifice, or being delivered over to a foreign power, their old one is gone, is only to tell them they may expect relief when it is too late, and the evil is past cure. This is in effect no more than to bid them first be slaves, and then to take care of their liberty; and when their chains are on, tell them they may act like free men. This, if barely so, is rather mockery than relief; and men can never be secure from tyranny if there be no means to escape it till they are perfectly under it: and therefore it is that they have not only a right to get out of it, but to prevent it.

221. There is therefore, secondly, another way whereby governments are dissolved, and that is when the legislative, or the prince, either of them act contrary to their trust.

First, the legislative acts against the trust reposed in them when they endeavour to invade the property of the subject, and to make themselves, or any part of the community, masters, or arbitrary disposers, of the lives, liberties, or fortunes of the people.

222. The reason why men enter into society is the preservation of their property; and the end why they choose and authorize a legislative is that there may be laws made and rules set as guards and fences to the properties of all the members of the society, to limit the power and moderate the dominion of every part and member of the society. For since it can never be supposed to be the will of the society that the legislative should have a power to destroy that which everyone designs to secure by entering into society, and for which the people submitted themselves to the

legislators of their own making, whenever the legislators endeavour to take away and destroy the property of the people, or to reduce them to slavery under arbitrary power, they put themselves into a state of war with the people, who are thereupon absolved from any further obedience, and are left to the common refuge which God hath provided for all men against force and violence. Whensoever, therefore, the legislative shall transgress this fundamental rule of society, and, either by ambition, fear, folly, or corruption, endeavour to grasp themselves, or put into the hands of any other, an absolute power over the lives, liberties, and estates of the people, by this breach of trust they forfeit the power the people had put into their hands for quite contrary ends, and it devolves to the people, who have a right to resume their original liberty, and, by the establishment of a new legislative (such as they shall think fit), provide for their own safety and security, which is the end for which they are in society. What I have said here, concerning the legislative, in general holds true also concerning the supreme executor, who, having a double trust put in him, both to have a part in the legislative, and the supreme execution of the law, acts against both when he goes about to set up his own arbitrary will as the law of the society. He acts also contrary to his trust when he either employs the force, treasure, and offices of the society to corrupt the representatives and gain them to his purposes, or openly pre-engages the electors, and prescribes to their choice such whom he has by solicitations, threats, promises, or otherwise won to his designs; and employs them to bring in such who have promised beforehand what to vote and what to enact. Thus to regulate candidates and electors, and new-model the ways of election, what is it but to cut up the government by the roots, and poison the very fountain of public security? For the people having reserved to themselves the choice of their representatives, as the fence to their properties, could do it for no other end but that they might always be freely chosen, and, so chosen, freely act and advise as the necessity of the commonwealth and the public good should, upon examination and mature debate, be judged to require. This those who give their votes before they hear the debate, and have weighed the reasons on all sides, are not capable of doing. To prepare such an assembly as this, and endeavour to set up the declared abettors of his own will for the true representatives of the people, and the law-makers of the society, is certainly as great a breach of trust, and as perfect a declaration of a design to subvert the government, as is possible to be met with. To which, if one shall add rewards and punishments visibly employed to the same end, and all the arts of perverted law made use of, to take off and destroy all that stand in the way of such a design, and will not comply and consent to betray the liberties of their country, 'twill be past doubt what is doing. What power they ought to have in the society, who thus employ it contrary to the trust that went along with it in its first institution, is easy to determine; and one cannot but see that he who has once attempted any such thing as this cannot any longer be trusted.

223. To this perhaps it will be said, that the people being ignorant, and always discontented, to lay the foundation of government in the unsteady opinion and uncertain humour of the people is to expose it to certain ruin; and no government will be able long to subsist if the people may set up a new legislative whenever they take offence at the old one. To this I answer: Quite the contrary. People are not so easily got out of their old forms as some are apt to suggest. They are hardly to be prevailed with to amend the acknowledged faults in the frame they have been accustomed to. And if there be any original defects, or adventitious ones introduced by time or corruption, 'tis not an easy thing to get them changed, even when all the world sees there is an opportunity for it. This slowness and aversion in the people to quit their old constitutions has, in the many revolutions which have been seen in this kingdom, in this and former ages, still kept us to, or, after some interval of fruitless attempts, still brought us back again to our old legislative of king, lords, and commons; and whatever provocations have made the crown be taken from some of our princes' heads, they never carried the people so far as to place it in another line.

224. But 'twill be said, this hypothesis lays a ferment for frequent rebellion. To which I answer:

First, no more than any other hypothesis. For when the people are made miserable, and find themselves exposed to the ill-usage of arbitrary power, cry up their governors as much as you will for sons of Jupiter, let them be sacred and divine, descended or authorized from heaven; give them out for whom or what you please, the same will happen. The people, generally ill-treated, and contrary to right, will be ready upon any occasion to ease themselves of a burden that sits heavy upon them. They will wish and seek for the opportunity which, in the change, weakness, and accidents of human affairs, seldom delays long to offer itself. He must have lived but a little while in the world who has not seen examples of this in his time, and he must have read very little who cannot produce examples of it in all sorts of governments in the world.

225. Secondly, I answer: Such revolutions happen not upon every little mismanagement in public affairs. Great mistakes in the ruling part, many wrong and inconvenient laws, and all the slips of human frailty will be born by the people without mutiny or murmur. But if a long train of abuses, prevarications, and artifices, all tending the same way, make the design visible to the people, and they cannot but feel what they lie under, and see whither they are going, 'tis not to be wondered that they should then rouse themselves, and endeavour to put the rule into such hands which may secure to them the ends for which government was at first erected, and without which ancient names, and specious forms, are so far from being better, that they are much worse than the state of nature, or pure anarchy: the inconveniences being all as great and as near, but the remedy further off and more difficult.

226. Thirdly, I answer: That this doctrine of a power in the people of providing for their safety anew by a new legislative, when their legislators have acted contrary to their trust by invading their property, is the best fence against rebellion, and the probablest means to hinder it. For rebellion being an opposition, not to persons, but authority, which is founded only in the constitutions and laws of the government, those, whoever they be, who by force break through, and by force justify their violation of them, are truly and properly rebels. For when men, by entering into society and civil government, have excluded force and introduced laws for the preservation of property, peace, and unity amongst themselves, those who set up force again in opposition to the laws do *rebellare*, that is, bring back again the state of war, and are properly rebels; which they who are in power (by the pretence they have to authority, the temptation of force they have in their hands, and the flattery of those about them) being likeliest to do, the properest

way to prevent the evil is to show them the danger and injustice of it, who are under the greatest temptation to run into it.

227. In both the forementioned cases, when either the legislative is changed, or the legislators act contrary to the end for which they were constituted, those who are guilty are guilty of rebellion. For if anyone by force takes away the established legislative of any society, and the laws by them made pursuant to their trust, he thereby takes away the umpirage which everyone had consented to for a peaceable decision of all their controversies, and a bar to the state of war amongst them. They who remove or change the legislative take away this decisive power, which nobody can have but by the appointment and consent of the people; and so destroying the authority which the people did and nobody else can set up, and introducing a power which the people hath not authorized, they actually introduce a state of war, which is that of force without authority. And thus by removing the legislative established by the society (in whose decisions the people acquiesced and united, as to that of their own will) they untie the knot, and expose the people anew to the state of war. And if those who by force take away the legislative are rebels, the legislators themselves, as has been shown, can be no less esteemed so when they, who were set up for the protection and preservation of the people, their liberties and properties, shall by force invade and endeavour to take them away; and so they, putting themselves into a state of war with those who made them the protectors and guardians of their peace, are properly, and with the greatest aggravation, *rebellantes*: rebels.

228. But if they who say it lays a foundation for rebellion mean that it may occasion civil wars, or intestine broils, to tell the people they are absolved from obedience when illegal attempts are made upon their liberties or properties, and may oppose the unlawful violence of those who were their magistrates when they invade their properties contrary to the trust put in them; and that therefore this doctrine is not to be allowed, being so destructive to the peace of the world; they may as well say upon the same ground that honest men may not oppose robbers or pirates, because this may occasion disorder or bloodshed. If any mischief come in such cases, it is not to be charged upon him who defends his own right, but on him that invades his neighbour's. If the innocent honest man must

quietly quit all he has, for peace' sake, to him who will lay violent hands upon it, I desire it may be considered what a kind of peace there will be in the world, which consists only in violence and rapine; and which is to be maintained only for the benefit of robbers and oppressors. Who would not think it an admirable peace betwixt the mighty and the mean when the lamb, without resistance, yielded his throat to be torn by the imperious wolf? Polyphemus's den gives us a perfect pattern of such a peace and such a government, wherein Ulysses and his companions had nothing to do, but quietly to suffer themselves to be devoured. And no doubt Ulysses, who was a prudent man, preached up passive obedience, and exhorted them to a quiet submission, by representing to them of what concernment peace was to mankind; and by showing the inconveniences might happen if they should offer to resist Polyphemus, who had now the power over them.

229. The end of government is the good of mankind; and which is best for mankind, that the people should be always exposed to the boundless will of tyranny, or that the rulers should be sometimes liable to be opposed when they grow exorbitant in the use of their power, and employ it for the destruction and not the preservation of the properties of their people?

230. Nor let anyone say that mischief can arise from hence as often as it shall please a busy head, or turbulent spirit, to desire the alteration of the government. 'Tis true, such men may stir whenever they please, but it will be only to their own just ruin and perdition. For till the mischief be grown general, and the ill designs of the rulers become visible, or their attempts sensible to the greater part, the people, who are more disposed to suffer than right themselves by resistance, are not apt to stir. The examples of particular injustice, or oppression of here and there an unfortunate man, moves them not. But if they universally have a persuasion, grounded upon manifest evidence, that designs are carrying on against their liberties, and the general course and tendency of things cannot but give them strong suspicions of the evil intentions of their governors, who is to be blamed for it? Who can help it if they, who might avoid it, bring themselves into this suspicion? Are the people to be blamed if they have the sense of rational creatures, and can think of

things no otherwise than as they find and feel them? And is it not rather their fault, who puts things in such a posture that they would not have them thought to be as they are? I grant that the pride, ambition, and turbulency of private men have sometimes caused great disorders in commonwealths, and factions have been fatal to states and kingdoms. But whether the mischief hath oftener begun in the people's wantonness, and a desire to cast off the lawful authority of their rulers; or in the rulers' insolence and endeavours to get and exercise an arbitrary power over their people; whether oppression or disobedience gave the first rise to the disorder, I leave it to impartial history to determine. This I am sure, whoever, either ruler or subject, by force goes about to invade the rights of either prince or people, and lays the foundation for overturning the constitution and frame of any just government, is guilty of the greatest crime, I think, a man is capable of, being to answer for all those mischiefs of blood, rapine, and desolation which the breaking to pieces of governments bring on a country. And he who does it is justly to be esteemed the common enemy and pest of mankind; and is to be treated accordingly.

231. That subjects (or foreigners) attempting by force on the properties of any people may be resisted with force is agreed on all hands. But that magistrates doing the same thing may be resisted hath of late been denied: as if those who had the greatest privileges and advantages by the law had thereby a power to break those laws by which alone they were set in a better place than their brethren. Whereas their offence is thereby the greater, both as being ungrateful for the greater share they have by the law, and breaking also that trust which is put into their hands by their brethren.

232. Whosoever uses force without right, as everyone does in society who does it without law, puts himself into a state of war with those against whom he so uses it; and in that state all former ties are cancelled, all other rights cease, and everyone has a right to defend himself, and to resist the aggressor. This is so evident that Barclay himself, that great asserter of the power and sacredness of kings, is forced to confess that it is lawful for the people, in some cases, to resist their king; and that too in a chapter wherein he pretends to show that the divine law shuts up the people from all manner of rebellion. Whereby it is evident, even by his own doctrine, that, since they

may in some cases resist, all resisting of princes is not rebellion. His words are these:

Quod siquis dicat, Ergone populus tyrannicae crudelitati et furori jugulum semper praebebit? Ergone multitudo civitates suas famae, ferro, et flammâ vastari, seque, conjuges, et liberos fortunae ludibrio et tyranni libidini exponi, inque omnia vitae pericula omnesque miserias et molestias à Rege deduci patientur? Num illis quod omni animantium generi est à naturâ tributum, denegari debet, ut scilicet vim vi repellant, seseque; ab iniuriâ tueantur? Huic breviter responsum sit, Populo universo non negari defensionem, quae iuris naturalis est, neque ultionem quae praeter naturam est adversus Regem concedi debere. Quapropter si Rex non in singulares tantum personas aliquot privatum odium exerceat, sed corpus etiam Reipublicae, cuius ipse caput est, i.e. totum populum, vel insignem aliquam eius partem immani et intolerandâ saevitiâ seu tyrannide divexet; populo, quidem hoc casu resistendi ac tuendi se ab iniuriâ potestas competit, sed tuendi se tantum, non enim in principem invadendi: et restituendae iniuriae illatae, non recedendi à debitâ reverentiâ propter acceptam iniuriam. Praesentem denique impteum propulsandi non vim praeteritam ulciscendi ius habet. Horum enim alterum à naturâ est, ut vitam scilicet corpusque tueamur. Alterum vero contra naturam, ut inferior de superiori supplicium sumat. Quod itaque populus malum, antequam factum sit, impedire potest, ne fiat, id postquam factum est, in Regem authorem sceleris vindicare von potest: Populus igitur hoc ampliùs quam privatus quisquam habet: Quod huic, vel ipsis adversariis iudicibus, excepto Buchanano, nullum nisi in patientia remedium superest. Cùm ille si intolerabilis tyrannis est (modicum enim ferre omnino debet) resistere cum reverentiâ possit. (Barclay, *Contra Monarchomachos*, lib. 3, c. 8)

In English thus:

233. But if anyone should ask, Must the people then always lay themselves open to the cruelty and rage of tyranny? Must they see their cities pillaged and laid in ashes, their wives and children exposed to the tyrant's lust and fury, and themselves and families reduced by their king to ruin and all the miseries of want and oppression, and yet sit still? Must men alone be debarred the common privilege of opposing force with force, which nature allows so freely to all other creatures for their preservation from injury? I answer: Self-defence is a part of the law of nature; nor can it be denied the community, even against the king

himself. But to revenge themselves upon him must by no means be allowed them; it being not agreeable to that law. Wherefore if the king shall show an hatred, not only to some particular persons, but sets himself against the body of the commonwealth whereof he is the head, and shall, with intolerable ill-usage, cruelly tyrannize over the whole or a considerable part of the people; in this case the people have a right to resist and defend themselves from injury. But it must be with this caution, that they only defend themselves, but do not attack their prince. They may repair the damages received, but must not for any provocation exceed the bounds of due reverence and respect. They may repulse the present attempt, but must not revenge past violences. For it is natural for us to defend life and limb, but that an inferior should punish a superior is against nature. The mischief which is designed them, the people may prevent before it be done, but when it is done they must not revenge it on the king, though author of the villainy. This therefore is the privilege of the people in general, above what any private person hath. That particular men are allowed by our adversaries themselves (Buchanan only excepted) to have no other remedy but patience; but the body of the people may with respect resist intolerable tyranny; for when it is but moderate they ought to endure it.

234. Thus far that great advocate of monarchical power allows of resistance.

235. 'Tis true he has annexed two limitations to it, to no purpose:

First, he says it must be with reverence.

Secondly, it must be without retribution, or punishment; and the reason he gives is 'because an inferior cannot punish a superior'.

First, how to resist force without striking again, or how to strike with reverence, will need some skill to make intelligible. He that shall oppose an assault only with a shield to receive the blows, or in any more respectful posture, without a sword in his hand to abate the confidence and force of the assailant, will quickly be at an end of his resistance, and will find such a defence serve only to draw on himself the worse usage. This is as ridiculous a way of resisting as Juvenal thought it of fighting, *ubi tu pulsas, ego vapulo tantum*. And the success of the combat will be unavoidably the same he there describes it:

> Libertas pauperis haec est:
> Pulsatus rogat, et pugnis concisus, adorat,
> Ut liceat paucis cum dentibus inde reverti.

[When you hit me, I simply take my beating. This is a poor man's freedom: when he is beaten, he begs, and when he is knocked down, he kneels, for his aim is only to escape with a few of his teeth in place.]

This will always be the event of such an imaginary resistance, where men may not strike again. He therefore who may resist must be allowed to strike. And then let our author, or anybody else, join a knock on the head, or a cut on the face, with as much reverence and respect as he thinks fit. He that can reconcile blows and reverence may, for ought I know, deserve for his pains a civil, respectful cudgelling wherever he can meet with it.

Secondly, as to his second – 'an inferior cannot punish a superior' – that's true, generally speaking, whilst he is his superior. But to resist force with force, being the state of war that levels the parties, cancels all former relations of reverence, respect, and superiority. And then the odds that remains is that he who opposes the unjust aggressor has this superiority over him, that he has a right, when he prevails, to punish the offender, both for the breach of the peace and all the evils that followed upon it. Barclay therefore, in another place, more coherently to himself, denies it to be lawful to resist a king in any case. But he there assigns two cases whereby a king may un-king himself. His words are:

Quid ergo nulline casus incidere possunt quibus populo sese erigere atque in Regem impotentius dominantem arma capere et invadere iure suo suâque authoritate liceat? Nulli certe quamdiu Rex manet. Semper enim ex divinis id obstat, Regem honorificato; et qui potestati resistit, Dei ordinationi resistit: Non aliàs igitur in eum populo potestas est quam si id committat propter quod ipso iure rex esse desinat. Tunc enim se ipse principatu exuit atque in privatis constituit liber: Hoc modo populus et superior efficitur, reverso ad eum scilicet iure illo quod ante regem inauguratum in interregno habuit. At sunt paucorum generum commissa eiusmodi quae hunc effectum pariunt. At ego cum plurima animo perlustrem, duo tantum invenio, duos, inquam, casus quibus rex ipso facto ex Rege non regem se facit et omni honore et dignitate regali atque in subditos potestate destituit; quorum etiam meminit Winzerus.

Horum unus est, Si regnum [et rempublicam evertere conetur, hoc est, si id ei propositum, eaque intentio fuerit ut] disperdat, quemadmodum de Nerone fertur, quod is nempe senatum populumque Romanum, atque adeo urbem ipsam ferro flammaque vastare, ac novas sibi sedes quaerere decrevisset. Et de Caligula, quod palam denunciarit se neque civem neque principem senatui amplius fore, inque animo habuerit, interempto utrisque ordinis Electissimo quoque Alexandriam commigrare, ac ut populum uno ictu interimeret, unam ei cervicem optavit. Talia cum rex aliquis meditatur et molitur serio, omnem regnandi curam et animum illico abiicit, ac proinde imperium in subditos amittit, ut dominus servi pro derelicto habiti, dominium.

236. *Alter casus est, Si rex in alicuius clientelam se contulit, ac regnum quod liberum à maioribus et populo traditum accepit, alienae ditioni mancipavit. Nam tunc quamvis forte non eâ mente id agit populo plane ut incommodet: Tamen quia quod praecipuum est regiae dignitatis amisit, ut summus scilicet in regno secundum Deum sit, et solo Deo inferior, atque populum etiam totum ignorantem vel invitum, cuius libertatem sartam et tectam conservare debuit, in alterius gentis ditionem et potestatem dedidit; hâc velut quadam regni ab alienatione effecit, ut nec quod ipse in regno imperium habuit retineat, nec in eum cui collatum voluit, iuris quicquam transferat; atque ita eo facto liberum jam et suae potestatis populum relinquit, cuius rei exemplum unum annales Scotici suppeditant.* (Barclay, *Contra Monarchomachos*, lib. 3, c. 16)

Which in English runs thus:

237. What then, can there no case happen wherein the people may of right, and by their own authority, help themselves, take arms and set upon their king, imperiously domineering over them? None at all, whilst he remains a king. 'Honour the king', and 'he that resists the power resists the ordinance of God' are divine oracles that will never permit it. The people therefore can never come by a power over him, unless he does something that makes him cease to be a king. For then he divests himself of his crown and dignity, and returns to the state of a private man, and the people become free and superior; the power which they had in the interregnum, before they crowned him king, devolving to them again. But there are but few miscarriages which bring the matter to this state. After considering it well on all sides, I can find but two. Two cases there are, I say, whereby a king, *ipso facto*, becomes no king, and

loses all power and regal authority over his people; which are also taken notice of by Winzerus.

The first is if he endeavour to overturn the government; that is, if he have a purpose and design to ruin the kingdom and commonwealth, as it is recorded of Nero, that he resolved to cut off the senate and people of Rome, lay the city waste with fire and sword, and then remove to some other place. And of Caligula, that he openly declared that he would be no longer a head to the people or senate, and that he had it in his thoughts to cut off the worthiest men of both ranks, and then retire to Alexandria; and he wished that the people had but one neck, that he might dispatch them all at a blow. Such designs as these, when any king harbours in his thoughts and seriously promotes, he immediately gives up all care and thought of the commonwealth, and consequently forfeits the power of governing his subjects, as a master does the dominion over his slaves whom he hath abandoned.

238. The other case is when a king makes himself the dependent of another, and subjects his kingdom, which his ancestors left him, and the people put free into his hands, to the dominion of another. For however perhaps it may not be in his intention to prejudice the people, yet because he has hereby lost the principal part of regal dignity, viz. to be, next and immediately under God, supreme in his kingdom; and also because he betrayed or forced his people, whose liberty he ought to have carefully preserved, into the power and dominion of a foreign nation. By this as it were alienation of his kingdom he himself loses the power he had in it before, without transferring any the least right to those on whom he would have bestowed it; and so by this act sets the people free, and leaves them at their own disposal. One example of this is to be found in the Scotch annals.

239. In these cases Barclay, the great champion of absolute monarchy, is forced to allow that a king may be resisted, and ceases to be a king. That is in short (not to multiply cases): in whatsoever he has no authority, there he is no king, and may be resisted. For wheresoever the authority ceases, the king ceases too, and becomes like other men who have no authority. And these two cases he instances in, differ little from those above mentioned to be destructive to governments, only that he has omitted the principle from which his doctrine flows; and that is the breach of trust in not

'reserving the form of government agreed on, and in not intending the end of government itself, which is the public good and preservation of property. When a king has dethroned himself, and put himself in a state of war with his people, what shall hinder them from prosecuting him who is no king as they would any other man who has put himself into a state of war with them? Barclay and those of his opinion would do well to tell us. This further I desire may be taken notice of out of Barclay, that he says 'The mischief that is designed them, the people may prevent before it be done,' whereby he allows resistance when tyranny is but in design. 'Such designs as these,' says he, 'when any king harbours in his thoughts and seriously promotes, he immediately gives up all care and thought of the commonwealth,' so that according to him the neglect of the public good is to be taken as an evidence of such a design, or at least for a sufficient cause of resistance. And the reason of all he gives in these words, 'because he betrayed or forced his people, whose liberty he ought carefully to have preserved'. What he adds – 'into the power and dominion of a foreign nation' – signifies nothing, the fault and forfeiture lying in the loss of their liberty, which he ought to have preserved, and not in any distinction of the persons to whose dominion they were subjected. The people's right is equally invaded, and their liberty lost, whether they are made slaves to any of their own, or a foreign nation; and in this lies the injury, and against this only have they the right of defence. And there are instances to be found in all countries which show that 'tis not the change of nations in the persons of their governors, but the change of government that gives the offence. Bilson, a bishop of our Church, and a great stickler for the power and prerogative of princes, does, if I mistake not, in his *Treatise of Christian Subjection* acknowledge that princes may forfeit their power and their title to the obedience of their subjects; and if there needed authority in a case where reason is so plain I could send my reader to Bracton, Fortescue, and the author of *The Mirror*, and others: writers who cannot be suspected to be ignorant of our government, or enemies to it. But I thought Hooker alone might be enough to satisfy those men who, relying on him for their ecclesiastical polity, are by strange fate carried to deny those principles upon which he builds it. Whether they are herein made the tools of cunninger workmen, to pull down their own fabric, they were best look. This I am sure, their civil polity is so new, so dangerous, and so destructive to both rulers and people, that as former ages never could bear the broaching of it, so it may be hoped those to come, redeemed from the impositions of those Egyptian under-taskmasters, will abhor the memory of such servile flatterers, who, whilst it seemed to serve their turn, resolved all government into absolute tyranny, and would have all men born to, what their mean souls fitted them for, slavery.

240. Here, 'tis like, the common question will be made: Who shall be judge whether the prince or legislative act contrary to their trust? This, perhaps, ill-affected and factious men may spread amongst the people, when the prince only makes use of his due prerogative. To this I reply: The people shall be judge. For who shall be judge whether his trustee or deputy acts well, and according to the trust reposed in him, but he who deputes him, and must, by having deputed him, have still a power to discard him when he fails in his trust? If this be reasonable in particular cases of private men, why should it be otherwise in that of the greatest moment, where the welfare of millions is concerned, and also where the evil, if not prevented, is greater, and the redress very difficult, dear, and dangerous?

241. But, further, this question ('Who shall be judge?') cannot mean that there is no judge at all, for where there is no judicature on earth to decide controversies amongst men, God in heaven is judge. He alone, 'tis true, is judge of the right. But every man is judge for himself, as in all other cases, so in this, whether another hath put himself into a state of war with him, and whether he should appeal to the supreme judge, as Jephtha did.

242. If a controversy arise betwixt a prince and some of the people, in a matter where the law is silent or doubtful, and the thing be of great consequence, I should think the proper umpire in such a case should be the body of the people. For in cases where the prince hath a trust reposed in him, and is dispensed from the common ordinary rules of the law, there if any men find themselves aggrieved, and think the prince acts contrary to or beyond that trust, who so proper to judge as the body of the people (who at first lodged that trust in him) how far they meant it should extend? But if the prince, or whoever they be in the administration, decline that

way of determination, the appeal then lies to nowhere but to heaven. Force, between either persons who have no known superior on earth, or which permits no appeal to a judge on earth, being properly a state of war, wherein the appeal lies only to heaven, and in that state the injured party must judge for himself when he will think fit to make use of that appeal, and put himself upon it.

243. To conclude, the power that every individual gave the society, when he entered into it, can never revert to the individuals again, as long as the society lasts, but will always remain in the community; because without this there can be no community, no commonwealth, which is contrary to the original agreement. So also when the society hath placed the legislative in any assembly of men, to continue in them and their successors, with direction and authority for providing such successors, the legislative can never revert to the people whilst that government lasts: because having provided a legislative with power to continue for ever, they have given up their political power to the legislative, and cannot resume it. But if they have set limits to the duration of their legislative, and made this supreme power in any person or assembly only temporary, or else when, by the miscarriages of those in authority, it is forfeited, upon the forfeiture of their rulers, or at the determination of the time set, it reverts to the society, and the people have a right to act as supreme, and continue the legislative in themselves, or erect a new form, or under the old form place it in new hands, as they think good.

20: Letter to Edward Clarke (27 January/6 February 1685)

6 Feb. 85

Sir

Though I writ to you the last post in answer to yours of 16th and 2d Jan., yet having therein in haste added some few further directions in reference to your son, but omitted other things I had to say to you about your garden and trees, I have ventured to put this note into Madam's letter.

First, then, since you so well like the roots of this country, I have got for you these following sorts which will be sent you by the first opportunity:

Seeds of White Sand turnips lb. 1/4
    Yellow Sand turnips lb. 1/4
    Early or Summer turnips oz. (ounces) 2
    Leiden carrots oz. 1
    Horn carrots oz. 1
    Early carrots oz. 1
    Wooden parsnips oz. 1
    Sarsafey oz. 1
    Sugar roots oz. 1
    Sugar Ray roots oz. 1.

What the last two sorts are I know not. They say the Sugar Ray roots, being boiled, may be either eaten hot, buttered, as turnips, or cold with oil and vinegar, as a salad. Sarsafey I have eaten in England. They are pleasant and commended for wholesome.

The lime and abele trees you desire I will take the best care I can of, and you shall have notice when they are sent.

If I had your coat of arms in colours, I would get it done in glass to be set up somewhere at Chipley, being very well acquainted with a good glass painter here.

I remember Adrian sent me word he could not get the key into the lock of a chest of mine wherein were some clothes. This has sometimes happened to me, for there is a square spike in the lock which goes into the hollow of the key, which if it stands not right the key will not go in, and then the spike in the lock must be turned a little with a pair of nippers or compasses so that the square of it may stand right with the square of the hollow of the key to go into it, and then the key will go in. But when the key is in there requires yet some skill to open the lock, to which purpose I left with him a circle drawn with marks. Pray remember that

this mark   stands for degrees and
this   for minutes.

I thank Susan for my flannel shirts. Pray appease her wrath, for I thought she would not be displeased with my recantation. To show her that I have no malice I desire her to get me four flannel shirts more just as the former, only the collars I would have single and at least three fingers broad, or more, whereas these I have were double and narrow. When they are done I would desire to have my scissors at John Hicks's, the little bottle Musidore left with you and another he has or will send you wrapped up and sent in them, and the shirts sent as the last were.

Now we are come to discourse of trees again, I cannot forbear to repeat what I think I mentioned formerly, that is, to be sure to set the inmost row of your trees that lead to your house on either side, 20 foot without the line of your house. This will be much best when the trees are grown up, and if you think it will be a fault to look along your walk by the side of your house in the meantime, that I think will be cured by planting one tree at the end of the walk next your house just in the line of your house. I do not approve abeles for walks up to your house: they will do better down about your ponds and by the brook's side. The walks leading to your house on the four sides I would have of these four sorts: lime in the front, and on the three other sides: oaks on one, elms on the other, and witch elms on the third as you like best, and for winter greens if you will be ruled by me use none but yew and holly. They will make hedges or standers as you please, will endure any cutting and weather, whereas all other, as phylyrea, alaternus, cypresses, etc., are commonly one in 20 years cut down to the ground by a severe winter. Examine the gardens and see how many of them were left last summer.

I am sir your most humble obedient servant

JL

Address: For Mr Clarke

Endorsed by Clarke: J.L. his letter received the 2d February 1684: with an account of seeds etc. and some ciphers on it etc.

21: *A Letter Concerning Toleration* (1685)

Honoured Sir,

Since you are pleased to inquire what are my thoughts about the mutual toleration of Christians in their different professions of religion, I must needs answer you freely, that I esteem that toleration to be the chief characteristical mark of the true Church. For whatsoever some people boast of the antiquity of places and names, or of the pomp of their outward worship; others, of the reformation of their discipline; all, of the orthodoxy of their faith (for everyone is orthodox to himself): these things, and all others of this nature, are much rather marks of men striving for power and empire over one another, than of the Church of Christ. Let anyone have never so true a claim to all these things, yet if he be destitute of charity, meekness, and good-will in general towards all mankind, even to those that are not Christians, he is certainly yet short of being a true Christian himself. 'The kings of the Gentiles exercise Lordship over them,' said our Saviour to his disciples, 'but ye shall not be so' (Luke 22.25). The business of true religion is quite another thing. It is not instituted in order to the erection of an external pomp, nor to the obtaining of ecclesiastical dominion, nor to the exercising of compulsive force; but to the regulating of men's lives according to the rules of virtue and piety. Whosoever will list himself under the banner of Christ must in the first place, and above all things, make war upon his own lusts and vices. It is in vain for any man to usurp the name of Christian without holiness of life, purity of manners, and benignity and meekness of spirit.

'Thou, when thou art converted, strengthen thy brethren' (Luke 22.32), said our Lord to Peter. It would indeed be very hard for one that appears careless about his own salvation to persuade me that he were extremely concerned for mine. For it is impossible that those should sincerely and heartily apply themselves to make other people Christians who have not really embraced the Christian religion in their own hearts. If the Gospel and the apostles may be credited, no man can be a Christian without charity, and without that faith which works, not by force, but by love. Now I appeal to the consciences of those that persecute, torment, destroy, and kill other men upon pretence of religion, whether they do it out of friendship and kindness towards them, or no? And I shall then indeed, and not till then, believe they do so, when I shall see those fiery zealots correcting, in the same manner, their friends and familiar acquaintance for the manifest sins they commit against the precepts of the Gospel; when I shall see them prosecute with fire and sword the members of their own communion that are tainted with enormous vices, and without amendment are in danger of eternal perdition; and when I shall see them thus express their love and desire of the salvation of their souls by the infliction of torments and exercise of all manner of cruelties. For if it be out of a principle of charity, as they pretend, and love to men's souls, that they deprive them of their estates, maim them with corporal punishments, starve and torment them in noisome prisons, and in the end even take away their lives; I say if all this be done merely to make men Christians, and procure their salvation, why then do they suffer 'whoredom, fraud, malice, and such like enormities' (Rom. 1), which (acccording to the apostle) manifestly relish of heathenish corruption, to predominate so much and abound amongst their flocks and people? These and suchlike things are certainly more contrary to the glory of God, to the purity of the Church, and to the salvation of souls than any conscientious dissent from ecclesiastical decisions, or separation from public worship, whilst accompanied with innocency of life. Why then does this burning zeal for God, for the Church, and for the salvation of souls (burning, I say, literally, with fire and faggot) pass by those moral vices and wickednesses without any chastisement, which are acknowledged by all men to be diametrically opposite to the profession of Christianity; and bend all its nerves either to the introducing of ceremonies, or to the establishment of opinions which for the most part are about nice and intricate matters that exceed the capacity of ordinary understandings? Which of the parties contending about these things is in the right, which of them is guilty of schism or heresy, whether those that domineer or those that suffer, will then at last be manifest when the cause of their separation comes to be judged of. He certainly that follows Christ, embraces his doctrine, and bears his yoke, though he forsake both father and mother, separate from the public assembly and ceremonies of his country, or whomsoever or whatsoever else he relinquishes, will not then be judged an heretic.

Now, though the divisions that are amongst sects should be allowed to be never so obstructive of the salvation of souls, yet nevertheless 'adultery, fornication, uncleanness, lasciviousness, idolatry, and such like things cannot be denied to be works of the flesh'; concerning which the apostle has expressly declared, that 'they who do them shall not inherit the kingdom of God' (Gal. 5). Whosoever, therefore, is sincerely solicitous about the kingdom of God, and thinks it his duty to endeavour the enlargement of it amongst men, ought to apply himself with no less care and industry to the rooting out of these immoralities than to the extirpation of sects. But if anyone do otherwise, and whilst he is cruel and implacable towards those that differ from him in opinion, he be indulgent to such iniquities and immoralities as are unbecoming the name of a Christian, let such a one talk never so much of the Church, he plainly demonstrates by his actions that 'tis another kingdom he aims at, and not the advancement of the kingdom of God.

That any man should think fit to cause another man whose salvation he heartily desires to expire in torments, and that even in an unconverted state, would, I confess, seem very strange to me, and, I think, to any other also. But nobody, surely, will ever believe that such a carriage can proceed from charity, love, or good-will. If anyone maintain that men ought to be compelled by fire and sword to profess certain doctrines, and conform to this or that exterior worship, without any regard had unto their morals; if anyone endeavour to convert those that are erroneous unto the faith by forcing them to profess things that they do not believe, and allowing them to practise things that the Gospel does not permit; it cannot be doubted indeed but such a one is desirous to have a numerous assembly joined in the same profession with himself; but that he principally intends by those means to compose a truly Christian Church is altogether incredible. It is not therefore to be wondered at if those who do not really contend for the advancement of the true religion, and of the Church of Christ, make use of arms that do not belong to the Christian warfare. If, like the captain of our salvation, they sincerely desired the good of souls, they would tread in the steps, and follow the perfect example, of that prince of peace who sent out his soldiers to the subduing of nations and gathering them into his Church, not armed with the sword, or other instruments of force, but prepared with the gospel of peace, and with the exemplary holiness of their conversation. This was his method. Though if infidels were to be converted by force, if those that are either blind or obstinate were to be drawn off from their errors by armed soldiers, we know very well that it was much more easy for him to do it with armies of heavenly legions, than for any son of the Church, how potent soever, with all his dragoons.

The toleration of those that differ from others in matters of religion is so agreeable to the Gospel of Jesus Christ, and to the genuine reason of mankind, that it seems monstrous for men to be so blind, as not to perceive the necessity and advantage of it in so clear a light. I will not here tax the pride and ambition of some, the passion and uncharitable zeal of others. These are faults from which human affairs can perhaps scarce ever be perfectly freed; but yet such as nobody will bear the plain imputation of, without covering them with some specious colour, and so pretend to commendation, whilst they are carried away by their own irregular passions. But however, that some may not colour their spirit of persecution and unchristian cruelty with a pretence of care for the public weal and observation of the laws; and that others, under pretence of religion, may not seek impunity for their libertinism and licentiousness; in a word, that none may impose either upon himself or others by the pretences of loyalty and obedience to the prince, or of tenderness and sincerity in the worship of God, I esteem it above all things necessary to distinguish exactly the business of civil government from that of religion, and to settle the just bounds that lie between the one and the other. If this be not done there can be no end put to the controversies that will be always arising between those that have, or at least pretend to have, on the one side, a concernment for the interest of men's souls, and, on the other side, a care of the commonwealth.

The commonwealth seems to me to be a society of men constituted only for the procuring, preserving, and advancing of their own civil interests.

Civil interests I call life, liberty, health, and indolency of body; and the possession of outward things, such as money, lands, houses, furniture, and the like.

It is the duty of the civil magistrate, by the impartial execution of equal laws, to secure unto all the people in general, and to every one of his subjects in particular, the just possession of these things belonging to this life. If anyone presume to violate the laws of public justice and equity, established for the preservation of these things, his presumption is to be checked by the fear of punishment, consisting in the deprivation or diminution of those civil interests, or goods, which otherwise he might and ought to enjoy. But seeing no man does willingly suffer himself to be punished by the deprivation of any part of his goods, and much less of his liberty or life, therefore is the magistrate armed with the force and strength of all his subjects, in order to the punishment of those that violate any other man's rights.

Now that the whole jurisdiction of the magistrate reaches only to these civil concernments, and that all civil power, right, and dominion is bounded and confined to the only care of promoting these things; and that it neither can nor ought in any manner to be extended to the salvation of souls, these following considerations seem unto me abundantly to demonstrate.

First, because the care of souls is not committed to the civil magistrate, any more than to other men. It is not committed unto him, I say, by God; because it appears not that God has ever given any such authority to one man over another as to compel anyone to his religion. Nor can any such power be vested in the magistrate by the consent of the people, because no man can so far abandon the care of his own salvation as blindly to leave it to the choice of any other, whether prince or subject, to prescribe to him what faith or worship he shall embrace. For no man can, if he would, conform his faith to the dictates of another. All the life and power of true religion consists in the inward and full persuasion of the mind; and faith is not faith without believing. Whatever profession we make, to whatever outward worship we conform, if we are not fully satisfied in our own mind that the one is true, and the other well pleasing unto God, such profession and such practice, far from being any furtherance, are indeed great obstacles to our salvation. For in this manner, instead of expiating other sins by the exercise of religion, I say in offering thus unto God Almighty such a worship as we esteem to be displeasing unto him, we add unto the number of our other sins those also of hypocrisy, and contempt of his divine majesty.

In the second place, the care of souls cannot belong to the civil magistrate, because his power consists only in outward force; but true and saving religion consists in the inward persuasion of the mind, without which nothing can be acceptable to God. And such is the nature of the understanding that it cannot be compelled to the belief of anything by outward force. Confiscation of estate, imprisonment, torments, nothing of that nature can have any such efficacy as to make men change the inward judgement that they have framed of things.

It may indeed be alleged that the magistrate may make use of arguments, and thereby draw the heterodox into the way of truth, and procure their salvation. I grant it; but this is common to him with other men. In teaching, instructing, and redressing the errone- ous by reason, he may certainly do what becomes any good man to do. Magistracy does not oblige him to put off either humanity or Christianity. But it is one thing to persuade, another to command; one thing to press with arguments, another with penalties. This the civil power alone has a right to do; to the other good-will is authority enough. Every man has commission to admonish, exhort, convince another of error, and by reasoning to draw him into truth: but to give laws, receive obedience, and compel with the sword, belongs to none but the magistrate. And upon this ground I affirm that the magistrate's power extends not to the establishing of any articles of faith, or forms of worship, by the force of his laws. For laws are of no force at all without penalties, and penalties in this case are absolutely impertinent, because they are not proper to convince the mind. Neither the profession of any articles of faith nor the conformity to any outward form of worship (as has already been said) can be available to the salvation of souls, unless the truth of the one, and the acceptableness of the other unto God, be thoroughly believed by those that so profess and practise. But penalties are no ways capable to produce such belief. It is only light and evidence that can work a change in men's opinions; and that light can in no manner proceed from corporal sufferings, or any other outward penalties.

In the third place, the care of the salvation of men's souls cannot belong to the magistrate, because, though the rigour of laws and the force of penalties were capable to convince and change men's minds, yet would not that help at all to the salvation of their souls. For there being but one truth, one way to heaven, what hopes is there that more men would be led into it, if they had no other rule to follow but the religion of the court, and were put under a necessity to quit the light of their own reason; to oppose the dictates of their own consciences; and blindly to resign up themselves to the will of their governors, and to the religion which either ignorance, ambition, or superstition had chanced to establish in the countries where they were born? In the variety and contradiction of opinions in religion, wherein the princes of the world are as much divided as in their secular interests, the narrow way would be much straitened: one country alone would be in the right, and all the rest of the world would be put under an obligation of following their princes in the ways that lead to destruction; and that which heightens the absurdity, and very ill suits the notion of a deity, men would owe their eternal happiness or misery to the places of their nativity.

These considerations, to omit many others that might have been urged to the same purpose, seem unto me sufficient to conclude that all the power of civil government relates only to men's civil interests, is confined to the care of the things of this world, and has nothing to do with the world to come.

Let us now consider what a Church is. A Church, then, I take to be a voluntary society of men, joining themselves together of their own accord in order to the public worshipping of God, in such a manner as they judge acceptable to him, and effectual to the salvation of their souls.

I say it is a free and voluntary society. Nobody is born a member of any Church; otherwise the religion of parents would descend unto children by the same right of inheritance as their temporal estates, and everyone would hold his faith by the same tenure he does his lands; than which nothing can be imagined more absurd. Thus therefore that matter stands: no man by nature is bound unto any particular Church or sect, but everyone joins himself voluntarily to that society in which he believes he has found that profession and worship which is truly acceptable to God. The hopes of salvation, as it was the only cause of his entrance into that communion, so it can be the only reason of his stay there. For if afterwards he discover anything either erroneous in the doctrine, or incongruous in the worship of that society to which he has joined himself, why should it not be as free for him to go out as it was to enter? No member of a religious society can be tied with any other bonds but what proceed from the certain expectation of eternal life. A Church then is a society of members voluntarily uniting to this end.

It follows now that we consider what is the power of this Church, and unto what laws it is subject.

Forasmuch as no society, how free soever, or upon whatsoever slight occasion instituted (whether of philosophers for learning, of merchants for commerce, or of men of leisure for mutual conversation and discourse), no Church or company, I say, can in the least subsist and hold together, but will presently dissolve and break to pieces, unless it be regulated by some laws, and the members all consent to observe some order. Place and time of meeting must be agreed on; rules for admitting and excluding members must be established; distinction of officers and putting things into a regular course, and suchlike, cannot be omitted. But since the joining together of several members into this Church society, as has already been demonstrated, is absolutely free and spontaneous, it necessarily follows that the right of making its laws can belong to none but the society itself, or at least (which is the same thing) to those whom the society by common consent has authorized thereunto.

Some perhaps may object that no such society can be said to be a true Church, unless it have in it a bishop, or presbyter, with ruling authority derived from the very apostles, and continued down unto the present times by an uninterrupted succession.

To these I answer, in the first place: let them show me the edict by which Christ has imposed that law upon his Church. And let not any man think me impertinent if, in a thing of this consequence, I require that the terms of that edict be very express and positive. For the promise he has made us that 'wheresoever two or three are gathered together in his name, he will be in the midst of them' (Matt. 18.20) seems to imply the contrary. Whether such an assembly want anything necessary to a true Church, pray do you consider.

Certain I am that nothing can be there wanting unto the salvation of souls, which is sufficient to our purpose.

Next, pray observe how great have always been the divisions amongst even those who lay so much stress upon the divine institution and continued succession of a certain order of rulers in the Church. Now their very dissension unavoidably puts us upon a necessity of deliberating, and consequently allows a liberty of choosing that which, upon consideration, we prefer.

And, in the last place, I consent that these men have a ruler of their Church, established by such a long series of succession as they judge necessary, provided I may have liberty at the same time to join myself to that society in which I am persuaded those things are to be found which are necessary to the salvation of my soul. In this manner ecclesiastical liberty will be preserved on all sides, and no man will have a legislator imposed upon him, but whom himself has chosen.

But since men are so solicitous about the true Church, I would only ask them, here by the way, if it be not more agreeable to the Church of Christ to make the conditions of her communion consist in such things, and such things only, as the Holy Spirit has in the Holy Scripture declared, in express words, to be necessary to salvation. I ask, I say, whether this be not more agreeable to the Church of Christ, than for men to impose their own inventions and interpretations upon others, as if they were of divine authority, and to establish by ecclesiastical laws as absolutely necessary to the profession of Christianity, such things as the Holy Scriptures do either not mention, or at least not expressly command? Whosoever requires those things in order to ecclesiastical communion which Christ does not require in order to life eternal, he may perhaps indeed constitute a society accommodated to his own opinion and his own advantage, but how that can be called the Church of Christ which is established upon laws that are not his, and which excludes such persons from its communion as he will one day receive into the Kingdom of Heaven, I understand not. But this being not a proper place to inquire into the marks of the true Church, I will only mind those that contend so earnestly for the decrees of their own society, and that cry out continually 'The Church! The Church!', with as much noise, and perhaps upon the same principle, as the Ephesian silversmiths did for their Diana; this, I say, I desire to mind them of: that the Gospel frequently declares that the true disciples of Christ must suffer persecution; but that the Church of Christ should persecute others, and force others by fire and sword to embrace her faith and doctrine, I could never yet find in any of the books of the New Testament.

The end of a religious society, as has already been said, is the public worship of God, and, by means thereof, the acquisition of eternal life. All discipline ought therefore to tend to that end, and all ecclesiastical laws to be thereunto confined. Nothing ought nor can be transacted in this society relating to the possession of civil and worldly goods. No force is here to be made use of, upon any occasion whatsoever. For force belongs wholly to the civil magistrate, and the possession of all outward goods is subject to his jurisdiction.

But it may be asked, by what means then shall ecclesiastical laws be established, if they must be thus destitute of all compulsive power? I answer, they must be established by means suitable to the nature of such things, whereof the external profession and observation, if not proceeding from a thorough conviction and approbation of the mind, is altogether useless and unprofitable. The arms by which the members of this society are to be kept within their duty are exhortations, admonitions, and advices. If by these means the offenders will not be reclaimed, and the erroneous convinced, there remains nothing further to be done, but that such stubborn and obstinate persons, who give no ground to hope for their reformation, should be cast out and separated from the society. This is the last and utmost force of ecclesiastical authority: no other punishment can thereby be inflicted than that, the relation ceasing between the body and the member which is cut off, the person so condemned ceases to be a part of that Church.

These things being thus determined, let us inquire in the next place how far the duty of toleration extends, and what is required from everyone by it.

And first, I hold that no Church is bound by the duty of toleration to retain any such person in her bosom as, after admonition, continues obstinately to offend against the laws of the society.

For these being the condition of communion, and the bond of the society, if the breach of them were permitted without any animadversion, the society would immediately be thereby dissolved. But nevertheless, in all such cases care is to be taken that the sentence of excommunication, and the execution thereof, carry with it no rough usage, of word or action, whereby the ejected person may any wise be damnified in body or estate. For all force (as has often been said) belongs only to the magistrate, nor ought any private persons, at any time, to use force, unless it be in self-defence against unjust violence. Excommunication neither does, nor can, deprive the excommunicated person of any of those civil goods that he formerly possessed. All those things belong to the civil government, and are under the magistrate's protection. The whole force of excommunication consists only in this, that the resolution of the society in that respect being declared, the union that was between the body and some member comes thereby to be dissolved, and, that relation ceasing, the participation of some certain things which the society communicated to its members, and unto which no man has any civil right, comes also to cease. For there is no civil injury done unto the excommunicated person by the Church minister's refusing him that bread and wine, in the celebration of the Lord's Supper, which was not bought with his, but other men's money.

Secondly, no private person has any right, in any manner, to prejudice another person in his civil enjoyments because he is of another Church or religion. All the rights and franchises that belong to him as a man, or as a denizen, are inviolably to be preserved to him. These are not the business of religion. No violence nor injury is to be offered him, whether he be Christian or pagan. Nay we must not content ourselves with the narrow measures of bare justice: charity, bounty, and liberality must be added to it. This the Gospel enjoins, this reason directs, and this that natural fellowship we are born into requires of us. If any man err from the right way, it is his own misfortune, no injury to thee: nor, therefore, art thou to punish him in the things of this life because thou supposest he will be miserable in that which is to come.

What I say concerning the mutual toleration of private persons differing from one another in religion, I understand also of particular Churches; which stand, as it were, in the same relation to each other as private persons among themselves, nor has any one of them any manner of jurisdiction over any other, no not even when the civil magistrate (as it sometimes happens) comes to be of this or the other communion. For the civil government can give no new right to the Church, nor the Church to the civil government. So that whether the magistrate join himself to any Church or separate from it, the Church remains always as it was before, a free and voluntary society. It neither acquires the power of the sword by the magistrate's coming to it, nor does it lose the right of instruction and excommunication by his going from it. This is the fundamental and immutable right of a spontaneous society, that it has power to remove any of its members who transgress the rules of its institution. But it cannot, by the accession of any new members, acquire any right of jurisdiction over those that are not joined with it. And therefore peace, equity, and friendship are always mutually to be observed by particular Churches, in the same manner as by private persons, without any pretence of superiority or jurisdiction over one another.

That the thing may be made yet clearer by an example, let us suppose two Churches, the one of Arminians, the other of Calvinists, residing in the city of Constantinople. Will anyone say that either of these Churches has right to deprive the members of the other of their estates and liberty (as we see practised elsewhere) because of their differing from it in some doctrines or ceremonies? Whilst the Turks in the meanwhile silently stand by, and laugh to see with what inhuman cruelty Christians thus rage against Christians? But if one of these Churches hath this power of treating the other ill, I ask which of them it is to whom that power belongs, and by what right? It will be answered undoubtedly, that it is the orthodox Church which has the right of authority over the erroneous or heretical. This is, in great and specious words, to say just nothing at all. For every Church is orthodox to itself; to other, erroneous or heretical. Whatsoever any Church believes, it believes to be true; and the contrary thereunto it pronounces to be error. So that the controversy between these Churches about the truth of their doctrines, and the purity of their worship, is on both sides equal; nor is there any judge, either at Constantinople or elsewhere upon earth, by whose sentence it can be determined. The decision of that question belongs only to the supreme judge of all men, to whom also alone belongs the punishment of the erroneous. In the meanwhile, let those men consider how heinously they sin, who, adding injustice, if not to their error yet certainly to their pride, do rashly and arrogantly take upon them to misuse the servants of another master, who are not at all accountable to them.

Nay, further: if it could be manifest which of these two dissenting Churches were in the right way, there would not accrue thereby to the orthodox any right of destroying the other. For Churches have neither any jurisdiction in worldly matters, nor are fire and sword any proper instruments wherewith to convince men's minds of error, and inform them of the truth. Let us suppose, nevertheless, that the civil magistrate inclined to favour one of them, and to put his sword into their hands, that (by his consent) they might chastise the dissenters as they pleased. Will any man say that any right can be derived unto a Christian Church, over its brethren, from a Turkish Emperor? An infidel, who has himself no authority to punish Christians for the articles of their faith, cannot confer such an authority upon any society of Christians, nor give unto them a right which he has not himself. This would be the case at Constantinople. And the reason of the thing is the same in any Christian kingdom. The civil power is the same in every place; nor can that power, in the hands of a Christian prince, confer any greater authority upon the Church, than in the hands of a heathen; which is to say, just none at all.

Nevertheless, it is worthy to be observed, and lamented, that the most violent of these defenders of the truth, the opposers of errors, the exclaimers against schism, do hardly ever let loose this their zeal for God, with which they are so warmed and inflamed, unless where they have the civil magistrate on their side. But so soon as ever court favour has given them the better end of the staff, and they begin to feel themselves the stronger, then presently peace and charity are to be laid aside; otherwise they are religiously to be observed. Where they have not the power to carry on persecution, and to become masters, there they desire to live upon fair terms, and preach up toleration. When they are not strengthened with the civil power, then they can bear most patiently, and unmovedly, the contagion of idolatry, superstition, and heresy in their neighbourhood; of which, in other occasions, the interest of religion makes them to be extremely apprehensive. They do not forwardly attack those errors which are in fashion at court, or are countenanced by the government. Here they can be content to spare their arguments: which yet (with their leave) is the only right method of propagating truth, which has no such way of prevailing, as when strong arguments and good reason are joined with the softness of civility and good usage.

Nobody therefore, in fine, neither single persons, nor Churches, nay, nor even commonwealths, have any just title to invade the civil rights and worldly goods of each other, upon pretence of religion. Those that are of another opinion would do well to consider with themselves how pernicious a seed of discord and war, how powerful a provocation to endless hatreds, rapines, and slaughters they thereby furnish unto mankind. No peace and security, no, not so much as common friendship, can ever be established or preserved amongst men, so long as this opinion prevails, that dominion is founded in grace, and that religion is to be propagated by force of arms.

In the third place, let us see what the duty of toleration requires from those who are distinguished from the rest of mankind (from the laity, as they please to call us) by some ecclesiastical character and office, whether they be bishops, priests, presbyters, ministers, or however else dignified or distinguished. It is not my business to inquire here into the original of the power or dignity of the clergy. This only I say, that whencesoever their authority be sprung, since it is ecclesiastical, it ought to be confined within the bounds of the Church, nor can it in any manner be extended to civil affairs; because the Church itself is a thing absolutely separate and distinct from the commonwealth. The boundaries on both sides are fixed and immovable. He jumbles heaven and earth together, the things most remote and opposite, who mixes these two societies, which are in their original, end, business, and in everything perfectly distinct, and infinitely different from each other. No man therefore, with whatsoever ecclesiastical office he be dignified, can deprive another man that is not of his Church and faith, either of liberty, or of any part of his worldly goods, upon the account of that difference which is between them in religion. For whatsoever is not lawful to the whole Church cannot, by any ecclesiastical right, become lawful to any of its members.

But this is not all. It is not enough that ecclesiastical men abstain from violence and rapine, and all manner of persecution. He that pretends to be a successor of the apostles, and takes upon him the office of teaching, is obliged also to admonish his hearers of the duties of peace and good-will towards all men; as well towards the erroneous as the orthodox; towards those that differ from them in faith and worship, as well as towards those that agree with them therein. And he ought industriously to exhort all men, whether private persons or magistrates (if any such there be in his Church), to charity, meekness, and toleration; and diligently endeavour to allay and temper all that heat, and unreasonable averseness of mind, which either any man's fiery zeal for his own sect, or the craft of others, has kindled against dissenters. I will not undertake to represent how happy and how great would be the fruit, both in Church and state, if the pulpits everywhere sounded with this doctrine of peace and toleration; lest I should seem to reflect too severely upon those men whose dignity I desire not to detract from, nor would have it diminished either by others or themselves. But this I say, that thus it ought to be. And if anyone that professes himself to be a minister of the word of God, a preacher of the Gospel of peace, teach otherwise, he either understands not, or neglects, the business of his calling, and shall one day give account thereof unto the Prince of Peace.

If Christians are to be admonished that they abstain from all manner of revenge, even after repeated provocations and multiplied injuries, how much more ought they who suffer nothing, who have had no harm done them, forbear violence, and abstain from all manner of ill-usage towards those from whom they have received none! This caution and temper they ought certainly to use towards those who mind only their own business, and are solicitous for nothing but that (whatever men think of them) they may worship God in that manner which they are persuaded is acceptable to him, and in which they have the strongest hopes of eternal salvation. In private domestic affairs, in the management of estates, in the conservation of bodily health, every man may consider what suits his own conveniency, and follow what course he likes best. No man complains of the ill-management of his neighbour's affairs. No man is angry with another for an error committed in sowing his land, or in marrying his daughter. Nobody corrects a spendthrift for consuming his substance in taverns. Let any man pull down, or build, or make whatsoever expenses he pleases, nobody murmurs, nobody controls him; he has his liberty. But if any man do not frequent the Church, if he do not there conform his behaviour exactly to the accustomed ceremonies, or if he brings not his children to be initiated in the sacred mysteries of this or the other congregation, this immediately causes an uproar, and the neighbourhood is filled with noise and clamour. Everyone is ready to be the avenger of so great a crime. And the zealots hardly have patience to refrain from violence and rapine so long till the cause be heard, and the poor man be, according to form, condemned to the loss of liberty, goods, or life.

Oh that our ecclesiastical orators, of every sect, would apply themselves with all the strength of arguments that they are able, to the confounding of men's errors! But let them spare their persons. Let them not supply their want of reasons with the instruments of force which belong to another jurisdiction, and do ill become a churchman's hands. Let them not call in the magistrate's authority to the aid of their eloquence, or learning; lest, perhaps, whilst they pretend only love for the truth, this their intemperate zeal, breathing nothing but fire and sword, betray their ambition, and show that what they desire is temporal dominion. For it will be very difficult to persuade men of sense, that he, who with dry eyes, and satisfaction of mind, can deliver his brother unto the executioner to be burnt alive, does sincerely and heartily concern himself to save that brother from the flames of hell in the world to come.

In the last place, let us now consider what is the magistrate's duty in the business of toleration: which certainly is very considerable.

We have already proved that the care of souls does not belong to the magistrate: not a magisterial care, I mean, (if I may so call it) which consists in prescribing by laws, and compelling by punishments. But a charitable care, which consists in teaching, admonishing, and persuading, cannot be denied unto any man. The care, therefore, of every man's soul belongs unto himself, and is to be left unto himself. But what if he neglect the care of his soul? I answer: What if he neglect the care of his health, or of his estate, which things are nearlier related to the government of the magistrate than the other? Will the magistrate provide by an express law, that such a one shall not become poor or sick? Laws provide, as much as is possible, that the goods and health of subjects be not injured by the fraud or violence of others; they do not guard them from the negligence or ill-husbandry of the possessors themselves. No man can be forced to be rich or healthful, whether he will or no. Nay, God himself will not save men against their wills. Let us suppose, however, that some prince were desirous to force his subjects to accumulate riches, or to preserve the health and strength of their bodies. Shall it be provided by law, that they must consult none but Roman physicians, and shall everyone be bound to live according to their prescriptions? What, shall no potion, no broth, be taken, but what is prepared either in the Vatican, suppose, or in a Geneva shop? Or, to make these subjects rich, shall they all be obliged by law to become merchants, or musicians? Or, shall everyone turn victualler, or smith, because there are some that maintain their families plentifully, and grow rich in those professions?

But it may be said, there are a thousand ways to wealth, but only one way to heaven. 'Tis well said indeed, especially by those that plead for compelling men into this or the other way. For if there were several ways that lead thither, there would not be so much as a pretence left for compulsion. But now if I be marching on with my utmost vigour, in that way which, according to the sacred geography, leads straight to Jerusalem, why am I beaten and ill-used by others; because, perhaps, I wear not buskins; because my hair is not of the right cut; because perhaps I have not been dipped [i.e. baptized] in the right fashion; because I eat flesh upon the road, or some other food which agrees with my stomach; because I avoid certain byways, which seem unto me to lead into briars or precipices; because amongst the several paths that are in the same road, I choose that to walk in which seems to be the straightest and cleanest; because I avoid to keep company with some travellers that are less grave, and others that are more sour than they ought to be; or, in fine, because I follow a guide that either is, or is not, clothed in white, and crowned with a mitre? Certainly, if we consider right, we shall find that for the most part they are such frivolous things as these that (without any prejudice to religion or the salvation of souls, if not accompanied with superstition or hypocrisy) might either be observed or omitted; I say they are such like things as these, which breed implacable enmities amongst Christian brethren, who are all agreed in the substantial and truly fundamental part of religion.

But let us grant unto these zealots, who condemn all things that are not of their mode, that from these circumstances arise different ends. What shall we conclude from thence? There is only one of these which is the true way to eternal happiness. But in this great variety of ways that men follow, it is still doubted which is this right one. Now neither the care of the commonwealth, nor the right of enacting laws, does discover this way that leads to heaven more certainly to the magistrate, than every private man's search and study discovers it unto himself. I have a weak body, sunk under a languishing disease, for which (I suppose) there is one only remedy, but that unknown. Does it therefore belong unto the magistrate to prescribe me a remedy, because there is but one, and because it is unknown? Because there is but one way for me to escape death, will it therefore be safe for me to do whatsoever the magistrate ordains? Those things that every man ought sincerely to inquire into himself, and by meditation, study, search, and his own endeavours, attain the knowledge of, cannot be looked upon as the peculiar possession of any one sort of men. Princes indeed are born superior unto other men in power, but in nature equal. Neither the right nor the art of ruling does necessarily carry along with it the certain knowledge of other things; and least of all of the true religion. For if it were so, how could it come to pass that the lords of the earth should differ so vastly as they do in religious matters? But let us grant that it is probable the way to eternal life may be better known by a prince than by his subjects; or at least, that in this incertitude of things, the safest and most commodious way for private persons is to follow his dictates. You will say, what then? If he should bid you follow merchandise for your livelihood, would you decline that course for fear it should not succeed? I answer: I would turn merchant upon the prince's command, because in case I should have ill-success in trade, he is abundantly able to make up my loss some other way. If it be true, as he pretends, that he desires I should thrive and grow rich, he can set me up again when unsuccessful voyages have broke me. But this is not the case, in the things that regard the life to come. If there I take a wrong course, if in that respect I am once undone, it is not in the magistrate's power to repair my loss, to ease my suffering, or to restore me in any measure, much less entirely, to a good estate. What security can be given for the Kingdom of Heaven?

Perhaps some will say that they do not suppose this infallible judgement, that all men are bound to follow in the affairs of religion, to be in the civil magistrate, but in the Church. What the Church has determined, that the civil magistrate orders to be observed; and he provides by his authority that nobody shall either act or believe, in the business of religion, otherwise than the Church teaches. So that the judgement of those things is in the Church. The magistrate himself yields obedience thereunto, and requires the like obedience from others. I answer: Who sees not how frequently the name of the Church, which was so venerable in the time of the apostles, has been made use of to throw dust in people's eyes, in following ages? But however, in the present case it helps us not. The one only narrow way which leads to heaven is not better known to the magistrate than to private persons, and therefore I cannot safely take him for my guide, who may probably be as ignorant of the way as myself, and who certainly is less concerned for my salvation than I myself am. Amongst so many kings of the Jews, how many of them were there whom any Israelite, thus blindly following, had not fallen into idolatry, and thereby into destruction? Yet nevertheless, you bid me be of good courage, and tell me that all is now safe and secure, because the magistrate does not now enjoin the observance of his own decrees in matters of religion, but only the decrees of the Church. Of what Church, I beseech you? Of, that certainly, which likes him best. As if he that compels me by laws and penalties to enter into this or the other Church did not interpose his own judgement in the matter. What difference is there whether he lead me himself, or deliver me over to be led by others? I depend both ways upon his will, and it is he that determines both ways of my eternal state. Would an Israelite, that had worshipped Baal upon the command of his king, have been in any better condition, because somebody had told him that the king ordered nothing in religion upon his own head, nor commanded anything to be done by his subjects in divine worship, but what was approved by the counsel of priests, and declared to be of divine right by the doctors of their Church? If the religion of any Church become therefore true and saving, because the head of that sect, the prelates and priests, and those of that tribe, do all of them, with all their might, extol and praise it, what religion can ever be accounted erroneous, false, and destructive? I am doubtful concerning the doctrine of the Socinians; I am suspicious of the way of worship practised by the papists or Lutherans; will it be ever a jot the safer for me to join unto the one or the other of those Churches, upon the magistrate's command, because he commands nothing in religion but by the authority and counsel of the doctors of that Church?

But, to speak the truth, we must acknowledge that the Church (if a convention of clergymen, making canons, must be called by that name) is for the most part more apt to be influenced by the court, than the court by the Church. How the Church was under the vicissitude of orthodox and Arian emperors is very well known. Or, if those things be too remote, the English history affords us fresher examples, in the reigns of Henry the 8th, Edward the 6th, Mary, and Elizabeth, how easily and smoothly the clergy changed their decrees, their articles of faith, their form of worship, everything, according to the inclination of those kings and queens. Yet were those kings and queens of such different minds, in point of religion, and enjoined thereupon such different things, that no man in his wits (I had almost said none but an atheist) will presume to say that any sincere and upright worshipper of God could, with a safe conscience, obey their several decrees. To conclude: it is the same thing whether a king that prescribes laws to another man's religion pretend to do it by his own judgement, or by the ecclesiastical authority and advice of others. The decisions of churchmen, whose differences and disputes are sufficiently known, cannot be any sounder, or safer, than his. Nor can all their suffrages joined together add any new strength unto the civil power. Though this also must be taken notice of, that princes seldom have any regard to the suffrages of ecclesiastics that are not favourers of their own faith and way of worship.

But after all, the principal consideration, and which absolutely determines this controversy, is this: although the magistrate's opinion in religion be sound, and the way that he appoints be truly evangelical, yet if I be not thoroughly persuaded thereof in my own mind, there will be no safety for me in following it. No way whatsoever that I shall walk in, against the dictates of my conscience, will ever bring me to the mansions of the blessed. I may grow rich by an art that I take not delight in; I may be cured of some disease by remedies that I have not faith in; but I cannot be saved by a religion that I distrust, and by a worship that I abhor. It is in vain for an unbeliever to take up the outward show of another man's profession. Faith only, and inward sincerity, are the things that procure acceptance with God. The most likely and most approved remedy can have no effect upon the patient, if his stomach reject it as soon as taken. And you will in vain cram a medicine down a sick man's throat, which his particular constitution will be sure to turn into poison. In a word: whatsoever may be doubtful in religion, yet this at least is certain, that no religion which I believe not to be true, can be either true or profitable unto me. In vain therefore do princes compel their subjects to come into their Church communion, under pretence of saving their souls. If they believe, they will come of their own accord; if they believe not, their coming will nothing avail them. How great soever, in fine, may be the pretence of good-will, and charity, and concern for the salvation of men's souls, men cannot be forced to be saved whether they will or no. And therefore, when all is done, they must be left to their own consciences.

Having thus at length freed men from all dominion over one another in matters of religion, let us now consider what they are to do. All men know and acknowledge that God ought to be publicly worshipped. Why otherwise do they compel one another unto the public assemblies? Men therefore constituted in this liberty are to enter into some religious society, that they may meet together, not only for mutual edification, but to own to the world that they worship God, and offer unto his Divine Majesty such service as they themselves are not ashamed of, and such as they think not unworthy of him, nor unacceptable to him; and finally that by the purity of doctrine, holiness of life, and decent form of worship, they may draw others unto the love of the true religion, and perform such other things in religion as cannot be done by each private man apart.

These religious societies I call Churches: and these I say the magistrate ought to tolerate. For the business of these assemblies of the people is nothing but what is lawful for every man in particular to take care of, I mean the salvation of their souls; nor, in this case, is there any difference between the national Church and other separated congregations.

But as in every Church there are two things especially to be considered – the outward form and rites of worship, and the doctrines and articles of faith – these things must be handled each distinctly; that so the whole matter of toleration may the more clearly be understood.

Concerning outward worship, I say (in the first place) that the magistrate has no power to enforce by law, either in his own Church, or much less in another, the use of any rites or ceremonies whatsoever in the worship of God. And this, not only because these Churches are free societies, but because whatsoever is practised in the worship of God is only so far justifiable as it is believed by those that practise it to be acceptable unto him. Whatsoever is not done with that assurance of faith, is neither well in itself, nor can it be acceptable to God. To impose such things, therefore, upon any people, contrary to their own judgement, is in effect to command them to offend God; which, considering that the end of all religion is to please him, and that liberty is essentially necessary to that end, appears to be absurd beyond expression.

But perhaps it may be concluded from hence, that I deny unto the magistrate all manner of power about indifferent things; which, if it be not granted, the whole subject-matter of law-making is taken away. No, I readily grant that indifferent things, and perhaps none but such, are subjected to the legislative power. But it does not therefore follow that the magistrate may ordain whatsoever he pleases concerning anything that is indifferent. The public good is the rule and measure of all law-making. If a thing be not useful to the commonwealth, though it be never so indifferent, it may not presently be established by law.

But further: things never so indifferent in their own nature, when they are brought into the Church and worship of God, are removed out of the reach of the magistrate's jurisdiction; because in that use they have no connection at all with civil affairs. The only business of the Church is the salvation of souls: and it no way concerns the commonwealth, or any member of it, that this or the other ceremony be there made use of. Neither the use nor the omission of any ceremonies, in those religious assemblies, does either advantage or prejudice the life, liberty, or estate of any man. For example, let it be granted that the washing of an infant with water is in itself an indifferent thing. Let it be granted also, that if the magistrate understand such washing to be profitable to the curing or preventing of any disease that children are subject unto, and esteem the matter weighty enough to be taken care of by a law, in that case he may order it to be done. But will anyone therefore say, that a magistrate has the same right to ordain, by law, that all children shall be baptized by priests, in the sacred font, in order to the purification of their souls? The extreme difference of these two cases is visible to everyone at first sight. Or let us apply the last case to the child of a Jew, and the thing will speak itself. For what hinders but a Christian magistrate may have subjects that are Jews? Now if we acknowledge that such an injury may not be done unto a Jew, as to compel him, against his own opinion, to practise in his religion a thing that is in its nature indifferent, how can we maintain that anything of this kind may be done to a Christian?

Again: things in their own nature indifferent cannot, by any human authority, be made any part of the worship of God; for this very reason, because they are indifferent. For since indifferent things are not capable, by any virtue of their own, to propitiate the Deity, no human power or authority can confer on them so much dignity and excellency as to enable them to do it. In the common affairs of life, that use of indifferent things which God has not forbidden is free and lawful, and therefore in those things human authority has place. But it is not so in matters of religion. Things indifferent are not otherwise lawful in the worship of God than as they are instituted by God himself; and as he, by some positive command, has ordained them to be made a part of that worship which he will vouchsafe to accept of at the hands of poor sinful men. Nor when an incensed deity shall ask us, 'Who has required these or such-like things at your hands?' will it be enough to answer him, that the magistrate commanded them. If civil jurisdiction extended thus far, what might not lawfully be introduced into religion? What hodge-podge of ceremonies, what superstitious inventions, built upon the magistrate's authority, might not (against conscience) be imposed upon the worshippers of God? For the greatest part of these ceremonies and superstitions consists in the religious use of such things as are in their own nature indifferent: nor are they sinful upon any other account, than because God is not the author of them. The sprinkling of water, and the use of bread and wine, are both in their own nature, and in the ordinary occasions of life, altogether indifferent. Will any man therefore say that these things could have been introduced into religion, and made a part of divine worship, if not by divine institution? If any human authority or civil power could have done this, why might it not also enjoin the eating of fish and drinking of ale in the holy banquet, as a part of divine worship? Why not the sprinkling of the blood of beasts in Churches, and expiations by water or fire, and abundance more of this kind? But these things, how indifferent soever they be in common uses, when they come to be annexed unto divine worship, without divine authority, they are as abominable to God, as the sacrifice of a dog. And why a dog so abominable? What difference is there between a dog and a goat, in respect of the divine nature, equally and infinitely distant from all affinity with matter; unless it be that God required the use of the one in his worship, and not of the other? We see therefore that indifferent things, how much soever they be under the power of the civil magistrate, yet cannot upon that pretence be introduced into religion, and imposed upon religious assemblies, because in the worship of God they wholly cease to be indifferent. He that worships God does it with design to please him and procure his favour. But that cannot be done by him who, upon the command of another, offers unto God that which he knows will be displeasing to him, because not commanded by himself. This is not to please God, or appease his wrath, but willingly and knowingly to provoke him by a manifest contempt, which is a thing absolutely repugnant to the nature and end of worship.

But it will here be asked: If nothing belonging to divine worship be left to human discretion, how is it then that Churches themselves have the power of ordering anything about the time and place of worship, and the like? To this I answer that in religious worship we must distinguish between what is part of the worship itself, and what is but a circumstance. That is a part of the worship which is believed to be appointed by God, and to be well-pleasing to him, and therefore that is necessary. Circumstances are such things which, though in general they cannot be separated from worship, yet the particular instances or modifications of them are not determined; and therefore they are indifferent. Of this sort are the time and place of worship, the habit and posture of him that worships. These are circumstances, and perfectly indifferent, where God has not given any express command about them. For example, amongst the Jews, the time and place of their worship, and the habits of those that officiated in it, were not mere circumstances, but a part of the worship itself; in which, if anything were defective, or different from that institution, they could not hope that it would be accepted by God. But these, to Christians under the liberty of the Gospel, are mere circumstances of worship, which the prudence of every Church may bring into such use as shall be judged most subservient to the end of order, decency, and edification. Though, even under the Gospel also, those who believe the first or the seventh day to be set apart by God, and consecrated still to his worship, to them that portion of time is not a simple circumstance, but a real part of divine worship, which can neither be changed nor neglected.

In the next place: as the magistrate has no power to impose by his laws the use of any rites and ceremonies in any Church, so neither has he any power to forbid the use of such rites and ceremonies as are already received, approved, and practised by any Church, because if he did so, he would destroy the Church itself, the end of whose institution is only to worship God with freedom, after its own manner.

You will say, by this rule, if some congregations should have a mind to sacrifice infants, or (as the primitive Christians were falsely accused) lustfully pollute themselves in promiscuous uncleanness, or practise any other such heinous enormities, is the magistrate obliged to tolerate them, because they are committed in a religious assembly? I answer, No. These things are not lawful in the ordinary course of life, nor in any private house; and therefore neither are they so in the worship of God, or in any religious meeting. But indeed if any people congregated upon account of religion should be desirous to sacrifice a calf, I deny that that ought to be prohibited by a law. Meliboeus, whose calf it is, may lawfully kill his own calf at home, and burn any part of it that he thinks fit, for no injury is thereby done to anyone, no prejudice to another man's goods. And for the same reason he may kill his calf also in a religious meeting. Whether the doing so be well-pleasing to God or no, it is their part to consider that do it. The part of the magistrate is only to take care that the commonwealth receive no prejudice, and that there be no injury done to any man, either in life or estate. And thus what may be spent on a feast, may be spent on a sacrifice. But if peradventure such were the state of things, that the interest of the commonwealth required all slaughter of beasts should be forborne for some while, in order to the increasing of the stock of cattle, that had been destroyed by some extraordinary murrain, who sees not that the magistrate, in such a case, may forbid all his subjects to kill any calves for any use whatsoever? Only 'tis to be observed that in this case the law is not made about a religious but a political matter; nor is the sacrifice but the slaughter of calves thereby prohibited.

By this we see what difference there is between the Church and the commonwealth. Whatsoever is lawful in the commonwealth cannot be prohibited by the magistrate in the Church. Whatsoever is permitted unto any of his subjects for their ordinary use, neither can nor ought to be forbidden by him to any sect of people for their religious uses. If any man may lawfully take bread or wine, either sitting or kneeling, in his own house, the law ought not to abridge him of the same liberty in his religious worship; though in the Church the use of bread and wine be very different, and be there applied to the mysteries of faith, and rites of divine worship. But those things that are prejudicial to the commonweal of a people in their ordinary use, and are therefore forbidden by laws, those things ought not to be permitted to Churches in their sacred rites. Only the magistrate ought always to be very careful that he do not misuse his authority, to the oppression of any Church, under pretence of public good.

It may be said: What if a Church be idolatrous, is that also to be tolerated by the magistrate? In answer I ask: What power can be given to the magistrate for the suppression of an idolatrous Church, which may not, in time and place, be made use of to the ruin of an orthodox one? For it must be remembered that the civil power is the same everywhere, and the religion of every prince is orthodox to himself. If, therefore, such a power be granted unto the civil magistrate in spirituals, as that at Geneva (for example), he may extirpate, by violence and blood, the religion which is there reputed idolatrous; by the same rule another magistrate, in some neighbouring country, may oppress the reformed religion; and, in India, the Christian. The civil power can either change everything in religion, according to the prince's pleasure, or it can change nothing. If it be once permitted to introduce anything into religion, by the means of laws and penalties, there can be no bounds put to it; but it will in the same manner be lawful to alter everything, according to that rule of truth which the magistrate has framed unto himself. No man whatsoever ought, therefore, to be deprived of his terrestrial enjoyments upon account of his religion. Not even Americans, subjected unto a Christian prince, are to be punished either in body or goods for not embracing our faith and worship. If they are persuaded that they please God in observing the rites of their own country, and that they shall obtain happiness by that means, they are to be left unto God and themselves. Let us trace this matter to the bottom. Thus it is: an inconsiderable and weak number of Christians, destitute of everything, arrive in a pagan country. These foreigners beseech the inhabitants, by the bowels of humanity, that they would succour them with the necessaries of life. Those necessaries are given them; habitations are granted; and they all join together and grow up into one body of people. The Christian religion by this means takes root in that country, and spreads itself; but does not suddenly grow the strongest. While things are in this condition, peace, friendship, faith, and equal justice are preserved amongst them. At length the magistrate becomes a Christian, and by that means their party becomes the most powerful. Then immediately all compacts are to be broken, all civil rights to be violated, that idolatry may be extirpated. And unless these innocent pagans, strict observers of the rules of equity and of the law of nature, and no ways offending against the laws of the society, I say unless they will forsake their ancient religion, and embrace a new and strange one, they are to be turned out of the lands and possessions of their forefathers, and perhaps deprived of life itself. Then at last it appears what zeal for the Church, joined with the desire of dominion, is capable to produce; and how easily the pretence of religion, and of the care of souls, serves for a cloak to covetousness, rapine, and ambition.

Now whosoever maintains that idolatry is to be rooted out of any place by laws, punishments, fire, and sword, may apply this story to himself, for the reason of the thing is equal, both in America and Europe. And neither pagans there, nor any dissenting Christians here, can with any right be deprived of their worldly goods by the predominating faction of a Court-Church; nor are any civil rights to be either changed or violated upon account of religion in one place more than another.

But idolatry (say some) is a sin, and therefore not to be tolerated. If they said it were therefore to be avoided, the inference were good. But it does not follow that, because it is a sin, it ought therefore to be punished by the magistrate. For it does not belong unto the magistrate to make use of his sword in punishing everything, indifferently, that he takes to be a sin against God. Covetousness, uncharitableness, idleness, and many other things are sins, by the consent of all men, which yet no man ever said were to be punished by the magistrate. The reason is, because they are not prejudicial to other men's rights, nor do they break the public peace of societies. Nay even the sins of lying and perjury are nowhere punishable by laws; unless in certain cases, in which the real turpitude of the thing, and the offence against God, are not considered, but only the injury done unto men's neighbours, and to the commonwealth. And what if in another country, to a Mahometan or a pagan prince, the Christian religion seem false and offensive to God; may not the Christians for the same reason, and after the same manner, be extirpated there?

But it may be urged further, that by the law of Moses idolaters were to be rooted out. True indeed, by the law of Moses. But that is not obligatory to us Christians. Nobody pretends that everything, generally, enjoined by the law of Moses, ought to be practised by

Christians. But there is nothing more frivolous than that common distinction of moral, judicial, and ceremonial law, which men ordinarily make use of. For no positive law whatsoever can oblige any people but those to whom it is given. 'Hear O Israel' sufficiently restrains the obligation of the law of Moses only to that people. And this consideration alone is answer enough unto those that urge the authority of the law of Moses for the inflicting of capital punishments upon idolaters. But, however, I will examine this argument a little more particularly.

The case of idolaters, in respect of the Jewish commonwealth, falls under a double consideration. The first is of those who, being initiated in the mosaical rites, and made citizens of that commonwealth, did afterwards apostatize from the worship of the God of Israel. These were proceeded against as traitors and rebels, guilty of no less than high treason. For the commonwealth of the Jews, different in that from all others, was an absolute theocracy; nor was there, or could there be, any difference between that commonwealth and the Church. The laws established there concerning the worship of one invisible deity were the civil laws of that people, and a part of their political government, in which God himself was the legislator. Now if anyone can show me where there is a commonwealth, at this time, constituted upon that foundation, I will acknowledge that the ecclesiastical laws do there unavoidably become a part of the civil; and that the subjects of that government both may and ought to be kept in strict conformity with that Church by the civil power. But there is absolutely no such thing, under the Gospel, as a Christian commonwealth. There are, indeed, many cities and kingdoms that have embraced the faith of Christ, but they have retained their ancient form of government, with which the law of Christ hath not at all meddled. He, indeed, hath taught men how, by faith and good works, they may attain eternal life. But he instituted no commonwealth; he prescribed unto his followers no new and peculiar form of government; nor put he the sword into any magistrate's hand, with commission to make use of it in forcing men to forsake their former religion, and receive his.

Secondly, foreigners, and such as were strangers to the commonwealth of Israel, were not compelled by force to observe the rites of the Mosaical law. But, on the contrary, in the very same place where it is ordered that 'an Israelite that was an idolater should be put to death', there it is provided that 'strangers should not be vexed nor oppressed' (Exod. 22.20, 21). I confess that the seven nations that possessed the land which was promised to the Israelites were utterly to be cut off. But this was not singly because they were idolaters. For if that had been the reason, why were the Moabites and other nations to be spared? No, the reason is this: God being in a peculiar manner the king of the Jews, he could not suffer the adoration of any other deity (which was properly an act of high treason against himself) in the land of Canaan, which was his kingdom. For such a manifest revolt could no ways consist with his dominion, which was perfectly political, in that country. All idolatry was therefore to be rooted out of the bounds of his kingdom; because it was an acknowledgement of another God, that is to say another king, against the laws of empire. The inhabitants were also to be driven out, that the entire possession of the land might be given to the Israelites. And for the like reason the Emims and the Horims were driven out of their countries by the children of Esau and Lot (Deut. 2); and their lands, upon the same grounds, given by God to the invaders. But though all idolatry was thus rooted out of the land of Canaan, yet every idolater was not brought to execution. The whole family of Rahab, the whole nation of the Gibeonites, articled with Joshua, and were allowed by treaty; and there were many captives amongst the Jews who were idolaters. David and Solomon subdued many countries without the confines of the Land of Promise, and carried their conquests as far as Euphrates. Amongst so many captives taken, so many nations reduced under their obedience, we find not one man forced into the Jewish religion and the worship of the true God, and punished for idolatry, though all of them were certainly guilty of it. If anyone, indeed, becoming a proselyte, desired to be made a denizen of their commonwealth, he was obliged to submit unto their laws, that is, to embrace their religion. But this he did willingly, on his own accord, not by constraint. He did not unwillingly submit, to show his obedience, but he sought and solicited for it, as a privilege. And as soon as he was admitted, he became subject to the laws of the commonwealth, by which all idolatry was forbidden within the borders of the land of Canaan. But that law (as I have said) did not reach to any of those regions, however subjected unto the Jews, that were situated without those bounds.

Thus far concerning outward worship. Let us now consider articles of faith.

The articles of religion are some of them practical, and some speculative. Now, though both sorts consist in the knowledge of truth, yet these terminate simply in the understanding, those influence the will and manners. Speculative opinions, therefore, and articles of faith, as they are called, which are required only to be believed, cannot be imposed on any Church by the law of the land. For it is absurd that things should be enjoined by laws which are not in men's power to perform. And to believe this or that to be true, does not depend upon our will. But of this enough has been said already. But (will some say) let men at least profess that they believe. A sweet religion, indeed, that obliges men to dissemble, and tell lies both to God and man, for the salvation of their souls! If the magistrate thinks to save men thus, he seems to understand little of the way of salvation. And if he does it not in order to save them, why is he so solicitous about the articles of faith as to enact them by a law?

Further, the magistrate ought not to forbid the preaching or professing of any speculative opinions in any Church, because they have no manner of relation to the civil rights of the subjects. If a Roman Catholic believe that to be really the body of Christ which another man calls bread, he does no injury thereby to his neighbour. If a Jew do not believe the New Testament to be the Word of God, he does not thereby alter anything in men's civil rights. If a heathen doubt of both Testaments, he is not therefore to be punished as a pernicious citizen. The power of the magistrate, and the estates of the people, may be equally secure, whether any man believe these things or no. I readily grant that these opinions are false and absurd. But the business of laws is not to provide for the truth of opinions, but for the safety and security of the commonwealth, and of every particular man's goods and person. And so it ought to be. For truth certainly would do well enough, if she were once left to shift for herself. She seldom has received, and I fear never will receive, much assistance from the power of great men, to whom she is but rarely known, and more rarely welcome. She is not taught by laws, nor has she any need of force to procure her entrance into the minds of men. Errors indeed prevail by the assistance of foreign and borrowed succours, but if truth makes not her way into the understanding by her own light, she will be but the weaker for any borrowed force violence can add to her. Thus much for speculative opinions. Let us now proceed to practical ones.

A good life, in which consists not the least part of religion and true piety, concerns also the civil government; and in it lies the safety both of men's souls and of the commonwealth. Moral actions belong therefore to the jurisdiction both of the outward and inward court; both of the civil and domestic governor; I mean, both of the magistrate and conscience. Here, therefore, is great danger, lest one of these jurisdictions entrench upon the other, and discord arise between the keeper of the public peace and the overseers of souls. But if what has been already said concerning the limits of both these governments be rightly considered, it will easily remove all difficulty in this matter.

Every man has an immortal soul, capable of eternal happiness or misery; whose happiness depending upon his believing and doing those things in this life which are necessary to the obtaining of God's favour, and are prescribed by God to that end, it follows from thence, first, that the observance of these things is the highest obligation that lies upon mankind, and that our utmost care, application, and diligence ought to be exercised in the search and performance of them, because there is nothing in this world that is of any consideration in comparison with eternity. Secondly, that seeing one man does not violate the right of another by his erroneous opinions, and undue manner of worship, nor is his perdition any prejudice to another man's affairs, therefore the care of each man's salvation belongs only to himself. But I would not have this understood, as if I meant hereby to condemn all charitable admonitions, and affectionate endeavours to reduce men from errors; which are indeed the greatest duty of a Christian. Anyone may employ as many exhortations and arguments as he pleases towards the promoting of another man's salvation. But all force and compulsion are to be forborne. Nothing is to be done imperiously. Nobody is obliged in that matter to yield obedience unto the admonitions or injunctions of another, further than he himself is persuaded. Every man, in that, has the supreme and absolute authority of judging for himself. And the reason is, because nobody else is concerned in it, nor can receive any prejudice from his conduct therein.

But besides their souls, which are immortal, men have also their temporal lives here upon earth; the state whereof being frail and fleeting, and the duration uncertain, they have need of several outward conveniences to the support thereof, which are to be procured or preserved by pains and industry. For those things that are necessary to the comfortable support of our lives are not the spontaneous products of nature, nor do offer themselves fit and prepared for our use. This part therefore draws on another care, and necessarily gives another employment. But the pravity of mankind being such that they had rather injuriously prey upon the fruits of other men's labours, than take pains to provide for themselves, the necessity of preserving men in the possession of what honest industry has already acquired, and also of preserving their liberty and strength, whereby they may acquire what they may further want, obliges men to enter into society with one another, that by mutual assistance, and joint force, they may secure unto each other their properties in the things that contribute to the comfort and happiness of this life; leaving in the meanwhile to every man the care of his own eternal happiness, the attainment whereof can neither be facilitated by another man's industry, nor can the loss of it turn to another man's prejudice, nor the hope of it be forced from him by any external violence. But forasmuch as men thus entering into societies, grounded upon their mutual compacts of assistance, for the defence of their temporal goods, may nevertheless be deprived of them, either by the rapine and fraud of their fellow-citizens, or by the hostile violence of foreigners, the remedy of this evil consists in arms, riches, and multitude of citizens; the remedy of the other in laws; and the care of all things relating both to the one and the other is committed by the society to the civil magistrate. This is the original, this is the use, and these are the bounds of the legislative, which is the supreme power in every commonwealth. I mean, that provision may be made for the security of each man's private possessions; for the peace, riches, and public commodities of the whole people; and, as much as possible, for the increase of their inward strength, against foreign invasions.

These things being thus explained, it is easy to understand to what end the legislative power ought to be directed, and by what measures regulated; and that is the temporal good and outward prosperity of the society; which is the sole reason of men's entering into society, and the only thing they seek and aim at in it. And it is also evident what liberty remains to men in reference to their eternal salvation, and that is, that everyone should do what he in his conscience is persuaded to be acceptable to the Almighty, on whose good pleasure and acceptance depends his eternal happiness. For obedience is due in the first place to God, and afterwards to the laws.

But some may ask, What if the magistrate should enjoin anything by his authority that appears unlawful to the conscience of a private person? I answer that if government be faithfully administered, and the counsels of the magistrate be indeed directed to the public good, this will seldom happen. But if perhaps it do so fall out, I say that such a private person is to abstain from the action that he judges unlawful; and he is to undergo the punishment, which it is not unlawful for him to bear. For the private judgement of any person concerning a law enacted in political matters, for the public good, does not take away the obligation of that law, nor deserve a dispensation. But if the law indeed be concerning things that lie not within the verge of the magistrate's authority (as, for example, that the people, or any party amongst them, should be compelled to embrace a strange religion, and join in the worship and ceremonies of another Church), men are not in these cases obliged by that law, against their consciences. For the political society is instituted for no other end but only to secure every man's possession of the things of this life. The care of each man's soul, and of the things of heaven, which neither does belong to the commonwealth nor can be subjected to it, is left entirely to every man's self. Thus the safeguard of men's lives, and of the things that belong unto this life, is the business of the commonwealth; and the preserving of those things unto their owners is the duty of the magistrate. And, therefore, the magistrate cannot take away these worldly things from this man, or party, and give them to that; nor change property amongst fellow-subjects (no, not even by a law) for a cause that has no relation to the end of civil government – I mean, for their religion, which, whether it be true or false, does no prejudice to the worldly concerns of their fellow-subjects, which are the things that only belong unto the care of the commonwealth.

But what if the magistrate believe such a law as this to be for the public good? I answer: As the private judgement of any particular person, if erroneous, does not exempt him from the obligation of law, so the private judgement (as I may call it) of the magistrate does not give him any new right of imposing laws upon his subjects, which neither was in the constitution of the government granted him, nor ever was in the power of the people to grant; and least of all if he make it his business to enrich and advance his followers and fellow-sectaries with the spoils of others. But what if the magistrate believe that he has a right to make such laws, and that they are for the public good; and his subjects believe the contrary? Who shall be judge between them? I answer, God alone. For there is no judge upon earth between the supreme magistrate and the people. God, I say, is the only judge in this case, who will retribute unto everyone at the last day according to his deserts; that is, according to his sincerity and uprightness in endeavouring to promote piety, and the public weal and peace of mankind. But what shall be done in the meanwhile? I answer: The principal and chief care of everyone ought to be of his own soul first, and in the next place of the public peace: though yet there are very few will think 'tis peace there, where they see all laid waste.

There are two sorts of contests amongst men: the one managed by law, the other by force; and these are of that nature, that where the one ends, the other always begins. But it is not my business to inquire into the power of the magistrate in the different constitutions of nations. I only know what usually happens where controversies arise without a judge to determine them. You will say, then the magistrate being the stronger will have his will, and carry his point. Without doubt; but the question is not here concerning the doubtfulness of the event, but the rule of right.

But to come to particulars. I say, first, no opinions contrary to human society, or to those moral rules which are necessary to the preservation of civil society, are to be tolerated by the magistrate. But of these, indeed, examples in any Church are rare. For no sect can usually arrive to such a degree of madness, as that it should think fit to teach, for doctrines of religion, such things as manifestly undermine the foundations of society, and are therefore condemned by the judgement of all mankind: because their own interest, peace, reputation, everything would be thereby endangered.

Another more secret evil, but more dangerous to the commonwealth, is when men arrogate to themselves, and to those of their own sect, some peculiar prerogative, covered over with a specious show of deceitful words, but in effect opposite to the civil right of the community. For example, we cannot find any sect that teaches expressly, and openly, that men are not obliged to keep their promise; that princes may be dethroned by those that differ from them in religion; or that the dominion of all things belongs only to themselves. For these things, proposed thus nakedly and plainly, would soon draw on them the eye and hand of the magistrate, and awaken all the care of the commonwealth to a watchfulness against the spreading of so dangerous an evil. But, nevertheless, we find those that say the same things, in other words. What else do they mean, who teach that faith is not to be kept with heretics? Their meaning, forsooth, is that the privilege of breaking faith belongs unto themselves. For they declare all that are not of their communion to be heretics, or at least may declare them so whensoever they think fit. What can be the meaning of their asserting that kings excommunicated forfeit their crowns and kingdoms? It is evident that they thereby arrogate unto themselves the power of deposing kings, because they challenge the power of excommunication as the peculiar right of their hierarchy. That dominion is founded in grace is also an assertion by which those that maintain it do plainly lay claim to the possession of all things, for they are not so wanting to themselves as not to believe, or at least as not to profess, themselves to be the truly pious and faithful. These, therefore, and the like, who attribute unto the faithful, religious, and orthodox, that is, in plain terms, unto themselves, any peculiar privilege or power above other mortals, in civil concernments; or who, upon pretence of religion, do challenge any manner of authority over such as are not associated with them in their ecclesiastical communion: I say these have no right to be tolerated by the magistrate; as neither those that will not own and teach the duty of tolerating all men in matters of mere religion. For what do all these and the like doctrines signify, but that those men may, and are ready upon any occasion to, seize the government, and possess themselves of the estates and fortunes of their fellow-subjects; and that they only ask leave to be tolerated by the magistrate so long, until they find themselves strong enough to effect it?

Again, that Church can have no right to be tolerated by the magistrate which is constituted upon such a bottom that all those who enter into it do thereby, *ipso facto*, deliver themselves up to the protection and service of another prince. For by this means the magistrate would give way to the settling of a foreign jurisdiction in his own country, and suffer his own people to be listed, as it were, for soldiers against his own government. Nor does the frivolous and fallacious distinction between the court and the Church afford any remedy to this inconvenience; especially when both the one and the other are equally subject to the absolute authority of the same person, who has not only power to persuade the members of his Church to whatsoever he lists, either as purely religious, or as in order thereunto, but can also enjoin it them on pain of eternal fire. It is ridiculous for anyone to profess himself to be a Mahometan only in his religion, but in everything else a faithful subject to a Christian magistrate, whilst at the same time he acknowledges himself bound to yield blind obedience to the Mufti of Constantinople, who himself is entirely obedient to the Ottoman emperor, and frames the feigned oracles of that religion according to his pleasure. But this Mahometan, living amongst Christians, would yet more apparently renounce their government if he acknowledged the same person to be head of his Church who is the supreme magistrate in the state.

Lastly, those are not at all to be tolerated who deny the being of a God. Promises, covenants, and oaths, which are the bonds of human society, can have no hold upon an atheist. The taking away of God, though but even in thought, dissolves all. Besides also, those that by their atheism undermine and destroy all religion can have no pretence of religion whereupon to challenge the privilege of a toleration. As for other practical opinions, though not absolutely free from all error, yet if they do not tend to establish domination over others, or civil impunity to the Church in which they are taught, there can be no reason why they should not be tolerated.

It remains that I say something concerning those assemblies, which being vulgarly called, and perhaps having sometimes been, conventicles, and nurseries of factions and seditions, are thought to afford the strongest matter of objection against this doctrine of toleration. But this has not happened by anything peculiar unto the genius of such assemblies, but by the unhappy circumstances of an oppressed or ill-settled liberty. These accusations would soon cease if the law of toleration were once so settled that all Churches were obliged to lay down toleration as the foundation of their own liberty; and teach that liberty of conscience is every man's natural right, equally belonging to dissenters as to themselves; and that nobody ought to be compelled in matters of religion, either by law or force. The establishment of this one thing would take away all ground of complaints and tumults upon account of conscience. And these causes of discontents and animosities being once removed, there would remain nothing in these assemblies that were not more peaceable, and less apt to produce disturbance of state, than in any other meetings whatsoever. But let us examine particularly the heads of these accusations.

You'll say that assemblies and meetings endanger the public peace, and threaten the commonwealth. I answer: If this be so, why are there daily such numerous meetings in markets, and courts of judicature? Why are crowds upon the exchange, and a concourse of people in cities suffered? You'll reply: These are civil assemblies, but those that we object against are ecclesiastical. I answer: 'Tis a likely thing indeed, that such assemblies as are altogether remote from civil affairs, should be most apt to embroil them. Oh, but civil assemblies are composed of men that differ from one another in matters of religion; but these ecclesiastical meetings are of persons that are all of one opinion. As if an agreement in matters of religion were in effect a conspiracy against the commonwealth; or as if men would not be so much the more warmly unanimous in religion, the less liberty they had of assembling. But it will be urged still, that civil assemblies are open, and free for anyone to enter into; whereas religious conventicles are more private, and thereby give opportunity to clandestine machinations. I answer: That this is not strictly true, for many civil assemblies are not open to everyone. And if some religious meetings be private, who are they (I beseech you) that are to be blamed for it? Those that desire or those that forbid their being public? Again, you'll say that religious communion does exceedingly unite men's minds and affections to one another, and is therefore the more dangerous. But if this be so, why is not the magistrate afraid of his own Church; and why does he not forbid their assemblies, as things dangerous to his government? You'll say: Because he himself is a part, and even the head of them. As if he were not also a part of the commonwealth, and the head of the whole people.

Let us, therefore, deal plainly. The magistrate is afraid of other Churches, but not of his own; because he is kind and favourable to the one, but severe and cruel to the other. These he treats like children, and indulges them even to wantonness. Those he uses as slaves; and, how blamelessly soever they demean themselves, recompenses them no otherwise than by galleys, prisons, confiscations, and death. These he cherishes and defends. Those he continually scourges and oppresses. Let him turn the tables; or let those dissenters enjoy but the same privileges in civils as his other subjects, and he will quickly find that these religious meetings will be no longer dangerous. For if men enter into seditious conspiracies, 'tis not religion that inspires them to it in their meetings, but their sufferings and oppressions that make them willing to ease themselves. Just and moderate governments are everywhere quiet, everywhere safe. But oppression raises ferments, and makes men struggle to cast off an uneasy and tyrannical yoke. I know that seditions are very frequently raised upon pretence of religion. But 'tis as true that, for religion, subjects are frequently ill-treated, and live miserably. Believe me, the stirs that are made, proceed not from any peculiar temper of this or that Church or religious society, but from the common disposition of all mankind, who, when they groan under any heavy burden, endeavour naturally to shake off the yoke that galls their necks. Suppose this business of religion were let alone, and that there were some other distinction made between men and men, upon account of their different complexions, shapes, and features, so that those who have black hair (for example), or grey eyes, should not enjoy the same privileges as other citizens; that they should not be permitted either to buy or sell, or live by their callings; that parents should not have the government and education of their own children; that they should either be excluded from the benefit of the laws, or meet with partial judges; can it be doubted but these persons, thus distinguished from others by the colour of their hair and eyes, and united together by one common persecution, would be as dangerous to the magistrate as any others that had associated themselves merely upon the account of religion? Some enter into company for trade and profit: others, for want of business, have their clubs for claret. Neighbourhood joins some, and religion others. But there is only one thing which gathers people into seditious commotions, and that is oppression.

You'll say: What, will you have people to meet at divine service against the magistrate's will? I answer: Why, I pray, against his will? Is it not both lawful and necessary that they should meet? Against his will, do you say? That's what I complain of. That is the very root of all the mischief. Why are assemblies less sufferable in a Church than in a theatre or market? Those that meet there are not either more vicious or more turbulent than those that meet else- where. The business in that is, that they are ill-used, and therefore they are not to be suffered. Take away the partiality that is used towards them in matters of common right; change the laws, take away the penalties unto which they are subjected; and all things will immediately become safe and peaceable. Nay, those that are averse to the religion of the magistrate will think themselves so much the more bound to maintain the peace of the commonwealth as their condition is better in that place than elsewhere. And all the several separate congregations, like so many guardians of the public peace, will watch one another, that nothing may be innovated or changed in the form of the government, because they can hope for nothing better than what they already enjoy; that is, an equal condition with their fellow-subjects, under a just and moderate government. Now if that Church which agrees in religion with the prince be esteemed the chief support of any civil government, and that for no other reason (as has already been shown) than because the prince is kind and the laws are favourable to it; how much greater will be the security of a government where all good subjects, of whatsoever Church they be, without any distinction upon account of religion, enjoying the same favour of the prince, and the same benefit of the laws, shall become the common support and guard of it; and where none will have any occasion to fear the severity of the laws, but those that do injuries to their neighbours, and offend against the civil peace?

That we may draw towards a conclusion: the sum of all we drive at is that every man may enjoy the same rights that are granted to others. Is it permitted to worship God in the Roman manner? Let it be permitted to do it in the Geneva form also. Is it permitted to speak Latin in the market-place? Let those that have a mind to it be permitted to do it also in the Church. Is it lawful for any man in his own house to kneel, stand, sit, or use any other posture; and to clothe himself in white or black, in short or in long garments? Let it not be made unlawful to eat bread, drink wine, or wash with water in the Church. In a word, whatsoever things are left free by law in the common occasions of life, let them remain free unto every Church in divine worship. Let no man's life, or body, or house, or estate suffer any manner of prejudice upon these accounts. Can you allow of the Presbyterian discipline? Why should not the Episcopal also have what they like? Ecclesiastical authority, whether it be administered by the hands of a single person, or many, is everywhere the same; and neither has any jurisdiction in things civil, nor any manner of power of compulsion, nor anything at all to do with riches and revenues.

Ecclesiastical assemblies and sermons are justified by daily experience and public allowance. These are allowed to people of some one persuasion. Why not to all? If anything pass in a religious meeting seditiously, and contrary to the public peace, it is to be punished in the same manner, and no otherwise, than as if it had happened in a fair or market. These meetings ought not to be sanctuaries for factious and flagitious fellows; nor ought it to be less lawful for men to meet in Churches than in halls; nor any one part of the subjects to be esteemed more blamable, for their meeting together, than others. Everyone is to be accountable for his own actions; and no man is to be laid under a suspicion, or odium, for the fault of another. Those that are seditious, murderers, thieves, robbers, adulterers, slanderers, etc., of whatsoever Church, whether national or not, ought to be punished and suppressed. But those whose doctrine is peaceable, and whose manners are pure and blameless, ought to be upon equal terms with their fellow-subjects.

Thus if solemn assemblies, observations of festivals, public worship be permitted to any one sort of professors, all these things ought to be permitted to the Presbyterians, Independents, Anabaptists, Arminians, Quakers, and others, with the same liberty. Nay, if we may openly speak the truth, and as becomes one man to another, neither pagan, nor Mahometan, nor Jew ought to be excluded from the civil rights of the commonwealth because of his religion. The Gospel commands no such thing. The Church, which 'judges not those that are without' (1 Cor. 5.12, 13), wants it not. And the commonwealth, which embraces indifferently all men that are honest, peaceable, and industrious, requires it not. Shall we suffer a pagan to deal and trade with us, and shall we not suffer him to pray unto and worship God? If we allow the Jews to have private houses and dwellings amongst us, why should we not allow them to have synagogues? Is their doctrine more false, their worship more abominable, or is the civil peace more endangered by their meeting in public than in their private houses? But if these things may be granted to Jews and pagans, surely the condition of any Christians ought not to be worse than theirs in a Christian commonwealth.

You'll say, perhaps: Yes, it ought to be. Because they are more inclinable to factions, tumults, and civil wars. I answer: Is this the fault of the Christian religion? If it be so, truly the Christian religion is the worst of all religions, and ought neither to be embraced by any particular person, nor tolerated by any commonwealth. For if this be the genius, this the nature of the Christian religion, to be turbulent, and destructive to the civil peace, that Church itself which the magistrate indulges will not always be innocent. But far be it from us to say any such thing of that religion which carries the greatest opposition to covetousness, ambition, discord, contention, and all manner of inordinate desires; and is the most modest and peaceable religion that ever was. We must therefore seek another cause of those evils that are charged upon religion. And if we consider right, we shall find it to consist wholly in the subject that I am treating of. It is not the diversity of opinions (which cannot be avoided), but the refusal of toleration to those that are of different opinions (which might have been granted), that has produced all the bustles and wars that have been in the Christian world upon account of religion. The heads and leaders of the

Church, moved by avarice and insatiable desire of dominion, making use of the immoderate ambition of magistrates, and the credulous superstition of the giddy multitude, have incensed and animated them against those that dissent from themselves, by preaching unto them, contrary to the laws of the Gospel and to the precepts of charity, that schismatics and heretics are to be outed of their possessions, and destroyed. And thus have they mixed together and confounded two things that are in themselves most different, the Church and the commonwealth. Now as it is very difficult for men patiently to suffer themselves to be stripped of the goods which they have got by their honest industry, and, contrary to all the laws of equity, both human and divine, to be delivered up for a prey to other men's violence and rapine, especially when they are otherwise altogether blameless, and that the occasion for which they are thus treated does not at all belong to the jurisdiction of the magistrate, but entirely to the conscience of every particular man, for the conduct of which he is accountable to God only; what else can be expected but that these men, growing weary of the evils under which they labour, should in the end think it lawful for them to resist force with force, and to defend their natural rights (which are not forfeitable upon account of religion) with arms as well as they can? That this has been hitherto the ordinary course of things is abundantly evident in history; and that it will continue to be so hereafter is but too apparent in reason. It cannot indeed be otherwise, so long as the principle of persecution for religion shall prevail, as it has done hitherto, with magistrate and people; and so long as those that ought to be the preachers of peace and concord shall continue, with all their art and strength, to excite men to arms, and sound the trumpet of war. But that magistrates should thus suffer these incendiaries, and disturbers of the public peace, might justly be wondered at, if it did not appear that they have been invited by them unto a participation of the spoil, and have therefore thought fit to make use of their covetousness and pride as means whereby to increase their own power. For who does not see that these good men are indeed more ministers of the government than ministers of the Gospel; and that by flattering the ambition and favouring the dominion of princes and men in authority, they endeavour with all their might to promote that tyranny in the commonwealth which otherwise they should not be able to establish in the Church? This is the unhappy agreement that we see between the Church and state. Whereas if each of them would contain itself within its own bounds, the one attending to the worldly welfare of the commonwealth, the other to the salvation of souls, it is impossible that any discord should ever have happened between them. *Sed, pudet haec opprobria,* etc. God Almighty grant, I beseech him, that the Gospel of Peace may at length be preached, and that civil magistrates growing more careful to conform their own consciences to the law of God, and less solicitous about the binding of other men's consciences by human laws, may, like fathers of their country, direct all their counsels and endeavours to promote universally the civil welfare of all their children; except only of such as are arrogant, ungovernable, and injurious to their brethren; and that all ecclesiastical men, who boast themselves to be the successors of the apostles, walking peaceably and modestly in the apostles' steps, without intermeddling with state affairs, may apply themselves wholly to promote the salvation of souls.

Farewell.

Postscript

Perhaps it may not be amiss to add a few things concerning heresy and schism. A Turk is not, nor can be, either heretic or schismatic to a Christian; and if any man fall off from the Christian faith to Mahometism, he does not thereby become a heretic or schismatic, but an apostate and an infidel. This nobody doubts of. And by this it appears that men of different religions cannot be heretics or schismatics to one another.

We are to inquire, therefore, what men are of the same religion. Concerning which it is manifest that those who have one and the same rule of faith and worship are of the same religion; and those who have not the same rule of faith and worship are of different religions. For since all things that belong unto that religion are contained in that rule, it follows necessarily that those who agree in one rule are of one and the same religion, and *vice versa*. Thus Turks and Christians are of different religions, because these take the Holy Scriptures to be the rule of their religion, and those the

Alcoran. And for the same reason there may be different religions also even amongst Christians. The Papists and the Lutherans, though both of them profess faith in Christ, and are therefore called Christians, yet are not both of the same religion, because these acknowledge nothing but the Holy Scriptures to be the rule and foundation of their religion, those take in also traditions and the decrees of popes, and of all these together make the rule of their religion. And thus the Christians of St John (as they are called) and the Christians of Geneva are of different religions, because these also take only the Scriptures, and those I know not what traditions, for the rule of their religion.

This being settled, it follows, first, that heresy is a separation made in ecclesiastical communion between men of the same religion, for some opinions no way contained in the rule itself. And, secondly, that amongst those who acknowledge nothing but the Holy Scriptures to be their rule of faith, heresy is a separation made in their Christian communion for opinions not contained in the express words of Scripture. Now this separation may be made in a twofold manner:

1. When the greater part, or (by the magistrate's patronage) the stronger part, of the Church separates itself from others by excluding them out of her communion because they will not profess their belief of certain opinions which are not to be found in the express words of Scripture. For it is not the paucity of those that are separated, nor the authority of the magistrate, that can make any man guilty of heresy. But he only is an heretic who divides the Church into parts, introduces names and marks of distinction, and voluntarily makes a separation because of such opinions.

2. When anyone separates himself from the communion of a Church because that Church does not publicly profess some certain opinions which the Holy Scriptures do not expressly teach.

Both these are heretics because they err in fundamentals, and they err obstinately against knowledge. For when they have determined the Holy Scriptures to be the only foundation of faith, they nevertheless lay down certain propositions as fundamental which are not in the Scripture; and because others will not acknowledge these additional opinions of theirs, nor build upon them as if they were necessary and fundamental, they therefore make a separation in the Church, either by withdrawing themselves from the others, or expelling the others from them. Nor does it signify anything for them to say that their confessions and symbols are agreeable to Scripture and to the analogy of faith. For if they be conceived in the express words of Scripture, there can be no question about them, because those are acknowledged by all Christians to be of divine inspiration, and therefore fundamental. But if they say that the articles which they require to be professed are consequences deduced from the Scripture, it is undoubtedly well done of them to believe and profess such things as seem unto them so agreeable to the rule of faith. But it would be very ill done to obtrude those things upon others, unto whom they do not seem to be the indubitable doctrines of the Scripture. And to make a separation for such things as these, which neither are nor can be fundamental, is to become heretics. For I do not think there is any man arrived to that degree of madness, as that he dare give out his consequences and interpretations of Scripture as divine inspirations, and compare the articles of faith that he has framed according to his own fancy with the authority of the Scripture. I know there are some propositions so evidently agreeable to Scripture that nobody can deny them to be drawn from thence: but about those, therefore, there can be no difference. This only I say, that however clearly we may think this or the other doctrine to be deduced from Scripture, we ought not therefore to impose it upon others as a necessary article of faith because we believe it to be agreeable to the rule of faith; unless we would be content also that other doctrines should be imposed upon us in the same manner; and that we should be compelled to receive and profess all the different and contradictory opinions of Lutherans, Calvinists, Remonstrants, Anabaptists, and other sects, which the contrivers of symbols, systems, and confessions are accustomed to deliver unto their followers as genuine and necessary deductions from the Holy Scripture. I cannot but wonder at the extravagant arrogance of those men who think that they themselves can explain things necessary to salvation more clearly than the Holy Ghost, the eternal and infinite wisdom of God.

Thus much concerning heresy, which word in common use is applied only to the doctrinal part of religion. Let us now consider schism, which is a crime near akin to it. For both these words seem unto me to signify an ill-grounded separation in ecclesiastical communion, made about things not necessary. But since use, which is the supreme law in matter of language, has determined that heresy relates to errors in faith, and schism to those in worship or discipline, we must consider them under that distinction.

Schism, then, for the same reasons that have already been alleged, is nothing else but a separation made in the communion of the Church upon account of something in divine worship, or ecclesiastical discipline, that is not any necessary part of it. Now nothing in worship or discipline can be necessary to Christian communion but what Christ our legislator, or the apostles by inspiration of the Holy Spirit, have commanded in express words.

In a word: he that denies not anything that the Holy Scriptures teach in express words, nor makes a separation upon occasion of anything that is not manifestly contained in the sacred text, however he may be nicknamed by any sect of Christians, and declared by some or all of them to be utterly void of true Christianity, yet in deed and in truth this man cannot be either a heretic or a schismatic.

These things might have been explained more largely, and more advantageously; but it is enough to have hinted at them thus, briefly, to a person of your parts.

22: Letter to Edward Clarke (29 January/8 February 1689)

Dear Sir

Yours of 22 Jan. is the third I received from you since your last coming to London, for which I cannot forbear to return you my thanks by the post this same day that I receive it, though it be a doubt to me whether as it may happen this or I shall get to you first.

I have seen the Prince's letter to the Convention, which carries weight and wisdom in it. But men very much wonder here to hear of Committees of Privileges, of Grievances, etc., as if this were a formal Parliament, and were not something of another nature, and had not business to do of greater moment and consequence, sufficiently pointed out to them by the Prince's letter.

People are astonished here to see them meddle with any small matters, when the settlement of the nation upon the sure grounds of peace and security is put into their hands, which can no way so well be done as by restoring our ancient government, the best possibly that ever was, if taken and put together all of a piece in its original constitution. If this has not been invaded men have done very ill to complain, and if it has, men must certainly be so wise by feeling as to know where the frame has been put out of order or is amiss, and for that now they have an opportunity offered to find remedies and set up a constitution that may be lasting, for the security of civil rights and the liberty and property of all the subjects of the nation. These are thoughts worthy such a convention as this, which if (as men suspect here) they think of themselves as a Parliament, and put themselves into the slow methods of proceeding usual therein, and think of mending some faults piecemeal, or anything less than the great frame of the government, they will let slip an opportunity which cannot even from things within last long. But if they consider foreign affairs I wonder any of them can sleep till they see the nation settled in a regular way of acting and putting itself in a posture of defence and support of the common interest of Europe. The spring comes on apace, and if we be, France will not be idle. And if France should prevail with the Emperor for an accommodation (which is more than feared) I beseech you consider how much time you have to lose in England. I mention not Ireland because that is in everybody's eye. I writ some time since to J.F. suspecting you might be out of town, concerning one point, which if gained will go a great way to keep all right: I desired him to communicate it with you if you were not gone into the country. I could tell you several other considerations I have, which I need not trouble you with, who I am sure will think of the very same or better. I do not perceive that you stood to be chosen anywhere, which when I see you I shall quarrel with you for not a little; make not the like omission the next election. I writ to you the same time I did to him, but supposing it would find you in the country it was only upon the old subject of your children. I am glad to hear their mother and they are well. I am their and

> Dear Sir
> Your most affectionate humble
> servant
> JL

The news comes just now from a good hand that the Emperor and the French King are agreed. I have by the two last posts remitted money to Mr Percivall. The bills of exchange are five that I have sent him, the sum how much you will see by the bills, pray whilst you are in town when you go that way look a little after it, and mind him to be careful of it. My service to Mrs Smithsby and the rest of my friends that are in town, especially your western neighbours amongst whom I reckon J.F.

23: Preface to *Two Treatises of Government* (1689)

Reader,

Thou hast here the beginning and end of a discourse concerning government; what fate has otherwise disposed of the papers that should have filled up the middle, and were more than all the rest, 'tis not worth while to tell thee. These which remain, I hope are sufficient to establish the throne of our great restorer, our present King William; to make good his title in the consent of the people, which being the only one of all lawful governments he has more fully and clearly than any prince in Christendom; and to justify to the world the people of England, whose love of their just and natural rights, with their resolution to preserve them, saved the nation when it was on the very brink of slavery and ruin. If these papers have that evidence I flatter myself is to be found in them, there will be no great miss of those which are lost, and my reader may be satisfied without them. For I imagine I shall have neither the time nor inclination to repeat my pains, and fill up the wanting part of my answer, by tracing Sir Robert again through all the windings and obscurities which are to be met with in the several branches of his wonderful system. The king, and body of the nation, have since so thoroughly confuted his hypothesis, that I suppose nobody hereafter will have either the confidence to appear against our common safety, and be again an advocate for slavery, or the weakness to be deceived with contradictions dressed up in a popular style, and well-turned periods. For if anyone will be at the pains himself, in those parts which are here untouched, to strip Sir Robert's Discourses of the flourish of doubtful expressions, and endeavour to reduce his words to direct, positive, intelligible propositions, and then compare them one with another, he will quickly be satisfied there was never so much glib nonsense put together in well-sounding English. If he think it not worth while to examine his works all through, let him make an experiment in that part where he treats of usurpation; and let him try whether he can, with all his skill, make Sir Robert intelligible and consistent with himself, or common sense. I should not speak so plainly of a gentleman long since past answering, had not the pulpit, of late years, publicly owned his doctrine, and made it the current divinity of the times. 'Tis necessary those men who, taking on them to be teachers, have so dangerously misled others, should be openly showed of what authority this their patriarch is, whom they have so blindly followed, that so they may either retract what upon so ill grounds they have vented, and cannot be maintained, or else justify those principles which they preached up for gospel, though they had no better an author than an English courtier. For I should not have writ against Sir Robert, or taken the pains to show his mistakes, inconsistencies, and want of (what he so much boasts of, and pretends wholly to build on) Scripture-proofs, were there not men amongst us who, by crying up his books and espousing his doctrine, save me from the reproach of writing against a dead adversary. They have been so zealous in this point, that if I have done him any wrong, I cannot hope they should spare me. I wish, where they have done the truth and the public wrong, they would be as ready to redress it and allow its just weight to this reflection, viz. that there cannot be done a greater mischief to prince and people, than the propagating wrong notions concerning government, that so at last all times might not have reason to complain of the drum ecclesiastic. If anyone, concerned really for truth, undertake the confutation of my hypothesis, I promise him either to recant my mistake, upon fair conviction, or to answer his difficulties. But he must remember two things:

First, that cavilling here and there, at some expression or little incident of my discourse, is not an answer to my book.

Secondly, that I shall not take railing for arguments, nor think either of these worth my notice. Though I shall always look on myself as bound to give satisfaction to anyone who shall appear to be conscientiously scrupulous in the point, and shall show any just grounds for his scruples.

24: 'Labour' (1693; from the 1661 Commonplace Book)

We ought to look on it as a mark of goodness in God that he has put us in this life under a necessity of labour: not only to keep mankind from the mischiefs that ill men at leisure are very apt to do; but it is a benefit even to the good and the virtuous, which are thereby preserved from the ills of idleness or the diseases that attend constant study in a sedentary life. Half the day employed in useful labour would supply the inhabitants of the earth with the necessaries and conveniences of life, in a full plenty, had not the luxury of courts, and by their example inferior grandees, found out idle and useless employments for themselves and others subservient to their pride and vanity, and so brought honest labour in useful and mechanical arts wholly into disgrace, whereby the studious and sedentary part of mankind as well as the rich and the noble have been deprived of that natural and true preservative against diseases. And 'tis to this that we may justly impute the spleen and the gout and those other decays of health under which the lazily voluptuous, or busily studious, part of men uselessly languish away a great part of their lives. How many shall we find amongst those who sit still either at their books or their pleasure, whom either the spleen or the gout does not rob of his thoughts or his limbs before he is got half his journey? And becomes a useless member of the commonwealth in that mature age which should make him most serviceable, whilst the sober and working artisan and the frugal laborious country man performs his part well, and cheerfully goes on in his business to a vigorous old age. So that when we have reckoned up how much of their time those who are intent on the improvements of their minds are robbed of either by the pains and languishing of their bodies, or the observance of medicinal rules to remove them, a very favourable calculation will show that if they had spent four, nay I think I may say six hours in a day in the constant exercise of some laborious calling, they would have had more hours of their lives to be employed in study than in that languishing estate of a broken health which the neglect of bodily labour seldom fails to bring them to.

He that exempts half his time from serious business may be thought to have made no scanty allowance for recreation and refreshment, and if the other twelve hours of the four and twenty are divided betwixt the body and the mind, I imagine the improvement of the one and the health of the other would be well enough provided for. I make account that six hours in the day well directed in study would carry a man as far in the improvement of his mind as his parts are capable of, and is more I think than most scholars that live to any age do or are able to employ in study. For as I have said, those who at their first setting out eager in the pursuit of knowledge spare as little as they can of their time to the necessities of life to bestow it all upon their minds, find it at last but an ill sort of husbandry, when they are fain to refund to the care of their decayed body a greater proportion of their time than what they improvidently robbed them of. Six hours thus allotted to the mind, the other six might be employed in the provisions for the body and the preservation of health. Six hours' labour every day in some honest calling would at once provide necessaries for the body and secure the health of it in the use of them.

If this distribution of the twelve hours seem not fair nor sufficiently to keep up the distinction that ought to be in the ranks of men, let us change it a little. Let the gentleman and scholar employ nine of the twelve on his mind in thought and reading, and the other three in some honest labour, and the man of manual labour nine in work and three in knowledge. By which all mankind might be supplied with what the real necessities and conveniency of life demand in a greater plenty than they have now, and be delivered from that horrid ignorance and brutality to which the bulk of them is now everywhere given up. If it be not so it is owing to the carelessness and negligence of the governments of the world, which, wholly intent upon the care of aggrandizing themselves, at the same time neglect the happiness of the people and with it their own peace and security. Would they suppress the arts and instruments of luxury and vanity, and bring those of honest and useful industry in fashion, there would be neither that temptation to ambition where the possession of power could not display itself in the distinctions and shows of pride and vanity, nor the well-instructed minds of the people suffered them to be the instruments of aspiring and turbulent men. The populace, well instructed in their duty, and removed from the implicit faith their ignorance submits them in to others, would not be so easy to be blown into tumults and popular commotions by the breath and artifice of designing or discontented grandees. To conclude, this is certain, that if the labour of the world were rightly directed and distributed there would be more knowledge, peace, health, and plenty in it than now there is. And mankind be much more happy than now it is.

25: 'Venditio' (1695; from the 1661 Commonplace Book)

Upon demand what is the measure that ought to regulate the price for which anyone sells so as to keep it within the bounds of equity and justice, I suppose it in short to be this: the market price at the place where he sells. Whosoever keeps to that in whatever he sells I think is free from cheat, extortion and oppression, or any guilt in whatever he sells, supposing no fallacy in his wares.

To explain this a little: A man will not sell the same wheat this year under 10s[hillings] per bushel which the last year he sold for 5s. This is no extortion by the above said rule, because it is this year the market price, and if he should sell under that rate he would not do a beneficial thing to the consumers, because others then would buy up his corn at his low rate and sell it again to others at the market rate, and so they make profit of his weakness and share a part of his money. If to prevent this he will sell his wheat only to the poor at this under rate, this indeed is charity, but not what strict justice requires. For that only requires that we should sell to all buyers at the market rate, for if it be unjust to sell it to a poor man at 10s per bushel it is also unjust to sell it to the rich for 10s, for justice has but one measure for all men. If you think him bound to sell it to the rich too, who is the consumer, under the market rate, but not to a jobber or engrosser, to this I answer he cannot know whether the rich buyer will not sell it again and so gain the money which he loses. But if it be said 'tis unlawful to sell the same corn for 10s this week which I sold the last year or week for 5s because it is worth no more now than it was then, having no new qualities put into it to make it better, I answer it is worth no more, 'tis true, in its natural value, because it will not feed more men nor better feed them than it did last year, but yet it is worth more in its political or marchand value, as I may so call it, which lies in the proportion of the quantity of wheat to the proportion of money in that place and the need of one and the other. This same market rate governs too in things sold in shops or private houses, and is known by this, that a man sells not dearer to one than he would to another. He that makes use of another's ignorance, fancy, or necessity to sell ribbon or cloth, etc. dearer to him than to another man at the same time, cheats him.

But in things that a man does not set to sale, this market price is not regulated by that of the next market, but by the value that the owner puts on it himself: v.g. x^1 has an horse that pleases him and is for his turn; this y would buy of him; x tells him he has no mind to sell; y presses him to set him a price, and thereupon x demands and takes £40 for his horse, which in a market or fair would not yield above twenty. But supposing y refusing to give £40, z comes the next day and desires to buy this horse, having such a necessity to have it that if he should fail of it, it would make him lose a business of much greater consequence, and this necessity x knows. If in this case he make z pay £50 for the horse which he would have sold to y for £40, he oppresses him and is guilty of extortion whereby he robs him of £10, because he does not sell the horse to him, as he would to another, at his own market rate, which was £40, but makes use of z's necessity to extort £10 from him above what in his own account was the just value, the one man's money being as good as the other's. But yet he had done no injury to y in taking his £40 for an horse which at the next market would not have yielded above £20 because he sold it at the market rate of the place where the horse was sold, viz. his own house, where he would not have sold it to any other at a cheaper rate than he did to y. For if by any artifice he had raised y's longing for that horse, or because of his great fancy sold it dearer to him than he would to another man, he had cheated him too. But what anyone has he may value at what rate he will, and transgresses not against justice if he sells it at any price, provided he makes no distinction of buyers, but parts with it as cheap to this as he would to any other buyer. I say he transgresses not against justice. What he may do against charity is another case.

To have a fuller view of this matter, let us suppose a merchant of Danzig sends two ships laden with corn, whereof the one puts into Dunkirk, where there is almost a famine for want of corn, and there he sells his wheat for 20s a bushel, whilst the other ship sells his at Ostend just by for 5s. Here it will be demanded whether it be not oppression and injustice to make such an advantage of their necessity at Dunkirk as to sell to them the same commodity at 20s per bushel which he sells for a quarter the price but twenty miles off? I answer no, because he sells at the market rate at the place where he is, but sells there no dearer to Thomas than he would to Richard. And if there he should sell for less than his corn would yield, he would only throw his profit into other men's hands, who buying of him under the market rate would sell it again to others at the full rate it would yield. Besides, as there can be no other measure set to a merchant's gain but the market price where he comes, so if there were any other measure, as 5 or 10 per cent as the utmost justifiable profit, there would be no commerce in the world, and mankind would be deprived of the supply of foreign mutual conveniences of life. For the buyer, not knowing what the commodity cost the merchant to purchase and bring thither, could be under no tie of giving him the profit of 5 or 10 per cent, and so can have no other rule but of buying as cheap as he can, which turning often to the merchant's downright loss when he comes to a bad market, if he has not the liberty on his side to sell as dear as he can when he comes to a good market. This obligation to certain loss often, without any certainty of reparation, will quickly put an end to merchandizing. The measure that is common to buyer and seller is just that if one should buy as cheap as he could in the market, the other should sell as dear as he could there, everyone running his venture and taking his chance, which by the mutual and perpetually changing wants of money and commodities in buyer and seller comes to a pretty equal and fair account.

But though he that sells his corn in a town pressed with famine at the utmost rate he can get for it does no injustice against the common rule of traffic, yet if he carry it away unless they will give him more than they are able, or extorts so much from their present necessity as not to leave them the means of subsistence afterwards, he offends against the common rule of charity as a man, and if they perish any of them by reason of his extortion is no doubt guilty of murder. For though all the selling merchant's gain arises only from the advantage he makes of the buyer's want, whether it be a want of necessity or fancy that's all one, yet he must not make use of his necessity to his destruction, and enrich himself so as to make another perish. He is so far from being permitted to gain to that degree, that he is bound to be at some loss, and impart of his own to save another from perishing.

Dunkirk is the market to which the English merchant has carried his corn, and by reason of their necessity it proves a good one, and there he may sell his corn as it will yield at the market rate, for 20s per bushel. But if a Dunkirker should at the same time come to England to buy corn, not to sell to him at the market rate, but to make him, because of the necessity of his country, pay 10s per bushel when you sold to others for five, would be extortion.

A ship at sea that has an anchor to spare meets another which has lost all her anchors. What here shall be the just price that she shall sell her anchor to the distressed ship? To this I answer the same price that she would sell the same anchor to a ship that was not in that distress. For that still is the market rate for which one would part with anything to anybody who was not in distress and absolute want of it. And in this case the master of the vessel must make his estimate by the length of his voyage, the season and seas he sails in, and so what risk he shall run himself by parting with his anchor, which all put together perhaps he would not part with it at any rate, but if he would, he must then take no more for it from a ship in distress than he would from any other. And here we see, the price which the anchor cost him, which is the market price at another place, makes no part of the measure of the price which he fairly sells it for at sea. And therefore I put in 'the place where the thing is sold': i.e. the measure of rating anything in selling is the market price where the thing is sold. Whereby it is evident that a thing may be lawfully sold for 10, 20, nay cent per cent, and ten times more in one place than is the market price in another place perhaps not far off. These are my extempory thought[s] concerning this matter.

Note

1. I have substituted letters from the Roman alphabet (x, y, z) for the Greek letters used by Locke.

26: *Draft of a Representation Containing a Scheme of Methods for the Employment of the Poor. Proposed by Mr Locke, the 26th October 1697*

To their Excellencies the Lords Justices:
May it please your Excellencies,
His Majesty having been pleased, by his commission, to require

us particularly to consider of some proper methods for setting on work and employing the poor of this kingdom, and making them useful to the public, and thereby easing others of that burden, and by what ways and means such design may be made most effectual; we humbly beg leave to lay before your Excellencies a scheme of such methods as seem unto us most proper for the attainment of those ends.

The multiplying of the poor, and the increase of the tax for their maintenance, is so general an observation and complaint, that it cannot be doubted of: nor has it been only since the last war that this evil has come upon us; it has been a growing burden on the kingdom these many years; and the two last reigns felt the increase of it, as well as the present.

If the causes of this evil be looked into, we humbly conceive it will be found to have proceeded neither from scarcity of provisions, nor from want of employment for the poor, since the goodness of God has blessed these times with plenty, no less than the former, and a long peace during those reigns gave us as plentiful a trade as ever. The growth of the poor must therefore have some other cause; and it can be nothing else but the relaxation of discipline, and corruption of manners: virtue and industry being as constant companions on the one side as vice and idleness are on the other.

The first step, therefore, towards the setting the poor on work, we humbly conceive, ought to be a restraint of their debauchery, by a strict execution of the laws provided against it; more particularly by the suppressing of superfluous brandy shops and unnecessary alehouses, especially in country parishes not lying upon great roads.

Could all the able hands in England be brought to work, the greatest part of the burden that lies upon the industrious for maintaining the poor would immediately cease: for, upon a very moderate computation, it may be concluded that above one half of those who receive relief from the parishes are able to get their livelihoods; and all of them who receive such relief from the parishes, we conceive, may be divided into these three sorts:

First, those who can do nothing at all towards their support.

Secondly, those who, though they cannot maintain themselves wholly, yet are able to do something towards it.

Thirdly, those who are able to maintain themselves by their own labour.

And these last may be again subdivided into two sorts: viz. either those who have numerous families of children, whom they cannot, or pretend they cannot, support by their labour; or those who pretend they cannot get work, and so live only by begging, or worse.

For the suppression of this last sort of begging drones, who live unnecessarily upon other people's labour, there are already good and wholesome laws, sufficient for the purpose if duly executed. We therefore humbly propose that the execution thereof may be at present revived by proclamation, till other remedies can be provided. As also, that order be taken every year, at the choosing of church wardens and overseers of the poor, that the statutes of the 39th Eliz. cap. 4 and 43 Eliz. cap. 2 be read and considered paragraph by paragraph, and the observation of them, in all their parts, pressed on those who are to be overseers. For we have reason to think that the greatest part of the overseers of the poor, everywhere, are wholly ignorant; and never so much as think that it is the greatest part, or so much as any part, of their duty, to set people to work.

But, for the more effectual restraining of idle vagabonds, we further humbly propose that a new law may be obtained, by which it be enacted:

That all men sound of limb and mind, above fourteen and under fifty years of age, begging in maritime counties out of their own parish without a pass, shall be seized on, either by any officer of the parish where they so beg (which officers, by virtue of their offices, shall be authorized, and under a penalty required to do it) or by the inhabitants of the house themselves where they beg; and be by them, or any of them, brought before the next justice of peace or guardian of the poor (to be chosen as hereafter mentioned), who in this case shall have the power of a justice of the peace; and by such justice of peace or guardian of the poor (after the due and usual correction in the case), be by a pass sent, not to the house of correction (since those houses are now in most counties complained of to be rather places of ease and preferment to the masters thereof, than of correction and reformation to those who are sent thither); nor to their places of habitation (since such idle vagabonds usually name some remote part, whereby the country is put to great charge;

and they usually make their escape from the negligent officers before they come thither, and so are at liberty for a new ramble). But, if it be in a maritime county, as aforesaid, that they be sent to the next sea-port town, there to be kept at hard labour till some of his Majesty's ships coming in or near there give an opportunity of putting them on board, where they shall serve three years under strict discipline, at soldier's pay (subsistence money being deducted for their victuals on board), and be punished as deserters if they go on shore without leave; or, when sent on shore, if they either go further, or stay longer, than they have leave.

That all men begging in maritime counties without passes, that are maimed, or above fifty years of age; and all of any age so begging without passes in inland counties nowhere bordering on the sea, shall be sent to the next house of correction, there to be kept at hard labour for three years.

And to the end that the true use of the houses of correction may not be perverted, as of late it has for the most part been, that the master of each such house shall be obliged to allow unto every one committed to his charge 4d per diem for their maintenance in and about London. But in remoter counties, where wages and provisions are much cheaper, there the rate to be settled by the grand jury and judge at the assizes: for which the said master shall have no other consideration nor allowance but what their labour shall produce; whom therefore he shall have power to employ according to his discretion, consideration being had of their age and strength.

That the justices of the peace shall, each quarter sessions, make a narrow inquiry into the state and management of the houses of correction within their district; and take a strict account of the carriage of all those who are there; and if they find that anyone is stubborn, and not at all mended by the discipline of the place, that they order him a longer stay there, and severer discipline; that so nobody may be dismissed till he has given manifest proof of amendment, the end for which he was sent thither.

That whoever shall counterfeit a pass shall lose his ears for the forgery the first time that he is found guilty thereof; and the second time, that he shall be transported to the plantations, as in case of felony.

That whatever female, above fourteen years old, shall be found begging out of her own parish without a pass (if she be an inhabitant of a parish within five miles distance of that she is found begging in) she shall be conducted home to her parish by the constable, tithing man, overseer of the poor, churchwarden, or other sworn officer of the parish wherein she was found begging; who by his place and office shall be required to do it, and to deliver her to the overseer of the poor of the parish to which she belongs, from whom he shall receive 12d for his pains; which 12d, if she be one that receives public relief, shall be deducted out of her parish allowance; or, if she be not relieved by the parish, shall be levied on her, or her parent's or master's, goods.

That whenever any such female, above fourteen years old, within the same distance, commits the same fault a second time; and whenever the same or any such other female is found begging without a lawful pass, the first time, at a greater distance than five miles from the place of her abode, it shall be lawful for any justice of peace or guardian of the poor, upon complaint made, to send her to the house of correction, there to be employed in hard work three months, and so much longer as shall be to the next quarter sessions after the determination of the said three months; and that then, after due correction, she have a pass made her by the sessions to carry her home to the place of her abode.

That if any boy or girl, under fourteen years of age, shall be found begging out of the parish where they dwell (if within five miles distance of the said parish) they shall be sent to the next working-school, there to be soundly whipped, and kept at work till evening, so that they may be dismissed time enough to get to their place of abode that night. Or, if they live farther than five miles off from the place where they are taken begging, that they be sent to the next house of correction, there to remain at work six weeks, and so much longer as till the next sessions after the end of the said six weeks.

These idle vagabonds being thus suppressed, there will not (we suppose) in most country parishes be many men who will have the pretence that they want work. However, in order to the taking away of that pretence whenever it happens, we humbly propose that it may be farther enacted:

That the guardian of the poor of the parish where any such

pretence is made shall, the next Sunday after complaint made to him, acquaint the parish that such a person complains he wants work, and shall then ask whether anyone is willing to employ him, at a lower rate than is usually given, which rate it shall be in the power of the said guardian to set; for it is not to be supposed that anyone should be refused to be employed by his neighbours, whilst others are set to work, but for some defect in his ability or honesty, for which it is reasonable he should suffer; and he that cannot be set on work for 12d per diem, must be content with 9d or 10d, rather than live idly. But, if nobody in the parish voluntarily accepts such a person at the rate proposed by the guardians of the poor, that then it shall be in the power of the said guardian, with the rest of the parish, to make a list of days, according to the proportion of everyone's tax in the parish to the poor; and that, according to such list, every inhabitant in the same parish shall be obliged in their turn to set such unemployed poor men of the same parish on work, at such under rates as the said guardian of the poor shall appoint: and if any person refuse to set the poor at work in his turn as thus directed, that such person shall be bound to pay them their appointed wages, whether he employ them or no.

That if any poor man, otherwise unemployed, refuse to work according to such order (if it be in a maritime county), he shall be sent to the next port, and there put on board some of his Majesty's ships, to serve there three years, as before proposed; and that what pay shall accrue to him for his service there, above his diet and clothes, be paid to the overseers of the poor of the parish to which he belongs, for the maintenance of his wife and children, if he have any, or else towards the relief of other poor of the same parish: but (if it be not in a maritime county) that every poor man, thus refusing to work, shall be sent to the house of correction.

These methods we humbly propose as proper to be enacted, in order to the employing of the poor who are able, but will not work; which sort, by the punctual execution of such a law, we humbly conceive may be quickly reduced to a very small number, or quite extirpated. But the greatest part of the poor maintained by parish rates are not absolutely unable, nor wholly unwilling, to do anything towards the getting of their livelihoods; yet even those, either through want of fit work provided for them, or their unskilfulness in working in what might be a public advantage, do little that turns to any account; but live idly upon the parish allowance, or begging, if not worse. Their labour, therefore, as far as they are able to work, should be saved to the public; and what their earnings come short of a full maintenance, should be supplied out of the labour of others; that is, out of the parish allowance.

These are of two sorts:

1. Grown people; who, being decayed from their full strength, could yet do something for their living, though, under pretence that they cannot get work, they generally do nothing. In the same case with these are most of the wives of day labourers, when they come to have two or three or more children: the looking after their children gives them not liberty to go abroad to seek for work; and so, having no work at home, in the broken intervals of their time they earn nothing. But the aid of the parish is fain to come in to their support; and their labour is wholly lost, which is so much loss to the public.

Everyone must have meat, drink, clothing, and firing; so much goes out of the stock of the kingdom, whether they work or no. Supposing, then, there be 100,000 poor in England that live upon the parish; that is, who are maintained by other people's labour (for so is everyone who lives upon alms without working); if care were taken that everyone of those, by some labour in the woollen or other manufacture, should earn but 1d per diem (which one with another they might well do, and more) this would gain to England £130,000 per annum, which in eight years would make England above a million of pounds richer.

This, rightly considered, shows us what is the true and proper relief of the poor: it consists in finding work for them, and taking care they do not live like drones upon the labour of others. And, in order to this end, we find the laws made for the relief of the poor were intended: however by an ignorance of their intention, or a neglect of their due execution, they are turned only to the maintenance of people in idleness, without at all examining into the lives, abilities, or industry of those who seek for relief.

In order to the suppression of these idle beggars, the corporations in England have beadles authorized and paid to prevent the breach of the law in that particular: yet, nevertheless, the streets everywhere

swarm with beggars, to the increase of idleness, poverty, and villainy, and to the shame of Christianity. And if it should be asked, in
any town in England, how many of these visible trespassers have
been taken up and brought to punishment by those officers this last
year, we have reason to think the number would be found to have
been very small; because that of beggars swarming in the streets is
manifestly very great,

But the remedy of this disorder is so well provided by the laws
now in force, that we can impute the continuance and increase of it
to nothing but a general neglect of their execution.

2. Besides the grown people above mentioned, the children of
labouring people are an ordinary burden to the parish, and are
usually maintained in idleness; so that their labour also is generally
lost to the public till they are twelve or fourteen years old.

The most effectual remedy for this that we are able to conceive,
and which we therefore humbly purpose, is, that in the forementioned new law to be enacted it be further provided that working-
schools be set up in every parish, to which the children of all such
as demand relief of the parish, above three and under fourteen
years of age, whilst they live at home with their parents, and are
not otherwise employed for their livelihood by the allowance of the
overseers of the poor, shall be obliged to come.

By this means the mother will be eased of a great part of her
trouble in looking after and providing for them at home, and so be
at more liberty to work; the children will be kept in much better
order, be better provided for, and from their infancy be inured to
work, which is of no small consequence to the making of them
sober and industrious all their lives after; and the parish will be
either eased of this burden, or at least of the misuse in the present
management of it: for a great number of children giving a poor man
a title to an allowance from the parish, this allowance is given once
a week, or once a month, to the father in money, which he not
seldom spends on himself at the alehouse, whilst his children (for
whose sake he had it) are left to suffer, or perish under the want of
necessaries, unless the charity of neighbours relieve them.

We humbly conceive, that a man and his wife, in health, may be
able by their ordinary labour to maintain themselves and two children. More than two children at one time, under the age of three

years, will seldom happen in one family: if, therefore, all the children above three years old be taken off from their hands, those who have never so many, whilst they remain themselves in health, will not need any allowance for them.

We do not suppose that children of three years old will be able at that age to get their livelihoods at the working-school; but we are sure that what is necessary for their relief will more effectually have that use, if it be distributed to them in bread at that school, than if it be given to their fathers in money. What they have at home from their parents is seldom more than bread and water, and that many of them very scantily too: if, therefore, care be taken that they have each of them their bellyful of bread daily at school, they will be in no danger of famishing; but, on the contrary, they will be healthier and stronger than those who are bred otherwise. Nor will this practice cost the overseers any trouble; for a baker may be agreed with to furnish and bring into the school-house, every day, the allowance of bread necessary for all the scholars that are there. And to this may be also added, without any trouble, in cold weather, if it be thought needful, a little warm-water gruel; for the same fire that warms the room may be made use of to boil a pot of it.

From this method, the children will not only reap the forementioned advantages with far less charge to the parish than what is now done for them, but they will be also thereby the more obliged to come to school and apply themselves to work, because otherwise they will have no victuals; and also the benefit thereby both to themselves and the parish will daily increase: for the earnings of their labour at school every day increasing, it may reasonably be concluded that, computing all the earnings of a child from three to fourteen years of age, the nourishment and teaching of such a child during that whole time will cost the parish nothing. Whereas there is no child now which from its birth is maintained by the parish, but, before the age of fourteen, costs the parish fifty or sixty pounds.

Another advantage also of bringing poor children thus to a working-school is that by this means they may be obliged to come constantly to church every Sunday along with their school-masters or dames, whereby they may be brought into some sense of religion; whereas ordinarily now, in their idle and loose way of breeding up, they are as utter strangers both to religion and morality as they are to industry.

In order, therefore, to the more effectual carrying on of this work to the advantage of this kingdom, we further humbly propose, that these schools be generally for spinning or knitting, or some other part of the woollen manufacture; unless in countries where the place shall furnish some other materials fitter for the employment of such poor children; in which places the choice of those materials for their employment may be left to the prudence and direction of the guardians of the poor of that hundred; and that the teachers in these schools be paid out of the poor's rate, as can be agreed.

This, though at first setting up, it may cost the parish a little, yet we humbly conceive that (the earnings of the children abating the charge of their maintenance, and as much work being required of each of them as they are reasonably able to perform) it will quickly pay its own charges, with an overplus.

That where the number of the poor children of any parish is greater than for them all to be employed in one school, they be there divided into two; and the boys and girls, if thought convenient, taught and kept to work separately.

That the handicraftsmen in each hundred be bound to take every other of their respective apprentices from amongst the boys in some one of the schools in the said hundred without any money, which boys they may so take at what age they please, to be bound to them till the age of twenty-three years, that so the length of time may more than make amends for the usual sums that are given to handicraftsmen with such apprentices.

That those also in the hundred who keep in their hands land of their own to the value of £25 per annum or upwards, or who rent £50 per annum or upwards, may choose out of the schools of the said hundred what boy each of them pleases to be his apprentice in husbandry, upon the same condition.

That whatever boys are not by this means bound out apprentices before they are full fourteen, shall, at the Easter meeting of the guardians of each hundred every year, be bound to such gentlemen, yeomen, or farmers, within the said hundred, as have the greatest number of acres of land in their hands; who shall be obliged to take them for their apprentices till the age of twenty-three, or bind them out at their own cost to some handicraftsmen; provided always that no such gentleman, yeoman, or farmer shall be bound to have two such apprentices at a time.

That grown people also (to take away their pretence of want of work) may come to the said working-schools to learn, where work shall accordingly be provided for them.

That the materials to be employed in these schools, and among other the poor people of the parish, be provided by a common stock in each hundred, to be raised out of a certain portion of the poor's rate of each parish as requisite; which stock, we humbly conceive, need be raised but once; for, if rightly managed, it will increase.

That some person, experienced and well-skilled in the particular manufacture which shall be judged fittest to set the poor of each hundred on work, be appointed store-keeper for that hundred, who shall accordingly buy in the wool or other materials necessary; that this store-keeper be chosen by the guardians of the poor of each hundred, and be under their direction, and have such salary as they shall appoint to be paid, *pro rata* upon the pound, out of the poor's tax of every parish; and over and above which salary, that he also have two shillings in the pound yearly for every twenty shillings that shall be lessened in the poor's tax of any parish, from the first year of his management.

To this store-keeper one of the overseers of the poor of every parish shall repair as often as there shall be occasion, to fetch from him the materials for the employment of the poor of each parish; which materials the said overseer shall distribute to the teachers of the children of each school; and also to other poor who demand relief of the said parish, to be wrought by them at home in such quantity as he or the guardian of the parish shall judge reasonable for each of them respectively to dispatch in one week; allowing unto each such poor person, for his or her work, what he and the store-keeper shall agree it to be worth. But if the said overseer and store-keeper do not agree about the price of any such work, that then any three or more of the guardians of that hundred (whereof the guardian of the same parish in which the contest arises [is] to be always one) do determine it.

That the sale of the materials thus manufactured be made by the store-keeper in the presence of one or more of the guardians of each hundred, and not otherwise; and that an exact account be kept by the said store-keeper of all that he buys in and sells out; as also of the several quantities of unwrought materials that he delivers to the respective overseers, and of the manufactured returns that he receives back again from them.

That if any person to whom wool or any other materials are delivered to be wrought shall spoil or embezzle the same, if it be one who receives alms from the parish, the overseers of the poor of that parish shall pay unto the store-keeper what it cost, and deduct that sum out of the parish allowance to the person who has so spoiled or embezzled any such materials; or if it be one that receives no allowance from the parish, then the said overseers shall demand it in money of the person that spoiled or embezzled it; and if the person so offending refuse to pay it, the guardian of the poor of that parish, upon oath made to him by any of the said overseers that he delivered such materials to such person, and that he paid for them such a sum to the store-keeper (which oath every such guardian may be empowered to administer), shall grant unto the said overseer a warrant to distrain upon the goods of the person so offending, and sell the goods so distrained, rendering the overplus.

That the guardian of the poor of every parish, to be chosen by those who pay to the relief of the poor of the said parish, shall be chosen, the first time, within three months after the passing of the act now proposed. That the guardians thus chosen by the respective parishes of each hundred shall have the inspection of all things relating to the employment and relief of the poor of the said hundred. That one-third part of the whole number of the guardians of every hundred thus chosen shall go out every year; the first year by lot, out of the whole number; the second year by lot out of the remaining two-thirds; and for ever afterwards in their turns: so that, after the first two years, everyone shall continue in three years successively, and no longer. And that, for the supply of any vacancy as it shall happen, a new guardian be chosen as aforesaid in any respective parish, at the same time that the overseers of the poor are usually chosen there, or at any other time within one month after any such vacancy.

That the guardians of the poor of each respective hundred shall meet every year in Easter week, in the place where the stores of that hundred are kept, to take an account of the stock; and as often, also, at other times as shall be necessary, to inspect the management of it, and to give directions therein, and in all other things relating to the poor of that hundred.

That no person in any parish shall be admitted to an allowance from the parish but by the joint consent of the guardian of the said parish and the vestry.

That the said guardians also, each of them, within the hundred whereof he is guardian, have the power of a justice of the peace over vagabonds and beggars, to make them passes, to send them to the sea-port towns, or houses of correction, as before proposed.

These foregoing rules and methods being what we humbly conceive most proper to be put in practice for the employment and relief of the poor generally throughout the country, we now further humbly propose, for the better and more easy attainment of the same, and in cities and towns corporate, that it may be enacted:

That in all cities and towns corporate, the poor's tax be not levied by distinct parishes, but by one equal tax throughout the whole corporation.

That in each corporation there be twelve guardians of the poor, chosen by the said corporation; whereof four to go out by lot at the end of the first year; other four of the remaining number to go out also by lot the next year; and the remaining four the third year; and a new four chosen every year in the rooms of those that go out, to keep up the number of twelve full; and that no one continue in above three years successively.

That these guardians have the power of setting up and ordering working-schools, as they see convenient, within each corporation respectively; to which schools the children of all that are relieved by the said corporation, from three to fourteen years of age, shall be bound to come, as long as they continue unemployed in some other settled service to be approved of by the overseers of the poor of that parish to which they belong.

That these guardians have also the sole power of ordering and disposing of the money raised in each corporation for the use of the poor, whether for the providing of materials to set them on work, or for the relieving of those who they judge not able to earn their own livelihoods; and that they be the sole judges who are, or are not, fit to receive public relief, and in what proportion.

That the said guardians have also the power to send any persons begging without a lawful pass to the next sea-port town, or house of correction, as before propounded.

That they have likewise power to appoint a treasurer to receive all money raised for the relief of the poor; which treasurer shall issue all such money only by their order, and shall once a year pass his accounts before them: and that they also appoint one or more store-keepers, as they shall see occasion, with such rewards or salaries as they think fit; which store-keepers shall in like manner be account-able unto them. Provided always that the mayor or bailiff, or other chief officer of each corporation, have notice given him that he may be present (which we humbly propose may be enjoined all such officers respectively) at the passing of the accounts both of the treasurer and store-keepers for the poor within each respective cor-poration.

That the teachers in each school, or some other person thereunto appointed, shall fetch from the respective store-keepers the materi-als they are appointed to work upon in that school, and in such quantities as they are ordered; which materials shall be manufac-tured accordingly, and then returned to the store-keeper, and by him be either given out to be further manufactured, or else disposed of to the best advantage, as the guardians shall direct.

That the overseers of the poor shall in like manner take from the store-keeper, and distribute unto those who are under the public relief, such materials, and in such proportions, as shall be ordered each of them for a week's work, and not pay unto any of the poor so employed the allowance appointed them, till they bring back their respective tasks well performed.

That the overseers of the poor of each parish shall be chosen as they are now, and have the same power to collect the poor's rates of their respective parishes as now: but that they issue out the money so collected for the relief and maintenance of the poor, according to such orders and directions as they shall receive from the guardians; and that the accounts of the overseers of the poor of each parish, at the end of their year, shall be laid before such persons as the parish shall appoint to inspect them, that they may make such observations on the said accounts, or exceptions against them, as they may be liable to. And that then the said accounts, with those observations and exceptions, be examined by the treasurer and two of the guardians (whereof one to be nominated by the guardians themselves, and the other by the parish); and that the said accounts be passed by the allowance of those three.

That the said guardians shall have power to appoint one or more beadles of beggars; which beadles shall be authorized and required to seize upon any stranger begging in the streets, or any one of the said corporation begging, either without the badge appointed to be worn, or at hours not allowed by the said guardians to beg in, and bring all such persons before any one of the said guardians: and that, if any of the said beadles neglect their said duty, so that strangers or other beggars not having the badge appointed, or at hours not allowed, be found frequenting the streets, the said guardians (upon complaint thereof made to them) shall have power and be required to punish the beadle so offending (for the first fault) according to their own discretion; but, upon a second complaint proved before them, that they send the said beadle to the house of correction, or (if it be in a maritime county, and the beadle offending be a lusty man, and under fifty years of age) to the next sea-port town, in order to the putting him aboard some of his Majesty's ships, to serve there three years, as before proposed.

That those who are not able to work at all, in corporations where there are no hospitals to receive them, be lodged three or four, or more, in one room, and yet more in one house, where one fire may serve, and one attendant may provide for many of them, with less charge than when they live at their own choice scatteringly.

And since the behaviour and want of the poor are best known amongst their neighbours, and that they may have the liberty to declare their wants, and receive broken bread and meat, or other charity, from well-disposed people; that it be therefore permitted to those whose names are entered in the poor's book, and who wear the badges required, to ask and receive alms, in their respective parishes, at certain hours of the day, to be appointed by the guardians. But if any of them are taken begging at any other hour than those allowed, or out of their respective parishes, though within the same corporation, they shall be sent immediately (if they are under fourteen years of age) to the working-school, to be whipped; and (if they are above fourteen) to the house of correction, to remain there six weeks, and so much longer as till the next quarter sessions after the said six weeks are expired.

That if any person die for want of due relief in any parish in which he ought to be relieved, the said parish be fined according to the circumstances of the fact and the heinousness of the crime.

That every master of the king's ships shall be bound to receive, without money, once every year (if offered him by the mayor or other officer of any place within the bounds of the port where his ship shall be) one boy, sound of limb, above thirteen years of age, who shall be his apprentice for nine years.

Bibliography

Andrews, Charles McLean (1934–8), *The Colonial Period of American History* (4 vols.), New Haven: Yale University Press.

Appleby, Joyce O. (1976), Locke, liberalism, and the natural law of money, *Past and Present* (71):43–69.

Ashcraft, Richard (1969), John Locke's library: Portrait of an intellectual, *Transactions of the Cambridge Bibliographical Society* 5:47–60.

   (1980), Revolutionary politics and Locke's *Two Treatises of Government*, *Political Theory* 8:429–86.

   (1986), *Revolutionary Politics and Locke's 'Two Treatises of Government'*, Princeton, NJ: Princeton University Press.

   (1987), *Locke's 'Two Treatises of Government'*, London: Allen and Unwin.

Ashcraft, Richard, and Goldsmith, Maurice M. (1983), Locke, revolution principles, and the formation of Whig ideology, *Historical Journal* 26:773–800.

Astbury, Raymond (1978), The renewal of the licensing act in 1693 and its lapse in 1695, *The Library* ser. V, 33:296–322.

Beier, A. L. (1988), 'Utter strangers to industry, morality and religion': John Locke on the poor, *Eighteenth Century Life* 12:28–41.

Boyle, Robert (1744), *The Works of the Honourable Robert Boyle*, ed. Thomas Birch (5 vols.), London: A. Millar.

Carlyle, C. Irving (1885–1900), Tyrrell, James, in *Dictionary of National Biography*, ed. Leslie Stephen and Sidney Lee (63 vols.), vol. 57, 441–2, London: Smith, Elder.

Charron, Pierre (1783; 1st edn 1601), *De la sagesse*, Paris: J.-F. Bastien.

Colie, Rosalie L. (1960), John Locke in the Republic of Letters, in *Britain and the Netherlands*, ed. J. S. Bromley and E. H. Kossman, 111–29, London: Chatto and Windus.

Collins, Anthony (1713), *A Discourse of Free-Thinking*, London.

Cox, Richard (1960), *Locke on War and Peace*, Oxford: Clarendon Press.

Cranston, Maurice (1957; paperback edn, Oxford, 1985), *John Locke: A Biography*, London: Longmans Green.

 (1987), John Locke and the case for toleration, in *On Toleration*, ed. Susan Mendus and David Edwards, 101–22, Oxford: Clarendon Press.

Culverwell, Nathaniel (1971; 1st edn 1652), *An Elegant and Learned Discourse of the Light of Nature*, ed. R. A. Greene and H. MacCallum, Toronto: Toronto University Press.

De Krey, Gary S. (1990), London radicals and revolutionary politics, 1675–1683, in *The Politics of Religion in Restoration England*, ed. Tim Harris, Paul Seaward, and Mark Goldie, 133–62, Oxford: Blackwell.

Dunn, John (1968), Justice and the interpretation of Locke's political theory, *Political Studies* 16:68–87.

 (1969a), *The Political Thought of John Locke*, Cambridge: Cambridge University Press.

 (1969b), The politics of Locke in England and America in the eighteenth century, in *John Locke: Problems and Perspectives*, ed. John W. Yolton, 45–80, Cambridge: Cambridge University Press.

 (1979), *Western Political Theory in the Face of the Future*, Cambridge: Cambridge University Press.

 (1981), Individuality and clientage in the formation of Locke's social imagination, in *John Locke: Symposium Wolfenbüttel 1979*, ed. Reinhard Brandt, 43–73, Berlin: Walter de Gruyter.

 (1985; 1st edn 1984), 'Trust' in the politics of John Locke, in John Dunn, *Rethinking Modern Political Theory: Essays 1979–83*, 34–54, Cambridge: Cambridge University Press.

 (1990), What is living and what is dead in the political theory of John Locke?, in John Dunn, *Interpreting Political Responsibility*, 9–25, Oxford: Polity.

Dworetz, Steven M. (1990), *The Unvarnished Doctrine: Locke, Liberalism and the American Revolution*, Durham: Duke University Press.

Filmer, Sir Robert (1991; 1st edn 1680), *Patriarcha and Other Writings*, ed. Johann P. Sommerville, Cambridge: Cambridge University Press.

Fox Bourne, H. R. (1876), *The Life of John Locke* (2 vols.), New York: Harper and Brothers.

Gauthier, David P. (1977), Why ought one obey God? Reflections on Hobbes and Locke, *Canadian Journal of Philosophy* 7:425–46, 35, 557–86.

Goldie, Mark (1992), John Locke's circle and James II, *Historical Journal*.

(forthcoming), John Locke, Jonas Proast, and religious toleration, 1688–1692, in *The Church of England 1689–1833: From Toleration to Tractarianism*, ed. J. Walsh, C. Haydon and S. Taylor, Oxford: Blackwell.

Gough, John W. (1956), *John Locke's Political Philosophy*, Oxford: Clarendon Press.

(1976), James Tyrrell, Whig historian and friend of John Locke, *Historical Journal* 19:581–610.

Grant, Ruth W. (1987), *John Locke's Liberalism*, Chicago: Chicago University Press.

Gregory, Tullio (1992), Pierre Charron's 'scandalous book', in *Atheism from the Reformation to the Enlightenment*, ed. Michael Hunter and David Wootton, 87–109, Oxford: Clarendon Press.

Grendler, Paul (1963), Pierre Charron: Precursor to Hobbes, *Review of Politics* 25:212–24.

Grotius, Hugo (1925; 1st edn 1625), *The Law of War and Peace*, trans. Francis W. Kelsey, Oxford: Clarendon Press.

Hacking, Ian (1975), *The Emergence of Probability*, Cambridge: Cambridge University Press.

Hale, Sir Matthew (1736), *Historia Placitorum Coronae: The History of the Pleas of the Crown* (2 vols.), London: E. & R. Nutt.

Haley, K. H. D. (1968), *The First Earl of Shaftesbury*, Oxford: Clarendon Press.

Hamowy, Ronald (1990), Cato's *Letters*, John Locke, and the republican paradigm, *History of Political Thought* 11:273–94.

Harrison, John, and Laslett, Peter (1965), *The Library of John Locke*, Oxford: Oxford University Press.

Hont, Istvan (1990), Free trade and the economic limits to national politics: Neo-Machiavellian political economy reconsidered, in *The Economic Limits to Modern Politics*, ed. John Dunn, 41–120, Cambridge: Cambridge University Press.

Horne, Thomas (1990), *Property Rights and Poverty*, Chapel Hill: University of North Carolina Press.

Houston, Alan Craig (1991), *Algernon Sidney and the Republican Heritage in England and America*, Princeton, NJ: Princeton University Press.

Jolley, Nicholas (1984), *Leibniz and Locke: A Study of the 'New Essays on Human Understanding'*, Oxford: Clarendon Press.

Kilcullen, John (1988), *Sincerity and Truth: Essays on Arnauld, Bayle and Toleration*, Oxford: Clarendon Press.

King, Peter (7th Lord King) (1829), *The Life of John Locke*, London.

Kraynak, Robert P. (1980), John Locke: From absolutism to toleration, *American Political Science Review* 74:53–69.

Locke, John (1720), *A Collection of Several Pieces of Mr John Locke*, ed. Pierre Desmaiseaux and Anthony Collins, London: R. Francklin.

(1789), Report of the Board of Trade to the Lords Justices in the Year 1697, in *An Account of the Origin, Proceedings, and Intentions of the Society for the Promotion of Industry in the Southern District of the Parts of Lindsey, in the County of Lincoln*, 101–26 (3rd edn, Louth, 1789).

(1823), *The Works of John Locke* (10 vols.), London.

(1872), First set of the constitutions for the government of Carolina, in *Thirty-Third Report of the Deputy Keeper of the Public Records*, 258–69, London: H. M. Stationery Office.

(1899(?)), *Four Letters on Toleration*, London: Ward, Locke.

(1927), *The Correspondence of John Locke and Edward Clarke*, ed. Benjamin Rand, London: Humphrey Milford.

(1936), *An Early Draft of Locke's 'Essay', Together with Excerpts from his Journals*, ed. R. I. Aaron and Jocelyn Gibb, Oxford: Clarendon Press.

(1954), *Essays on the Law of Nature*, ed. W. von Leyden, Oxford: Clarendon Press.

(1961), *Scritti editi e inediti sulla tolleranza*, ed. C. A. Viano, Turin: Laterza.

(1963), *A Letter Concerning Toleration*, ed. Mario Montuori, The Hague: Martinus Nijhoff.

(1967a), *Two Tracts on Government*, ed. Philip Abrams, Cambridge: Cambridge University Press.

(1967b; revision of 1st edn, 1960), *Two Treatises of Government*, ed. Peter Laslett, Cambridge: Cambridge University Press.

(1968), *Epistola de Tolerantia: A Letter on Toleration*, ed. Raymond Klibansky and John W. Gough, Oxford: Clarendon Press.

(1972), Testi teologico-filosofici Lockiani dal Ms. Locke c. 27 della Lovelace Collection, ed. Mario Sina, *Rivista di filosofia neo-scolastica* 64:54–75, 400–427.

(1974a), '*An Essay Concerning Toleration*' and '*Toleratio*', ed. K. Inoue, Nara, Japan: Nara Women's University.

(1974b), Locke and ethical theory: Two Ms pieces, ed. T. Sargentich, *Locke Newsletter* 5:24–31.

(1975), *An Essay Concerning Human Understanding*, ed. Peter Nidditch, Oxford: Clarendon Press.

(1976–89), *Correspondence*, ed. E. S. de Beer (8 vols.), Oxford: Clarendon Press.

(1983), *A Letter Concerning Toleration*, ed. James Tully, Indianapolis: Hackett.

(1985), John Locke on the Glorious Revolution: A rediscovered document, ed. James Farr and Clayton Roberts, *Historical Journal* 38:385–98.

(1987), *A Paraphrase and Notes on the Epistles of St Paul*, ed. Andrew W. Wainright, Oxford: Clarendon Press.

(1988; rev. edn of Locke 1967b), *Two Treatises of Government*, ed. Peter Laslett, Cambridge: Cambridge University Press.

(1989), *Some Thoughts Concerning Education*, ed. John W. and Jean S. Yolton, Oxford: Clarendon Press.

(1990), *Questions Concerning the Law of Nature*, ed. R. Horwitz, J. Strauss Clay and D. Clay, Ithaca: Cornell University Press.

(1991), *Locke on Money*, ed. Patrick H. Kelly (2 vols.), Oxford: Clarendon Press.

Long, P. (1959), *A Summary Catalogue of the Lovelace Collection of the Papers of John Locke in the Bodleian Library*, Oxford: Bodleian Library.

McGuinness, C. (1989), The *Fundamental Constitutions of Carolina* as a tool for Lockean scholarship, *Interpretation* 17:127–43.

Marshall, John (1990), *John Locke in Context: Religion, Ethics and Politics*, Ph.D. Thesis, Johns Hopkins University.

(1992), John Locke and latitudinarianism, in *Philosophy, Science, and Religion in England, 1640–1700*, ed. Richard Ashcraft, Richard Kroll, and Perez Zagorin, 253–82, Cambridge: Cambridge University Press.

(forthcoming), John Locke and Socinianism, in *Seventeenth Century Philosophy in Historical Context*, ed. M. A. Stewart, Oxford: Clarendon Press.

Menake, G. T. (1981), Research note and query on the dating of Locke's *Two Treatises*, *Political Theory* 9: 547–50.

(1982), . . . a sequel, *Political Theory* 10:609–12.

Mendus, Susan (1989), *Toleration and the Limits of Liberalism*, Basingstoke: Macmillan.

Milton, John (1991), *Political Writings*, ed. Martin Dzelzainis, Cambridge: Cambridge University Press.

Molyneux, William (1968), *The Case of Ireland's Being Bound by Acts of Parliament in England*, Dublin: J. Ray.

More, St Thomas (1989; 1st edn 1516), *Utopia*, ed. Robert M. Adams and George M. Logan, Cambridge: Cambridge University Press.

Mulligan, Lotte, Richards, Judith, and Graham, John K. (1982), A concern for understanding: A case of Locke's precepts and practice, *Historical Journal* 25:841–57.

Nelson, Jeffrey (1978), Unlocking Locke's legacy: A comment, *Political Studies* 26:101–4.

Noonan, Harold W. (1989), *Personal Identity*, London: Routledge.

Pangle, Thomas (1988), *The Spirit of Modern Republicanism*, Chicago: University of Chicago Press.

Patterson, Annabel (1990), Miscellaneous Marvell?, in *The Political Identity of Andrew Marvell*, ed. Conal Condren and A. D. Cousins, 188–212, Aldershot: Scolar.

Pocock, J. G. A. (1975), *The Machiavellian Moment: Florentine Political Thought and the Atlantic Republican Tradition*, Princeton, NJ: Princeton University Press.

(1988), The fourth English Civil War: Dissolution, desertion and alternative histories in the Glorious Revolution, *Government and Opposition* 23:151–62.

Proast, Jonas (1984; 1st edns 1690, 1691, 1704), *Letters Concerning Toleration*, New York: Garland.

Pufendorf, Samuel (1934; 1st edn 1672), *De Jure Naturae et Gentium Libri Octo*, ed. C. H. Oldfather and W. A. Oldfather, Oxford: Clarendon Press.

(1991; 1st edn 1673), *On the Duty of Man and Citizen*, ed. James Tully; trans. Michael Silverthorne, Cambridge: Cambridge University Press.

Rahn, B. J. (1972), A ra-ree show – a rare cartoon: Revolutionary propaganda in the treason trial of Stephen College, in *Studies in Change and Revolution*, ed. Paul J. Korshin, 77–98, Menston: Scolar Press.

Scott, Jonathan (1991a), *Algernon Sidney and the Restoration Crisis, 1677–1683*, Cambridge: Cambridge University Press.

(1991b), The law of war: Grotius, Sidney, Locke and the political theory of rebellion, Paper to the 10th Congress of Anglo-Dutch Historians, Oxford.

Seliger, Martin (1968), *The Liberal Politics of John Locke*, London: Allen and Unwin.

Spellman, W. M. (1988), *John Locke and the Problem of Depravity*, Oxford: Clarendon Press.

State Tracts (1689), London.

State Tracts: in Two Parts (1693) (2 vols.), London: R. Baldwin.

Sterne, Laurence (1760–67), *The Life and Opinions of Tristram Shandy* (9 vols.), York and London.

Strauss, Leo (1953), *Natural Right and History*, Chicago: University of Chicago Press.

Tarcov, Nathan (1984), *Locke's Education for Liberty*, Chicago: University of Chicago Press.

Thompson, Martyn P. (1976), The reception of Locke's *Two Treatises of Government*, *Political Studies* 24:184–91.

(1979), Reception and influence: A reply to Nelson on Locke's *Two Treatises of Government*, *Political Studies* 28:100–108.

(1987), *Ideas of Contract in English Political Thought in the Age of John Locke*, New York: Garland.

Toland, John (1696), *Christianity not Mysterious*, London.

Tuck, Richard (1979), *Natural Rights Theories: Their Origin and Development*, Cambridge: Cambridge University Press.

(1983), Grotius, Carneades and Hobbes, *Grotiana* 4:43–62.

(1987), The 'modern' theory of natural law, in *The Languages of*

Political Theory in Early-Modern Europe, ed. Anthony Pagden, 99–119, Cambridge: Cambridge University Press.

(1988), Optics and sceptics: The philosophical foundations of Hobbes's political thought, in *Conscience and Casuistry in Early Modern Europe*, ed. Edmund Leites, 235–63, Cambridge: Cambridge University Press.

Tyrrell, James (1681), *Patriarcha non Monarcha*, London: R. Janeway.

(1694), *Bibliotheca Politica*, London: R. Baldwin.

[Tyrrell, James] (1705), Locke (John), in 'Addenda' to *A Supplement to the Great Historical, Geographical, Genealogical and Poetical Dictionary*, ed. Jeremy Collier, London: Henry Rhodes.

Viano, Carlo A. (1960), *John Locke, dal razionalismo all'illuminismo*, Turin: Taylor.

Waldron, Jeremy (1988), Locke: Toleration and the rationality of persecution, in *Justifying Toleration: Conceptual and Historical Perspectives*, ed. Susan Mendus, 61–86, Cambridge: Cambridge University Press.

Wallace, John (1980), The date of Sir Robert Filmer's *Patriarcha*, *Historical Journal* 23:155–65.

Wood, Neal (1983), *The Politics of Locke's Philosophy: A Social Study of 'An Essay Concerning Human Understanding'*, Berkeley: University of California Press.

(1984), *John Locke and Agrarian Capitalism*, Berkeley: University of California Press.

Wootton, David, ed. (1986), *Divine Right and Democracy: An Anthology of Political Thought in Stuart England*, Harmondsworth: Penguin Books.

(1989), John Locke: Socinian or natural law theorist?, in *Religion, Secularization, and Political Thought*, ed. James Crimmins, 39–67, London: Routledge.

(1990), The crisis of the winter of 1642/3 and the birth of Civil War radicalism, *English Historical Review* 105:654–69.

(1991), Leveller democracy and Puritan revolution, in *The Cambridge History of Political Thought*, vol. II, ed. J. H. Burns, 412–42, Cambridge: Cambridge University Press.

(1992a), John Locke and Richard Ashcraft's *Revolutionary Politics*, *Political Studies* 40:79–98.

(1992b), New histories of atheism, in *Atheism from the Reformation to the Enlightenment*, ed. David Wootton and Michael Hunter, 13–53, Oxford: Clarendon Press.

Worden, Blair (1985), The Commonwealth kidney of Algernon Sidney, *Journal of British Studies* 24:1–40.

Yolton, John W. (1956), *John Locke and the Way of Ideas*, Oxford: Clarendon Press.

(1985), *Locke: An Introduction*, Oxford: Blackwell.

Zuckert, Michael P. (1979), An introduction to Locke's First Treatise, *Interpretation* 8:58–74.